Three Further Clinical Faces of Childhood

Edited by
E. James Anthony, M.D.
and
Doris C. Gilpin, M.D.
Division of Child Psychiatry
Washington University School of Medicine
St. Louis, Missouri

RJ499
T55
1981

SP

SP MEDICAL & SCIENTIFIC BOOKS

New York

376049

To Cadell,
a child of the future

Copyright © 1981 Spectrum Publications

All rights reserved. No part of this book may be reproduced in any form, by photostat, microform, retrieval system, or any other means without prior written permission of the copyright holder or his licensee.

SPECTRUM PUBLICATIONS, INC.
175-20 Wexford Terrace, Jamaica, N.Y. 11432

Library of Congress Cataloging in Publication Data
Main entry under title:
Three further clinical faces of childhood.
    Includes index.
    1. Child psychopathology. 2. Hysteria.
3. Anxiety. 4. Pseudoneurotic schizophrenia.
I. Anthony, Elwyn James. II. Gilpin, Doris C.
[DNLM: 1. Hysteria—In infancy and childhood—
Congresses. 2. Anxiety—In infancy and childhood
—Congresses. 3. Mental disorders—In infancy
and childhood—Congresses. WS350 T532 1977–78]
RJ499.T55   618.9′28′9   79–23860
ISBN 0-89335-110-5

CONTRIBUTORS

EBRAHIM AMANAT, M.D.
Washington University School of Medicine
St. Louis, Missouri

E. JAMES ANTHONY, M.D.
Blanche F. Ittleson Professor of Child
   Psychiatry
Director, William Greenleaf Eliot Division of
   Child Psychiatry
Director, Edison Child Development
   Research Center
Washington University School of Medicine
St. Louis, Missouri

HENRY P. COPPOLILLO, M.D.
Division of Child Psychiatry
University of Colorado
Denver, Colorado

RUDOLF EKSTEIN, PH.D.
University of California
Los Angeles, California

BERNARD FEINBERG, M.D.
Child Guidance Clinic
Washington University School of Medicine
St. Louis, Missouri

JEREMY FIALKOV, M.D.
Child Guidance Clinic
Washington University School of Medicine
St. Louis, Missouri

PRAVIN GANDHY, M.D.
Child Guidance Clinic
Washington University School of Medicine
St. Louis, Missouri

DORIS C. GILPIN, M.D.
Division of Child Psychiatry
Child Guidance Clinic
Washington University School of Medicine
St. Louis, Missouri

JAMES H. GRUBBS, M.D.
Division of Child Psychiatry
University of Texas Southwestern Medical
   School
Dallas, Texas

CLAIRE IRWIN, M.D.
Child Guidance Clinic
Washington University School of Medicine
St. Louis, Missouri

CYNTHIA JANES, PH.D.
Edison Child Development Research Center
Washington University School of Medicine
St. Louis, Missouri

PAULINA F. KERNBERG, M.D.
Albert Einstein College of Medicine
Bronx, New York

ELAINE KORNBLUM, M.S.W.
Child Guidance Clinic
Washington University School of Medicine
St. Louis, Missouri

RICHARD J. LAITMAN, PH.D.
Child Guidance Clinic
Washington University School of Medicine
St. Louis, Missouri

KATE MATTES, M.S.W., A.C.S.W.
Child Guidance Clinic
Washington University School of Medicine
St. Louis, Missouri

JULIO MORALES, M.D.
Child Guidance Clinic
Washington University School of Medicine
St. Louis, Missouri

GAIL OVERBEY, PH.D.
Child Guidance Clinic
Washington University School of Medicine
St. Louis, Missouri

SANDRA SEXSON, M.D.
Child Guidance Clinic
Washington University School of Medicine
St. Louis, Missouri

HARINDER SINGH, M.D.
Child Guidance Clinic
Washington University School of Medicine
St. Louis, Missouri

CAROL WALD
Child Guidance Clinic
Washington University School of Medicine
St. Louis, Missouri

LILLIAN WEGER, M.S.W.
Child Guidance Clinic

Washington University School of Medicine
St. Louis, Missouri

ANNEMARIE P. WEIL, M.D.
Clinic for Training and
   Research
Columbia University
New York, New York

DAVID T. WELLS, PH.D.
The Orchard Place
Des Moines, Iowa

JULIEN WORLAND, PH.D.
Child Guidance Clinic
Washington University
   School of Medicine
St. Louis, Missouri

PREFACE

The university clinic such as ours keeps one foot in academia and the other in the community. Its teachers are expected to treat and its therapists are expected to teach. Its researchers are meant to be steeped in clinical experience and understanding so that they can investigate what is relevant to the life of the clinic. The staff—psychiatrists, psychologists, social workers, researchers, and administrators—is dedicated to the aphorism that there will be no research and training without good treatment, and no treatment without good research and training. This volume, like the previous one, attempts to exemplify this guiding principle. The format remains the same: The clinic workers expose their clinical ideas, their clinical techniques, and their clinical results to an outside public made up of invited consultants and a wide variety of city professionals. The workshop is regarded as cross-fertilizing. On these two days, the clinic plays consultant to the municipal agencies, who in turn play consultant to the clinic. Both share in the superordinate wisdom of the visiting "firemen" and "firewomen." The periodic evaluation of the clinic's performance by both self and others seems to us to provide a needed monitoring to ensure the maintenance of excellence. To paraphrase a classical quotation, one would have to say that the unexamined clinic is not worth running.

As will be evident from these pages, staff and trainees from every discipline have worked synergistically to demonstrate the value of coordinated efforts both in understanding and in treating the disordered child.

The success of any conference, together with the publication of its proceedings, is also a collaborative process, involving in this case Mr. Lee Judy, the executive director of the Washington University Child Guidance Clinic; Miss Doris Diephouse, the administrative secretary of the Washington University Division of Child Psychiatry; the many leading professionals from the metropolitan area who gave generously of their time to lead discussion groups; and the unnamed members of the treatment, training, and research staffs who continued to hold the fort and carry out essential clinic duties while some of their colleagues devoted themselves to the running of the workshop.

Finally, our gratitude goes to Janet Ferguson and Jane Reidelberger, who have been largely responsible for the production of this book.

E. JAMES ANTHONY, M.D.
DORIS C. GILPIN, M.D.

CONTENTS

INTRODUCTION

It is hard for adults to take the psychopathology of childhood seriously. Freud had to teach clinicians to do so, and we in turn must continue to tell parents that it exists, that it is not naughtiness but neurosis (although sometimes, with the oversophisticated, we may also need to say that it is not neurosis but naughtiness, because naughtiness continues to exist and may need to exist as an essential ingredient, within limits, of childhood). All this is true not only of psychopathology, but of childhood itself. For many centuries until the last few, adults have not taken children seriously or given them much thought, for the most part waiting impatiently for them to grow up, to become reasonable and to respond to the inviolable logic that is assumed to govern the grown-up world. As clinicians with a special understanding of childhood, it is up to us to remind parents that children need to be children and to behave like children rather than like miniature adults. (But once again we may have to caution the oversophisticated not to take childhood so seriously that it seems to become the end of human development and not its beginning. Children should be an accepted part of the world, not its center; their thoughts and feelings must be taken into consideration in the shaping of that world, but not to the exclusion of the adult viewpoint.)

The main reason, explicit or implicit, that adults have for not taking childhood too seriously is that it is evanescent. Its stages rapidly give place to others before the adult has time to come to terms specific to any of them. There is, therefore, a kernel of reality to this common point of view. Children do grow up and do grow out of their psychological clothes, and shed their symptoms as they do their successive developmental "skins." How can one take such human kaleidoscopes seriously when every chronological shift sets up a new pattern of responses, making us forget that the earlier patterns ever existed and that they ever meant anything? The wet beds are now dry; the soiled underclothes are now clean; the emotional storms have disappeared mysteriously into the past; and the magical thinking that gave rise to little phobias and obsessions have given way to the encroachments of reality. How can such symptoms be taken seriously when they are here today and gone tomorrow? Again, as clinicians, we soon come to realize that the present never fades into nothingness, but that traces of all these developmental events are stored within the vast memory system of the mind and may continue to influence further development. Contemporaneous psychopathology may portend the future disturbances and even help to form and pattern them.

The plasticity of children is not unlimited, and although their chances of recovery from emotional disturbances are for the most part better than adults', one has to remember that they are less knowledgeable, less experienced, less defended, and more vulnerable than their parents. By the same token, they are often able to blossom under conditions that would completely hamper adults' productivity. They have not yet become so "rhinocerized" that, to borrow Ionesco's expression, a single flower could not be grown on them. Because of this, child clinicians remain perpetually optimistic and hopeful.

These six clinical faces that we have so far portrayed in this series are meant to be taken for what they are—far from complete clinical pictures of common clinical states accumulated over the years from various sources. They represent an attempt on our part to share our clinical findings with other clinicians so that more finished and accurate portraits may gradually emerge. This is about as much as the state of the field can provide at the present time, but, like childhood itself, the art and science of child psychiatry is still in the process of growth. This volume represents at best another stage in this development.

E. JAMES ANTHONY, M.D.

PART I: THE HYSTERICAL CHILD

Chapter 1

The Flowers of Mankind

E. JAMES ANTHONY

Hysterics are the flowers of mankind, sterile,
no doubt, but beautiful as double flowers.
Freud, 1893–95

One of the fascinations for the clinician is to meet the familiar psychopathology of the adult in its less fully developed childhood form. It may not be as distinctive or as stable, but being nearer the roots, it is etiologically more illuminating. The childhood face of the hysteric is already elusive and enigmatic, but as in the adult disorder, there are a wide variety of sensory, motor and psychic disturbances that either may make their appearance in the absence of any known organic pathology or may accompany organic illness and grossly exaggerate its effects.

The diagnosis is at first made on the basis of eliminating all possible physical causalities. When these symptoms without apparent cause are counted, a critical quantity is supposed to establish the diagnosis. More dynamic clinicians search for specific types of personality and conflict that conduce to the hysterical reaction. For many physicians operating in a busy medical clinic, the diagnosis of hysteria is often viewed as a victory for the doctor and a defeat for the patient, whose bizarre business is seemingly to bluff the doctor into the belief that he is suffering from a physical disorder. The label is therefore not too clearly distinguished from that of frank malingering. Once the hysterical patient is "found out," he is often treated with a humiliating lack of respect as some sort of imposter, and the naïveté of his anatomical understanding might be demonstrated to the students as a cautionary lesson in how not to be medically misled. The patient might then be summarily dismissed from the clinic or referred to the psychiatrist. Less than a hundred years ago, if he was living in Vienna he might have been

1

fortunate enough to have fallen into the clinical hands of Freud and Breuer, and the underlying reasons for his mysterious malady would have been systematically and respectfully explored.

The history of childhood hysteria is a short one, whereas the adult counterpart was already well recognized in ancient times. The Greek term *hystera* related initially to the frenetic emotional state into which the devotees of the goddess Aphrodite worked themselves during the orgies at the start of every new year. Later, Greek physicians would account for unstable and mobile disturbances in young females with the intriguing theory of a wandering uterus that created a variety of symptoms during the course of its itinerary through the abdominal cavity. Galen pulled together this conglomerate of medical and folk lore around 200 A.D., and defined the "hysterical passion" as a generic label for "varied and innumerable forms" that at times affected even men, in whom it led to the retention of sperm. What is most surprising in this history is that seventeen hundred years later, hysteria was once again reconnected to the sexual apparatus, first by Charcot and then by Freud and Breuer.

Charcot laid down several principles: that hysteria ran in families; that it frequently had a sexual etiology; that it occurred in major and minor forms, with the latter being frequently overlooked; and that it was commoner in men, especially working-class men, than even Galen had supposed. The rest of Europe was scandalized by this French insouciance, since, according to them, the male was by definition nonhysterical; so-called male hysteria could therefore only be a French ailment. Charcot retaliated by diagnosing, at a distance, a case of "reflex epilepsy" in a German grenadier as hysterical.

Freud was very much on the side of his mentor, and declared unequivocally that Charcot's work entitled him "for all time to the glory of being the first to elucidate hysteria."

In addition to this powerful influence on his ideas, Freud was also interested in the views put forward by Moebius, who believed that hysteria was ubiquitous, that almost everyone had a touch of it, some more than others, and that the essential change in hysteria was similar to what took place under hypnosis.

While allowing for its commonality in minor forms, Freud and Breuer felt that clinical hysteria had to have some additional dispositional characteristics that created an "innate breeding ground" for hysteria and cultivated an abnormal expression of emotions. This took the form of a certain liveliness, a restlessness, a craving for sensation, an intolerance of monotony and boredom, a tendency to exaggerate and dramatize, and an intense inhancement of sensory experience that made every pain and pleasure excruciating.

In those early exciting days of psychoanalytic discovery, Freud was well aware that his concepts were still in relatively rudimentary form, although the formulation was not without some portion of the truth, and he was equally aware that there were other acute contemporary minds making excellent observations. "A future exposition of the true state of affairs," he said, "will certainly include them all and will merely combine all the one-sided views of the subject into a corporate reality. Eclecticism, therefore, seems to me nothing to be ashamed of."

Times, however, have changed; and psychoanalysts today are prone to fight shy of any hint of eclecticism and are often ashamed to acknowledge the findings from other disciplines. In these presentations, we will try to adhere to Freud's declaration that eclecticism is not only nothing to be ashamed of, but is something to be considered within the dimensions of a corporate reality.

Since children and adolescents are our main concern, we must ask ourselves a number of crucial questions:

1. Is there such an entity as childhood hysteria, and can it be defined in a distinctive way and diagnosed reliably?

2. Is it related to adult hysteria, and does it become transformed into adult hysteria during the course of time?

3. Is it as common as other disorders in childhood but tending to be confused with them because of its variegated manifestations?

4. Is there any evidence that it is generically determined or that it is sex-linked?

5. Is there a special kind of developmental environment generated by the interplay of constitutional factors, psychosexual conflicts, and abnormal attitudes and behavior on the part of the parents?

6. Are the subtypes—such as conversion hysteria (in which the psychical conflict is expressed symbolically in somatic terms), paroxysmal hysteria (in which emotional crises are accompanied by theatricality), and hysterical phobias—seen during childhood, and if so, at what stage?

7. If there is a major etiopathogenic mechanism at work in hysteria to the extent of affecting the personality organization as a whole, is this apparent at some time during childhood when there are no phobic symptoms or conversions?

According to psychoanalytic theory, the specificity of hysteria is to be found in the prevalence of a particular kind of identification and of particular mechanisms of defense, especially repression, and in the emergence of oedipal conflict in the phallic and oral libidinal spheres. When phobic characteristics were predominant, Freud diagnosed the condition as anxiety hysteria, and pronounced this to be the major neurosis of childhood.

There are certain attributes of childhood that might readily lead to hypnoid hysteria. (That, according to Freud's earlier views, along with retention and defense hysteria, is a form of the disorder in which ideas associated with the hypnoid state remain unintegrated with the everyday self and consciousness.) Children are suggestible, submissive, emotionally less

controlled, and immature in their personality development, so that it might
be expected that a dissociation of conscious and unconscious may easily take
place. This is in fact not the case, and it is difficult to explain why
dissociation (except for some hypnagogic and hypnopompic states on falling
asleep and waking up) is not a frequent feature of childhood psychopathology. Several reasons may be offered as explanations: The child's narcissism
and egocentrism, his lack of introspection, his propensity for reverie, and his
inability to maintain a set of associations may all disqualify him as a
candidate for hysteria. These would stem mostly from those of Breuer's ideas
with which Freud did not agree and which in fact, he found superfluous and
misleading. Nor did he find any value in Janet's notion of a weakness of
synthetic function, a condition also likely to be more prevalent in childhood.
The notion of defense hysteria, favored by Freud, would render the child,
once repression became a major factor in his post-oedipal life, as susceptible
as the adult to the formation of hysteria.

According to Freud (Anthony, 1967), phobic reactions tend to start in
children about four or five years old, obsessional reactions between six and
seven, and the conversion reactions at eight. The amount of background
disturbance is greatest in the conversion reaction and the mixed neurosis,
and seems only slight in the phobic and obsessional reactions. The course of
the phobic reaction seems little influenced by the traumatic factors, whereas
these, such as sexual seduction, play an important role in the three other
subgroups. During the time that he elaborated his seduction hypothesis,
Freud held to the belief that hysterical reactions originated in passive sexual
experiences. The variety of disorders observed in hysteria is well illustrated
in the case of Dora, the adolescent girl that he treated. She masturbated and
wet the bed from the age of 6 until she was 8, developed migraine, a nervous
cough, and hoarseness at the age of twelve, and lost her voice at the age of
sixteen, at which time she also had marked functional abdominal pain and
convulsions. At the end of her teenage period, she developed a very painful
facial neuralgia. What was striking in her history was the change of
personality at the age of eight (the critical age for hysteria, according to
Freud) from uncontrolled tempestuousness to quietness. The symptoms
served to lessen conscious anxiety and to symbolize the underlying mental
conflict, but since they also met the immediate need of the patient, they
served as a source of secondary gain.

At the time when Freud still believed in the role of recent trauma, he
mentioned the case of a little girl who developed convulsions and had
convulsive attacks under hypnosis when she "saw" a dog coming toward her.
Her first attack had occurred soon after she was chased by a mad dog. The
hypnotic abreaction was followed by the disappearance of the symptom,
confirming its hysterical nature. This causal chain was soon to appear too
simplistic in the light of the new complexity with which Freud was regarding

neurosis. He began to postulate the presence of an unbearable idea, a capacity for conversion or somatization, a readiness to dissociate, and early memories that antedated the precipitating traumatic event. He began to feel convinced of the sexual etiology, and at first looked toward sexual experience at puberty and then, beyond puberty, into the dark period of childhood. At this time children were regarded as asexual, and it seemed to him that he must abandon either his sexual hypothesis or his childhood hypothesis. He decided to abandon neither, but rather to incorporate both in a fresh theory that attributed the development of hysteria to the occurrence of actual sexual experience in childhood before the age of eight years (which coincided, he noted, with the appearance of the second dentition).

Soon, however, he was faced with another critical decision when he found that many of the seduction stories told him by his patients had never in fact taken place. He now had to either sacrifice his theory of neurosis based on childhood sexual experience or take a closer look at the "lies." It was at this point in history that he reached his "Copernican" conclusion, that lies—or fantasies, as he now recognized them to be—were even more potent in generating neurotic reactions than reality itself. In the final etiological step, he brought the infantile sexual fantasies into the overall framework of the Oedipus complex, and traced the development of hysteria to the repression of unresolved oedipal wishes that coincided with the early phase of masturbation. Dora's hysteria began, therefore, not at the age of eight, but at the age of six, when her unresolved oedipal fantasies were at their height.

Thus, in psychoanalytic history, child and adult hysterias are intermingled in the same dynamic context. Attempts to let childhood hysteria stand by itself as a clinical entity have not been as successful. As a clinical condition, it was first mentioned by Lepois in 1618, and from 1873 until 1915 there were thirty-six publications devoted to the topic of childhood hysteria. From these publications it is clear that nearly every conceivable form of disturbed behavior was included under the concept. (We have seen the same tendency to inundate a new diagnosis, such as childhood depression, with every disturbance to be observed in the literature.) In 1954 an entire issue of *The Nervous Child* was devoted to the subject, but thereafter references to it gradually subsided to less than a trickle. About three to five cases of hysterical contractures, aphonias, and amblyopias can be expected in the outpatient department of a children's hospital every year, while milder forms of conversion are usually seen as part of a mixed neurotic disturbance with phobic, obsessional, depressive, and sometimes even psychotic elements.

Various psychoanalytic authors have also suggested that hysteria is not as phase-specific as was once thought, and that it may well have its roots in a primary disturbance at the oral level that furnishes it with a paranoid substructure and adds malignant aspects to the hysterical personality.

As the occurrence of hysteria has become less frequent, the hysterical profile has been delineated both dynamically and descriptively. Dynamically, one can observe the strange and even bizarre somatizations, the pseudosexualizations of attitudes and behavior, the metaphoric symbolizations, the denotative pantomimic movements, and the condensation of identifications. The hysteric emerges as the great imitator, the great rememberer, and the great actor with more than his share of histrionic talent.

Freud liked to compare his theory of hysteria to a many-storied building with a psychophysiological base, upon which was erected the minor hysterias, to be followed by the major hysterias, and ultimately by the hysterical psychoses. He felt that the increased frequency of hysteria at puberty was due in part to the emergence of biological sexuality, for which the child was unprepared, to the high degree of suggestibility that conduced at times to autohypnosis, and to the facility for dissociation characteristic of the period.

Descriptively, the so-called Renard school of psychiatry has attempted to add precision to the diagnosis of hysteria, and even to that of childhood hysteria, by providing a checklist with a critical threshold that would lead different observers to a diagnostic consensus. The argument is that one can only investigate hysteria if one first agrees as to what it is. The drawback to this point of view is that the descriptive psychiatrist tends to regard the dynamic profile as speculative and inferential, apart from being inexact, while the dynamic psychiatrist looks upon the checklist not only as simpleminded and devoid of meaning, but also as likely to confound further investigation by an emphasis on observable criteria.

Anthony (1967) has described the type of conversion response—hysterical paresis—that is common at puberty and is sometimes brought about by a strongly worded suggestion from a parental figure. In the girl there is often a marked ambivalent attitude toward boys, alternatively rejecting and inviting. She is at once contemptuous, disparaging, rejecting, and crudely masculine in her behavior, envious of boys and resentful of their unfair advantages. On the other side, she may be seductive and inviting, but in ways that carry a double message. There is no doubt that the biological thrusts of puberty resulting from endocrinological changes often upset the neurotic equilibrium, and previously successful defenses, such as masculine identification in the girl and feminine identification in the boy, are no longer adequate. Anthony (1967) has attempted to illustrate this development:

> An 11-year-old girl, described as having been previously always bright and cheerful, collapsed suddenly in school before an examination and had to be carried home because her legs were "paralyzed." On arriving at her house, she set the whole family in turmoil while she herself remained curiously dispassionate, although she reiterated in a flat tone of voice that it was "all very terrible." On examination, she had a typical glove-and-stocking anesthesia of all four limbs, associated with normal tendon and Babinski responses. There was a history of a less serious attack some months previously, when she had

tried to get to her father's bed after a nightmare and her legs had given away. Her father had carried her back to her own room and had sat with her, but she seemed confused and did not know who he was. The next morning she had no recollection of what had happened. During treatment, which was conducted at home, she developed a strong rapport with the male therapist and felt that he alone could cure her. She talked of becoming increasingly upset before the examination and of fearing that her father would be disappointed with her if she did not do well. She always did all her work "for Daddy" because her mother did not appear to appreciate her school achievements and even deprecated them. She hated her mother for this attitude, as well as for the way she treated her husband. She would quite understand if her father decided to leave home and take her with him, since she was certain she could do a much better job of looking after him than her mother did. As these ideas came into consciousness, and she became increasingly anxious, her paresis rapidly disappeared.

The prognosis for both conversion and dissociative states in children and adolescents is generally good, since the condition often disappears spontaneously in the course of a few months, to be replaced by some other symptomatic expression, usually from the same reactive group. One occasionally sees alternations of fugue states, somnambulisms, and twilight states.

Once the personality becomes "hysterical" in configuration, the prognosis tends to become less favorable, and repeated attacks may occur. The dictum that hysterical parents have hysterical children is probably truer for associative reactions than for other hysterical states. In the entire series of *The Psychoanalytic Study of the Child*, which offers us, to some extent, the clinical history of childhood since 1945, hysterical states were described in their first few years and then mysteriously disappeared from the scene. The analysis of a hysterical eight-year-old girl by Bornstein (1945) and of a hysterical eight-year-old boy by Waelder Hall (1945) offers us at least some idea of how such children behave in treatment, what mechanisms are at play in the hysterogenesis, and what meanings of the symbolic manifestations are uncovered.

Sonya had her first attack at the age of six, in which she ran out on the road and beckoned to men driving by on the highway in a very seductive and coquettish manner. The episodes were repeated and when her mother tried to stop her, she became hostile and threatened her and herself with a knife. She responded when called by her name, recognized people (except for her father) and when the attack was over, she whimpered and whined and clung affectionately to her mother pleading for protection. She appeared to have a complete amnesia for what she referred to as her "foolishness." The history prior to six was traumatic. At the age of four, a sister was born, and at the age of four and a half, she was seduced by a maternal uncle who also infected her at the same time with gonorrhea. The mother covered up the incident and blamed herself for leaving the girl unsupervised, but Sonya experienced the vaginal discharge as an aspect of her badness and that [*sic*] she would be punished by not being able to have children. She was also very upset that her mother appeared to spend endless time with her baby sister and to neglect her. The dream material brought by the girl to treatment repeated the various aspects of the attack and Bornstein asked herself, many years after Freud had abandoned his seduction theory for the genesis of neurosis, the part the actual seduction played in Sonya's hysteria. What the child remembered and brought back into the treatment was the remark made by her mother that Sonya and her young uncle were just foolish children who did not know what they were doing. The fugue state then represented in a dramatic fashion the act of not knowing what she was doing and for which she could therefore not be held accountable. After 11 months of analysis, the child was freed from her symptoms but treatment had to be terminated. The setting of the stage by the pre-Oedipal experiences could only be inferred but it did seem that the discontinuation of indirect sexual gratification by the parents was important in the formation of the hysterical symptom. The intolerance of frustration of the need to leave the place of temptation seemed crucial in generating the twilight state.

The case described by Waelder Hall was also, curiously enough, related to actual seduction: The only two analyzed cases of childhood hysteria to be fully reported agreed in this one important respect almost as if they had set out to confirm Freud's older theory.

Anton began to have severe night terrors (*pavor nocturnus*) at the age of seven years for which he had complete amnesia when he woke to full consciousness. The marital relationship between the parents was not a happy one. The father was given to sudden menacing rages and his mother turned instead to her son whom she declared that she loved more than anybody else in the world and who made up for her unsatisfactory marriage. The boy's fears related more to losing his mother's love than to being beaten by his father. He insisted on sleeping with his mother because of his night terrors and when the therapist suggested to him that it was also because he wanted his mother to himself, Anton replied: "Yes, of course; she belongs to me," adding, after a short pause, "Oh, and to my father." The therapist then went on to suggest further that Anton wanted his mother all to himself to which he replied: "Yes, because he is bad. He torments my mother and there's never peace when he's around. He tickles her on the neck in bed." While coming out with this material he got very hot and excited.

What was extraordinary about this child analysis carried out 50 years ago was that a complete transference neurosis developed in the patient. He first confessed about his sexual seduction by another boy, throwing himself upon the couch and, in a state of surrender, demanded what else she wanted to know about him. Then his mood changed, and he became extremely aggressive toward her, threatening to attack her, behaving toward her like his father behaved toward his mother. He then revealed that he had the idea that his father was trying to take the therapist away from him and he suspected that his father had kissed the therapist when he saw her and was going to do even more. He began to devise sadistic tortures, one of which involved never being allowed to lie down. That was the forbidden (especially lying down in bed with his mother or therapist!). He became increasingly entranced with the analyst and said to her that he loved her and wanted to marry her. This declaration was accompanied by a fantasy in which she would be walking down the street on an icy day and would suddenly slip so that her skirt would fly up and he would see what lay under it. With the analysis of his castration anxieties, his masturbation guilt, his concern between differences between males and females and his curiosity about what happened in the parental bedroom, the transference neurosis was gradually resolved. Six years later, he was going through a very normal, non-turbulent puberty, had no memory of his treatment and was regarded as a very nice child.

What is evident from these case studies is that the hysterical child is eminently treatable, responds well to insight, and is inclined to develop intense transference manifestations, during which the hysterical attack may repeat itself in blatant form. We are becoming increasingly aware of the shifts in psychopathology that take place with the passage of years: Psychoneuroses have given place to character disorders even before we have completed our understanding of the psychoneuroses. Childhood neurosis seems to have dwindled to an even greater extent, and it may be that every step in a developing civilization generates its own idiosyncratic types of disturbance. As the culture advances, the clinical phases of children and adolescents undergo change. The psychopathologist is forever trying to correlate the clinical realities with which he is confronted and the underlying psychological mechanisms that appear to cause them, but he is never sure how closely the shadow and the substance are related. Before we have time to complete our investigations of the particular neurosis, the century hurries by, the culture is transformed, and a new psychopathology makes its appearance. The best we can do theoretically may help to improve our clinical practice, but it may not correspond to the truth. Speaking of hysteria, Freud quotes Theseus from *A Midsummer Night's Dream*:

> The best in this kind are but shadows, and even the weakest is not without value, if it honestly and modestly tries to hold on to the outline to the shadows which the unknown real objects throw upon the wall. For then, in spite of everything, the hope is always justified that there may be some degree of correspondence and similarity between the real processes as they occur and our idea of them.

In this section, we shall try "honestly and modestly" to construct an outline that may help a little toward an explanation of this most mysterious malady.

REFERENCES

Anthony, E. J. (1967) Psychoneurotic disorders. In *Comprehensive Textbook of Psychiatry*, A. M. Freedman and H. I. Kaplan, eds. Baltimore: Williams and Wilkins.

Bornstein, B. (1945) Clinical notes on child analysis. In *The Psychoanalytic Study of the Child*, Vol. I, A. Freud, H. Hartmann, and E. Kris, eds. New York: International Universities Press.

Breuer, J., and Freud, S. (1955) *Studies on Hysteria*, Standard ed., Vol. 2. London: Hogarth Press.

Waelder Hall, Jenny (1945) The analysis of a case of night terror. In *The Psychoanalytic Study of the Child*, Vol. II, A. Freud, H. Hartmann, and E. Kris, eds. New York: International Universities Press.

Chapter 2

The Hysterical Child

HENRY P. COPPOLILLO

INTRODUCTORY CONCEPTS

Hysteria has been a subject of fascination to humanity since the time of Hippocrates, and while many of its puzzles have been investigated and solved in the last hundred and fifty years, we would be guilty of complacency if we did not acknowledge that aspects of the condition continue to perplex us. Once named the Proteus of pathology, it has lived up to its reputation of changing its form and appearance from place to place and from age to age.

Recently we have become aware that our descriptions and our explanations regarding the etiology and pathogenesis of hysteria have become a psychological Tower of Babel. I have become convinced that one reason for this confusion is that hysteria can be viewed from different perspectives while using different frames of reference. This diversity is desirable and perhaps even necessary if we are to achieve a satisfactory understanding of hysteria. We have gotten into trouble, however, when an investigator viewing the condition from one point of view, and using the techniques of investigation appropriate for that point of view, seeks to translate the findings into explanations and arguments directed at concepts pertinent to an entirely different frame of reference. For example, hysteria can be studied in relation to the culture in which it occurs (Kaufman, 1962); or a descriptive approach can be used, and the symptoms by which it is manifested can be described microscopically. They can then be clustered, correlated, and listed in order of their frequency (Liskow et al. 1977; Hartmann and Loewenstein, 1946). Patterns of interpersonal relatedness of the hysteric can be studied (Celani, 1976), or the intraorganismic forces that comprise the psychodynamics of the individual hysteric can be unraveled from his or her diagnostic evaluation and therapy (Federn, 1940). It is, however, as scientifically naïve

11

to attempt to describe or argue for or against psychodynamic considerations using a strictly descriptive approach to the study of hysteria as it would be to attempt to use even the most artistically taken and detailed photograph of the human torso instead of an X-ray to document or describe fractures of the ribs. By the same token, even the most technically perfect X-ray would not do full justice to Racquel Welch's torso.

In the area of psychoanalytic considerations (an area I should like to address in this paper), we have wandered into obscure ground on several issues, especially in considering children. Let me mention just a couple of these areas. In speaking of childhood hysteria, we have often lumped all of its manifestations together and failed to consider whether we were speaking of transitory hysterical manifestations, such as phobias of early childhood, or of the more stable and stubborn conversions, the more ominous and rare dissociative states, or the life-style condition that we call the hysterical character. Do these conditions have a common etiology and pathogenesis? Are they different illnesses? Are they different phases of the same condition? Is it the biogenetic endowment of the individual that will determine what form the hysteria will take? These are questions that have not been satisfactorily answered. Yet there are times when hysteria in children is discussed as if these were settled issues and the people interested in behavior had come to a common acceptance and understanding of the terms involved.

In psychoanalytic thinking, hysteria was first conceptualized as one of the transference neuroses. Transference was used here by Freud as it was used in *The Interpretation of Dreams* (1953). In this context it is a psychological observation describing the unconscious *transfer* of the memory of a wish, impulse, affect, or conviction from the past into a current life situation. The phenomenon of transference was then explained through the use of metapsychological concepts, such as cathexis, energic imbalances, displacements, countercathexis, etc. Unfortunately, the term and concept changed, and "transference" became more narrowly used to describe some of the ways the patient perceived his or her analyst. Since a number of child analysts felt that children could not develop a transference neurosis if their parents were still real and active forces in their lives, it appears that a number of people began to confuse the transference neuroses, transference neurosis, and symptoms predicated on transference. This added to the confusion in conceptualizing pathogenesis in children. I would like to return to the concept of transference in a few minutes.

CLINICAL CONSIDERATIONS AND DIFFERENTIAL DIAGNOSIS

For our purposes we will attempt to define a number of conditions that are seen in childhood and then attempt to differentiate them from other psychological or behavioral states that may be superficially similar but may have very different implications in terms of the child's prognosis or state of his personality. In speaking of hysteria in children, we will include phobias or phobic states, conversions, dissociative states or reactions, and a particular disturbance of personality or character organization called the hysterical character.

We may define "phobia" as the irrational fear of an object or a class of objects that the child then attempts to avoid. When the fear includes a group or class of objects, the link that connects them may be patently clear, as in the case of a child's fear of all large animals. Or the connecting links may be obscure on superficial examination and revealed only when the child's associations are microscopically examined and unconscious or suppressed connections are elicited. A child with a phobia usually cannot be comforted by the usual rational reassurances, and the quality ascribed to the objects that renders them frightening is generated from the child's unconscious fantasies, wishes, or experiences. I consider this latter consideration to be the pathonomic quality of a phobia even if the manifest reason given for the fear is a rational and realistic one. If, for example, a child states that he will not leave his home because he is afraid that a dog in the neighborhood will bite him and we discover that the fear had its origin in an unconscious wish or in the conviction that retaliation would ensue from an unacceptable wish, we are forced to conclude that the child suffers from a phobia, even if there is a large Doberman pinscher perched on his front stoop. If the evidence is that there is no such wish or fear of retaliation, then the child's fear of the Doberman may safely be called good sense. The presence or absence of a phobic state cannot be determined from the apparent rationality or irrationality alone. But wait. Some will say by this definition phobias are ubiquitous—and indeed I think they are. I would like to return to this later.

For this presentation, "conversion symptoms" may be described as those conditions in which an unconscious conflict is expressed by physical symptoms that represent the unconscious conflict symbolically. The alteration of function or appearance of the body part that is affected is not caused by an anatomical or physiological change, although anatomical or physiological changes can accompany or follow the conversion phenomena.

"Dissociative states" are states of experiences or a sequence of behaviors which either remain completely out of awareness of the core personality of the patient or are experienced as having been lived by one other than the self. Multiple personality is a severe form of dissociation.

Fiinally, we shall consider the "hysterical character" or "hysterical personality" as the descriptive term for people whose mode of reacting and interacting follows a relatively stable and predictable pattern. They are people who are inordinately preoccupied with themselves and how they appear to others. They are dramatic, somewhat given to hyperbole in their interpersonal affairs, and often accompany their emotional lability with superficiality in their capacity for insight and understanding. Frequently they infer sexual or aggressive intent in the communications of others, and while they see sexuality or hostility everywhere, they disavow their own sexual or aggressive feelings or impulses. Despite their constant demand for approbation, attention, and support from others, they frequently have very little to give themselves. This style of interacting with the world is essentially the only one they have available to them, and their relationships are monotonously alike.

Having described the condition or group of conditions that we will be discussing, I should like to discuss briefly the current concepts of pathogenesis of the various conditions; to use these concepts to help us differentiate the various conditions from other psychopathological states; and finally, to see if adding a new conceptualization may help us to understand another aspect of the pathology in hysteria.

In order to review the psychodynamic pathogenesis of hysteria, a brief review of ego development and symptom formation is necessary. Many of Freud's early contributions to the psychodynamic understanding of hysterical symptoms came within the context of the topographic model of the mental apparatus. In this context he conceived of consciousness as an organ of internal perception, and the mental content that was conscious at any given moment as but a miniscule part of the content of the whole mental apparatus. This organ of perception, called consciousness, could be turned and directed to a number of percepts, body sensations, memory traces, wishes, etc., that were available to conscious scrutiny and were governed and regulated by the reality principle (or in Western civilization, by Aristotelian logic). A man who is determined to acquire a certain amount of economic well-being by working knows, for example, that he has to arise from bed at a certain time in the morning, and because he is hungry, goes to the kitchen to light the gas to warm the coffee. Following this, he goes to the bathroom to shower and shave, then back to the kitchen to drink his coffee, eat breakfast, finish dressing and leave his home to catch the bus to work. One day this logical, adaptive, and well-rehearsed chain of events is interrupted by the intrusion of an unforeseen experience: Let us say that after all of his preparations, while he is walking down his front stairs, our serene and adaptable man is assailed by the conviction that he left the gas on under the coffee. Although he is relatively sure that he turned the gas off, a nagging doubt about the accuracy of his memory and an inordinate fear about the possible consequences of a mistake force him to return to the kitchen, reach over to the gas jet, and touch it to make sure it is off. Again our worker sets off to reestablish the logical and purposive activity of his typical day, only to again encounter the doubt and anxiety on the staircase. He may remark to himself that the anxiety is absurd, and that when he reached over to touch the gas jet, it was indeed off and he did not accidentally turn it on. Perhaps he can find the strength to overcome his anxiety and proceed to work, or perhaps he finds he must once more return upstairs to restart the touching doubting cycle. In any event the stable, logical, adaptive patterns of behavior regulated by the memory traces stored in that part of the mind that is readily available to conscious scrutiny have been disrupted by the intrusion of a maladaptively disturbing thought.

Through the use of hypnosis and free association, Freud discovered that there was another part of the mental apparatus, not readily available to conscious scrutiny, in which thoughts, wishes, feelings, convictions, and images seethed in apparent chaos, waiting to make their presence felt by disrupting the processes that humans use to adapt to external reality. As you are aware, he called this group of thought fragments the unconscious. By the systematic study of slips of the tongue and other parapraxes, by the interpretation of dreams and the study of wit, he demonstrated that the unconscious was filled with experiences from the past which the human organism attempted to *actively* bar from conscious scrutiny and which were regulated by a set of laws that followed their own logic; these laws were called the primary process. He demonstrated that under certain conditions these thoughts escaped the barrier that the organism had erected in an effort to impede their capacity to capture consciousness, and they affected the way their unwitting host perceived or adapted to situations in the present. The process by which attitudes, wishes, percepts, or convictions from the past affect objects, thoughts, convictions, or adaptations in the present was called transference. We will return to this concept of transference as we address the pathogenesis of some forms of hysteria.

The other concept that needs exploration is that of the structural model as modified by Hartmann (1939) and Hartmann et al. (1946). We must then conceptualize that as ego and id evolve from an undifferentiated matrix, one group of functions develops from the stimulation that impinges on them from external reality. It appears that although these functions can be directed and stimulated by drive activity, they do not depend on drives per se for their maturation. They are, however, dependent on stimulation from the external world. Hartmann called these the autonomous functions of the ego, because they are relatively autonomous from the id and drive activity. Perceptual ability, motoric ability, capacity to lay down and retrieve memory traces, are a few of these functions.

There are, however, a number of other ego functions that are dependent for their development on the interplay between the drives and external reality. Let us take a grossly simplified example: Suppose that Johnny, age four, driven by voyeuristic impulses, is peeking through the keyhole in the bathroom door at his mother or an older sister, who is taking a bath. This rapturous interlude is interrupted by the footfall of that hobnail-booted giant who is known as "Dad" around the house. As Johnny stands there quaking internally, let us contemplate only two of the infinite number of possible parental responses as perceived by the boy. Suppose that in one instance, either because of the father's conflicts about sexuality or because of cultural or moral convictions, or possibly because of Johnny's perception, his father's response appears massively threatening. Johnny, under this threat, must avoid expressing his impulse. Remembering that a four-year-old's capacity for abstraction does not permit him to differentiate between wish and deed, we must assume that in most instances he will soon find it necessary to turn away, not only from the deed but also from the wish. In this way repression has begun, and at least a part of the drive is lost for further use as a force in ego development.

In the second example, Johnny's father may approach him and say, "Look, buddy, you can't go peeking at people through bathroom doors. Everyone has a right to privacy. You'll be able to see what nude women look like when you're older." Or perhaps, as happens in more intellectually oriented people, he shows his child a picture of a nude woman. This latter response, while still prohibiting the direct expression of the child's wish, offers in addition two important bits of communication: It says that while the wish could not be gratified in the manner Johnny was using, Johnny would have the right to gratify the wish in the culturally proper way and at the proper time. Secondly, the communication underlines that there are culturally sanctioned ways of gratifying wishes and drives. With these communications, Johnny is not only authorized and encouraged to avoid squelching and repressing an impulse or desire, he is also invited to imitate, discover, or invent socially acceptable ways of meeting these wishes. Father has acted as a mediator between the impulses, the ego, and reality. He has assumed the role of a temporary auxiliary ego and fostered sublimation and neutralization. These new-found culturally acceptable ways of gratifying drives and component instincts will one day again be subjected to optimal frustration, and the process of acquiring increasingly more mature and productive techniques for adaptation will continue.

Having reviewed some fundamental concepts of ego development, we may use these concepts as a frame of reference to consider a number of ways that symptoms develop in the ego and to attempt to correlate these with the forms of hysteria as we have defined them. When either externally precipitated or internally perceived trauma occurs, the individual passes through a number of steps before the full-blown symptom appears. In the first of these steps, the traumatized individual may go over and over the event in fantasy to attempt to master the pain or to find a more satisfactory way of adapting. Who of us has not been in a social situation, perhaps holding forth on a favorite topic, where we felt that for one brief, shining moment every ear was straining to gather every pearl of wisdom that we uttered. At just about that time, a gross, insensitive, intellectual bully—and especially one that comes equipped with facts, figures, and the memory of a bull elephant—shoots us out of orbit with one deft, cruel, and beautifully articulated phrase. Try as we may, no retort comes to our lips, and the evening is ruined. Have you noticed what happens next? During the drive home and perhaps, if the wound is deep and grievous enough, for the next couple of days, the recurring fantasy is, "I should have said . . . " and a scathing, flaying rejoinder worthy of an Oscar Wilde or a Shaw presents itself to us—alas, too late. This happens frequently enough to merit a special phrase for it in French. They call it *espirit d'escalier*, "the wit that occurs to you on the staircase going home." This is an example of the first reaction to a traumatic event, one that, fortunately for most of us, is reversible in that we tire of the fantasy in a couple of days, resolve to become the best-informed member of that social set by subscribing to *Time*, *Newsweek*, or *Playboy*, and proceed about our business.

If, however, the adaptive techniques we attempt to employ to reestablish our former state of psychological equilibrium or equanimity are not successful or are no longer available, a second step in the process occurs that is more difficult to control. The individual thus suffering psychic pain attempts to return to modes of relating or adapting that had worked for him in the past. In a word, he regresses. With regression, the person not only invests in adaptive styles that had once been successful; he also, without wanting to do so, invests in the conflicts and impulses that had to be banned from awareness by repression and also perhaps by some mechanisms of defense. In the face of this renewed investment, the impulses become more powerful than the mental mechanisms that were used to bar them from awareness, and a psychological imbalance occurs. It is in this state of imbalance that wishes and attitudes from the past transfer themselves onto objects or situations in the here-and-now. Since the original attitude or impulse had to be banned from awareness in the past because it had elicited fear or anxiety, it is not surprising that as it tends to reemerge, even in disguised form, it is accompanied by signals of discomfort and anxiety. The ego at this point no longer attempts to solve the problem of the original hurt, but reacts to the more immediate and compelling need to alleviate the threatening anxiety, and additional defenses are called into play. The symbolic representation of impulse and the defenses that the anxiety has mobilized constitute the neurotic symptom. It can therefore also be called a compromise formation.

Although in later writings Freud substituted the term "displacement" for "transference," this model of symptom formation has been the classical model to describe the pathogenesis of neurotic symptoms, and continues to serve us well. In the case of phobias, we can conceive that an unwelcome impulse or the defenses used to control it were transferred from the child's past to a discrete object in its current life. The monsters of the latency-age child are often thinly disguised derivatives of the ogre to whom the child was valiantly but inexorably losing the oedipal battle. The impulse in the compromise formation of the monster phobia is represented by both the aggression projected onto the monster and the child's justified anger and hostility toward him. The defense is represented by the relative control the child has over all monsters as he runs to his mother, flips on the night-light switch, or turns off the television set.

To return now to the issue of the ubiquity of phobias, a glance at development and at everyday adaptation should dispel any doubt that phobias are ubiquitous. What is equally clear, however, is that *most* phobias are easily controlled. Either through the adaptive use of knowledge or through appropriate motor behavior, the child or the adult learns to stay away from places where snakes or spiders may lurk. By controlling fascination and turning it into curiosity, a self-devised program of desensitization may reduce phobias. The important issue is that the ego may marshal its resources not only to defend against the anxiety elicited by the original impulse that generated the phobia, but also to reorganize the resources so that the phobia disappears or becomes innocuous.

Understanding and classifying the conversion symptom has not been as linear as in the case of phobias. Conversion symptoms were originally thought to be confined only to the perceptual apparatus and to the voluntary musculature. A number of observations have led us to acknowledge that involuntary processes, such as those that occur in the digestive tract or cardiovascular system, can meet the criteria of conversion symptoms. Engel has addressed himself to this problem, maintaining that any function that can be perceived by the individual and acquires mental representation is capable of being disrupted by a psychological process and of serving as the symbolic representation of an unconscious conflict (1962). I would submit, therefore, that in the case of conversion, the unconscious impulse is transferred or displaced, but not onto an external object, as in the case of a phobia; rather, the process is directed toward any body process that has been represented by a memory trace in the patient. Thus motor or sensory activity can become affected as well as the borborygmi or peristaltic movements of the gastrointestinal tract if it has been perceived and associated with an unconscious conflictual wish.

Prugh (1963) helped to reduce the confusion in this area by articulating a number of criteria for the diagnosis of a conversion symptom in a child. He insists (1) that the diagnostician find an unconscious unresolved conflict, (2) that he find a demonstrable precipitating event or events, (3) that the symptoms symbolically represent the repressed impulses and defenses, and (4) that there be unconscious secondary gain from the illness.

At this point it would be good to present a case illustration of conversion hysteria in a twelve-year-old boy. Larry was referred to a community mental health center after being worked up for ataxia in the pediatrics section of a community hospital. Since they could find no demonstrable organic lesion, they assumed that his problem was psychogenic. Our own evaluation revealed that Larry was the third child born in his family. He had a sister four years older than he and one that was six years older. The eldest sister was married and had been out of the home for about a year prior to the onset of the illness. The household until just before the illness had consisted of father, who was a steelworker; mother, a full-time homemaker who had worked for only a brief period some years before when the father had been on strike; the older sister, and Larry. The information that we elicited indicated that both mother and father had been devoted and stable parents for the better part of the children's lives.

Larry had been born following an unremarkable pregnancy and delivery. His development was well within normal limits both psychologically and physiologically until he was about five years of age. At that time he began to exhibit some irritability in kindergarten and began having nightmares two or three times per week. Mother, from whom we obtained the developmental history, stated that she thought that Larry was most afraid when father worked the evening and night shifts, because it was then that he was most likely to awaken with a nightmare and insist on sleeping in her bed. These problems went on for about a year and then gradually disappeared. For the most part, however, mother stated that Larry was a bright, communicative, and active little boy. At about six-and-one-half, and almost coincidentally with the disappearance of the nightmares, Larry became quieter, less joyful, and perhaps a bit withdrawn, mother noticed. He continued to do well in school, and mother thought that the change in him was principally due to maturation.

Larry's paternal grandmother died approximately one year before the onset of Larry's symptoms. Following the grandmother's death, a marked change occurred in Larry's father. He began to delay his arrival home from work more and more frequently and arrived home drunk several times a week. He became truculent when drunk, and after a number of months became physically violent in the home. By the end of that year he had begun to beat Larry's mother, and on one occasion threatened to hit Larry. One day, following one of these violent episodes, while father was at work mother packed her bags, and with the children, went to the small town where her eldest daughter lived. She called her husband from there, telling him that she would return home only after he could demonstrate to himself and to her that he would drink no more. She rented a small apartment near her daughter's home and found a job. The eldest daughter was to mind the children for the hour or so between the time school was dismissed and the time mother could come home from her job. One evening about a week after they were in their own apartment, there was a disturbance in the apartment next to them. Their next-door neighbors had a family quarrel, during which voices were raised, and there were sounds of doors being slammed. At this time Larry became extremely fearful and agitated, saying that "Daddy's come to get us." Mother states that he was so frightened and agitated that she felt it necessary to hold him. After she had calmed him down a bit she suggested that he go to bed. The next morning she noticed the peculiar ataxia that brought him first to the pediatrician and then to see us.

When we saw Larry we found a very sober and quiet child who looked a bit younger than his stated age. He was extremely uncommunicative and could tell us very little about his illness or about his feelings regarding the move, the separation from his father, or even how he felt about seeing the doctors he had seen. In an extremely bland manner he was perfectly willing to demonstrate his difficulty to us but was literally incapable or unwilling to say one word about the incapacity to walk comfortably.

While walking there were very dramatic losses of balance, and he would sometimes career from one piece of furniture to the other in the room. The difficulty was all caused by a peculiar oscillatorylike movement of his thighs while the lower parts of his legs took ineffective and erratic small steps. In contrast to the dramatic losses of balance and the agonizing ineffectiveness of his attempts to walk, Larry's equanimity remained intact. While we suspected that the problem was a conversion reaction, we could not get enough information from Larry to permit us to demonstrate the psychological underpinnings of the symptoms. This, plus the fact that we attempted to interview him, with very scant results, countless times over a three-week period and the mother's conviction that Larry was getting worse, led us to rehospitalize the boy, reexamine him, and at the same time conduct an Amytal interview. During the Amytal interview we discovered a number of concerns that Larry had that were repressed or suppressed. He said that he had urged his mother to leave and take him with her because he was afraid of his father. He thought his father would hurt him if he became aware that Larry was the cause of his mother's running away from home. He was also afraid that father would find out where they were staying and would come to hurt him. Finally, he revealed that when they decided to leave home, he wanted his mother to run with him. At this point his thighs began to oscillate rapidly even as he was on the table. He said that he should have stayed home even though he wanted to run away; otherwise his father would say he was a bad boy and would come to kill him. We thus found the symbolic significance of the rapid leg movements. They expressed both the wish to run with the oscillating movements of the thighs and the defense against the impulse through the ineffectiveness of the total movement and the helplessness that made him dependent on the mother. The secondary gain was the amount of attention he was getting and the control he exercised over his mother.

Of all the forms of hysteria, conversion is the one that requires the most finely tuned differential diagnosis. I believe this is true both because of the need to understand the pathology and because management of a number of conditions that simulate it is very different.

First, conversion hysteria must be differentiated from the psychosomatic conditions. In these the autonomic nervous system plays a much more important role, and the physiologic changes that ensue may gradually evolve toward irreversibility. The prevention of irreversible tissue changes with medication and physical means when necessary is as urgent a consideration as the alleviation of the psychological condition that may have been a contributory or precipitating cause. Furthermore, despite some picturesque language used in describing psychosomatic illness some three decades past (such as "the asthmatic wheeze is the unconscious cry for the mother"), the psychosomatic symptom has never been demonstrated to have consistent symbolic significance.

Hysteria must also be differentiated from the kind of somatic symptoms that, for lack of a better term, can be called somatization. Among these symptoms I would include those that are the direct physical expression of a distressing psychological state. These symptoms may or may not involve autonomic innervation, but they have no symbolic communicative value. The headache or the stomachache that the school-age child experiences Monday through Friday may be because the child is so concerned about going to school that he has slept badly and indeed has a headache. Or it may also be that he has no words in his repertoire to express experiences such as anxiety, terror, or sadness, and finds that the words of physical illness are the closest he can come to communicating feelings. I mention somatization because my clinical experience tells me that especially in adolescence, somatization is frequently the expression for a depression. Despite the fact that some of our colleagues have in the past doubted or been unconcerned about depression existing in children and adolescents, I have come to take it very seriously. Somatic complaints in children, as in adults for that matter, may be the way these unhappy people plead for relief. In differentiating the two conditions, it is helpful to remember the dramatic communicative élan of the hysteric. The symptoms are described in terms that are bigger than life and in a style designed to rivet you to your chair and your attention to the ailing part. Not so in somatization: The patient communicates the draining, corrosive quality of his saddened and weary state. The effect on the diagnostician is one of being drained or wearied.

Finally, conversion symptoms must be separated from another phenomenon that may be the harbinger of a more ominous and serious condition. I am speaking now of the hypochondriacal concerns of the person who is undergoing prepsychotic decompensation. In this situation, the person buffered and removed from external stimuli by his withdrawal from the world of reality begins to perceive proprioceptive and enteroceptive sensations as intrusive and compelling. In an attempt to give these internally generated sensations meaning and thus master them, he invokes his already damaged cognitive equipment. The result is a grotesque and bizarre admixture of descriptions and causal explanations that convey that his own body is a repository of terror and horror for the patient, from which the only escape seems madness.

To illustrate, the following is one of a series of themes written in an English class by a twelve-year-old girl who was in the process of psychotic decompensation. By way of background, we discovered that the child's mother had died in a state hospital about a year before the decompensation had begun. Her father had recently remarried (Coppolillo, 1965).*

OLD MAN MASHER

Long ago, in a village, lived Old Man Masher. They called him Old Man Masher because he had the horrible reputation of mashing other people.

This is how it worked. Anytime anyone came to his bone-fenced house he would tell them to come in. Then he would take them down to a dingy dark cellar, where he kept his gigantic potatoe masher. Then he would merely chop off their heads and shove them under his potatoe masher. When they were done being mashed they made the best hash you ever tasted. Or at least he thought so.

If anyone tried to run away he'd simply chase them around with his devil's pitchfork until he caught them. He had got the pitchfork from Santa Clause last Christmas.

One day a little beggar girl came to his house. She was pretty scrawny, but he decided to use her anyway. And her head was pretty hollow so he knew it would make a splendid cooky jar.

Another day a square came to his house. Old Man Masher decided to use him for a chair because he was so square. So he did.

Old Man Masher was always seen waring [sic] a different color of eyes to match the hair ribbon he happened to be waring on his beautiful green hair. He kept all his eyes in a drawer, which he called his own "Private Eye Drawer." The next day a soldier, which was coming home from the war, came to his frightening house. So Old Man Masher took him down to the cellar. Just as he was about to chop the solder's head off. He fell through the trap door which he used for disposal of the heads that were slightly cracked. So that was the end of Old Man Masher. But it was very unfortunate because after that the soldier took Old Man Mashers place and it happened all over again.

As is evident, in addition to the bizarre, macabre quality of relationships, the ambivalences and the pessimism expressed in this theme, the child's concepts of body integrity and body functions are filled with primitive ideas

---

*Reprinted from the *Journal of the Arkansas Medical Society.*

of shifting images and dissolution. A far cry from the dramatic but structured images the hysterical child presents of his body and its functions.

While we have been able to use rather classical theories of drive and defense to conceptualize the pathogenesis of phobias and conversions, I feel we need new models and paradigms to understand dissociative states and the concept of the hysterical character. Libido theory and the descriptions of the defense mechanisms have served us well for eighty years. We would be unwise to abandon or denigrate the insights they provide. Conversely, it would be equally unwise to feel that behavior and mentation could only be explained in terms of a model of drive-defense conflict. Elucidation of the hysterical character and the dissociative states may give us an opportunity to try on some alternative models for size.

In the case of the dissociative reactions, it appears almost obvious that the failure in this condition is one of integration. We can see a child or an adult who has integrated many ego functions to adapt to a number of situations, but the integration is incomplete in that ego functions are lumped in clusters that the patient uses in different ego states; they are not, however, integrated with each other. They may, for example, be very competent and creative in expressing positive feelings to others and in being the recipient of approbation. They conceive of their core identity as that of a person who likes and is liked by people. In their development they become convinced that aggression or hostility is not part of their lives. Somehow, however, they also become quite adept in developing techniques of expressing aggression. This group of functions never becomes integrated with other personality functions, and through repeated disavowals they develop a blind spot in their *self* observation (or more appropriately stated, in the observation of their self system) for their own potential for anger and aggression.

Suppose, then, that a situation arises in which they become enraged at their mother or father. The anger is sufficient to cause behaviors that terrify or repel the person who has an image of himself that does not contemplate anger or aggression. To maintain this image intact, there is a literal alteration of awareness regarding his behavior, and the angry or aggressive act either is not remembered at all or is remembered as if another person had committed it. We could say that this person's ego was organized with more than one cluster of functions that were or were not integrated with a sense of self. In our case example, the sweet, amiable behaviors that seduce love and approbation from others are closely integrated with the sense of self, and the behaviors are regulated by this image of self as the observer sees it interact with the world. The raging angry behavior is not integrated with a sense of self and is therefore not regulated by the total personality. It seems to the observer as though this behavior has escaped the control of the personality and is regulated by the drives.

Thus, the concepts of organization and regulation, primitive as they are at present, become crucial issues in understanding dissociative states if we use this frame of reference.

In thinking of the hysterical character, we find that here, too, an issue of organization is important. No single impulse or wish can be invoked as pathogenic in the hysteric. Rather, we see a whole life style that emerges as certain ego functions, such as self-observation, modulation of affects, or tolerance of frustration, fail to become integrated into the repertoire of activities the person uses to relate and adapt to the world. As we interact with these people, we find that many of their behaviors and reactions are unconsciously designed to control their environment. As we study their histories, we can often demonstrate that they perceived their early lives as so unpredictable and uncontrollable that they despaired of ever being their own masters. As a result, in order to predict their world they provoke predictable responses from it. They then perceive that the regulation of their behavior comes from without and not from within themselves. This calls forth even more provocative behavior, and the hysterical character finds himself in a never-ending spiral of action and reaction that cannot contemplate serenity or gratification.

Again, then, concepts of organization and regulation may be invoked to shed some light on a group of conditions that clamor for elucidation.

Obviously I make no pretense at an exhaustive conceptual treatment of hysteria. I only plead in this presentation for two principles: The first is that we recognize that a human phenomenon can be viewed from a number of points of view and within the context of various frames of reference. If we are to avoid perpetuating chaotic fragmentation of our field, we must be disciplined in our use of these frames of reference and techniques of inquiry, and be even more disciplined in terms of what we feel our findings can prove or disprove when other frames of reference are contemplated.

Secondly, our frames of reference are tools for our use and not masters to which we bow. In the psychoanalytic field we must examine the notion closely that the time has come for us to broaden our conceptual framework beyond that which we already have without destroying the basic tenets of our original frame of reference. While libido theory and conflict psychology have served us well and will continue to do so in years to come, surely we can see that children, the hysterical child included, are more than merely the sum of their conflicts.

REFERENCES

Celani, D. (1976) An interpersonal approach to hysteria. *Am. J. Psychiatry*, 133:12.
Chodoff, P., and Lyons, H. (1958) Hysteria, the hysterical personality and "hysterical" conversion. *Am. J. Psychiatry*, 114:734.

Coppolillo, H.P. (1965) Conversion, hypochondriasis and somatization: A diagnostic problem for internists. *J. Ark. Med. Soc.*, 62 (2):67–71.

Engel, G. (1962) *Psychological Development in Health and Disease.* Philadelphia: W.B. Saunders.

Federn, P. (1940) The determination of hysteria versus obsessional neurosis. *Psychoanal. Rev.*, 27:265–270.

Freud, S. (1900) *The Interpretation of Dreams*, Standard eds. 4 and 5. London: Hogarth Press, 1953.

Gillette, W.R. (1882) Hysteria in early childhood. *N.Y. Med. J.*, 36:66–67.

Hartmann, H. (1939) *Ego Psychology and the Problem of Adaptation.* New York: International Universities Press (1958).

——, Kris, E., and Loewenstein, R. M. (1946) Comments on the formation of psychic structure. *The Psychoanalytic Study of the Child*, 2:11–38. New York: International Universities Press.

Kaufman, I. (1962) Conversion hysteria in latency. *J. Am. Acad. Child Psychiatry*, 1:385.

Liskow, B., Clayton, P., Woodruff, R., Guze, S., and Cloninger, R. (1977) Briquet's syndrome, hysterical personality and MMPI. *Am. J. Psychiatry*, 134 (10):1137–1139.

Marmor, J. (1953) Orality in the hysterical personality. *J. Am. Psychoanal. Assn.*, 1:656.

Perley, M. J., and Guze, S. B. (1962) Hysteria—the stability and usefulness of clinical criteria. *N. Eng. J. Med.*, 266:421–426.

Proctor, J. T. (1959) Hysteria in childhood. *Am. J. Orthopsychiatry*, 28:395.

Prugh, D. G. (1963) Towards an understanding of psychosomatic concepts in relation to illness in childhood. In *Modern Perspectives in Child Development*, Solnit, A. J., and Provence, S.A., eds. New York: International Universities Press.

—— (in press, 1979) *Psychosocial Aspects of Pediatrics.* Philadelphia: Lea and Febiger.

Chapter 3

The Hysterical Personality in Child and Adolescent Analysis

PAULINA F. KERNBERG

GENERAL COMMENTS ABOUT CHARACTER AND CHARACTER FORMATION

A brief review of key concepts concerning character and character formation may be useful for a discussion of the hysterical character in children and adolescents. Glover, cited by Beres (1969), defines character as a set of organized behavioral reactions intended to preserve a stable equilibrium between instinctual drives and the demands of reality. Fenichel (1945) defines character as the ego's habitual modes of adjustment to the external world, the id, and the superego, and the characteristic way of combining these modes with one another. Thus, character disturbances are "limitations or pathological forms of treating the external world, internal drives and demands of the superego, or disturbances of the way in which these various tasks are combined." Fenichel divides character in sublimatory and reactive types according to what in ego psychological terms corresponds to aspects of primary and secondary autonomy structures. With the reactive types, in contrast to the sublimatory types, Fenichel proposes that any subdivisions be made in connection with the corresponding symptomatic neurosis, as mechanisms similar to those involved in symptom formation are operative in "the formation of character traits." For example, he describes phobic and hysterical characters as the characterological equivalents of their respective symptomatic neuroses.

Beres (1969) refers to character development as a consistent pattern of adaptation to reality, whether normal or pathological. According to Beres, the fixed patterns of response characterizing the adult are foreshadowed in the behavior and responses of the small child and pass through recognizable vicissitudes at different phases of the individual's life. Indeed, I would suggest that character styles are present in the child and may be stabilized very early in childhood; that changes are the symptomatic manifestations of character rather than the underlying structure, especially in neurotic and more serious forms of pathological character. A hypothetical chronology of development of character structures would have the following sequence: psychotic and borderline character, zero to two years; hysterical character, three to five years; depressive and compulsive character, the latency-age years. From this perspective, adolescence serves mostly as the stage in which additional refinements are made to already quasi-stable structures.

Beres proposes that the young child deals with his conflict by constantly varying defenses. According to him, this is the reason we see such rapid shifts in the clinical manifestations of children. Beres states that "too early fixity of response in the child may presage serious psychopathology." He believes it is possible to recognize in the child the increasing predominance of certain defenses that indicate the direction of later character structure. Beres in fact attempts to differentiate normal character from pathological character by the predominance of certain defenses, such as projection in the paranoid character, action-proneness in the acting-out character, reaction formation in the obsessive character, and repression in the hysterical character. What is important is the precocious fixity of these defense patterns. The stabilization of these defenses serves to keep the individual free from neurotic symptoms. The resultant behavior patterns, however, are clinically pathological. Whether or not the person seeks professional intervention will depend on the degree of ego dystomicity, the intensity of the effects of the patient's character pathology in interpersonal relations, the availability of treatment resources, and the cultural context.

FACTORS DETERMINING THE FORMATION OF CHARACTER CONFIGURATIONS EARLY IN LIFE

In this section I shall discuss the contribution of endowment to the formation of character (Brazelton, 1973; Korner, 1964; Gardner et al., 1968). In a later section I shall examine the influences of early interaction with the mother, the family, and the cultural environment (Metcalf, 1977; Mahler and Kaplan, 1977). Korner (1964), in her introduction to her classic paper, quotes Freud as stating that "each individual ego is endowed from the beginning with its own peculiar dispositions and tendencies." Korner also adds that Hartmann expands this concept, linking individual differences in the primary ego apparatuses to later choice of defense and, by implication, to choice of illness. Hartmann also introduces the hypothesis of individual differences at birth with regard to the infant's state of adaptedness—that is, his inherent adaptive capacities—and with regard to the inherent degree of differentiation between the ego and the id.

Korner points out the difficulty in building a bridge between neonatal and later behavior. This difficulty is not surprising, because developmental factors proceed toward an ever-increasing complexity and differentiation, which, along with a constantly changing behavioral context, obscure continuities. She suggests, therefore, that the variables studied reflect the formal characteristics of behavior rather than its continuously changing content. Thus, it is "the study of the style of development rather than of the developmental process itself which may provide the continuities in behavior for which we are searching."

Responses to External Stimuli

In the newborn there are already some variables that may relate to the development of hysterical character—for example, the frequency and length of periods of alert inactivity, which is an index of availability to external stimuli. In the first days of life there are periods of alert inactivity in which the infant's eyes are wide open and appear to focus. When observed over twenty-four hours, there are individual differences in the length and frequency of these periods as well as in the infant's capacity for visual and auditory pursuit. Wolff (1959) indicates that the state of alert inactivity may presage a later capacity to pay attention and to concentrate.

Singular or global versus multiple responses to external stimuli may be, as Korner has suggested, a sensorimotor antecedent of later "leveling perceptual modes" (Gardner et al., 1968) and of repressive tendencies. Gardner et al. (1968) demonstrated the capacity of babies to respond to auditory stimulation either with a large repertoire of reactions or with single responses or global bodily response. Thus, at an early age babies *differ in their perceptual styles, cognitive controls, and types of defenses.* Gardner and his colleagues found that "levelers," in contrast to "sharpeners," show more difficulty in perceiving similar stimuli as distinct in various sensory modalities; this incapacity negatively affects learning tasks and recall. In later observations of children between ages nine and thirteen, Gardner et al. found that perceptual style is quite constant over time and shows sex differences. Girls are more characteristically levelers, while boys are more characteristically sharpeners.

Another trait of the infant possibly related to a predisposition to hysterical personality is the response to multiple and competing stimuli. During opthalmological examinations, some babies suck more strenuously when the eye examination begins, others stop completely. This variable may relate to later tendencies of the hysterical child toward motor discharge, or to displacement behavior aimed at tension reduction. It may foreshadow the need for warding-off mechanisms or a propensity to flood the ego apparatuses in the face of massive stimulation.

Influence of Internal State on Behavior, Particularly Sensory Responsiveness

Sensory thresholds vary greatly with deep sleep, irregular sleep, drowsiness, alert inactivity, waking activity, and crying. Babies vary in their autonomy from internal states. The relative strengths of internal and external stimuli can be inferred from the baby's response to external stimuli while under various degrees of hunger tension and during various states of arousal. The more state-bound the infant, the less available he may be to external stimuli and to perceiving mother as differentiated from himself. This latter trait may contribute to the intensity or prolongation of dependency needs, a component of the hysterical character organization.

Distinctness of state. According to Korner, "Some babies demonstrate more clearly than others when they are hungry or sleepy. Some pass from one state of arousal to another without spending much time in transitional indeterminate states." It seems to be another early individual difference. This characteristic permits the mother to attend to the cues given by the infant with more precision. It is interesting to speculate that if mother does not attend to these cues, the child may have to exaggerate them to communicate them and avoid a sense of frustration and deprivation.

Zone reliance is another factor affecting character formation. Drive tension may originate from internal stimuli other than hunger. Already at birth one can observe individual differences in the baby's drive expression. Some babies mouth much more than others, irrespective of hunger. The incidence of erections, which are common among baby boys, also may differ. Thus, individual differences exist in the choice of discharge channels, and hypothetically, this choice may reflect a zone preference, which may predispose to greater difficulties in resolving certain specific conflicts and psychosexual fixations.

Mode reliance is yet another factor that must be taken into account. Observations of neonates show that there are individual differences in the quality of mouthing—some clearly prefer sucking or tonguing, others prefer chewing. Some infants are spitters, others droolers, still others hardly ever spit. In Erikson's (1950) terms, the infant's mouthing may be primarily incorporative, retentive, eliminative, or intrusive in character. The question arises whether early preferential-mode reliance reflects a lasting and distinctive drive quality, which then finds expression in later development. Is early mode reliance transferred to later psychosexual stages, and does mode fixation thus influence character development? For example, is the eliminative mode related to the tendency toward dissociation in the hysterical character? Or the incorporative mode to the demandingness and penis envy of these patients? Another factor to be considered is *self-consistency*. It refers to the capacity to respond to a stimuli in a predictable manner. Some infants, for example, respond quite predictably to auditory stimulation, while others do not. (Hypothetically, this variable may be crucial to the ease with which a mother can learn to understand her infant's needs.) Possibly, unpredictability is a function of fluctuations in the strength of internal stimuli impinging on behavior. The hysterical personality displays sudden, abrupt changes in behavior and moods in the form of temper tantrums, and these may well be rooted, at least in part, in this particular factor of self-consistency.

Brazelton's (1973) scale lists some other factors that may be relevant to hysterical characters. The degree of orientation to animate, visual, and auditory stimuli, and to motor maturity may contribute to zone reliance and hence to possible points of fixation. Peak excitement is also a factor of heuristic interest. The infant may go from a low level of response to all stimuli to reactions of excitement, such as screaming, where some quieting may occur with consoling, to an insulating crying state where the infant is unable to be quieted or soothed. A predisposition to intensive affective reactions is indeed suggestive of the histrionics and affective outbursts of the hysterical personality.

Rapidity of build-up is another factor in the Brazelton scale. This can range from the infant's not being upset at all by noxious stimuli to his being extremely sensitive and irritable. Hand-to-mouth facility and self-quieting activity are adaptive coping devices for self-soothing. Both factors may contribute to various aspects of the hysterical personality—in particular, the predisposition to emotional outbursts and the sensitivity to oral frustration. Tremulousness in its mild form may be an antecedent to epilepticlike activity.

THE RELATION OF EARLY MODES TO COGNITIVE CONTROLS

Korner (1964) ends her paper by stating that a continuity "between the early modes and the cognitive control principles seems particularly plausible, because cognitive functioning is largely determined by the way stimuli are taken in, internally elaborated, organized and synthesized." Gardner and his collaborators (1968) have found a definite correlation between the cognitive controls and the defenses. Much of their evidence suggests that the cognitive-control principles are structures antecedent to the formation of the defenses. The study of variations in the way neonates deal with external and internal stimuli may thus carry us back one step further in finding antecedents to the formation of defenses.

In the research conducted by Gardner et al. (1968), middle-class and Midwestern children participated in various cross-sectional and longitudinal studies, including clinical interviews, psychological testing, and some experimental tests related to cognitive structures. Gardner and his colleagues found that characteristics of ego organization seemed as clearly apparent in the clinical test performance of the younger children studied (average age of 9.6) as in the performance of the older children (average age of 13.4). These findings seem to hint at the possibility that even in normal children, defense mechanisms are employed in a more crystallized way than assumed by Beres (1969). What does seem to increase as a function of age is the overall ego autonomy.

Gardner et al. found that those children who were levelers, that is, who lagged behind in the capacity for discrimination of similar stimuli, showed an inaccuracy of reality testing, demonstrating relatively high degrees of sporadic disruption of control in the clinical testing situation. Their impulse-control problem concerned the maintenance of reality-attuned orientations over considerable periods of time rather than the degree of effectiveness and motor control measured in extremely short periods. These lapses occurred in a context of specific ego weaknesses and were not attributable to the kinds of ego primitivity of more serious pathology.

Gardner et al. also suggest that there is a difference in the capacity of boys and girls to articulate experience, with boys being more articulate. This capacity is linked to relatively limited repression and relatively high scores on the WISC verbal factor. Children with low verbal scores, more often girls than boys, responded more quickly and willingly to the ink blots and gave responses to smaller areas; they also used repression to a greater degree. The link between field articulation and repression corresponds with findings of other authors, as does the superiority of boys over girls in the cognitive-control tasks specifically requiring articulation under relatively difficult conditions.*

In addition, Gardner et al. found that girls showed less explorative behavior; they seemed to be more placid and less open to new experience, less projective, and less verbally skilled. Similar descriptions are included in

---

*This general pattern of behavior was also more apparent in Catholic than in Protestant children. Beres (1969) stresses that character pathology needs to be assessed within the context of culture, and the value of doing so is amply illustrated here. Indeed, those children who were more open, uninhibited, and cooperative and who employed generalized repression to a lesser degree were more often Protestant than Catholic. This has interesting implications in that in predominantly Catholic countries or in Catholic subcultures, the incidence of classical forms of hysterical neurosis is higher than in Protestant countries and subcultures.

Horowitz's (1977) discussion of the cognitive styles of the hysterical personality, suggesting a continuity into adulthood of these patterns.

As we have seen, various studies of individual differences in infancy and latency suggest that specific endowment factors may contribute to the formation of the hysterical character structure. Before turning to the development of the hysterical personality in childhood and adolescence, it seems important to clarify, for purposes of comparison, the characteristics of the hysterical personality as it applies to adults.

The hysterical neurotic personality, what Zetzel (1968) calls the "good hysteric," implies a well-integrated but severe and punitive superego, a well-integrated ego identity, a stable self-concept, and a stable representational world. Excessive defense operations against unconscious conflicts center on repression. The character defenses are largely of an inhibitory or phobic nature or are reaction formations against repressed instinctual needs. There is very little or no instinctual infiltration into the defensive character traits. The ego at this level is somewhat constricted by its excessive use of neurotic defense mechanisms, but the patient's overall social adaptation is not seriously impaired.

The hysterical personality has fairly deep, stable object relations and is capable of experiencing guilt, mourning, and a wide variety of affective responses. His sexual and/or aggressive drive derivatives are partially inhibited; however, the infantile genital phase and oedipal conflicts are clearly predominant, and there is no pathological condensation of genital sexual strivings with pregenital aggression in which the latter predominates (Abraham, 1920; Easser and Lesser, 1965).

Horowitz (1977) describes some common patterns found in the adult hysterical personality. He has subdivided these patterns in long-, medium-, and short-order patterns according to the time period in which they become evident.

1. *Long-order patterns*: *Interpersonal relations* are repetitive, impulsive, and stereotyped. They are often characterized by victim-aggressor, child-parent, and rescue-rape interaction. The hysterical personality creates *"cardboard" fantasies* and conceives of *caricaturelike roles*. He leads a drifting but possibly dramatic life with an existential sense that reality is not really real; there is a frequent experience of self as not in control and not responsible.

2. *Medium-order patterns*: The hysterical personality shows attention-seeking behavior, which may include demands for attention and/or the use of charm, vivacity, displays of sex appeal, childlikeness, passivity, or infirmity. There are fluid changes in mood and in motion, with excitability and an episodic flooding with feeling. Inconsistency of attitudes and suggestibility are also present.

3. *Short-order patterns*: The information-processing style involves global

deployment of attention and unclear, inhibited, or incomplete statements of ideas and feelings, possibly with a lack of details or clear labels in communication. Nonverbal communication is not further translated into words or conscious meanings; there are only partial or unidirectional associational lines with a short-circuiting of apparent completion of problematic thoughts.

In looking at these various characteristics one can see that the experience of self as not in control, the demands for attention, the fluid change in mood and in motion, the excitability, the episodic flooding with feeling, the inconsistency of attitudes, the global deployment of attention with the lack of details or clear labels in communication, are all quite possibly related to the endowment factors outlined above.

THE HYSTERICAL PERSONALITY IN CHILDHOOD AND ADOLESCENCE

Metcalf (1977) provides a fairly comprehensive discussion of the childhood hysterical phenomena. What follows is a summary of the salient points in her paper. Although she begins by stating that what is ordinarily meant by character disorder does not occur in children of preschool and grammer-school age, she notes that even small children have predictable characteristic ways of responding—that they have character "styles" that can be recognized throughout their development even if their manifest behavior is different. She points out, however, that prospective studies indicate it is difficult to predict outcome from childhood to adulthood in terms of personality; moreover, the difficulty at prediction is compounded by the fact that character styles are frequently mixed.

Metcalf stresses that it is important to remember that when we talk about character styles in the child, we have to consider the potential resilience of the child relative to the adult. I would suggest, however, that the difference in such resilience between the child and adult character is less wide if we are talking about pathological character formations in the child. In this case the treatment presents similar difficulties, as does the treatment of adults. In my opinion, psychoanalysis of obsessive neurosis and hysterical character problems in children may not necessarily be briefer than an adult psychoanalysis just because the patient is younger.

There has not been a sharp differentiation of hysterical psychoneurosis from hysterical personality in childhood. The Group for the Advancement of Psychiatry in fact does not list hysterical psychoneurosis at all; it provides "hysterical personality disorder" as a diagnostic category instead. GAP's position follows the general philosophy that diagnostic categories in childhood are in general more transitory.

Since the cardinal features of the adult disorders—egocentric and urgent attention-seeking behavior—are developmentally more appropriate in school-age children, the "good hysterical traits" present no problem during school years. Those unusual children whose traits are reminiscent of the highly disturbed or "oral" adult hysterical characters described by Zetzel (1968) and Easser and Lesser (1965) appear infantile for their age in their provocative sexual play, their aggressive cuteness, and their childish demands for attention.

Yet it is important to differentiate hysterical personality from the phenomenon of conversion. I would agree with Rangell (1959) that conversion is an expression of forbidden wishes in symbolic form or via body language, or it may serve as a way of escaping life-threatening stress at almost any age or stage of development and in almost any pathological personality configuration. Another point to consider is that the sicker patients are in terms of their level of object relations, use of primitive mechanisms of defense, early fixation, and problems in the integration and maturity of the ego's synthetic functions, the more blatant and infantile will be the conversion symptoms they show.

The relationship between symptomatic hysteria and the hysterical personality type is unclear. There are reports in the literature of overt hysteria, but this has not been related to character style. Robbins (1966), for example, shows that girls diagnosed as having hysteria during childhood were only slightly more susceptible than nonhysteric girls to falling ill with hysteria in adult life. None of the boys with hysteria in childhood had such symptoms when they grew up. In this study, however, there is no reference to the hysterical personality.

At this point we shall turn to Metcalf's (1977) review of the cultural, interpersonal, and intrapsychic conflictual factors that may contribute to a child's developing a "hysterical style of behavior."

Culture and Character Pathology

That cultural practices may foster hysterical symptomatology and character seems evident from the study of some social structures. In Puerto Rican–American culture, a particular child is prepared to become a *santero*, or priest, of a religion that is a mixture of *Yoruba* practices and Catholicism. The child chosen to become a *santero* has been identified as specially suggestible, exhibitionistic, and predisposed to excitement peaks and hallucinatory experiences, both visual and auditory. As another example, La-Barre and LaBarre (1965) report the case of a twelve-year-old prepubertal child raised in the Bible belt of the South. In this case, the *conditioning* the child received eventually led to hysterical blindness.

Interpersonal Factors

Mother-child attachment bond. Ainsworth (1973) studied a group of young children in whom she was able to demonstrate three general types of attachment by the age of one year: secure, insecure, and unattached. In the insecure group the infant averted his gaze upon reunion with the mother after a brief separation; in the unattached group the aversion of gaze persisted for some time after the mother's return. It seems possible that the insatiable attention-seeking of the hysteric may originate in part from the "insecure" experience, where there is a partially frustrated attachment behavior. The partial frustration has the paradoxical effect of increasing the behavior rather than extinguishing it.

This interactional pattern may thus be an early precursor of hysterical personality development. In addition, the inner picture of what one is apparently grows in each child as the precipitate of physical experiences with the social partner. Psychic representations of these early impressions color the experience of subsequent development throughout life. In the productions of children in psychotic experiences and in the regression of the psychoanalytic treatment, derivatives of these early physical experiences may appear. This factor may be particularly relevant to the tendency to somatize in the easily excitable hysterical personality.

Overt parental example and the shaping effects of parental intervention. Learning from the environment begins early after birth and becomes the most important source of all personality traits. The learning begins in simple mirroring of fragments of adult and sibling behavior or of certain body movements, especially those involving the mouth, face, and head. Head bobbing, mouth opening, lip smacking, and tongue play are a few of these early mimicry behaviors.

The type of learning situation relevant here is one that becomes progressively more important as object relations mature. The child's perceptions of overt and covert inhibition, combined with reenforcement from his parents, cause him to shape his behavior, to some extent, to conform to their intervention. Included here is the child's acting out of unconscious impulses on the parents' part. This process reaches its greatest intensity after the age of two, when the child begins to grasp his mother's intentions and plans, especially her affects in relation to his own impulses and feelings.

It seems possible that there may be a congenital-activity type or inborn temperament that influences the direction and quality of the early interaction between parents and child. Nevertheless, the greater frequency of hysterical traits in women than in men seems to be satisfactorily explained by the fact that parents tolerate or encourage dependency more in girls than in boys. The gender of the child, his or her physical appearance, his or her assertiveness or passivity, tend to elicit different responses from the parents.

These responses feed back into the child's developing behavioral systems in a way that shapes the direction taken by the child's own responses and later his or her attitude about him or her self. Girls are often described as sweet, shy, and in need of their father's protection, and boys as tough, aggressive, and destined for success in sports. These descriptions may persist in spite of the fact that the children in question appear to an objective observer as identical in size and behavior.

Reactions to physical illness. Abse (1974) points out that the parents of a hysterical child are often neglectful when the child is healthy and then remorsefully attentive when he is sick or distressed. Such a primary focus on the body may be another impetus toward seeking attention to and through the physical modalities.

Irregular stimulus gratification. Millon (1969) feels that the persistent, yet erratic dependency behavior of the hysterically inclined child, whom he refers to as the "active dependent" personality type, may reflect a pathological form of intense stimulus-seeking traceable to highly charged, varied, and irregular stimulus reenforcements associated with early attachment. He suggests that the child may have had many different caretakers in infancy who supplied him with intense, short-lived stimulus gratifications that came at irregular intervals. From a purely behavioral point of view, he notes that irregular schedules of reinforcement establish deeply ingrained habits that are highly resistant to extinction.

Encouragement to look to others for fulfillment and help. A predominant constellation in the early life of a child with hysterical traits is the parent's overt encouragement to expect and demand help, guidance, and the good things of life while covertly signaling that these are beyond the child's competence to obtain and can only be supplied by the parent. In this regard, the parent treats the child as he or she would have like to have been treated as an indulged child.

The suppression of anger and assertiveness. Sperling (1973) describes how certain mothers, caught in an unconscious conflict, do not permit expression of anger, assertiveness, or anxiety in their child, but encourage dependency and passivity instead. At the same time the mothers do not expect the child to be able to cope with anxiety-provoking situations without their help.

Inappropriate sexualization of the parent-child relationship. When parents have been physically overstimulating, especially when they infantilize the child as a projection of themselves, the child may show an early and intense development of sexuality, which may divert him from other exploratory interests. Since this inappropriate sexuality is connected with social interaction, it may lead in later life to the need to maintain a similarly high level of egocentric and sexually oriented interactions typical of the hysterical personality.

HYSTERICAL TYPES IN CHILDHOOD

According to Metcalf (1977), there is a spectrum of the "hysterically inclined child." The first and most mature of these types is a youngster who would not ordinarily be seen as suffering from a disorder, since he or she rarely presents any disturbance or distress within the family during latency. Such a child is like an early edition of the good, or healthy, hysteric. There is a predominance of oedipal over oral conflicts, and if the youngster in question is a girl, she will focus on her relationship with her father, which will be colorfully romanticized. The child may have some difficulties in mastering the cognitive part of school work because of a tendency to overgeneralize, a lack of acute attention to detail, and a deficiency in analytical ability. He or she, however, more than makes up for this socially by animation and attentiveness to others. The child's social skills, which are apt to be precocious, equip him or her to get along well with peers and teachers alike. The child may be quite artistic.

In this child's background one would expect to find a relatively intact family group and good attachment as an infant. In the case of the girl, one tends to find intense, emotional relationships with her father and brothers and a depreciated relationship with her mother, whom she sees as drab and uninteresting compared to herself. As an example of this type, I shall present Gardner et al.'s (1968) observations of Jane, from early infancy through preadolescence.

Background

Jane was the younger of two girls born to middle-class, college-educated, intelligent parents. Mrs. K., Jane's mother, expressed her wish that her child would learn to behave in socially appropriate ways and was concerned lest Jane become too willful, tempestuous, or spirited. She showed feelings of social obligations with definite codes of correct, refined, mannerly, and controlled behavior. At the time of the infant observations, when Jane was twenty-four weeks old, Mrs. K. was an attractive, well-groomed woman in her late twenties. Although cooperative, she had a deliberate, reserved demeanor which allowed her to say pleasantly but firmly of matters she considered too personal to share (such as her feelings about pregnancy and delivery), "I can't see that it has any bearing on this." The father, a professional in an executive position, found time for daily play with his daughter and was appreciative of the staff's interest in her. His play involved talking and laughing with Jane, entertaining her by whistling and making a variety of noises, which seemed to delight her thoroughly. He never took care of the child.

Infancy

At twenty-four weeks Jane was a healthy feminine-looking baby who, despite very mobile facial features, was less active in general bodily movement than many babies and unusually pliant during the manipulations involved in caring for or examining her. Although vigorous and loud, her vocalizations were relatively undifferentiated, consisting predominantly of rather throaty "vowel sounds." She was capable of expressing feeling, getting "just plain mad" when she could not get at her thumb or when a prolonged nap made her hungrier than usual and therefore less willing to wait for the preparation of food. She was capable of protest but was not irritable for extended periods.

Psychological tests at twenty-four weeks showed that her postural adjustments and fine motor coordination were well advanced for her age, as were her language and social responses. Her relatively low (for her) adaptive skills were seen by an observer as reflecting "a lack of interest in performing." In connection with cognitive styles already present at this age, the following observation is quoted: "The most conspicuous aspect of her test behavior was the unusual delay between clear perception of a stimulus and response to it. If one waited, however, she eventually reached, always with one hand, and in a very slow motion would grasp the object in question with impressive skill." Thumbsucking acted as a kind of screen against outside stimulation, in that while sucking, her eyes might be focused in the direction of another object, but except for mildly regarding it, she would make no response to it. If the thumb was playfully removed or if one waited until she herself had ceased sucking, the same object would be responded to in the expected manner. This may be, as described above, a precursor of the cognitive control of leveling and partial reactions to stimuli described by Korner (1964).

The Preschool Years

At about four years, Jane suffered from headaches; loss of appetite, facial pallor, and lack of energy were also observed. These symptoms disappeared after her tonsils and adenoids were removed. She was well prepared for the operation and met the experience calmly. At four years, eleven months, Jane was described by a psychologist as a child of softly feminine beauty and good manners. Her movements were graceful; her voice, although usually gentle and well modulated, like that of her mother, was at times rough and guttural. There was also about her something of a tomboyish quality, suggesting some embarrassment in being observed or some conflict in the expression of the aggression she appeared to avoid so carefully in projective tests and play sessions. The projective tests further suggested conflict or lack of clarity about her role in her family and society. She enjoyed being the cute, charming baby of the family, but felt pressures to conform. She was cognitively alert and assured, but was at the same time moderately socially remote and emotionally unspontaneous. Jane's preschool Rorschach responses demonstrated "precise reality testing and an effective capacity for distinction of fantasy from reality," but they also suggested generalized "repression as a characteristic coping mode with a likelihood of impulsive breakthrough," probably appearing in the form of minor naughtiness, teasing, and occasional temper outbursts. She engaged in teasing interactions with her father and enjoyed the role of the playful, attractive, admired little girl.

Latency

During the latency years, Jane mobilized motor skills with a faultless grace. In addition, her test scores revealed superior cognitive resources. At age 7.5 her WISC performance I.Q. of 129 was the same as it had been at age 4.11; it was also consistent with the preschool Stanford-Binet I.Q. of 132 and the latency Stanford-Binet I.Q. of 130. A change did occur, however, in Jane's score on the verbal subtests of the WISC from preschool to latency, her verbal I.Q. jumping from 103 to 116. It was largely her deficits in arithmetic and rote memory for digits that prevented her verbal I.Q. from being even higher and brought the full-scale WISC I.Q. down to 125. Her information and interest, although broad, were not outstanding for one at her superior intellectual level.

During the latency Jane was capable of imaginative play but was more likely to remain concrete in her thinking. There were some remnants of hostility toward her mother and feelings of deprivation from her, which probably carried over from unresolved aspects of the oedipal conflicts, but these did not seem to be unusually marked in degree.

Preadolescence

At preadolescence Jane was reported as being relatively pleasant at school. She liked physical education and art. Her limited achievement drive was reflected in her consistently average grades in most subjects, in contrast to her superior ability on tests. At age thirteen, her average-level verbal I.Q. of 103 and her superior performance I.Q. of 131 reproduced the pattern of her WISC scores at the preschool age. Her vocabulary score had dropped a dramatic six points, and her comprehension and digit-span scores dropped four and three points respectively. Her information score dropped two points.

Thus at preadolescence there was a notable contrast between Jane's enduring interest and her articulated skills in motoric behavior as opposed to thoughts and words. There was also at this time a somewhat strange effort to behave in a proper and ladylike manner. In summary, Jane could be described as a girl with a high-level hysterical character configuration.

PATHOLOGICAL CHILDHOOD HYSTERICAL DISORDERS

We shall now turn to the more severe childhood hysterical disorders formulated by Metcalf (1977). Children of these types have obvious hysterical traits and thus are most commonly brought to pediatricians and child psychiatrists for evaluation and treatment. They produce disequilibrium within the family or have provoked such negative response outside the family that help is sought. The similarity with Zetzel's (1968) so-called good hysteric is striking.

General Characteristics

Initially these children tend to be outgoing, engaging, and charming, but are soon seen as irritating and intrusive, impulsive, and more selfish than is normal for their age. They are more than usually emotional, but in a superficial way, yielding quickly to indications that others have different feelings by abruptly changing their tack. This trait gives them a fickle and capricious quality, which loses friends for them as fast as their gregarious but shallow friendliness gains them. Above all, these youngsters seek approval and attention as if they were trying to fill themselves up.

The pronounced oral quality accounts for the striking pregenital impression these children make on the observer despite whatever overt sexual behaviors they may mimick. They have learned that their satisfactions are dependent on others and that this satisfaction is variable and may be withdrawn at any time. They therefore press for more. They crave stimulation and excitement and seek it through interpersonal contacts, often with much younger children, who are liable to give them more attention. They are uneasy in the give-and-take with peers. Their emotions are labile, and they either erupt in inappropriate and sometimes bizarre outbursts or else withdraw.

One of the most impressive traits of these children is an uncanny sensitivity to the moods and unexpressed thoughts of the adults with whom they have relationships. If the unconscious attention of the adult is focused on eroticized topics, such a youngster will not fail to become excited. They give the impression of being used to receiving some sort of positive response from adults and become confused or frightened when it is not forthcoming. Genital exposure and confused sexual play mixed with aggressive components are frequently among the presenting complaints of these children. Their sexual provocations with both adults and peers seem to result not in satisfaction but in a heightening of diffuse tension and excitement, which is then discharged in tantrums and aggressive motor behavior that is often self-hurtful.

Sexual Behavior

The sexuality of the hysterical personality in childhood is deceptive. The "overly feminine" or seductive traits are only superficially sexual; they really express the identifications with the orally seductive parents as a means of retrieving or maintaining love or as the acting out of hostile manipulations. The hysterical child seldom seeks a sexual partner in the adult sense, but absorbs instead the eroticized positive or negative attention of the parents. If the mother herself is hysterical or infantilizing or encourages competitiveness in her pretty child, any fixation of the child in these character styles is easy to understand.

A hysterical personality can result if the little girl manages to turn her father into a substitute mother by developing abnormally close ties with him because she is or feels deprived of adequate mothering. If this relationship becomes sexualized because of her father's conflicts, the child learns this technique and uses it to earn dependent gratification from future father figures at the cost of submission and passivity. If it is the father who initiates the excessive mothering, he tends to see his daughter as weak and young, projecting his own oral neediness onto her. If he leads her into petting games, thinking of her as a less threatening sexual partner than her mother, her flirtatiousness will reflect this sexualized interaction with her father. Perhaps the strongest, most persuasive setting for the development of the hysterical personality in childhood involves both parents' participation in the relationship just described.

Learning Skills

The ego abilities of these patients vary. Most suffer from some deficit in their cognitive development with the inevitable limitations in learning tasks. They are so busy acting on their sexual and aggressive impulses and repressing these actions that they have little time or interest in the mastery of learning.

Mechanisms of Defense

The less disordered hysterical child uses relatively mature defenses due to identification with the mother—i.e., repression of the awareness of the sexual elements in her own behavior, reaction formation, and intellectualization to handle the self-assertive impulses and the anger at frustration. "I don't know" is likely to be the first answer that comes to her lips on being questioned on practically any topic. This reply is not simply employed to avoid self-incrimination, but is often a fact, for memories are frequently not accessible to such a child, and when they are, they are vague and impressionistic. For the more disturbed and immature child, the defenses are more primitive, such as projection, somatization, passive aggression, and schizoid fantasies.

At times only a trial of treatment will differentiate between the more seriously ill child, with her immature defenses and intense parental stimulation, and the less-disordered child, with her defenses dominated by repression but with greater development concealed behind her symptoms. While it may be that the more developed child can be successfully treated alone, therapy for the parents is a great adjunct to accurate diagnosis and good outcome and may be virtually the only treatment method short of residential placement for the sicker child.

This description of the childhood hysterical personality, then, conforms with the general classification of high-level and low-level character organizations described by Otto Kernberg (1976) as well as, more specifically, with the high-level and low-level hysteric described by Easser and Lesser (1965) and by Zetzel (1968).

From an epidemiological perspective, Robins's (1966) work, cited in Sadock et al.'s (1976) review of the literature, is noteworthy. Robbins found that children from a child-guidance clinic who received an adult diagnosis of either hysteria or antisocial personality had similar characteristics in childhood. Females who became adult hysterics had a very high rate of juvenile sexual offenses, as did the sociopathic group (80% and 86% respectively). An episode of rape before age eighteen was reported by one third of the girls who became hysterics, as compared with a quarter of the future sociopathic woman. Seventy-five percent of the hysterics had voluntary premarital sexual experiences. Accompanying such behavior were reports of incorrigibility, associations with undesirable company, and a history of running away and vagrancy. However, the incidents of stealing and, correspondingly, the number of arrests were lower in the future antisocial women. Other characteristics of the future hysterics included lack of energy and apparent laziness, which was more prevalent than in any other future psychiatric diagnostic category studied. In addition, somatic symptoms were recorded in about one third of the cases. Forty-one percent of the children who became either hysterics or sociopaths as adults experienced some somatic symptoms prior to the age of eight.

The longitudinal history with childhood antecedents resembling those of antisocial behavior supports the conclusion that hysteria belongs among the personality disorders rather than among the symptomatic neuroses.

I shall now present two cases of hysterical personality, in a child and in an adolescent, as seen through psychoanalytic observation in a treatment process. After describing briefly the background and chief complaint of the case, I shall illustrate the characteristics of these patients' functioning which led me to hypothesize the existence of hysterical character structure.

JEANNIE

Jeannie, a fifteen-year-old, was referred to me for psychoanalysis. During the initial interview no specific symptoms were described by her parents or herself; they were only uncovered as the process of treatment unfolded. At the beginning, both Jeannie and her parents talked about chronic unhappiness with herself, tension and anger, and negative and hypercritical attitudes toward others and herself.

Overall quite a good student, Jeannie excelled in dramatics and foreign languages. She liked acting, playing the piano, skiing, and horseback riding, although lately she had become increasingly afraid of horses. The second of four siblings of college-educated parents, Jeannie had longed for her real father, whom she lost in her early childhood through divorce. Although her mother remarried after a few years, she deeply resented her stepfather and the children born during the second marriage, a girl and a boy, five and seven years her junior.

Overview of Development

There were no medical complications in pregnancy and delivery. At that time the parents were in intense marital distress, characterized by violently angry scenes. Her mother described Jeannie as a healthy, vigorous, easy baby who screamed loudly.

At as young as two years of age, she would favor her brother over mother whenever he was around. Developmental landmarks were within normal limits. When she began to speak, she spoke clearly and was able to read, teaching herself phonics. The mother said that as she was in the process of divorce, her relationship with the older child in the family, a boy, was easier than with Jeannie.

Jeannie went to preschool and elementary school with no apparent problems. In first grade, however, she got lost in the park; after she was found, it took her a couple of days to recover. As she entered adolescence, she became more distant from her mother, her relationship with peers was inconsistent and scarce, she showed contempt for others and was haughty and superior with those around her. She was competitive with her peers and siblings and complained of being frequently short-changed by her parents in relation to her siblings. Although generally she seemed to control her affects, she had intense temper tantrums if something did not go her way.

As a teenager she was stern, rigorous, and prudish. Although at times she liked to exhibit herself by lying in the roof garden of the building in a bikini or by showing off pretty clothes, she would get outraged if the boys made comments about her looks. She had a boyfriend, whom she just liked as a friend. She liked to be held by him. She complained that he only wanted to neck with her and was concerned that her reputation might be spoiled by her going steady with him.

She described her two sets of parents in a rather generalized, nonspecific manner; the most blurred figure in her description was the father. She had chronic difficulties with her family and felt she didn't get along with either her mother and stepfather or with her father and stepmother. Lately she felt she had no close friends.

She had no use for leisure-time activities, spending most of her days doing homework and not allowing herself to go to sleep before midnight— allegedly because of her chronic tendency to procrastinate in doing home- work. She complained that she could not get herself organized, she forgot things, and got mad at herself for not being responsible. Last but not least, she said, "I eat too much and now I have lost my willpower to follow a diet." It was striking to observe that in spite of Jeannie's attractive appearance, with her black hair, light skin, and well-developed secondary feminine characteristics, she behaved as a sexless, frozen, stereotyped person.

She was controlled, talking with a certain deliberateness that served the purpose of suppressing many intermediary thoughts. In addition, she selected words that would be the most global and least specifically descrip- tive. Although she had originally accepted the recommendation of the referring psychiatrist, a few months later she admitted she had pushed away any reservations or anxieties about the beginning of treatment.

In what follows I shall present process material of the actual psychoanalytic sessions. (These sessions occurred after Jeannie had been coming four times a week for six months.) By focusing not only on the contents but also on the characteristic styles revealed, the reader may see how this material connects to the discussions of the literature presented earlier.

Session 1

Jeannie began:

This has been a bad day; had a quarrel with Mother about driving. I walked out of the house. I came back and took a nap and I had a dream. I don't know what to tell about this dream, but I was with Dee, my brother's girlfriend. Dee was supposed to go away to Wyoming; instead we went to the basement, perhaps to the wine cellar. We drank wine. My mother was angry, and the housekeeper was too noisy, shouting at me. I went to my own room and took off my slippers. Then I went to the third floor to Richard's room [her brother]. It was neat and quiet. There was a bookcase used as a divider for the bedroom part of the room. I did not like the bedroom; it was dark, so I got scared and ran but it was as if I was running in the same place. I went to the top of the stairs, bounced up and down, and finally got to the foot of the stairs after bouncing up and down several times. It was like a dream, but it was so real I felt as if I was moving myself.

In the next scene, Jeannie explained, she was back in her bedroom. There was a card with red pieces of thread written for Dee, and something about a strange boy being her new boyfriend. She was dating him. Then she said that she decided to keep the card so people would not believe that it was a dream.

Jeannie told the dream with great difficulty. She was surprised she was able to remember it at all, as usually she forgot her dreams "quite easily." She complained that the analysis was not changing her, nothing in her behavior had changed: "I could be here three and four years and it still will be the same." In fact it really had not been her idea to be in analysis. She mentioned that she had to come to her session by taxi that day because her mother was taking the younger children for their music lessons. She complained that she felt abandoned by her mother to have to come by taxi here.

In this particular session I would like to stress her impulsivity in spite of her usual control, and her sense of frustration and disappointment in her mother with her resultant demandingness. In her dream she looks to her older brother as the maternal figure (comforting, soothing), but he is relatively unavailable to her because he has a girlfriend. Her wish to get rid of the oedipal competitor is displaced onto the brother's girlfriend. The combination of unresolved oedipal conflicts, with the demanding orality, is illustrated by her going down to the basement with the oedipal competitor to drink wine. Her feeling left out because her mother did not drive her instead of her younger stepsiblings also illustrates the frustrating relationship with the mother and her infantile dependency.

The contributing factors of Jeannie's sense of maternal deprivation needs to be specified. In Jeannie's case, maternal deprivation meant intermittent emotional unavailability, due to the mother's stress in her first marriage and divorce. In addition, the mother showed a preference for Jeannie's half siblings. Furthermore, there was a special kind of deprivation in that mother tended to relate to her child in a narcissistic manner. The mother, for example, gave Jeannie medication for what later developed into various somatic complaints which both shared. Because her mother anticipated many of Jeannie's concerns, she became quite dependent on her mother to find out how she felt about things. The mother also gave Jeannie a pair of earrings (a gift of her first husband for their official engagement) right after she divorced her husband. Jeannie has worn these earrings ever since, which in a certain way left her more at the mercy of her oedipal fantasies. The following session illustrates Jeannie's style of expression and her characteristic oedipal conflict around the love object and in relation to male figures.

Session 2

Jeannie reported:

I had a bizarre weekend. Yesterday was very rotten. I had a falling-out with Peter [her boyfriend]. I had a day off; there were teachers' conferences. There was something about Peter's way of explaining to me the problems in the math book. He seemed aggressive and hostile, impatient and condescending with me. Later in the evening I was talking with my brother. Peter came in and I only felt like talking to my brother. My brother and I talked for 45 minutes. Peter told me he had to leave and we got into another fight. He said I was getting him depressed. I continued to talk with my brother and it was a nice talk. We discussed many things.

Later on Jeannie explained that she wanted to show how well she got along with her brother in front of her boyfriend. She felt her boyfriend was jealous because he didn't have that kind of relationship with his own sister.

Session 3

These vignettes may illustrate the progressive transformation of character configuration into symptomatic productions. Jeannie reported:

I am in an awful mood today since I went to a checkup with my new doctor. I weigh 140 pounds, twisted my ankle, my favorite coat ripped. I've had a migraine for three days; it's getting better; my boyfriend came with me. It would have been worse. I got out of the doctor's office and felt violent; I felt like bashing into somebody's car—I was driving pretty fast—I am still uptight—the whole trip was weird.

Dad had a problem on Christmas day. His second wife had been drinking too much. [She proceeded to tell details about the visit in a rather calm manner, which surprised me in view of the content of what she was telling.] When I got back, my stomach started to act up. I also had blotches and pimples all over the place, which hardly ever happens—stomach, heartburn, a monumental case of it. I got my whole face broken out and I ate like crazy. I also have tension in my head, vague headaches, awful, pain in my left eye, throbbing. It's got better and then it got worse. I also have a tension headache when I am here (in session), and it goes away when I leave. The migraine is going away, though.

Jeannie commented that the doctor had insisted on calling her migraines tension headaches. She said he smoked like a chimney and he himself had a twitch. He was slimy—not a nice sort of person. "I had to go to see another doctor," Jeannie continued. "He said he didn't like to see kids my age on medication. I used to have gas problems in my stomach, just like my mother."

The following excerpts of two successive sessions have been selected to illustrate the patient's intense inhibitions and guilt over her sexual strivings, expressed both toward the boyfriend and in the analytic situations. These were dealt with by repression and a dissociative experience reminiscent in its qualitative aspects to derivatives of endowment and early childhood factors outlined above, such as change in mood, peak of excitement, impulsivity, global responses, such as her verbal expressions—"all was quiet, horrible, blah—I was completely upset . . . ."

Sessions 4 and 5 (4 Weeks Later)

Jeannie had just returned from a week's vacation with her boyfriend and his family. She complained:

I feel depressed. There is nothing different. It is nice to be in a different place. We had nice moments (with her boyfriend). Toward the end of the vacation I did a lot of thinking. I had distressing dreams. I have been thinking a lot about the analysis. My face is worse, I have been picking at it. I am in a constant worry. The night I got back home it was horrendous. I was completely upset when I was coming home. I guess I have been kicking around for a long time. I am in a quandary about what to do about myself this summer, what I ought to do.

Returning to the vacation, she said, "A couple of things happened that I did not want to think about. Peter and I, we did a little more experimenting in our sexual life, which I regret. I don't want to think about it." There was a long pause—I wondered whether she was finding it hard to talk about this and whether what she was reflecting to me was her reaction to what had happened—her feelings of discouragement. Jeannie replied that her boyfriend was happy about it, but she was regretful and upset. She acknowledged that it was very hard to talk about. "One of the things I was going to talk with you about . . . sometimes I rehearse what I am going to say here, but it is not so good to be open. After all, how I feel is none of your business."

She had commented initially that she had enjoyed herself with her boyfriend and I wondered whether her enjoyment made her feel very bad. "Whenever I think about it", she explained, "I reach a complete block which prevents any further look at what is going on. I don't want to talk about it, it's hard to get any further." I asked whether she was surprised that she could have some enjoyment, perhaps an intense experience, and felt bad about it. She repeated that she had thought a lot about the analysis while she was away. "Everything I do with other people, I start to think what's behind it, what it means, whether I can figure out things about myself." I then said that she seemed to have taken me with her on her vacation. In response, Jeannie mentioned that she had had a dream about me. She became silent. Again there was a pause. I wondered whether the dream was also hard to talk about. Only then did Jeannie begin to describe the dream:

> It was weird, strange. There were other people. You and I were in a library, and I was waiting for you to come in. You were in another room with another patient. I was poking around in the office. In the middle of the room there was a big blue book—it was a physician's desk reference. I looked up stomach medication. I wanted to look for Valium. Instead I thought it was a book about diseases. We were trying to classify what my disease was. It was very strange. You turned the pages, you read all the symptoms—excessive eating, not sleeping—that always sounds like you. I am repressing something. There was a light-brown chair. We were looking at my disease. There were awful symptoms that described me. It is strange talking about it.

I wondered whether her association to her intense sexual experience with Peter was linked to the wish for punishment as expressed in her fear of the terrible disease in the dream.

Session 6

Jeannie commented:

> Weird. I didn't know how to think about the session. Not everything is concrete at all. I hadn't thought enough about what I have been saying—a

session isn't worthwhile unless it is very difficult. Yesterday it felt *as if I was in a trance*. I felt as if I had been listening to myself in a trance; I came out of it confused, embarrassed, not sure what you were going to say about it. I felt spacy, not all there—scared. While I was talking a wave of strong feelings came over me; I felt confused. I wonder, was it like a sensation? It was very sudden, a big wave just hit me very strong. I felt like laughing and crying—mostly in my head, I guess. Like my thinking about something which is very wide and blank—it is peculiar and hard to describe. It was when you were looking through this book to find out what disease I had. Again I feel peculiar, giddy, faint, like crying. I was like in a trance, yet I kept talking; when I was finished with the dream I kept talking. I wonder if I made the whole thing up . . .

I asked her whether it was similar to the experience she had had with Peter that she could not describe. She said it was similar; she did not feel good at all. "I felt seasick. I also regret it at the same time. Now he has some control over me that he didn't have before. I have a large grudge against men in general. I felt like fainting too. It would prevent me from losing control, not doing anything else. For a while he has necked, petted, but he felt that he wanted to be working for my climax. If I told him my feelings, he would have more power over me than I think he should. I didn't like to give him the idea that he matters more to me than he does. It would make him feel good. He should not think he was so wonderful for me. He should think that it was mostly my doing. I feel that I am not going to solve it, what does it matter, anyhow."

After a brief comment on my part she mentioned that she had hinted about something having occurred with her boyfriend, something similar to when she stayed overnight at his house. "I resent my boyfriend more these days. Some of his mannerisms seem to bother me more. I started to have a headache now, like my head would fall apart when I leave here. I am going to regret bringing this up."

Session 7 (Following Day)

Jeannie came twenty minutes late. She had overslept. She blamed her boyfriend, with whom she had been taking a nap, for not waking her on time to come to the session. "I am sure you are going to think that it has a meaning. You always think that there may be something subconscious. I sort of dreaded the session, but today it was not like that. I didn't seem to mind it as much. I feel stupid, I really do— I have a lot of trouble figuring out something important in something superficial. I told myself it was ridiculous to have something have a meaning when it may really not have a meaning."

Jeannie then talked about her driving to the session here. It felt as if she was going very fast, although she really was driving within the speed limit.

She could not remember what had occurred in the previous session. She felt rather futile, that she is trying to find meaning in her life but she doesn't believe in "all that garbage." All the various stupid things that occur to her day in and day out are "sort of ridiculous." I wondered whether her calling all of this meaningless arose out of guilt for her experiences with her boyfriend.

Session 8

The sense of loss following the termination of her relationship to her boyfriend arose from a displaced feeling toward her father, whom she had also felt as lost, through the divorce. This time, however, she had turned passive into active, and had induced the separation herself. Later, as it turned out, the relation to both boyfriend and father had a parallel as she continued to see them intermittently.

I asked Jeannie about the color black, and she explained she wears black when she feels in a bad mood, when she wants someone to feel sorry for her. I said black is a color for mourning, as if she had lost somebody. She asked me whether I meant her boyfriend. At the same time she started to touch her earrings her mother had given her—originally a gift from her father to her mother. I then drew the parallel of her expressing the feelings about her boyfriend and, at the same time, similar feelings about her father by recalling him through his gift, the earrings. She said, "It doesn't do any good—what does it help to know what belongs to what relationship?" She doesn't want to believe, to understand.

Sighing, Jeannie murmured that she didn't feel that her boyfriend or her father would change. "What's the use of understanding all of this?" She then began reproaching me for pointing out things that did not change anything. She just wanted to say that what happened with her boyfriend was clear and simple.

Session 9

I include a fragment of Jeannie's description of her subjective experiences:

I am pretty tense all the time. I never seem to get the grasp of the idea of a conversation. [This in spite of the fact that she was an outstanding student.] I have an act that I have to keep up—I can be more relaxed with some people, but I want to make sure that people will like me. Sometimes it is worse with friends. It is more important that I appear favorable to them. [Sigh.] Usually it results in my feeling false most of the time—I think sometimes friends like you for what you really are. The person I seem to be is nonexistent." Here I commented that this was a sad thing to say. "What else can I say? I have a very hard time—I can't never tell what is fair and what is unfair. It is really a defense against really knowing; that is the way it is really for me. Almost everything I do I drop out—running, swimming, guitar, ballet. I would have been a very good piano player if I hadn't dropped it. Everything I do has fizzled away, and at school I am not doing much of anything anymore. My brother, he has kept his interest throughout the years, and by now he is a good guitar player.

At this point I bring her back to her sense that everything is fizzling out, as if there was something missing in her that her brother has.

I have it all there, but I can't seem to do anything with it; I have all the qualities, I know, but I don't read enough, I don't think enough. I could be a good musician. I haven't done anything with my talents. It is almost as if you didn't have them. I hope that that will change . . . I could have been president of the Spanish Club, chairman of the Model UN, and I just didn't do it. I called my daddy and didn't have much to say to him; my brother, he can talk with him and be closer to him than I.

Toward the end of the session I elaborated on her comparison between herself and her brother in terms of their pursuits and their abilities. This was one of the sessions in which we began to connect with her sense of her depression, diffuseness about feeling that something is missing in her—the roots of her being a girl.

These various sessions highlight the character style of Jeannie as well as the progression of the transference neurosis. At first we see the expression of character traits in the transference and then the transformation of some of these character styles into symptoms (tension headaches and the trancelike experience described in detail in one of the sessions). What is interesting is the patient's subjective awareness of her cognitive style, which fits so well the descriptive characteristics of these patients.

TINA

I will now present the case of Tina, a six-year-old child, as there are some striking similarities to the hysterical character structure described in Jeannie in spite of Tina's much younger age.

When Tina's parents came to see me they felt that Tina needed treatment because of her extremely negative reaction to the birth of her younger brother, two years her junior. She had found his presence overwhelming; she had teased him, provoked him, and agitated him. When she had seen her baby brother being diapered for the first time, she had shouted, "What is that?" from the threshold of the door. She now asks for things to be done for her, to be given to her, and yet no matter how much her parents do for her she always feels that it is not enough.

She doesn't get along with other children. She initiates contact, but after a few minutes she manages to antagonize all her peers. This has happened with eight girls in her class. Nobody wants to sit next to her. The teacher, in fact, had to persuade somebody to sit next to her, and the child who sat next to her eventually hated her. She reads very well at school, but her desk is an absolute mess and she is forever losing her pencils. She is always asking for another pencil. She has no sense of responsibility. Although at times she shows some creativeness, she does not apply herself and is described in the class as a drifter. She is always losing her library books, her milk money, and her notebook. Earlier, in nursery school, Tina was described as wonderful, creative, although somehow shy with other children. Toward the end of nursery school, however, she began to be more withdrawn, as if something was bothering her.

There is a driven quality to Tina. As mentioned above, initially she can be charming with other children, but then she lets them know that she can do better than they can, that they are stupid. Often she says, "That's not right, stupid," to any child who is doing something contrary to her wishes. She finds herself compelled to needle other children. She refuses to share her toys. The only friend she has is a boy at school who can stand her provocativeness because he doesn't seem to care. With her brother, she is extremely provocative. She stirs him up, and when he brings his friends home she goads them to antagonize him: "See that little boy? Don't let him in. Let's punish him." Although her behavior with her parents is better when her brother is not around, she still is quite unpleasant. This behavior has grown worse.

Tina's parents reported repeatedly during the consultation session that she was never satisfied. Even on her birthday her mood was completely spoiled because she worried about not receiving enough or the same as the rest. She eats voraciously. She piles up her plate even though there is already a lot on it.

Developmentally, the parents described a normal pregnancy and delivery. Tina weighed seven pounds at birth. She was a wonderful baby—responsive and active; she ate extremely well. This good appetite did not cause her to be overweight. She was breast-fed for two months, but did not gain enough weight. During her first year of life she was kept on a rigid schedule of feedings every four hours. When Tina was one month old, the mother went back to work and a nurse took care of her for the next three years. As Tina got older, however, her mother always found it hard to leave her, as the young toddler clung to her blouse when she was about to leave. As a young infant Tina had had a transitional object (a blanket). She clung to different stuffed animals, and recently she has used another blanket.

Language development was advanced, and at two years Tina was able to talk in rather long sentences and to carry on advanced conversations. When she was five years old, she had gone to camp and developed a stiff neck. It was thought that it could be a viral or bacterial meningitis syndrome. She was thoroughly evaluated, but the examination was negative. Since that time, she has taken special gym classes where she is quite reserved. She thinks she can be the best dancer and the best gymnast, but she does not do as well as the average child and seems to have some problems with coordination. She wants very badly to have friends, but children reject her. Sometimes she wets herself—about once every two or three weeks during the day. A couple of times during the month she has nightmares in which a monster runs after her.

During the diagnostic evaluation Tina drew herself consistently in relation to her parents and her brother with the same quality of self-enhancement. In fact, in the drawings, she took two large pages to draw herself at a size of approximately 20 inches. In contrast, her brother was meekly drawn as a fragmentary stick figure without arms and hands, two inches tall.

Tina came from a family of professional people with both mother and father working. When I met Tina for the first time, she was of average size, with big eyes and honey-colored hair. She moved and dressed rather unattractively. Her shoulders were humped; she had a runny nose and would wipe her nose with her sleeve. She breathed rather heavily with a frequent cough. There was a quality of suffering about her that reminded me of a miniature madonna. She conducted herself in such a way that I was concerned she had some real difficulty in gross motor coordination. She moved in a stiff manner with a cogwheel quality to her arm movements, which were quite slow in initiation and completion. Often she came in dragging a long red-and-white kerchief on the floor. Then, when she entered the playroom, she put it on; she looked like a grand dame wearing her stole.

She was indeed unhappy, and it was only after several months of my seeing her in analysis that she began to come out of her tragic mood. She was greedy, and for several months I concentrated on her sense of dissatisfaction in connection with her feelings about her mother and her envy of her brother. Whenever we talked about this greedy feeling that came up and spoiled everything for her—her meals, her games, her being with her mother and father, her liking herself—she started literally to relax her body. I heard then that she had learned to ski and to go bike riding and to ice skate with tremendous ease, and she took a lot of pride in these new achievements. Her compulsivity also lessened. On one occasion she just coudn't resist, and threw all the Monopoly game money in a kind of shower of little papers flowing all over the room, saying this was a snowstorm that helped her "cool down." (Tina always expressed her feelings in a histrionic manner.)

The Sessions

During a session well toward the end of our first year, Tina sat and proceeded to paint a flower. She then painted another flower, and progressively this flower turned into a messy, brownish surface. She did the same with a third flower. She then proceeded to paint her hands and her elbows. At this point I told her that maybe she at times felt good about herself—like a pretty flower, but maybe then she thought she had done something that made her feel all messy like this brownish stuff she was smearing all over her.

Tina had consistently omitted any talk about masturbatory activity. At this point I commented on this omission, saying that maybe there is something that makes her feel so dirty and bad, such as her playing with her genitals, rubbing herself, touching herself. She looked at me with a sense of surprise and said, "No, I never do it. My brother does it, pulls his penis hard and he hurts it. He does it all the time, even in concerts." She added, "I really like to watch it." I pointed out that she never talked to me about it—maybe she felt it was something very bad to talk about or do. She replied that nobody does it at school. "When I go to the bathroom I do it and it hurts a lot you know, it really hurts. I am the only one at school who does it." We talked about how difficult it must be, and how if she did not know that other boys or girls also did it she must feel even worse.

At this point she proceeded to paint her face like a clown, while looking at herself in a portable mirror that I have in my office. She painted her mouth big in red and continued to paint all over her face. She then went out into the corridor to be with her father, who was waiting for her. I commented before she left that she wanted to let her dad know that she and I had been talking about these things that she felt were messy and she wanted to know whether her dad would disapprove of this mess or not. How would he like this face with big red lips that were like the red lips in between her legs? She looked at me again and proceeded to leave the room, as our time was up. Later it was reported to me that she made a deliberate effort to show her face to her mother and father and was quite relieved to see that they were not shocked by this experience.

The following day Tina proceeded to paint her face again. I commented on her wanting to make sure that what we had talked about was all right with me. She then washed her face carefully and began to play with the bowling pins. She filled up the holes of the bowling ball with pink liquid mixed with glue and commented, "Your fingers can get stuck in the ball." I wondered about her fears that her fingers would get stuck in her genitals when she touches them. She giggled with some relief and then proceeded to play a regular bowling pin game with me until the end of the hour, showing enjoyment and an increasing sense of spontaneity.

A couple of weeks later Tina was playing with her fingers, moving them up and down. She told me that she has two joints in each finger, but in one finger she has less joints and that was the thumb. I commented that something was missing again, according to her. She proceeded to tell me that of all the superheroes she likes Wonder Woman the best. She is better than any of the other superheroes. She knocks the torch down from the Torchman, she catches Spiderman, she can do anything the Bionic Woman can do and more. I asked her whether she would like to be like her. "I would like to play her on the TV series, but somebody already took her place. Twenty years ago [meaning twenty years into the future], she [the actress] would be too old" and maybe she can be in her role.

Tina then played with the toy bowling pins, but this time she hid them in the corners and nooks in the office so it was practically impossible to knock them down. I wondered whether she felt she had something hiding within her that was now giving her the feeling she could do many things and maybe even play Wonder Woman.

The previous day Tina had commented that she was like her mother: "She has pretty blue eyes [she has brown eyes], she has the same hair, the same nose." Tina mentioned, with some slight derision, that her father always holds his hat and it is embarrassing, especially when she is at a birthday party. This was the first comment of some admiration for her mother and depreciation of her father.

As an indication of the beginning resolution of her oral needs, I shall mention another session. On this day she came in in a good mood. We had had previous sessions where it was rather rough, all centered around her greediness. She told me that she had gone to a goodbye party for a friend. She then announced with pride that she got twelve Halloween cards. In fact her improvement with her peers had already begun toward the end of the first year. Tina said that she was selling cookies for the Girl Scouts, that she had left a Valentine card on my desk, and that her grandparents were going to buy her a gift. Maybe, she thought, she could sell me some cookies. I asked her whether I seemed to be a tough, special person who did not give her gifts or candy. She said, "Well, my grandparents are worth a thousand families."

She began to read a book on how babies are made. She looked with considerable interest at the drawings of flowers and puppies, but when human examples came up she closed the book rather hurriedly and said she knew all about that because she had seen a TV show. When she saw the rooster on top of the hen she said, "They can't do it like that," with a sense of disbelief. Then she commented that she doesn't know how it is with humans because she has not seen it. On the TV show there was a real woman. They had an adopted child. She is not adopted.

At this point Tina began to play with some musical instruments. She remembered that when she was two years old her harmonica was squashed by her brother. She then got a bigger one. She also remembered that she had scissors with a bird on the scissors and they were also squashed by her brother because she had lent them to him. I wondered whether she was afraid to look at the pictures about mommies and daddys making babies, feeling that if the daddy was on top of mommy he might hurt her or *squash* her, just as her harmonica and her scissors had been squashed. Her own aggression projected on her brother was an important element of this communication.

Her particular links to father (seductive) and to mother (dependent) are illustrated in a nightly ritual. Tina has a special way of saying goodnight to her parents. With her father, according to him, she kisses him on the mouth and with her mother she complains of her aches and pains. Tina referred to it by saying she liked to talk with mommy and that she had nothing to say to daddy. She has a boyfriend now; he used to set all the boys against the girls. But "sometimes I still like him outside of school." The treatment is still in process.

CONCLUSION AND SUMMARY

In this paper I have presented a definition of hysterical character. I have described the origins of the character structure as stemming from endowment, familial, and cultural factors, the similarities in the description of high-level or "good" hysteric and low-level or "so-called good hysteric" and childhood description of hysteria. Clinical observations in the psychoanalytic setting seem to justify the existence of hysterical character neurosis in childhood.

REFERENCES

Abse, W. (1974) Hysteria within the context of the family. *J. Oper. Psychiatry*, 6:31–42.

Abraham, K. (1920) Manifestations of the female castration complex. In *Selected Papers on Psychoanalysis*. London: Hogarth, Press, pp. 338–369.

Ainsworth, M. (1973) The development of infant-mother attachment. In *Review of Child Development Research, No. 3*, B. Caldwell and H. Ricciuti, eds. pp. 1–94. Chicago: University of Chicago Press.

Beres, D. (1969) Character formation. In *Adolescent: Psychoanalytic Approach to Problems and Therapy*, S. Lorand and H. Schneer, eds. New York: Delta Books, pp. 1–9.

Brazelton, B. (1973) Clinics in developmental medicine, No. 50: neonatal behavioral assessment scale. In *Spatics International Medical Publications*. Philadelphia: J.B. Lippincott.

Easser, B.R., and Lesser, S.R. (1965) Hysterical personality: a re-evaluation. *Psychoanal. Quart.*, 34:390–405.

Erikson, E. H. (1950) The theory of infantile sexuality. In *Childhood and Society*. New York: Norton, pp. 42–92.

Fenichel, O. (1945) *The Psychoanalytic Theory of the Neurosis*. New York: Norton, pp. 42–92.

Gardner, R., Riley, W., and Monarty, A. (1968) *Personality Development at Preadolescence: Exploration of Structure Formation*. Seattle: University of Washington Press.

Horowitz, M.J. (1977) The core characteristics of hysterical personality. In *Hysterical Personality*, M.J. Horowitz, ed. New York: Jason Aronson, pp. 3–6.

Kernberg, O. (1976) *Object Relations Theory and Clinical Psychoanalysis*. New York: Jason Aronson.

Korner, A. (1964) Significance of primary ego and drive endowment for later development. In *Exceptional Infant, Vol. I: The Normal Infant*, J.H. Ellmuth, ed. New York: Bruner/Mazel.

La Barre, M., and La Barre, W. (1965) The worm in the honeysuckle. *Social Casework*, 46:399–413.

Mahler, M.S., and Kaplan, L. (1977) Developmental aspects in the assessment of narcissistic and so-called borderline personalities. In *Borderline Personality Disorders: The Concept, the Syndrome, the Patient*, P. Hartocollis, ed. New York: International Universities Press, pp. 71–85.

Metcalf, A. (1977) Childhood Process to structure. In *Hysterical Personality*, M.J. Horowitz, ed. New York: Jason Aronson.

Millon, T. (1969) *Modern Psychopathology*. Philadelphia: W.B. Saunders.

Rangell, L. (1959) The nature of conversion. *J. Am. Psychoanal. Assn.*, 17:632–662.

Robins, L. (1966) Childhood behavior predicting later diagnosis. In *Deviant Children Grown Up; A Sociological and Psychiatric Study of Sociopathic Personality*. Baltimore: Williams and Wilkins, pp. 135–158.

Sadock, J.H., Kaplan, T., and Freedman, M. (1976) *The Sexual Experience*. Baltimore: Williams and Wilkins.

Sperling, M. (1973) Conversion hysteria and conversion symptoms. *Am. Psychoanal. Assn.*, 21:745–771.

Wolff, P. H. (1959) Observations on newborn infants. *Psychosom. Med.*, 21:110–118.

Zetzel, E. (1968) The so-called good hysteric. *Int. J. Psycho-Anal.*, 49:256–260.

Chapter 4

Hysterical Disorders Observed in a University Child Guidance Clinic

DORIS C. GILPIN *

The records of 30 cases, covering a period of 20 years, 1959–79, and diagnosed as either hysterical character disorder or hysterical neurosis, were obtained from the clinic files. Since only four of the number were male, these were excluded from the present review, so that the final sample was made up of 26 females. The data were further collapsed under a uniform rubric of hysterical disorder when it was found that 18 had been labeled hysterical personality and 8 hysterical neurosis, and that on inspection nothing was likely to be obtained by treating the data separately, in addition to the fact that the neurotic cell was very small. For similar reasons, the prepubertal and pubertal subjects were also lumped together. The control set of charts was pulled by taking the one next in file to the experimental chart that corresponded with respect to age and sex.

Methodologically, two lots of information were extracted from the records: first, direct data elicited from demographic sheets, standard developmental questionnaires and standard symptom checklists devised for general clinic use. This ensured that the same questions were asked of all the parents, and although not all the questions were answered, all those that were answered were used in the analysis. No attempt was made to distinguish between "no" and "unknown" responses. Second, more inferential data were obtained by consensus of the working group from the social histories, the psychological examinations, and the psychiatric interviews,

* In association with Pravin Gandhy, Jeremy Fialkov, Harinder Singh, Claire Irwin, and Gail Overbey, with statistical help provided by Cynthia Janes.

some of which were relevant to the task at hand, some irrelevant, and a great deal redundant.

RESULTS

Demographic Findings

In general Chi Square analyses were carried out unless the numbers were too small, and recourse was made to Fisher's treatment. Some degree of bias could also be attributed to preconceived notions about the nature of hysteria with possible unconscious tendencies to favor the experimental group. In favor of the investigators, it should be pointed out that the data were collected by others, many of whom had long since left the clinic. Nonetheless, these past collectors may also have been biased by some preconceived notion regarding the etiology of hysteria.

Ethnically, there were 18 white to 8 black subjects in the hysterical group, the number of blacks being in smaller proportion (30%) than what was usual for the clinic (40%) or what was found in the control group of patients (37%). The average income of the families (around $7,500) was the same for both groups, but since the records go back to 1959, the income levels from the first to the second decade were in no way comparable. There were also no significant differences in the marital status of the two groups or in the nature of the referring sources. Regarding the latter, one might have expected, if the factor of "conversion" was prominent, that more medical referrals would have taken place for the experimental group.

With respect to the age of onset, however, some interesting differences were revealed with possibly a theoretical importance. For example, there was a clear clustering around the ages of 7 to 9 in the hysterical group, as compared with the controls; this corresponds "closely" with Freud's findings almost 70 years ago and might be regarded as lending support to the degenerative concept of an unresolved oedipal conflict disposing to hysteria.

Family Relationships

The closeness of the hysterical girl to her father provides one of the most significant items of difference with 62% of the experimental group manifesting this attribute to only 17% of the control group. Although the data were anecdotal, the impact of the material was no less convincing. A typical example from which the assessment was made would be the following: Father talked freely about an early-morning "ritual" that he had with his daughter; she would come into his bed and scratch and massage his back, and he would tell her how good these physical manipulations felt. This procedure started when she was about six or seven years old. The competition with the mother differentiated the two groups almost as strikingly. The girls were openly rivalrous with the mother and would tell her that she did not know how to raise the children, the inference being that they could do a much better job (54% of the experimental group: 21% of the control group). A clear profile of the mother of the hysterical girl emerged from the contrast with the mothers of control patients: They were more strictly religious (31% to 8%), more emotional (46%), more hysterical (27% to 4%), and more narcissistic. (During the interviews, the mothers would focus mainly on their own background, their own concerns, their own problems, their own appraisals of the situation, and would dominate the interview in a garrulous and gushing way.)

Religion appeared to play an important role for both parents; in many instances, they had met through religious experiences, at church functions and through mutual religious interests. ("We fell in love because we had so much in common, such as religion.") The fathers, however, were not always faithful to their wives in spite of this religious background. While 38% of them were religious, 35% of them ran around with other women. This contrasted sharply with the control fathers, who professed no strong religious beliefs or tendencies and of whom only 4% were unfaithful.

Developmental Findings

The only item that distinguished the two groups was the history of gastrointestinal illness, which was much greater in the control subjects (82% to 38%). As far as emotional problems in infancy, developmental deviations, or difficulties of any kind, no significant differences occurred between the groups either in terms of the presence or absence of problems or in terms of severity.

During the toddler phase, there seemed to be a later beginning of bowel training in the hysterical group, but no difference in the time of completion. In psychosexual terminology, there is just the slightest suggestion that the hysteric child experiences less concentration and therefore less fixation at the anal level.

Symptomatology

The analysis of the symptom list yielded three items indicating *less* pathology on the part of the hysterical child in the areas of aggressiveness or show of anger (0% to 78%), eating problems (10% to 78%) and negativism (19% to 67%). Furthermore, the hysterical child had the greater sense of humor (71% to 11%), a fact that has also been noted in the adult hysteric. Even though somatic symptoms were not significantly more frequent than in the controls, they often took a somewhat unusual form: "She sees things squeezing down and getting tinier and tinier [micropsia]."

As one might have expected from impressionistic clinical material, although the hysterical child seems singularly free from aggressiveness, 27% of them (as compared with 0% of controls) have displays of temper as one of the presenting symptoms. Such paradoxes are inevitable in this type of retrospective clinical research when the evidence cannot be reexamined.

Clinical Examination

Seven items were found to be significant on clinical examination out of a pool of thirty-six items. The hysterical child was found to be more impulsive than the control child (56% to 15%), more narcissistic (52% to 20%), more histrionic (48% to 15%), more seductive (43% to 5%), and more demanding of nurturance by the father (43% to 10%). It is of interest that negative feelings (aggression, anger, and hostility) were not noted in the psychiatric and psychological interviews as being salient for hysterical subjects, whereas the parents complained about them. They were present in the girls no more than in the control patients. The discrepancy is probably a function of parental expectation and related to moralistic ideas about the control of negative affects.

Some quotations from the test responses did help to convey a flavor of hysteria:

From the WISC: In response to losing a friend's doll, one would cry, be ashamed.

From the examiner's observation: "She appears to see herself as the center of the universe"; "She sees sexuality, seductiveness, and flirtatious cuteness as the only ways to induce others to meet her needs"; "There was an excited fleeting around the room. She made exaggerated exclamations of affected pleasure in tasks that were obviously difficult for her and was somewhat ingratiating in her awed compliments"; "She emphasized her needs, the examiner's luck and abundance of supplies as if to put the examiner in a position of being selfish or thoughtless if he did not provide for her. Her fantasies reflected her feeling that if you are a helpless little baby doll, you will get more."

From the Rorschach response: A tendency to see wholes, not details (30% in the hysterical group, and 0% in the controls). One response was "a nest of baby birds waiting to be fed." "The most striking characteristic of her thinking is the overwhelming immaturity. Her defensive avoidance, repression and denial lead to a kind of global, undifferentiated impressionistic perception. She does not seem to allow herself to consider details; instead she derives conclusions from her first quick impressions of a stimulus."

On TAT cards: "He's just met her a few days before. They both love each other and she finally gets him to stay and they go to the back room. The boy loved this girl and they were going steady for a few months and he never told his mother, and so one day he decided to come home and tell his mother but his mother then said 'no' and he was sort of mad." And again: "Looks like these two girls hated each other a whole lot. They were both after the same boy. One came out from behind a tree and scared the other. This girl hated her a whole lot because she was so beautiful."

The narcissism, the need for supplies, the seductiveness and the dramatic quality are all very evident. Thirty percent of the hysterical girls tended to see their mothers as narcissistic, whereas only 5% of the controls had this perspective. There also appeared to be more evidence of latency (as manifested by repression) in the experimental group (43%) to 10% in the controls).

Some examiner bias was clearly operating with regard to certain of the items. For example, female examiners detected 50% more competitiveness with mothers than male examiners, while male examiners detected 50% more seductiveness in the hysterical child than the female examiners.

The Profile of the Hysterical Child

Based on the symptom list and on the psychiatric-psychological examination, the following 19 items were found in over half the hysterical girls, and 10 of them significantly differentiated the hysterical subject from the control:

1. The hysterical girl is closer to her father: significant.
2. The hysterical girl is more competitive with her mother: significant.
3. There is usually a precipitating factor present in hysteria: nonsignificant.
4. The hysterical girl is more emotional, hysterical, and narcissistic: significant.
5. The hysterical girl has a greater sense of humor: significant.
6. The hysterical girl is more narcissistic: trend.
7. The hysterical girl wants more nurturance: nonsignificant.
8. The hysterical girl wants more nurturance from her father: significant.
9. The hysterical girl shows evidence of oedipal attachment to her father: nonsignificant.
10. The hysterical girl shows evidence of a strong superego: nonsignificant.

11. The hysterical girl is more anxious: nonsignificant.

12. The hysterical girl is impulsive: significant.

13. The hysterical girl is histrionic: significant.

14. The hysterical girl is seductive: significant.

15. The hysterical girl has a problem with aggressiveness: nonsignificant.

16. The hysterical girl provides an abundance of oral material: nonsignificant.

17. The hysterical girl provides an abundance of phallic-oedipal material: nonsignificant.

18. The hysterical girl manifests a strong latency: significant.

19. The hysterical girl shows more phallic-oedipal than oral material: significant.

Although there was some degree of overlap between the experimental and control groups, it was surprising how clear-cut the profiles turned out to be. A histrionic tendency, as a significant item, and the need for nurturance by the father were found in only two of the controls, but in both these cases the final diagnosis following discharge was hysteria. In one of them there must have been an appreciable degree of seductiveness, since there was a reference to her in the text as being a Lolita.

The material from the clinic was also reassessed in terms of the Perle-Guze checklist, designed to distinguish Briquets syndrome in adults, a condition said to be linked to hysteria. This measure did not distinguish significantly between the hysterical and the nonhysterical groups, but there were indications that with further refinement, it might prove of some value pathognomically, as a clustering did occur around either "no symptoms" or "many symptoms" in the hysterical group.

Using the Perle-Guze list, the clinic symptom list, and the symptoms discovered during the psychiatric-psychological examinations (and, statistically, making use of the *t*-test), the symptomatic profile based on significantly differentiating items did seem to emerge as a clinically stable and non-overlapping personality picture that might be summed up as a peculiar literary combination of *Lolita* and *Alice in Wonderland*. The triad of traits contributing predominantly to the hysterical profile in childhood would seem to be histrionicity, seductiveness, and the need for nurturance from the father. It is obvious that a prospective study beginning with rigorous operational definitions would confirm or disconfirm some of these tentative retrospective conclusions. One small piece of confirmation did help to bolster the findings of this pilot study. On a further review of the past records, three fresh cases were turned up, again all girls, diagnosed as hysterical neurosis on the basis of a single conversion symptom. As mentioned earlier, the overall average in the hysterical group had been 10.8 of the profile items. These three had 11 to 12 of the items and 3 to 6 of the significantly differentiating items. All three wanted nurturance from the father.

SOME FOLLOW-UP AND THERAPEUTIC IMPLICATIONS

As compared with previous studies on male patients at this clinic, the female children and their families in the hysterical group accepted treatment more frequently and remained in treatment for longer periods. Compared with nonhysterical female patients, there was much less forced termination with the experimental group as a result of failures to keep appointments or to pay for the treatments. Ethnicity played no role in the choice of treatment: Psychotherapy was recommended to 33% of the white sample and to 31% of the black sample.

With such small numbers, it is difficult to assess the efficacy of different treatment modalities. The treatment plans vary from individual case work, conjoint treatment of the parents, group treatment of the parents, special tutoring, and family therapy. As a general rule, those that remained in treatment showed improvements. The remainder of the group were placed in other treatment facilities, dropped out of treatment, or refused treatment. There is no doubt that family treatment does seem to work with a certain number of the hysterical girls, but improvements have also been obtained with various forms of collaborative therapy. From our experience, therapy suited to the needs of a particular child and his family is as important in the management of these cases as with other patients seen in the clinic. The recommendations should be individualized and tailored to the particular needs. What we are trying to do here is to present a model by means of which a clinic can evaluate its own work, and in so doing also make a contribution to general psychiatric knowledge.

DISCUSSION OF CHAPTER 4

PAULINA F. KERNBERG
HENRY P. COPPOLILLO

Dr. Kernberg

I was impressed by the fact that 18 out of the 26 children had a characterological label, because the question of character and character pathology in childhood is still a controversial issue, and my paper addresses itself to this. What further emphasizes the permanence of character structure is the finding that there are no differences between pre- and post-pubertal characteristics in these patients. The age of onset of the hysterical state was found to be 8 or 9 years, which is also the age of onset for hysteria given by Freud in his early etiological papers. Related to this are the findings by Neubauer that 20% of apparently normal preschool children from a middle-class mid-Manhattan population had reached the level of the classical Oedipal complex. In 80%, therefore, there was a failure of conflict resolution and consequently, according to psychoanalytic theory, a predisposition to hysteria.

There are clearly other factors involved, since 80% of normal preschool children do not develop hysterical pathology. Returning to the clinic sample, I was also struck by the absence of pre-oedipal problems around eating, bowel, and bladder training, and the relative absense of anger. All this speaks to the type of mother-child relationship that has been described in the literature as typifying the tie between mothers and their hysterical daughters. The suppression of anger, leading to compliance, makes it harder for the girl to resolve the early developmental issues with the mother, and this may lead to problems involving gender identity later on. The presentation also highlights, as I do in my own paper, the importance of the cognitive style, the leveling type, in shaping the psychopathological responses. The finding that seductiveness is directed toward the male and competitiveness toward the female should not, I think, discourage us unduly with regard to the impingement of the sex of the therapist on the therapy. It is largely a question of the unfolding of transference over the course of time: The female therapist will experience the seductiveness when the father transference is uppermost, the competitiveness when the mother transference is uppermost, and vice versa. The matter also has importance in terms of countertransference risks for therapists who may feel uncomfortable with these contrasexual projections.

The research also supports the contention that symptomatic criteria are not enough by themselves to sort out these patients. If we take conversion, for example, as clearly defined by Dr. Coppolillo, it emerges as a phenomenon that can occur at any stage and any disorder, and it is not, therefore, pathognomonic of hysteria. In order to differentiate hysteria from other groups, one needs to look at the totality of the person as reflected in the characteristics of his ego, his self-identity, his interpersonal relations, the state of intrapsychic conflicts in relation to superego and defenses, and cognitive style. With the help of these, we can begin to sort out the psychopathology and the resulting different aspects of hysteria.

Dr. Coppolillo

The research is impressive and, like most good research, it is disturbing. It disturbs us because it shadows some of the clinical illusions that each one of us cherishes and that is based on a small personal sample of experience. Research like this shakes us out of our complacency and also serves the important function of raising questions that need to be investigated further. The process has its frustrations. When one looks at the findings as presented one invariably searches for information that has not been collected. One should regard it not as an end in itself but as stimulus to further inquiry. One should also not allow oneself in any way to prejudge questions that may require a chain of investigations before one can arrive at convincing answers. One must also not consider a particular constellation of symptoms as eternal and unchanging. When we examine a symptom picture, we should keep in mind the timing of our evaluation: At what stage in the evolution of the disturbance was the child? How does the present state compare with the child's state a year ago or a year later? This is to remind us that we are evaluating state and not process. Let me try and illustrate this point:

The onset of symptoms clustering around the period of eight or nine years is an important finding that confirms previous similar findings. I think we would be remiss, however, if we left it at that. Why eight or nine years? It is tempting to speculate that this is when the resolution of the oedipal conflict begins or fails to begin, but there are other events that are taking place at about the same time. This is when the child starts to recognize that in place of assigned work, he now needs actively to acquire work, and that in place of the self-esteem that is assigned to him in the family, he now needs to cultivate his own self-esteem. It marks the passage from passivity to activity, from assignment to accomplishment. In the child moving toward hysteria, the holdup may lie in the resolution of the oedipal conflict or in the resolution of self-centeredness. These kinds of questions can be answered not by research such as this but by individual in-depth treatment.

I was also interested in the finding of religiosity in the parents of hysterical children. We must remember that we do not know precisely what religion means to such people or what part it plays in their internal and external economy. I recently heard about a primitive revivalist meeting in which the participants all seemed to be caught up in various stages of ecstasy and trance. There happened to be one man standing aside who did not appear to be moved at all, so much so that someone asked him, "What are you doing here?" His answer was that this was the best place to come to make out! The point is that we do not know what religion means to different patients. It could mean a set of rules rigidly operated as part of the regulatory system, or a gratifying regression associated with fantasies of primal reunion. With some religions ego competence may be emphasized and preached, while with others empathic feeling may be enhanced.

Another problem facing this kind of research has to do not with the presence but with the absence of significant differences—the noncontributory findings. One always has to ask whether there were no significant differences, or whether the instrument failed to reveal them, or even whether the differences were so short-lived that they were not present at the time of measurement. A conversion sympton, for example, has a psychic goal to accomplish, and once this is done the conversion becomes unnecessary and disappears.

Let me move to another area. When the mothers of these hysterical children are described as narcissistic, does this really mean that they cannot differentiate themselves from object at times, or does it mean that they are exaggeratedly self-centered? The two concepts are frequently confused. The self-centered people are able to differentiate self from object, but the object is always there as a handmaiden to the self; the narcissistic person often cannot differentiate self from object, and the object becomes a mere extension of the self.

In the issue of sexual gratification, it is sometimes difficult to determine to what level the impulse belongs: whether the longings are mature and related to tender and sexual wishes toward the object, or whether the longings are primitive and preoedipal. I recall one adolescent girl saying, in relation to a passed period of promiscuity: "No, it wasn't very sexually gratifying, but being held and being close to another human being was the most important part of it."

Like Dr. Kernberg, I was much taken with the fascinating differences found with regard to male and female psychiatrists, and I think that this should be taken seriously. It underlines the fact that we are the instrument of treatment and that we should never give up the process of keeping one eye on ourselves as the other eye focuses on the patient.

I would also like to comment on the fathers in the hysterical triangle, particularly on their participation in sports; this is connected with the myth that hysteria is a woman's illness, which is, in my opinion, neither theoretically nor clinically sound. I think that we simply tend not to recognize male hysteria. If we are indeed convinced of the bisexual nature of human beings, and there is much evidence to support this, then I think one has to concede that males have as much chance as females to develop hysteria, although they may show a different pattern of traits. Many men who are daredevils and who carry out dangerous stunts in a flamboyant way are possibly hysterical; similarly, *macho* characters, who are constantly preoccupied with their masculinity, potency, and body integrity (like some of Hemingway's characters) are among the most poignant hysterics around.

The research also serves to remind us how important it is to keep our records systematically so that we can use them with an increasing degree of sophistication. In this same context, it might be possible to enlarge our sample of hysterics with a central clinic, like the Washington University Clinic, soliciting the help of other agencies in collecting cases and using the same format for evaluating them. This simple but fundamental research strategy could be duplicated without great pains throughout the country.

Finally, with regard to treatment, my experience has been that it is not difficult to get the hysteric into therapy, but it is less easy to keep him there. The most difficult patient in this category that one has to treat is the one who derives his major gratification from the illness itself. The fact that the patients who did best were those whose whole family was involved in treatment must mean that this is a powerful way to prevent the continued acting out of inner conflicts within the provocative hysterical family milieu.

The danger for the family members as well as for the therapist is to get into a reciprocal pathological interchange from which the patient obtains much secondary gain. One has, in a way, to build therapeutic fences around hysterics so that transference entanglements do not constantly stimulate countertransference responses. You will recall that Freud, in his treatment of Dora, became furious with her and described her as "one of the most repulsive hysterics I have ever treated," and that when certain issues came up, he "did not fail to use them against her." Although interpersonal relations may aggravate the hysterical state in family life, one should never overlook the fact that it is the internal representations that determine the pathology rather than physical reality. It does not matter, therefore, for genesis of hysteria that the father is "out of the picture" through separation, divorce, or death, because it is a fantasized father and not the real father that is at work in the child's mind. I think that in the early days of child analysis some of the people who felt that the child could not develop transference because of the presence of the parents in the home were confusing geographic with psychological space.

However, although I believe that hysteria is intrapsychically determined, I am well aware of the shaping effect of culture. I saw many conversion reactions in Tennessee; I can well remember the hysterical child being brought from the hills to the unit at Vanderbilt, for the first time mixing with a fairly sophisticated milieu. Within two weeks the conversions had disappeared, but, of course, forces within the personality that permitted such symptoms to emerge in the first place remained. As Dr. Kernberg emphasized, one has to take both internal and external influences into consideration when looking at any psychopathology.

Chapter 5

The Hysterical Child in the Doe Family: A Multifaceted Approach to the Problem of Hysteria

5.1 PSYCHOTHERAPY OF THE HYSTERICAL GIRL

DORIS C. GILPIN
KATE MATTES

There are many potential pitfalls for the psychotherapist of the girl with a hysterical character disorder. These can be understood in a global way by realizing that these children have a style of getting along with people that is by and large rewarding, by and large acceptable, and that by and large makes sense of their environment. Therefore, it is not easy to demonstrate a need to change. One can ask why these children should be treated at all. The answer lies in the human need to respect oneself and one's fellow man, which is not met when one exploits or is exploited. The reasons that parents bring these children to the clinic are not stated in those terms, nor are the children clearly aware of this. They are aware of something unsatisfying and unfulfilling in relationships, of a hunger which they try to fill by using their exploiting tactics, but which is never assuaged. Their bodies, their movements, their affects are tools to manage others and are ignored as being part of themselves. They do not let themselves be "real" to others, and they do not let inner messages be real to themselves.

They argue with mother, not aware of the conflicted pull to take on mother's feminity. They tickle father and blot out the focus of their excited feelings. Because they are often verbal, charming, entertaining, and clever, it is easy for others to respond to these "surface" characteristics and not pay attention to the insecure and denigrated child underneath. The therapist can be "seduced" into reinforcing the surface and ignoring the underlying disturbance.

There is another aspect, too, that makes the therapist's role a difficult one: This is that the hysterical child has gained a certain amount of power over others and does not give it up easily. Setting up a therapeutic alliance, therefore, needs to be seen and felt by both participants as an alliance leading to choices, not an alliance to force changes. As the child recognizes how much more meaningful life is when she is recognized and cared about for herself and not for her performances, she may willingly give up treating others in less meaningful ways. Being able to perform, of course, will always remain as part of her repertoire of coping skills.

Excerpts from once-a-week therapy of an eleven-year-old girl who shall be called Stephanie Doe may illustrate some of these points. This girl had seen two previous therapists before this therapist began with her. At this first session, the girl, standing on a toilet seat, refused to come out of the bathroom to meet the new therapist. The latter went in alone, stood outside her booth, and introduced herself, saying that she could see that Stephanie really had some strong feelings about being there that day and not wanting to see her, since the two were strangers. The doctor said she knew some things about Stephanie from Stephanie's previous therapist and from her mother's reports about her, but that she really didn't know Stephanie. She could see that Stephanie felt she didn't need to be there, and asked her directly whether she felt that she needed to be here. She received a curt "No." The therapist, Dr. Gilpin, now continues to relate her own experiences of this disconcerting child:

I said to her that I could understand how that would make her pretty angry if she thought she didn't need to be here and yet somebody was pushing her to get here. I knew she had seen a previous therapist for a long time, and wondered if she felt that had been any help at all to her. She again responded with a curt "no." I said that I understood that this would also make her angry. If coming here hadn't helped her and yet someone was still making her come, I could see why she'd be angry. I gathered that it was her mother that was making her come, and she acknowledged that this was so. I then asked if her mother had explained to her why she felt that Stephanie needed to come, but she did not answer. I said that it was quite a situation when some grown-up made someone like her do things that she didn't feel like she needed to do; that really was a maddening situation and I could see that. At different times I discussed the fact of our being in the bathroom, pointing out that it must be uncomfortable to just be standing there all this time and that it might be more comfortable if we could go to my office and sit down. There was no immediate response to this, although after a while she did get off the toilet seat. I then pointed out that it was hot in the bathroom because there was no air conditioning there, and that it was cooler in my office. I said that I did not know about her, but I knew that I would be more comfortable if I could sit down where it was nice and cool; however, I was willing to stay in the bathroom if she felt that this was what she had to do. I added that I didn't necessarily take anybody else's word about her and that I would need to make up my own mind by actually getting to know Stephanie herself. I could then figure out whether I thought she needed help, and if so, whether I would be the one who could help her. I knew that she might not trust that I would be any different from anybody else who was telling her what she should do when she felt that it was something she didn't want to do. Later I said that it looked as if we were stuck with each other for forty-five minutes, and it seemed to me that as long as we were stuck with each other, we might as well be comfortable with it. I really didn't see that it was worse being stuck with each other in my office rather than here in the bathroom. At this point she very slowly and sullenly, and with a defiant toss of her head, came out, and we went upstairs to my office.

Clearly the girl was not being challenged in her oppositional behavior toward her mother, who had brought her, nor in her denial of a need to be there. I was trying to ally with the part of her that wanted to be taken care of or to take care of itself. Her histrionic gesture of stubborn withdrawal could well defeat a therapist who fell into the position of competing with her over how her needs were best met.

(Mother at this time, in her work with a social worker, was dealing with depressed feelings about losses.)

At the next session the girl came readily, bringing her kitten. She told me that her mother gave her sister more than she gave her. I was actively interested in the kitten, and the following process occurred around this:

I said that she could see that I really enjoyed having the kitten, but I wondered if there was something I should know about why she had wanted to bring the kitten. She said she kind of wanted to show it off because it was so cute and funny. I agreed that it was cute and funny and added that it did make one feel good to have something to show off. I wondered whether her parents ever showed her off like she was showing off the kitten. She thought her father used to when he would take her to bars and have her dance and sing to the jukebox on the bar. He still shows her off to his friends by at least introducing her. She didn't think her mother showed her off . . .

The therapist can be seen appreciating some of the impulse to show off, but at the same time making a beginning at helping the girl think about the reasons behind her actions, and to notice if these reasons are linked to her past.

Following this there was a session in which she talked of how both she and her mother had responded to the death of Elvis Presley. (Mother, in her sessions, was dealing with her relationship with men.) Then came an interaction that was important both for keeping the alliance and for understanding the transference.

Stephanie said that she had missed some of her favorite TV programs and missed seeing her girlfriend by coming here today, but that it was okay. I remarked that she was very nice about it, but that I detected hints that she really didn't want to be here today. She again insisted it was okay, but proceeded to say she really hated her mother for making her miss her favorite programs. I agreed that this must be maddening.

The therapist is understanding of the "niceness," and by implication the "reasonableness," of the roundabout approach to expressing one's self, but is dealing right away with exposing whatever negative may wreck a therapeutic alliance. This in turn exposes the transference to the therapist as the depriving mother.

(Mother was concurrently in her sessions recognizing how she felt deprived by her mother of her father.)

The kitten was brought again for the next session. She called it her "daughter" and said she liked to aggravate it. She wondered if she could bring her tape recorder. I asked if there was any reason why she shouldn't. We discussed this as well as the things she did to aggravate her mother.

The therapist is again trying to help the girl think about her behavior as well as support her responsibility for herself. She, for her part, was apparently checking to see if the therapist would be aggravated. There followed a session in which oedipal material was prominent, and the girl's identification and transference were seen in fluctuation. The therapist continued to enter into the interaction in a real way, while at the same time assisting the girl to be curious about herself.

(In her session, mother was trying to extricate herself from allowing her husband to continue to run her life.)

She got out a huge half-colored outlined picture of Mickey Mouse and showed it to me proudly. I said that it was well done and asked if she had done it. She said it was her boyfriend who had drawn it, and I said he was apparently good at drawing. She got out some felt-tipped pens and spent the rest of the session, as we talked, coloring in the drawing. I asked if he had been her boyfriend very long, and she said she had known him since first grade. In response to my next question she said he was a pretty nice guy, and I wondered what he did to make him so nice. At first she was rather vague, but then, with much laughter, launched into a story. He used to come to their house and bring bones for their dog, and on one occasion when he came, her mother was in the front room watching a soap opera. She and her sister told him to climb in through the kitchen window, which he did, and they gave him a popsicle. He then climbed back out the window. They then told him to go around to the front door and ring it and say he had the bone for the dog. He did this, and her mother answered the door and had him take the bone back to the kitchen for the dog. The mother noticed that one popsicle was missing. She asked who had had it, and they all denied they had. The mother said, "Well, it couldn't just melt without leaving a trace." Stephanie then explained the joke to her.

I confessed that I was a bit confused as to why they had him climb in through the window and whether her mother did not allow boys in the house. She became vague about this and said something about being younger then and afraid her mother might not give him a popsicle. She had also been afraid to tell her mother about this . . .

She also hated Larry, a grown relative. When asked why, she said he was big and fat and that he was always playing tricks on people. She just didn't like him. I inquired if that was the way she always felt about people who played tricks. She said, "Well, I play tricks," and I told her I remembered that but that she liked herself; at least I hoped she did. I also recalled that she had said she was like her father and that he played tricks. She said that was true.

She then said that her father had given her mother a dozen roses and they cost twenty-three dollars. She quoted the note that had come with the roses: "Darling, let's forget all that has been begotten and get together again. I love you." She said her father wanted to marry her mother again. He told Stephanie the other day that he wanted to come back in the family so that he could take them to ball games and to go roller skating and to do all kinds of things. He had two cars, and she thought that he made about two-hundred dollars a week. He chased her mother's boyfriend off. She really hated her mother's boyfriend and would chase him off. He could be really mean.

Her father took the whole family to breakfast the other day after she had had a friend stay the night, and she and her sister had bought him a present. I said that it sounded like she wanted to give him something after the things that he had been doing for them, and she agreed. He used to take them out to eat a lot when he was in the family, and they got good food. Her mother always served food that was just awful. She named about twenty items and made a horrible face after each one. I asked why mother served meals that she didn't like, and she said that her mother liked these foods. She said that Polish sausage and sauerkraut go well together, and that Polish sausage was from Poland, as was her mother, and sauerkraut was from Germany, as was her father. Her mother and father should go well together. I said that it sounded as if she wanted her father and mother to get back together again, and I wondered what had happened so that they weren't together. She said that her father used to drink a lot and would then beat up her mother. She didn't think he drank much anymore, maybe a beer every once in a while. She also didn't think he would get angry that way anymore. I asked her what she thought he would do with his anger now, and she answered huffily,

"How should I know?" I said that I was not saying she *should* know, but I thought it was pretty important, because if he hadn't found some different way of handling his anger, then the whole thing could happen all over again.

She suddenly and unexpectedly told a joke. I said to her that we had been talking about what her father did with his anger now, and she had sort of tricked me with a joke. I wondered if she was trying to find out something about my anger. She said she was really going to show me a trick; it was from a magic set she had. I asked if it was the kind of trick that I might get mad about, and she said that I might get sore for a while, but that I would then calm down. I wondered what she thought I might do if I got angry, and she said, "You might yell but not for very long!"

At the next session she somewhat dramatically ignored me but later asked me to help with her homework, and then demonstrated she didn't really need the help. At one point I confessed to being mixed up, and she said, "Everybody is mixed up. I've got a mixed-up old man and a mixed-up old lady." Clearly she had been thinking over the realities regarding her parents; she was dropping some of her one-sided thinking over the realities regarding her parents—her one-sided rejection of her mother and her over-idealization of her father. (In her sessions, mother was working at improving her self-esteem during this same period.)

We then entered the Christmas period and tried together to understand and deal with the question of gifts so that no one was exploited, no one was rejected in her personhood, and an alliance for therapy was maintained. She brought presents her first therapist had given her as a gambit in the delicate negotiations.

Then came a session where she talked of receiving rewards for making good grades from her father, of things she was making for her mother, and of what she wanted for Christmas. She tried to get me to buy her a cologne bottle cat from the Avon catalog that she brought. At the next session, she asked if I was going to order that. I said that I wanted to talk with her about it and that I had been trying hard to figure out whether it was really going to be helpful for her. Her mother was selling Avon products, and I pointed out she was not really here for her mother. She then asked if I would buy some stamps from her school. Again I said that I heard her trying to be helpful, but that I didn't know how it would help her. She said if she sold five of them she would be able to get a present for her mother. I said that since I knew how she felt about her mother, which was partly positive and partly not positive, I imagined that she probably had mixed feelings about giving her a present, that she partly wanted to and partly didn't want to. I could not see how it would be good for her for me to help her to give her mother a present. She said that if she sold eight of the sets of stamps, then she would get a couple of things for herself. I then bought some.

The therapist felt the girl needed some reinforcement for her honest facing of where she was in wishes for herself.

(During her sessions, mother was beginning to recognize her own manipulations.)

Stephanie got out a doll wearing a T-shirt. The T-shirt had printed all over it, "I love you." She said it was the doll that her first therapist had given her, and that she had been going to give him a present, but she didn't get to do so because her mother had neglected to buy it. I guessed that she had some pretty strong feelings about her previous therapist, but she gave no answer. I noted that the T-shirt said "I love you" all over it and wondered if love was one of the feelings she felt about him. She changed the subject. She said that he let her do anything. He would let her bring records and sing along with her records. The therapist observed that she was talking about her previous therapist, but she hadn't said anything about her feelings about him. She showed me a drawing she had made at school of a fantastic animal. I said she had really invented something there, but noted that she still didn't seem to want to talk about her feelings about her first therapist.

She then read some stories she'd written about a girl who wanted lots of things.

At the next session discussion of presents got more into the open.

She said she was going to buy me a present and bring it. I said that maybe she was trying to think of some way to talk about wanting me to give her a present. I reminded her how she had shown me in the catalog what she would like and that she had also brought the presents that her other therapist had given her; she talked about what her father wouldn't buy her, about someone giving her a kitten, and now she was talking about getting me a present. It all seemed that maybe she would really like to talk about my giving her a present. She said she gets presents for everyone she knows, and then she named off the presents she had already bought.

I acknowledged that she certainly did have presents for a lot of people, but she had said "everyone," and surely that couldn't be everyone she knew. She said, "Just about." I said that it sounded as if her father was the only person she was mad at because he was the only one that she was not going to give a present to. She said that he didn't like what they gave him anyway. They gave him a necktie, and he left it at their house because he didn't even want it.

There was more talk of music and books, and I then noted that she hadn't really talked about her wish for a present. She totally ignored this comment in a very obvious way, getting out a pencil from her pencil case and correcting something in her story after looking up a word in the dictionary. I observed that she seemed to be avoiding the subject of my giving her a present. She said, "I don't ask people to give me a present." I asked her about this, but she totally ignored this. I again reminded her that she was keeping from talking about not asking people to give her a present. But this also drew a blank and she talked instead of a TV program she didn't understand. I discovered that she didn't feel she had enough facts and said that this was the way I was feeling today—that I didn't have enough facts about whatever her wish was for me to give her a present. I didn't know how she would feel if different things happened: Say, for instance, you gave me a present and I didn't give you one; would you feel cheated? Or say you gave me a present and I gave you a present; would you think I did it just because I had to so as to keep it even and that I really wouldn't have wanted to? Or say you didn't give me a present and I didn't give you one; would you think I was mad at you and that would be the reason why I wasn't doing it? Or say you didn't give a present and I gave you one; would you feel I was being kind just to keep you from being angry? She said, "I don't understand what you are talking about." I asked her if she didn't understand all of it or just part of it. She repeated, "I just don't understand." I said that now I was not sure how to go on—whether she really wanted to understand, whether I should try to explain more, whether it would be worth her time if I did? She said, "I don't listen to people usually," to which I replied that this meant that she thought that what I was saying was not very worthwhile . . .

Clearly, the therapeutic alliance was tenuous at this point.

She brought D., her cat, to the following session, and this was useful in reaching more understanding.

A couple of times during the session she would address a few remarks to the animal. At one point Stephanie was saying she hoped the cat didn't do anything on the floor. She said something about having brought a present for me, and I reminded her that we hadn't really settled the matter about my giving her a present, but that it had become clear that she wanted one from me. She began listing all the presents that she had gotten for different people, and I said that it seemed that she was planning to give lots of presents. She then showed me a picture of herself as a baby, and I remarked on its cuteness. She said it was taken before her sister was born, and I asked if she remembered when this had happened. She said that she did and remembered being mad and stomping around the room, demonstrating this to me. I said I understood that she would be mad at not getting all the attention of her mother and father. She said she had always been her father's favorite, and I sympathized with her fear that this would no longer be the case when her sister was born. She asked, "Should I have worried?" and I said that it would have been natural to worry about it. I then remarked that she was always giving me things, such as bringing her cat, her pictures, and her stories, and I wondered if that had something to do with her wanting to be given something back. She said that people who didn't give were dumb. I said that this meant I'd be dumb if I didn't give her something. She said, "Yeah, you would be dumb like my other therapist. I used to sit and call her dumb, dumb, dumb." I asked her how she had felt about having a dumb therapist, and she said, "She was weird." I pointed out that this was a thought about it, but what about a feeling? "On Christmas she only gave me a card," and even though I encouraged her, she refused to say how she felt about that.

I then told her that I could hear her saying two things: that I'd be dumb if I didn't give her a present and dumb if I did because it would look as if I was trying to get her to keep entertaining and giving me things by my giving her things, but that this was not what we were here for—for her to be taking care of me. I was supposed to be helping her. I'd be dumb if I made her think that she was here to entertain me and keep me happy. She said she brought the stuff because it would be boring here if she didn't. I wondered about her doing it for that reason, since the impression she gave me was that she was doing it to keep me happy and entertained. Perhaps part of it was the way she thought it was, but I also thought she really meant to please me. She said, "Yeah, that's right."

I then said that what I could get her that might really be of help would be something that would make the sessions here more interesting. She began cutting out paper letters to spell "noel," said it was for her mother and kept saying she wasn't doing it very well. I talked about how she was feeling more like giving her mother things; I knew she kept wanting her mother and others to give her things and wondered if she was just trying to do for other people what she would really like done for herself. She agreed, and I remarked supportingly that this was not a bad way to handle those feelings of wanting something for oneself, adding a little later that I knew how much she wanted gifts from her parents and that I was trying to find out if she had kind of turned me into a better mother or a better father. Of course, that really wouldn't in the long run be helpful because she was living in a real world with her real mom and her real dad, and what she really needed help with was how to handle all that stuff in her life that was already there.

She said she didn't need any help. She already knew about handling her life. She figured out what she wanted and she got it. I asked if she had figured out I was to give her a gift. She said no, but that when she grew up she was going to have a big house and a Cadillac, and she was going to have twins, and a pool, and many other things. I asked whether she was going to get all these things by getting people to give them to her like Christmas presents, and she answered that she was going to get them from her singing. I used this to point out that in a way this was what had been going on here. She had been constantly trying to entertain, not by singing, but in other ways; maybe she felt she was supposed to be paid by getting a Christmas gift. I again emphasized that I didn't think that this would be a good idea because it would give her the idea that I thought that she was really here to entertain me and keep me pleased, and that was not really it. She asked me to draw an "n" that she could cut out, and I told her that this was really interesting in view of her saying she didn't need me for anything. I drew one and she cut it out . . .

At one point the kitten was climbing up on the back of the couch. She said, "You better be good or Santa won't give you anything." Again this was turned to therapeutic account by my reminding her that this was also kind of the way that she acted with me, as if she had to be good with me and as if I was the Santa Claus who wouldn't give her something unless she was good. It was fine with me that she wanted to be good, but I was also supposed to be here for that part of her that didn't feel like being good. So far, I could not see that giving her a present was really going to be of help for the things that she needed help with. She said that it was thoughtful and nice to give presents. I wondered whether she thought that by giving her a present I would feel I was being thoughtful and nice, that I would be doing it for me and not for her. At this point she indicated in a humorous way that she felt driven up the wall! When I asked her what would happen if I didn't give her a present, she said that maybe she would get mad. I said that that was something that I could help with. I could help her with being mad. She said, "You are crazy like this whole place and all the people in it." I asked if she thought I was crazy because I said I would help her with being mad. She said, "Nobody can help with mad, you just have it." She went on: "When I get mad, I get stubborn." I said that it was sometimes useful to be stubborn. At first she disagreed with that until I asked if she meant that she really would like some help or would like to change from being stubborn. She said, "No, it could be useful." Toward the end of the hour, I said that there were just a few minutes left and I thought there was one other thing we still needed to talk about—her giving me a present. If she gave me a present and I took it, it would look as if I was telling her that she was here to please me instead of me being here to do something for her. She said, "Well, I could give it to my girlfriend. Maybe I will just bring you cookies." I said that I would have to think about whether I would take any of those or not. She said seductively, "I made them myself," and I replied that she was probably a good cook but that would not be the reason why I would turn them down. She said that what she had bought but was now going to give her girlfriend was a candle that said, "To a special friend." I said that that was a very nice thing to say.

The underlying wish for a phallus was not being discussed openly, but was coloring the interaction.

(In her sessions, mother was getting in touch with the causes underlying her childhood depression in addition to losing her father. For reasons stemming from mother's dynamics and the reality situation, there was a two-month interval with no sessions.)

When therapy resumed, it again focused on gift-giving, with the therapist clarifying the difference between the naturalness with which friends could exchange gifts and its unhelpfulness in a therapeutic relationship.

In the session we talked of her angry frustration. She said, "You are not like anyone I've ever known. You are not like my mother, you're not like my father, you're not like my sister," and continued to list all the people she knew that I was unlike.

We dealt next with the issue of her feelings about coming to therapy, and she reported discomfort because the sessions always made her wonder why whenever she had a question. She now seemed to be observing herself and trying to understand what was taking place between the therapist and herself and in herself. She gradually began to check the therapist out as an object of identification. She was able, through her kitten, to inform the therapist she liked her because she had "gotten used" to her. However, she continued to show off her skills, as in guitar playing, and got very haughty on occasion. But she really seemed to be thinking a lot about her therapy.

(Mother began to focus on her sexual feelings during this same interval.)

GENERAL COMMENT

Stephanie illustrates well the seductiveness, the histrionics, and the wish for nurturance from the father that the hysterical child manifests. She also illustrates very well the problem of making a therapeutic alliance with these "gimme" girls who are easily rejecting of nongivers but who need gifts to help their deeper needs, not their superficial wants. The parallels between the mother's and the daughter's therapy are also fairly typical.

The therapy has been aimed at helping the girl's self-esteem about herself as a person and not as a show or a sex object, so that she in turn can see others the same way and become able to develop deeper relationships. It was also designed to enable her to look at her thoughts and behavior and to become generally more introspective and insightful.

This, we hope, will reduce the impulsiveness, as well as the stereotyped ways, she has of dealing with people and the world. Her unconscious wish to be given a phallus cannot be dealt with in this kind of once-a-week therapy. Repressions about this are not really being lifted, nor are other aspects of her sexual feelings. However, mother's ability to explore this may prognosticate similar possibilities for Stephanie as well. In collaborative therapy of this sort, one may be able to transcend some of the built-in limitations of individual psychotherapy.

5.2 A FAMILY THERAPY PERSPECTIVE ON HYSTERICAL DYNAMICS IN CHILDHOOD

RICHARD J. LAITMAN

Intake Situation

Stephanie Doe, age nine, has made two suicide gestures. Two years ago, she hanged herself from a coat hook, first telling her sister to go and get her mother. Several months ago, Stephanie took a knife to bed with her.

Stephanie's family consists of Mrs. Doe, Henrietta (girl, age six), and Jody (boy, age 2). Mr. Doe left the family several months before the first suicide gesture, and their divorce was finalized soon after it. Mr. and Mrs. Doe have frequently engaged in violent disputes in front of their children. Stephanie has been "daddy's girl," but she has also tried to protect her mother during violent scenes. Mr. Doe continues to keep intrusive contact with the family, particularly trying to keep Mrs. Doe away from other men.

Stephanie is afraid of storms. She is described as "moody," at times outgoing and seeking the spotlight and at times seeming to be angrily sulking. Stephanie's schoolwork is adequate, and she has peer contacts.

The clinician who is faced with this presenting problem needs a framework within which to understand Stephanie's behavior and organize a treatment plan. This paper will begin by presenting some of the concepts that a family therapist uses to understand a presenting situation. Particular emphasis will then be placed on how these concepts may relate to hysterical dynamics. Next, a fictional script will be presented suggesting how the Doe family might respond in a diagnostic interview. Finally, several characteristics of the Does will be highlighted and possible intervention techniques will be discussed.

Family Observation

Stephanie Doe did not display the florid conversion symptoms commonly associated with hysteria. Her behavior did, however, contain many characteristics of children with hysterical dynamics. Aubrey Metcalf (1977) has pointed out several of these behavioral characteristics, including (1) initial charm, which may soon give way to negativism and self-centeredness; (2) superficial emotionality and capriciousness in friendships and opinions; (3) attention- and approval-seeking, but withdrawal or emotional scenes when needs are thwarted; and (4) presenting problems such as inappropriate sex play or frightening emotional displays.

Metcalf's statements refer to how the child deals with his environment, and individual evaluation can further illuminate how the child perceives his environment. For the family therapist, crucial questions are likely to be, What is the nature of the transactions in the child's family environment, and how are the child's symptoms related to the family system?

If one were to watch Mrs. Doe, Stephanie, Henrietta, and Jody interacting, the potential data for observation would be enormous. People would be talking, moving, and gesturing in response to one another. These would be only the most gross observable data. Each communication could be broken down as to how it is expressed, how it is heard, how it is understood, and how it is answered. For example, Mrs. Doe could tell Stephanie, "It's cloudy today." Stephanie might hear her mother also saying, "And its going to rain." She might then understand that her mother "really" means, "Take an umbrella and why do I always have to remind you?" Stephanie might respond with, "Get off my back," and this will certainly seem like a peculiar response to "It's cloudy." However, the close observer may also note a critical tone in Mrs. Doe's voice when she says, "It's cloudy," and indirectness may be her characteristic style to which Stephanie has become accustomed. The amount of observational data can be overwhelming. Thus the family therapist must have organizing concepts to aid her: (1) understanding the family system, (2) understanding how the system is producing stress, and (3) planning effective intervention.

The structure of the family can be looked at in terms of *subsystems* and *boundaries* (Minuchin, 1974). A subsystem is a unit within a family that is created to differentiate its members and perform certain functions. When two people marry, the *spouse* subsystem is created. Its function is mutual gratification and personal enrichment. When the couple has their first child, the *parental* subsystem is formed, as husband and wife also become father and mother. The function of parenting is both socialization of the child and promoting his or her unique development. If another child is born, the *sibling* subsystem comes into being; and this subsystem becomes the testing ground for peer relationships. There are many other subsystems formed by sex, interest, function or combinations of these (e.g., dad and the boys go fishing, grandma and mom make the rules in the house).

The boundaries of a subsystem are the rules that govern how transactions will take place among subsystems members and those outside. Effective boundaries protect subsystem members from undue interference while also permitting sufficient communication to allow for flexibility when necessary. For example, each spouse subsystem has a boundary around it which permits more or less access. In some families the boundary is quite *enmeshed* and too much access is permitted. This would likely be the case where a mother would let her daughter sleep with her if the girl complained of a stomach ache—even though this may require or "force" her husband to sleep on the living-room sofa. In other families this boundary may be disengaged and too little access permitted. In this situation real emergencies may not be attended to, and family members may appear emotionally cut off from one another. Minuchin (1974) points out that boundaries form a continuum from enmeshed to clear to disengaged. The nature of these boundaries may change over time; and at any one time, some family boundaries may be enmeshed, some clear, and some disengaged.

When families are in distress and children are symptomatic, there is often trouble within the spouse subsystem and/or dysfunctional parent/child boundaries. When the parent/child boundary is enmeshed, the parent(s) may become overidentified and overinvolved with the child and vice versa. The child may sacrifice individuation to be part of the group. When this parent/child boundary is disengaged, the child may have to sacrifice normal dependency and feelings of belonging for pseudomaturity. This child may also lack models for identification and act out his unmet needs.

The family therapist discerns the subsystem and boundary qualities of a family through observation of the rules that govern their transactions. One area of observation is the flow of communication itself—who talks to whom, about what, who listens, who interrupts, who yawns. There may be subtle rules governing these interchanges which have meaning in defining boundaries. When mother and father are talking, a child may interrupt in a seemingly tangential way. One of the parents may say, "Not now, son, we're talking." This possibly offhand comment may underscore a rule and a spouse boundary in an important way.

Often families have stated or covert rules governing the awareness and expression of feelings. The author has worked with one family where there was a previously unstated rule of "only Dad can get mad." Whenever anyone else became even mildly irritated, father moved in to squelch any expression. It turned out that this father had had an out-of-control hostile father of his own and that any angry expression reminded him of the terror of his early life. The parent/child boundaries were enmeshed, and the children had learned that the price of belonging was the inhibition of their aggression. Thus the family therapist needs to observe the rules governing feeling expression—who can express what, to whom and when.

After such detailed observation, repeated interactional patterns begin to emerge. The outcome of these patterns is that each family member develops habitual ways of feeling, responding, viewing him or herself, and viewing other family members. These ways of viewing the other become the foundation for family roles. Once a role becomes fixed, the parent or child continues in the role to maintain the family homeostasis and the continued integrity of the family patterns. The nature of the role also has implications for which behaviors are encouraged and which are ignored or suppressed. Thus the child who is labeled "bad" will be pounced upon for noncompliance, while his cooperative behavior may be ignored or interpreted as manipulative. These roles are difficult to alter.

Given this brief background regarding some of the types of observations that family therapists make, let us move to what types of family dynamics might be particularly germane to the child displaying the behavioral characteristics of hysteria.

Family Dynamics and Hysteria

The family system of the child with hysterical behaviors appears to have enmeshed boundaries between parents and child. Abse (1974) terms this "the family soup" with the ingredients being "insufficient basic individuation . . . and an excessively deep collective family dependency."

One way that this enmeshment appears to come about is through difficulty in the spouse subsystem and concomitant *triangulation* of the child. Triangulation refers to the inclusion of a third person as a means of handling conflict between two people.

MacKinnon and Michels (1971) note that the child developing hysterical characteristics may be involved in two types of triangulation. Both are based upon a dysfunctional spouse subsystem. The first type of triangulation is the situation where the father, experiencing the distance between him and his wife, may turn to the female child for substitute gratification. This gratification may be nurturant or teasingly sexual, giving the child the hint of more to come and the concomitant need to repress her own feelings of participation. The second type of triangulation is the situation where the child experiences both inadequate gratification from her mother and an awareness of martial conflict. She is thus pulled toward her father for recognition of her adequacy and desirability. When both of these forces are at work, the child may become flirtatious, moody, and self-centered, and may tend toward the use of repression—the hallmarks of hysteria. Stephanie was blatantly and frighteningly introduced to her parents' marital conflict, and there are many references in the history to her perception of a mutually "special" relationship with Mr. Doe.

Another mechanism that contributes to the enmeshment of the child with hysterical symptomatology is *parental projection*. Parental projection refers to the parents' perception of their own traits, needs, or conflicts as residing in the child. Upon seeing these characteristics, the parent may gratify the child as they wish to have been gratified, reject the child for having certain attributes, or behave in confusing and inconsistent ways. The child may stimulate these projections on the part of her parents through her gender, her ordinal position in the family, or a particular physical characteristic or frailty. The impression that the social worker described in her report about Mrs. Doe clearly points to parental projections. She wrote, "Although Stephanie is 'daddy's girl,' Mrs. Doe identifies strongly with many of Stephanie's traits: fear of the dark, of men, of wanting a father figure, and the ambivalence over divorce. Looking into Stephanie's problems, for mother, is somehow looking into her own."

It may be "human nature" to love in another what we love in ourselves and reject in another what we reject in ourselves. However, a confusingly strong mixture of "come closer" and "go away" behaviors seems to characterize the parent/child relationships of children with hysterical-type symptoms. These children are seen as dependent, oriented toward adults for gratification, and yet insecurely attached. They receive alternations of approval and disgust, which keep them other-directed, hoping to please but unsure how (Metcalf, 1977).

When the decision is made for family therapy, the decision is made to treat these powerful interactional forces. The data for the therapist's attention and intervention are the interactions among those present. To provide the reader with such data, the author has written a fictional script of how the Does might respond in a family diagnostic interview. This script is based upon the author's conceptualization of the case after consultation with Stephanie's and Mrs. Doe's therapists.

A FICTIONAL DIAGNOSTIC EXCERPT

The Doe family consists of Mrs. Doe, Stephanie (age nine), Henrietta (age six), and Jody (a boy, age two). Mrs. Doe is small, attractive, and in her late twenties. Stephanie is thin with long, straight blond hair. Henrietta is also thin with short dark hair and a forlorn demeanor. Jody is an active two-year-old who will be moving around but not speaking in this vignette. The therapist is male and in his thirties. We begin with the family walking into the interview room—Jody is carrying a toy, Stephanie is carrying her schoolbooks, Henrietta is carrying nothing, and Mrs. Doe looks like she is carrying "the weight of the world."

Therapist: I think one way I could learn about your family would be to ask you a question about how you decide things. Let's pretend it's Saturday morning, and you are together and you can plan whatever you'd like to do that day. Go ahead. I'll just watch.

Mrs. Doe: Jody, stay over there and play . . . I'm sorry, I didn't quite get you . . . Stephanie, put the books down and listen. You're not being polite.

Therapist: Pretend it's Saturday morning, and you all can plan whatever you'd like to do together.

Stephanie: (*To therapist, coyly*) Will you give us the money so we can do stuff?

Therapist: No . . .

Stephanie: (*Interrupts*) I didn't think so.

Mrs. Doe: We can never make decisions.

Stephanie: All right, let's go to Six Flags [amusement park].

Mrs. Doe: We can't afford that. You know we can't.

Stephanie: You always fix it so I can't have what I want, and anyway, we could go if Dad gave us the money. He took me there once by myself.

Mrs. Doe: (*Sharply*) I said we're not going to ask him.

Stephanie: Why not? I could say it's for a school project.

Mrs. Doe: We aren't going to ask this time.

Stephanie: You only ask him when *you* want something. It's all your fault we even have to ask.

Henrietta: (*Pleadingly*) C'mon, Stephanie.

Stephanie: (*To Henrietta*) Well, what do *you* want, Miss Goody Two Shoes.

Mrs. Doe: Don't talk to her with that voice.

Stephanie: (*Snappish*) Then I'll just read and make notes on my hand.

Mrs. Doe: (*Leans toward Henrietta and says gently*) Henrietta, what's your idea?

Henrietta: Oh, most anything . . . Six Flags . . . I could just watch TV . . . Really, I just want us to do something together.

Stephanie: (*Pokes self*) Ouch!

Mrs. Doe: (*Sharply*) Be careful. Put those books down.

Henrietta: Could we take Jody along . . . I know he's kind of hard to handle (Jody comes over to mother).

Mrs. Doe: Oh, huh. (*To therapist*) Do we take Jody along too?

Therapist: Well, I think it's your Saturday plan to decide anyway you like.

Stephanie: When do we leave?

Mrs. Doe: When the doctor says . . .

Henrietta: What do *you* want, Mommy?

Mrs. Doe: (*Surprised at first*) Oh, well, I don't know . . . maybe a picnic in Forest Park.

Stephanie: (*Teasingly*) What if it rains?

Henrietta: It might not.

Mrs. Doe: We're going on a picnic.

Stephanie: (*Blurts out*) I want Kentucky friend chicken. Dad took me there . . . I had the biggest piece. I think it was a leg. Okay, can we leave here now?

Mrs. Doe: (*To therapist, irritated, but smiling*) I told you we had trouble making decisions.

Discussion

Stephanie has been characterized as coy, demanding, and competitive with Mrs. Doe regarding Mr. Doe. She begins by teasingly asking the therapist for money and then proceeds to "subtly" remind her mother that she and Mr. Doe had been to Six Flags. Stephanie then blames her mother and also lashes out at Henrietta, who she feels is coming on like the "good daughter." Stephanie goes through a long series of behaviors to gain recognition—demanding, competing, blaming, guilt-invoking, teasing, withdrawing, and self-injuring.

Henrietta is depicted in a placating, peacemaking posture. She tries to cool Stephanie down from a conflict with her mother, and she pleads for family togetherness. Henrietta is willing to sacrifice her own needs ("I could just watch TV"), and she is the one who asks Mrs. Doe what *she* wants.

Mrs. Doe perhaps feels nervous with the male therapist, has trouble hearing the task, and has little confidence it can be done. She and Henrietta are protective and nuturing of each other, while she and Stephanie are mutually competitive and critical. Mr. Doe, while not physically present, is the central character of Stephanie and Mrs. Doe's competition.

From this excerpt, one can perhaps view Stephanie's suicidal gesture with some perspective. It appears that Stephanie experienced great loss when Mr. Doe left the home. Before the marital breakup, Stephanie hints, she and her father had a "special" relationship which excluded Mrs. Doe and all others. It may be that Mrs. Doe and Henrietta had created their own mutually supportive subsystem. Stephanie's suicidal gesture occurred several months after her parents' separation and just following an argument with her mother over not being able to have her own room. It is likely that Stephanie felt enranged and abandoned. She wanted her father, but he was gone. She wanted her mother but may have felt her mother "belonged" to Henrietta. Desperately she wanted something for herself (her own room), but she could not get it. Speaking symbolically, she was at the "end of her rope." Yet before Stephanie hanged herself, she told Henrietta to go and get her mother. What incredible faith in the family system! Stephanie may have trusted with her life that Henrietta would be the dutiful daughter and that her mother would believe her and come running.

THERAPY WITH THE DOE FAMILY

To put it simply, family therapists are each quite different. The field is relatively new, having only gained wide acceptance in the 1960's. Beels and Ferber (1973) provide an excellent summary of the diversity of family-therapy approaches. These authors also explore the theoretical and technical differences now present in the field. This author's framework is closest to that of Virginia Satir (1964) in the emphasis on (1) here-and-now experience (including action techniques, such as role playing and sculpting), (2) clarifying communication, (3) facilitating congruent feeling expression, and (4) attention to how past models are affecting interaction in the present.

Family therapy with the Does would need to begin with certain therapist characteristics and then address the issues of (1) locked-in roles, (2) feelings toward Mr. Doe, and (3) the projective enmeshment of Mrs. Doe with her two daughters. Regarding therapist characteristics, it would be best to begin family therapy with a male/female co-therapy team. Mrs. Doe has had extremely unpleasant *early* and *recent* experiences with men that influence her toward seeing them as powerful, brutal, abandoning, and violent. Since Mrs. Doe has had such destructive experiences with men, I suggest both sexes be represented in the co-therapy team; and that the female therapist sit near her and pay special attention to her feelings and views. A male therapist should also be involved, as eventually Mrs. Doe may come to differentiate men ("they're not all alike") and test out different ways of relating. Also, a co-therapy team that is experienced working together can provide useful male-female modeling.

One problem in the Doe family is stereotyped roles. In markedly oversim-plified terms, Stephanie has the role of "demanding problem child," Henrietta the role of "quiet, good child," while Mrs. Doe is the "overburdened mother." Mrs. Doe, feeling overburdened and without the support of a spouse subsystem, has likely formed a mutually nurturant subsystem with Henrietta. Henrietta remains in her role to both give to her mother and receive love herself. Stephanie's demands come from her position as the outsider.

Therapeutic effort must be geared toward creating a climate where family members can express feelings that are outside their role. This can move each person toward greater individuation as well as influence the family system. Stephanie needs to express her true feelings of rage, pain, loss, and fright. These feelings need not come out only in criticism of Mrs. Doe, competition for her father, and demanding behavior. Henrietta needs to express her own anger and fright while having less fear that such expression would mean the end of maternal nurturance. Mrs. Doe needs most of all to express her adult needs and find more success in the adult world. For this reason, the therapists' acceptance of her is vital, as is their encouragement for her to pursue adult social and intellectual experiences. In this regard, if Mrs. Doe indicated an interest in separate individual sessions, these would be highly desirable.

A second area of focus with the Does would be feelings about Mr. Doe. They need him. They fight for him. They fear him. They hate him. They aren't legally attached, but they can't get loose. Each of them has very complex and understandable feelings regarding Mr. Doe, but they find it very difficult to express them in straightforward ways. They fight among each other, not realizing how in many ways they share common feelings.

There are several techniques that can be used to facilitate expression and understanding of feelings toward Mr. Doe. One would be through *family sculpting* (Duhl et al., 1973). Sculpting is the physical representation of how a person experiences the relationships and feelings within the family. A person is asked to physically arrange the members of the family into a sculpture that represents how she sees the people in relation to each other. Sculptures can include people at opposite ends of the room, two people each pulling on a third person in the middle and many other representations. A person not in the family can be represented by a therapist or even by a piece of furniture. We can speculate how different members of the Doe family would sculpt their own relationships and how they would represent Mr. Doe's place in the family. Another potential technique would be to imagine that Mr. Doe was actually in the room, perhaps fantasizing that he was sitting in a specific chair. Family members could then express their feelings and their views of Mr. Doe's responses.

A third issue to be dealt with in the Doe family is Mrs. Doe's projections upon her daughters. Mrs. Doe is enmeshed with Stephanie and Henrietta, and each of the girls represents and expresses a part of her. Stephanie expresses Mrs. Doe's feelings of anger, deprivation, and the need to manipulate to get what she wants. Henrietta expresses Mrs. Doe's feelings of low self-esteem, conflict over assertion, and yearnings to be nurtured. These projections make the roles that Henrietta and Stephanie play necessary for the family system and all the harder to change. We can only speculate as to why Stephanie has received the majority of Mrs. Doe's projected anger. Becoming pregnant with Stephanie was, in fact, Mrs. Doe's stated reason for marrying. This could result in very strong unconscious feelings of "if it weren't for you." Above all, Mrs. Doe needs help in meeting her needs in more successful ways. The more she is able to do, the less she will need her daughters to express her suppressed feelings.

In this regard, the therapists' relationship with Mrs. Doe is again crucial. There may be a time in treatment, when Stephanie is demanding attention, that Mrs. Doe can gain some insight into her reactions or understanding of Stephanie's behavior. The therapist can ask Mrs. Doe and Stephanie to switch roles and repeat an interaction. The therapist might also ask Mrs. Doe if she herself has ever had such "I want it and I want it now" feelings. If the therapeutic relationship is strong, Mrs. Doe may be able to reach the insight that she may give Stephanie double messages regarding nurturance because she herself is in conflict over it. Sometimes such insight is powerful in producing change. Insight need not be undervalued in family therapy. The crucial observation is whether insight promotes change in the particular family's interactional system.

SUMMARY

The family is the arena in which most of us have developed our first answers to the basic emotional questions of life: (1) What kind of person am I? (2) What kinds of feelings do I have, and how can I usefully and safely express them? (3) How safe is it for me to be an individual and express my own opinions and uniqueness? (4) How can I get close to another person, and what are the rewards and consequences of intimacy? (5) How can I meet my needs to achieve and to love?

The child with hysterical symptoms may have arrived at some painful and dysfunctional early answers to these questions, such as "I am worthless unless others give to me," "I can get whatever I want if I act a certain way," and "intimacy means abuse." Family therapy may offer a means for changing some of the relationships, boundaries, rules, communication patterns, and roles toward more satisfying outcomes.

REFERENCES

Abse, W. (1974) Hysteria within the context of the family. *J. Operational Psychiatry*, 6:31–42.
Beels, C., and Ferber, A. (1973) What family therapists do. In *The Book of Family Therapy*, A. Ferber, M. Mendelsohn, and A. Napier, eds. Boston: Houghton Mifflin.
Duhl, F., Kantor, D., and Duhl, B. (1973) Learning, space, and action in family therapy: A primer of sculpture. In *Techniques of Family Therapy: A Primer*, D. Bloch, ed. New York: Grune and Sratton.
MacKinnon, R., and Michels, R. (1971) *The Psychiatric Interview in Clinical Practice*. Philadelphia: W. B. Saunders.
Metcalfs, A. (1977) Childhood: From process to structure. In *Hysterical Personality*, M. J. Horowitz, ed. New York: Jason Aronson.
Minuchin, S. (1974) *Families and Family Therapy*. Cambridge: Harvard University Press.
Satir, V. (1964) *Conjoint Family Therapy*. Palo Alto: Science and Behavior Books.

5.3 THE CASE OF STEPHANIE DOE AS VIEWED BY A TRANSACTIONAL ANALYST

ELAINE KORNBLUM

Transactional analysis can be a useful therapeutic modality in at least two basic ways: first and foremost, as a diagnostic tool which can help a skilled therapist to define quickly and clearly problem areas from which a specific treatment plan can be derived; and second, as a language which can be communicated easily and clearly to the client. The transactional analyst believes that the more a person can be taught about himself and about what is appropriate behavior to get needs met in a healthy way, the more he can eliminate pathology and take charge of his life. The T.A. therapist also agrees with the humanistic psychologist that there is a basic drive toward health which may be tapped into and worked with to achieve therapeutic results.

Transactional analysis is an eclectic therapeutic system in both its theoretical and its clinical expression, and tends to be inclusive rather than exclusive of other modalities.

Specifically, transactional analysis utilizes four diagnostic areas:

Script analysis	Uncovering basic decisions, attitudes and life plan of the client (usually determined by age eight)
Structural analysis	The analysis of ego states
Transactional analysis	Analyses of what goes on between or among the ego states internally or with other persons
Game analysis	Identifying repetitious behavior patterns with bad-feeling payoffs

SCRIPT ANALYSIS

Below are presented some of the major script messages of Mrs. Doe and Stephanie, as deduced from the available case material:

MRS. DOE:
> I'm not important . . . my needs don't count.
> I can get help only if I'm desperate.
> I shouldn't ask for help for myself.
> I have to sacrifice for my kids.
> I can't give enough to my kids.
> I'm okay only if I'm taking good care of others.
> I shouldn't make mistakes.
> I'm nobody without a man.
> Divorce is bad.
> You have to let men use you to get what you need.
> Men are scary. You can't count on them.
> If only Dad were here, things would be okay.
> If only Mother would take care of me . . . protect me . . . I'd be okay.

STEPHANIE:
> I can manipulate to get what I want.
> I have to control everything . . . no one else will.
> I can trick you.
> I can get my parents to disagree and get what I want from both of them.
> Men are scary . . . they won't come through for you.
> Men will use you to get what they want. I can do that too.
> If things don't work out, it's your fault.

Using this analysis to bring these attitudes and decisions to the attention of the client may help her to understand her present behaviors, feelings, and problems. These can then be reexamined in the light of the present objective reality, and redecisions can be made on a cognitive and emotional level with the help of the therapist.

STRUCTURAL ANALYSIS

Another way to understand the problems of the Does is to take a look at what's going on internally and with other people. The transactional analyst uses the concept of ego states to help elucidate these complex processes.

Ego states are the three observable forms of ego functions, which we call Parent, Adult, and Child. They may seem to resemble the psychoanalytic concepts of superego, ego, and id, but they are in fact quite different. The Parent, Adult, and Child are all manifestations of the ego. Thus, they represent visible behavior rather than hypothetical constructs. The Parent acts like a parent, either imitating one's own parents or borrowing from other models. It makes rules, defines the world, and nurtures, criticizes, or controls the Child. The Adult ego state is a computer. Only when the Parent or Child requests that the Adult think about something does it do so. Most people keep their Adult functioning to some extent all of the time because thinking is a primary survival adaptation. The Child contains all of the experiences that people have had and all urges and feelings that come naturally to the individual.

Below is a diagram of the ego states as they are functionally described:

STRUCTURAL ANALYSIS

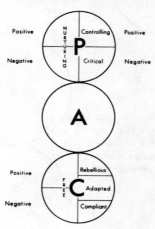

The Parent is divided into four types, two positive and two negative. The positive nurturing and critical parts of the Parent take care of the Child in helpful ways, providing the needs that children have for nurture, control and protection. The negative nurturing and critical parts of the Parent are destructive, either condemning or belittling, or overprotecting, all of which inhibit growth and healthy self-reliance.

Diagram B shows how Mrs. Doe's Parent functions for her children and how it functions for herself. As you can see, it is perceived that Mrs. Doe is transmitting to Stephanie a good deal of positive nurturing and negative nurturing, as well as some negative critical Parent, and very little positive controlling Parent; whereas for herself, the situation is reversed: not enough positive nurturing and too much negative critical Parent is seen.

The Child is divided into five functional parts to help us understand how the energy can be distributed (see Diagram A). The free Child is that spontaneous and uninhibited part of the person which we often think of as a positive, but which may be negative in terms of unchecked impulsive behavior. The adapted parts of the Child include the healthy adaptations, which help the individual function in the community; the rebellious part, which is reacting (often blindly) against the Parent; and the compliant part, which also blindly conforms to Parent expectations.

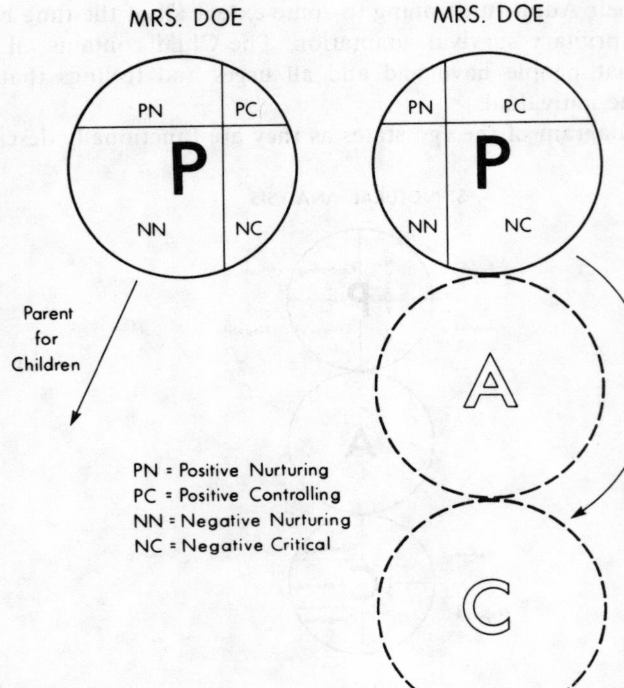
MRS. DOE
PN
PC
P
NN
NC
MRS. DOE
PN
PC
P
NN
NC
Parent for Children
A
Parent for Self
C
PN = Positive Nurturing
PC = Positive Controlling
NN = Negative Nurturing
NC = Negative Critical

Diagram C shows the Child ego states of Mrs. Doe and Stephanie. The overlapping circles indicate what we call contaminations—that is, the Adult

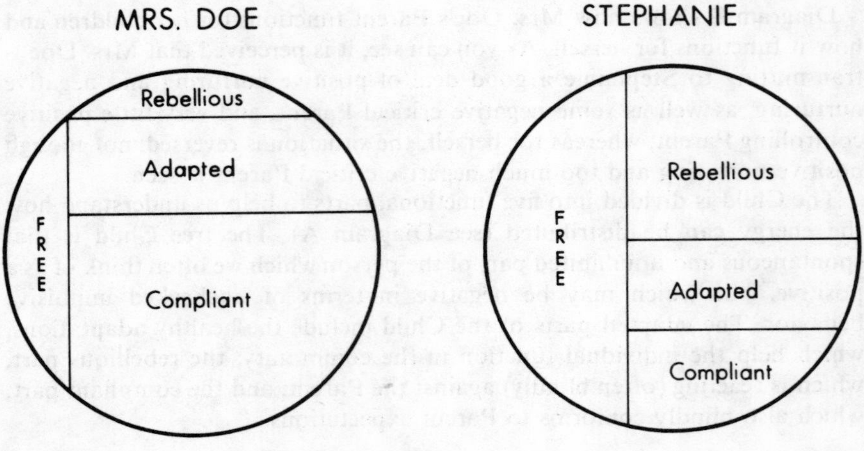
MRS. DOE
Rebellious
Adapted
FREE
Compliant
STEPHANIE
Rebellious
FREE
Adapted
Compliant

ego state has information, much of which is untrue, as it is distorted by false ideas from the Parent and Child.

The T.A. therapist works with the client to see and correct these distortions, such as the ones we have seen in the script messages presented earlier (e.g., "All men are scary").

As the diagram shows, the energy in Mrs. Doe's Child ego state is largely tied up on compliance to others' expectations, whereas the energy in Stephanie's Child is primarily distributed between Free Child and Rebellious Child.

These diagrams are useful in focusing on what areas of the personality need to be strengthened or weakened, both in Mrs. Doe and in Stephanie, recognizing that helping Mrs. Doe to change her internal structure will affect Stephanie's structure as well.

TRANSACTIONAL ANALYSIS

In terms of the structural and transactional relationship between Mrs. Doe and Stephanie, there is clear evidence of what we call in T.A. a symbiotic relationship. Diagrammatically, this looks like the following:

This means simply that two people function as if they were one . . . or that they are not sufficiently differentiated and are discounting parts of themselves.

Thus, Mrs. Doe often discounts her own Child feelings because of her script, and instead sees Stephanie's Child as identical to her own. She then overidentifies and attributes feelings to Stephanie that are really her own suppressed feelings. She sees Stephanie as needful, deprived, suffering from the loss of father and inadequacies of mother. These feelings seem more appropriately to describe herself than Stephanie.

Stephanie accepts some of this projection in an adaptive way, and also attributes as her own feelings those of her mother. An example of this is her expressed feelings about the death of Elvis Presley, which were borrowed from mother, as Dr. Gilpin implicitly noted in her process with Stephanie.

The symbiotic dynamic is clearly described in the process notes of the previous social worker in her transfer summary, where she states: "In the middle phase of treatment, Mrs. Doe began to experience a growing awareness of her self as differentiated from her children. This therapist encouraged this by consistently pointing out the differences between her childhood and her children's, and attempted to be as supportive as possible to Mrs. Doe in her role as mother, while emphasizing her own needs as a woman and individual."

In T.A., this therapeutic process would be called the breaking up of the

SYMBIOSIS

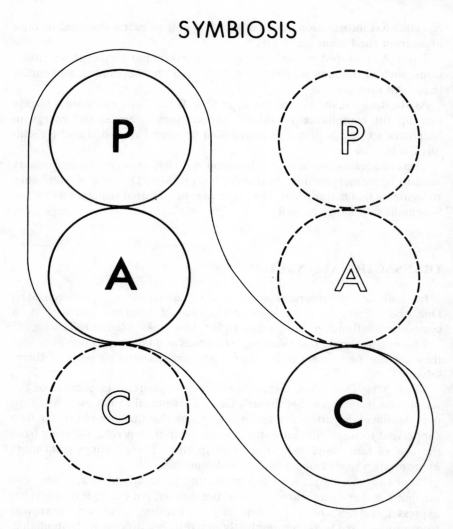

unhealthy symbiosis so that each person would have her own thoughts and feelings.

GAME ANALYSIS

One of the easiest ways to demonstrate games in transactional analysis is the "drama triangle," a concept developed by Dr. Steve Karpman. Diagram E illustrates the triangle. According to this theory, people who are playing games are assuming one or more of the three basic game positions or attitudes: Rescuer (I have to help you because you can't help yourself), Persecutor (I'm better than you; you are inferior), or Victim (I am inadequate; you are better than me). Once a person takes on one of these positions, he relates to himself and others in a distorted way, giving them more or less power than is the reality. Also, whenever a person gets on the triangle by assuming one of the positions, she will move to the other positions at some point . . . thus the denotation "drama."

Looking at the Doe family relationships in this context, it is not difficult to see where each family member is on the triangle at any particular time. Mrs. Doe spends most of her time between Rescuer and Victim, Stephanie is mostly in Persecutor or Rescuer, and Mr. Doe is the same.

It is important to remember that when discussing games and the drama triangle, no one assumes that one position is better or worse than any other, and that once one assumes one of the positions, he will be playing them all.

DRAMA TRIANGLE

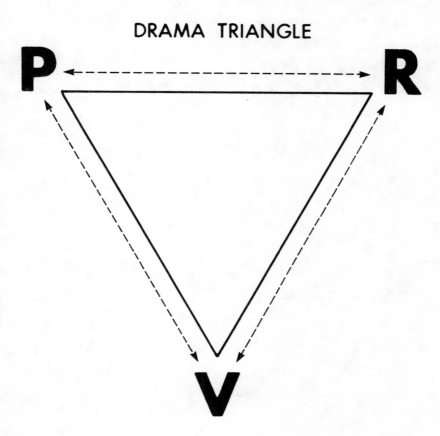

To put it more simply, Rescuers and Victims always Persecute themselves and others by preventing problem-solving, growth, and healthy interactions.

TREATMENT PLAN

On the basis of the above analysis, it would seem that Mrs. Doe should be identified as the client and treatment should be focused toward working with her to break up the symbiotic relationship with Stephanie and to take care of her own Child needs. This would include being helped to set appropriate limits with Stephanie, the other children, and her ex-husband, and it would also include being helped to develop her confidence in herself as a mother and person in her own right.

Positive experiences with a male therapist could also be helpful at a future time for all family members.

5.4 A SOCIAL LEARNING APPROACH TO HYSTERIA IN CHILDHOOD

JULIEN WORLAND

My goal is to provide an alternative conceptualization and intervention plan for Stephanie Doe and her family. That is, I will try to describe how a behaviorally oriented psychologist or mental health worker would try to (1) understand the etiology of Stephanie's behavior and (2) provide help to alleviate this family's distress. I will try to do this by developing an etiological picture of Stephanie's behavior from a behavioral viewpoint; by mentioning the requirements that are necessary for an operant intervention, giving examples of applications of social learning principles to cases similar to Stephanie's; and finally, by explaining how these interventions might apply to Stephanie's case.

ETIOLOGY

A behaviorally oriented clinician has an approach to clinical problems that is distinctly different from the approach of other therapists. Eysenck (1959) emphasizes these differences between psychotherapy and behavior therapy:

> I have called these methods "behavior therapy" to contrast them with methods of psychotherapy. This contrast of terms is meant to indicate two things. According to psychoanalytic doctrine, there is a psychological complex, situated in the unconscious mind, underlying all the manifest symptoms of neurotic disorder. Hence the necessity of therapy for the psyche. According to learning theory, we are dealing with unadaptive behaviour conditioned to certain classes of stimuli; no reference is made to any underlying disorders or complexes in the psyche. Following on this analysis, it is not surprising that psychoanalysts show a preoccupation with psychological methods involving mainly speech, while behavior therapy concentrates on actual behavior as most likely to lead to the extinction of the unadaptive conditioned responses. The two terms express rather concisely the opposing viewpoints of the two schools.

With this point of view, we can examine the record of Stephanie Doe to develop an understanding of how Stephanie came to be showing the behaviors that she was demonstrating at the beginning of treatment.

The first thing we need to know is, What is Stephanie doing that made her mother bring her to the clinic? We know, for example, that one of her behaviors was hanging herself from a coat hook. Although this is sufficient reason to approach treatment, it is hard to understand what the specific behavior problems were because the data collected do not lend themselves to a behavioral analysis. For example, although there are hints throughout the psychological evaluation, the social history, and the psychiatric evaluation that Stephanie's relationship with her mother is very important in the development of Stephanie's problems, no systematic observations of Stephanie and her mother's behavioral interactions were carried out. A behaviorist would be very interested in knowing how Mrs. Doe responded to Stephanie's behavior, and vice versa.

There are few statements in the data about what her problems were in behavioral terms. However, we do have a mixture of a few behaviors and a number of judgments. For example, the case materials list fearfulness, moodiness, selfishness, etc.

Table 1 provides a list of the statements made about Stephanie when she was first evaluated. As can be seen, there are few behaviors listed in the first column and a great number of judgments in the second. In the third column under "Possible Behavioral Referents," I have listed what I consider to be likely behavioral explanations for the judgments that were made in column 2.

One distinguishing characteristic between judgments and behaviors is that judgments are adjectives and behaviors are verbs. This is not just a semantic difference. Note that the behaviors that I have listed in column 3 are much longer than the judgments listed in column 2. Therefore, another characteristic of judgments is that they are more economical than the list of behaviors. However, the difficulty with this gain in economy is that there may be a great deal of error, as seen in a number of judgments which required several possible alternative explanations and the fact that others might disagree with a number of interpretations that I have made.

Beyond these problems, however, is the fact that we are dealing in this case with hysteria, one characteristic of which is that situations and judgments tend to be exaggerated. Again, systematic observation of Stephanie and her mother might have helped us decide if the behaviors of complaint are real or exaggerated, which can be seen, for example, in the four different interpretations that I have listed for the judgment about fearfulness. It may be that the behavioral referent of fearfulness is (at most) crying, avoidance, or running away, or (at a lesser level) talking about the fears obsessively or maybe only mentioning them.

Table 1. Labels and Behaviors in Repertoire of Stephanie Doe Given at Intake and in Social History

Behaviors	Judgments (Labels)	Possible Behavioral Referents
1. Takes knife to bed		
2. Hangs self from coat hook		
3. Argues to have own room		
4.	Is fearful (monster, spiders, dark rooms, storms, etc.)	Cries, avoids, runs away, talks about, mentions
5. Bites nails		
6.	Is poor and finicky eater	Eats only meat and potatoes, does not eat vegetables or Eats less than mother expects, but eats good variety or Refuses to eat unless coaxed
7.	Needs praise	Asks for reinforcement or Repeats behaviors that are reinforced or (maybe) Repeats behaviors that are punished
8.	Is moody	Yells, hits, talks back, cries
9.	Is selfish	Refuses to share toys
10.	Has "chip on shoulder"	Responds with angry statements
11.	Feels mother unfair	Complains about mother's rules
12.	Has rivalry with younger sister	Teases, hits, complains about sister
13.	Is orderly as to room	Cleans room frequently or Complains when room messy
14.	Is headstrong	Disagrees, argues, does not comply
15.	Has physical complaints	Complains of physical ailments
16.	Makes suicidal gesture	(See 1, 2)

Now, how would a behaviorally oriented clinician go about understanding this list of behaviors, assuming that they are the ones that really occurred? This can be understood by considering four behavioral axioms:

1. Behavior is a function of its consequences.
2. The events immediately following a behavior in time affect the probability that a behavior will be repeated in the future.

3. A behavior frequently repeated must be being followed (at least sometimes) by a consequence that is maintaining it (positive reinforcement).

4. Maintaining consequences are usually (but not always) apparently pleasurable.

The consequences that maintain (or "reinforce") a behavior may be internal (like good feelings), external (like attention from other people), or both. Presumably elements of both would almost always be present. For example, in Stephanie's case (Table 2) her taking a knife to bed may be maintained or increased by the fact that taking a knife to bed decreases her anxiety, an internal positive consequence.

It often happens that the *situation* (or "cue") is important; in this example, bedtime and an increase in anxiety are the important cues. Similarly, her complaints about her mother's not being fair, which occur in the situation of perceiving that her mother has slighted her in some way (the cue), are probably being maintained by her mother's making excuses, protesting her love, and trying harder, which we would consider to be external positive consequences. Of course, there are usually internal and external components to both cues and consequences.

INTERVENTION PLAN

Mrs. Doe was involved in a parent training class at the clinic beginning in August 1976. She came to three of the first four sessions, and then dropped out because she joined a vocational education class on Monday and Wednesday evenings. The parent training class was taught on Tuesday evenings, and she did not want to be absent from the home for three nights in a row. It is also suspected that she dropped out because she was the only single parent in the group and it was led by a male.

Table 2. Examples of Functional Analyses of Two of Stephanie's Behaviors

Situation ("Cue")	Behavior	Consequence
Bedtime, increase in anxiety	1. Takes knife to bed	Decrease anxiety (internal positive consequence)
Perceived slight by mother	11. Complains mother not fair	Mother makes excuses, protests her love, tries harder (external positive consequence)

Note: Numbers refer to Table 1

In planning a behavioral intervention, a worker must keep in mind that it is triadic (Tharp and Wetzel, 1969). It involves a therapist, a parent, and a child. Therefore, the characteristics of the parents are very important and must be assessed before assuming that an operant intervention will be possible.

First, a parent must be available when the problem behavior occurs. This doesn't seem to be a problem in the case of Mrs. Doe and Stephanie, since Stephanie's problem behaviors usually occurred in response to her mother's presence. Second, the parent must be a reliable informant. This may be a problem in this case because of the question of mother/child differentiation and of hysteria, indicating that some of the information might be exaggerated, or that Mrs. Doe's attention to one topic may not be long enough to allow a full exploration of it. Third, the parent must control the reinforcers the child wants. This again may be difficult with someone like Mrs. Doe, who appears to have felt depleted in her own life and consequently may be unable to give reinforcers at times when they would be most appropriate. Finally, the parent must be able to give and withhold reinforcers when requested by the worker. This requires that Mrs. Doe be systematic and have a certain degree of self-control. Another complicating factor in this case is whether Mr. Doe's violent visits to the home might interrupt and prevent Mrs. Doe from a consistent application of the procedures that would be taught her in this kind of an intervention.

If the parent is appropriate for parent training, then the steps for the intervention can be begun. First, a successful intervention requires that the behavior problem be defined in operationalized terms, that is, by stating it as a behavior and not as a judgment. Second, we need to determine how often the problem behavior is occurring before we begin our intervention.

This is done to allow the worker and the parent together to have a means to evaluate whether goals are reached after the implementation of a behavior-change program. Third, in the process of determining the pretreatment frequency of the problem behavior, we ask the parent to become aware of the cues and consequences that are maintaining the behavior—that is, what is occurring immediately before and immediately after the behavior that can be considered to be the maintaining events or "causes" of the behavior. These first three steps allow the worker and the parent to develop a "functional analysis" of the problem. Fourth, we help the parent to design and implement a plan to alter the consequences and/or the cues. This is a crucial and difficult step. The plan selected by the parent and the therapist together needs to match general characteristics in the parent and in the child to maximize the likelihood of success. Characteristics in the parents (such as the ability to ignore problem behavior, for example) and characteristics in the child (such as age and the dangerousness of the problem behavior) all are typically taken into account. A decision-making model for selecting intervention plans (Worland et al., 1975) operationalizes these steps to increase the chances that parents will be successful with an intervention plan.

After the plan is put into effect, we reevaluate the situation and compare the frequency of the behavior problem after the intervention with its pretreatment frequency. Finally, we continue, fade the plan, or begin again, depending on whether or not we have been successful with our first effort.

INTERVENTION IN A SIMILAR CASE

This was an eight-year-old white female brought to a pediatric hospital emergency room for loss of feeling on one side of her body. Neurological examination the morning after admission was negative. She was referred to Psychology, where the mother gave a history of "spells" since the age of two. Her current "spells" were twenty- to thirty-minute periods of uncontrolled anger. The mother usually recognized their onset because of a changed look in her daughter's eyes. At these times, the mother sent the other children away for protection to other rooms and held the daughter on her lap. The girl had other problems in the area of fear of being away from home and a fear of being attacked by men on the street. The onset of the recent experience coincided with the father's absence from the home.

> **Target behavior:** The "spells" were selected as the behavior to be reduced.
> **Functional analysis:** Her "spells" were being reinforced by the mother's holding and restraining her.
> **Goal:** Goal was to decrease her spells and increase her play with peers.
> **Method:** The daughter was to be sent from the room at the time of the onset of each spell. She was allowed to return when the spell terminated.
> **Reinforcer:** The mother's praise for terminating the spell was used as a reinforcer.
> **Results:** After two weeks, there was an elimination of spells, increased play with peers at home, decreased fear about going to friends' homes, and an increase in self-esteem.

SUMMARY OF INTERVENTION STRATEGIES

All operant interventions have two purposes: to decrease maladaptive behavior, and to increase more adaptive behavior. This is important because if (in Stephanie's case) a program was formulated to stop reinforcing Stephanie's negative behaviors, such as arguing, without simultaneously providing an equal amount of reinforcement for some prosocial behavior, the result would be that Stephanie would have to find a new (probably maladaptive) behavior to earn back her missing reinforcement. So simply ignoring "moodiness" might lead to crying spells, and ignoring complaints that the mother is unfair might lead to a conversion symptom, if not to a suicide attempt. This "symptom substitution" always occurs if the symptom is eliminated without a simultaneous reinforcement for a prosocial behavior that we hope to see replace the original symptom.

INTERVENTION IN THE CASE OF STEPHANIE

These procedures could easily have been applied to reducing Stephanie's complaints, spells, and specific fears. For example, Stephanie's complaints that her mother was unfair would be handled by a solution similar to the one given before—that is, by giving systematic reinforcement for positive statements about her mother and by ignoring her negative statements. Success, however, would require that Mrs. Doe be psychologically able to deal with this kind of treatment.

We need to address ourselves also to what would be done about Stephanie's suicide gesture, the problem of original complaint. This life-threatening low-frequency behavior is not readily amenable to an operant intervention. An operant approach to such a problem is to determine whether this behavior occurs in temporal relationship to some other behaviors that we could directly intervene with. For example, does the suicide gesture occur at the termination of a long chain of obnoxious behaviors? In this case, it appeared that the suicide gesture was the result of a very unsatisfying argument between Stephanie and her mother about whether she could have her own room. Here our intervention would be to help alleviate the less noxious, more frequent behaviors (like arguments about her room) to decrease her need for suicide gestures. Stephanie's history of escalating to the point of a self-destructive act is good reason for us to avoid such procedures as timeout or ignoring as operant methods. Such a case requires a reliance almost exclusively on positive reinforcement.

REFERENCES

Eysenck, H.J. (1959) Learning theory and behavior therapy. *J. Med. Sci.*, 105:61–75.
Tharp, R., and Wetzel, R. (1969) *Behavior Modification in the Natural Environment*. New York: Academic Press.
Worland, J., Behrendt W., and Talent, B. (unpublished, 1975) *Helping Parents Help Children: A Decision Making Guide for Social Service Workers*. Available from the authors at 369 N. Taylor, St. Louis, Mo. 63108.

5.5 DISCUSSION

RICHARD J. LAITMAN
JULIEN WORLAND
DORIS C. GILPIN
PAULINA F. KERNBERG
ELAINE KORNBLUM

Dr. Kernberg:

In my own clinic in New York, it sometimes happens that we do misdiagnose and place a child erroneously in individual therapy when he might have benefited more from family therapy. However, the procedure is such that we try to keep our minds as open as possible so as to be able to shift the child from one or the other treatment modality, depending on whether the patient is motivated for knowledge in depth or whether the interactions with the family have become so structuralized that the mother in the here-and-now is no longer the mother with whom the conflict originated.

I do not want to make the complex even more complicated, but it so happens that the child and his family come to us with their major conflicts and a huge number of experiences well entrenched in the past. In such cases, family therapy, with its therapeutic strategies bearing mainly on present-day transactions, is not the choice of treatment. However, an experience in family therapy may contribute positively to the clarification of this sort of limitation. Family therapy may, therefore, indicate that individual therapy is necessary, or sometimes vice versa.

I found the interactions in the Doe family fascinating since the script was well put together and indicated just what family therapy can do well. (There is always something more evocative in doing rather than in talking and in playing rather than in doing.) What comes through from the little drama was the idealized image that Stephanie has of her father. She had identified with this image in the way described by Kohut, and she seems to be already on the way to developing a grandoise self that is a synthesis of herself with the idealized image of her father. To bring this to the forefront of consciousness is a task for both the individual and the family approach, and both are able to cope with it. The applications of behavior therapy to the Doe family was also of great interest.

111

One of the advantages of being in a university milieu is that one constantly has the opportunity to learn from other disciplines or other approaches. It is the business of a university to contain a completely open house so that dynamic therapists can learn from behavior therapists about the need for careful observational and descriptive material in their work. The former tend sometimes to short-cut the process of observation, and before establishing the data, are already involved in third or fourth order of inference.

For example, when confronted with anxiousness or fearfulness, we need to begin by clarifying the how, what, and where of the presenting phenomena if we are to have any success of eliciting the underlying fantasies. If we take, for instance, the suicidal act, we notice in this case that the child has attempted to hang herself. Now this is a form of suicidal behavior that is much more frequently seen in boys than in girls, and so this consideration already begins to tell us that hysterical girls may have problems with gender identities. Interwoven with this inference will be fantasies relating to the masculine identification.

Let me make a further comment on the exploration of methodologies of treatment, which has the advantage of allowing us to study them and even, perhaps, to study their efficacy. Having a spectrum of therapies at one's disposal and guides that allow one to prescribe the appropriate therapy for a particular child can be very useful devices both for clinical practice and for training.

It is also very reassuring for a patient who may not be at all psychologically minded to have the feeling that the staff knows what it is doing and that the approach has a positivistic quality about it, unlike [the situation] analysis, where [it] is left open-ended and is consequently often very anxiety-producing. In these more directed methods, questions are asked and feelings explored, communicating both concern and support, which are in themselves very therapuetically helpful. The big problem would come if a negative therapeutic reaction, in psychoanalytic terminology, comes up, with the patient getting steadily worse and the parents getting increasingly uncooperative. How does one handle such situations with the more directive type of therapy?

Transactional analysis is, again, an appealing theory to me because it is easily transmitted and easily assimilated. One can take up issues of being a child, of being a parent, of setting up and crystalizing goals, and of writing scripts. There is no doubt that people make up stories unconsciously about their goals, their personal styles, the direction that they want their lives to take, and their anticipation of what is going to happen. Take, for instance, the wife of an alcoholic who marries again another alcoholic, again another alcoholic; she has a repetitive script. There is a fine paper by Kris, entitled "The Personal Me," which throws a different light on the transactional situation. It should be acknowledged that this approach does help the patient to clarify his aims and to come to realistic conclusions as to whether they are realizable or not. It is also, I think, an excellent discipline for trainees in the mental health field, chiefly because the participant is rewarded by what he learns and by the specific changes that he detects within himself rather than by some global change in personality.

My last remarks have to do with the absence of symptom substitution in these cases of hysteria. I think that by now we know that symptom substitution is not automatic, but in addition, the substitution may be difficult to detect, since the symptoms that are substituted may range from simple conditioned responses to complex symptom formation. When substitution does not occur, it may be that we are dealing with rather simple symptomatic structures or reactive monosymptomatic ones that are not susceptible to substitution.

Dr. Worland:

Dr. Kernberg has asked what we do in behavior therapy when things do not go too well. I can answer this in a couple of ways: The first is that there is a value in carrying out behavioral intervention, because the goals are very specified and operationalized in the mind of the therapist and in the mind of the parent; and the question of whether one is going to reach one's goals is decided ahead of time. For instance, one frequent method that we use is to pick some specific piece of behavior and contract with the mother to keep a record of its frequency. Thus, we may call on a daily basis to find out how often there are fights between the children, what percentage of requests was complied with, and what percentage was not complied with. Consequently when things go badly after you have started an intervention, you get to know it very quickly.

Furthermore, when things go badly they do so in a very typical way. The parents may have worked with you to the point of deciding on the target behavior and the program on which they are going to work. They go home eager to start. You call on the first night to ask how things are going, and they tell you that they will be starting on the next day. You call the next day, and they tell you that they "sort of" carried it out, but then decided that they would do something else instead. By the end of the week they may return to let you know, although not directly, that your therapeutic suggestions make sense but that they cannot carry them out. They do not quite have it in them at this point.

My tendency in such a case is to try a couple of weeks longer, keeping the expectations the same; and then, if this does not work, to radically change course and say to the parents, "All right, let us put all this away, and talk instead about what is stopping you from being able to do this."

Let me offer a case in point: An adolescent girl complained that her mother was not giving her sufficient money, and constantly badgered her to raise her allowance, "nickle-and-diming her" all through the week. I set up what seemed to be a very simple program, and the mother informed me that she simply could not carry it out. She had been saying essentially the same thing in other ways for many years. I was able to wait. Eventually she felt up to it; she did indeed carry out the simple program of putting the girl on an allowance that seemed to satisfy her, and then decreasing the allowance by twenty-five cents every time the girl made a complaint about not having enough money. This went well for about three weeks and then decayed. She was unable to keep it up, and so we are still working on why it is so difficult for her to set limits for her daughter. You will observe that we start with the behavioral approach and then fall back to a casework approach when the former fails to work.

Dr. Laitman:

It is quite true to say that at times the image that a child has of his mother is different from who she actually is, and that the child is reacting to the image. Certainly this happens, and when it does, individual treatment can be very useful in resolving the confusion. In family therapy, it is possible to flesh out such distortions and give the opportunity of looking at the members of the family in different ways.

For example, I am currently working with a family in which the father has custody of his four sons. The mother remained a destructive influence on the boys, promising them gifts and not delivering, promising visits and not coming. In the session, we let the boys air their views about their mother, and all of them were different. They were given to understand that it was all right to have such different views and that one had different views based on who one was and the particular experiences one had undergone. We were also able to let the stepmother realize that the children did have different views about their mother and that she did not have to feel threatened or defensive or to point out the children the many faults of mother and the reasons why they should not love her. In doing this, it would cause the children to protect and idealize the mother.

Sometimes parents may react to their children as they once reacted to their own parents, and this can be demonstrated and treated in the family session. In one case of a mother, son, and daughter, the boy was totally unable to say anything negative about his mother and usually ended up the session feeling quite depressed. In one of the sessions, she invited him to tell her what she did wrong; he took the chance because it seemed to be a safe place in which to come out with feelings, to let her know that he sometimes experienced her as "grumpy." This made her extremely angry, and so I asked her to tell us about why she felt so mad. She talked about her sensitivity to criticism and the fact she felt that she had been criticized all her life starting with her mother. So it was her mother's voice that she heard in her child, and it was the wish to suppress that voice that led her to suppress any possible criticism coming from the child. The child, who was having to cope with a heavy load of parental projections, then felt free to talk more direclty to his mother. On the way home in the car, what they discussed was not related to the theme of the session, but was of their early lives together, which had never been broached before.

Mrs. Kornblum:

I also would like to make a comment about what happens when things go wrong in the session. In transactional analysis, we also make use of contracts, give assignments, and expect certain results. For our theory and practice we borrow from other sources, and here we have borrowed from behavior theory. We define our different plans very specifically in behavioral terms, and when these are sabotaged by the clients, we make use of a technique devised by Haley ["Strategies of Psychotherapy"], in which we take up the advantages agained by sabotaging the plan, by not succeeding, by permitting children to act out, and by not wanting to have the symptoms cured. The advantages may not be positive, but they look as if they are. For example, by keeping the child symptomatic, one keeps the focus on the child's problem and not on the shaky marriage. The script decision may be reinforced by the parent's wish to remain a victim and not do a good job as a parent, to allow the child to act out because this is what the parent has always wanted to do and was never able to do. Thus, it is therapeutically profitable to find out all the advantages to be gained when therapy is not succeeding.

Haley has also devised another technique to be used under similar circumstances: When resistance is high, he goes with the resistance so that he accentuates and even aggravates the behavior; he invites the family, since they are not being constructive, to engage in further sabotage, to do badly and not follow through with the plan that has been arranged. Or he will invite them to say, every hour on the hour, "I'll never be able to solve this problem." This will gratify the immature ego state of the patients, at least for a while, until they begin to become disgusted with themselves about what they are doing and then insist that they do want to solve the problem. This is an example of going with the resistance until the person decides to give up the resistance and cooperate in a healthy fashion with the therapist.

Dr. Kernberg:

When a child comes into treatment, the therapist needs to be very much aware of where the parents stand in the matter of cooperation with the process. When the mother is forcing the child to come and the father wants her not to come, not only is the patient a pawn between the two, but she also derives a lot of narcissistic gratification from the role. The situation makes her feel important, and so, in the beginning of therapy, the therapist should endeavor to bring such matters into the therapeutic situation. As someone who is constantly dealing with transference phenomena, I was most intrigued by the girl's behavior with the kitten, blowing into his ear. I think that here she was reenacting the way in which she had felt treated, especially in connection with her father.

The trick that she plays on the therapist reminds me of a paper by Arlow of the tricks that latency children play. A very typical and appropriately developmental game has to do with the wish to reverse roles with the adult: to catch them by surprise rather than the other way around. It is not I, the child, who gets scared by the anatomical differences that exist between the sexes—it is you, the adult. It is not I, the child, who is being caught masturbating; it is I who tricks you. All this is based, of course, on illusion. In the case of Stephanie, I think she was using the trick quite adaptively, because in a way she wished that all this play between her father and herself would be an illusion. It is, but at the same time it is not. It is true that the father has left, but in a way it is not because he is still very much in the play through her identification with him.

The question of giving gifts seems to be a universal problem in child therapy. As in the case of Stephanie, it can become a real predicament for the therapist. I would just like to state my view that we may sometimes go overboard in being so neutral in our therapeutic attitude and behavior that we may deprive the child of a healthy need to be good to the therapist. This young girl really tortured her therapist; from the very beginning it took a long while before she developed a wish to bring a gift for this special friend. Since this therapy was not psychoanalytic, I myself would have tended to accept it, to observe her reactions and to help her develop spontaneous fantasies about what she did and did not expect to receive in return. Stephanie's wish to make reparation or compensation was an acknowledgment that she had developed a good feeling, for which she wanted to be grateful. It is very important for our child patients (and this is also true for adults) to reach the stage of being able to acknowledge gratitude as a real aspect of human normality.

With regard to the family therapy, I tend to view it as an interesting application of object relations therapy, I tend to view it as an interesting application of object relations theory in that the characters, instead of being talked about or replayed in the transference, as would be the case in individual therapy, actually come to life and act their individual parts in manifest relation to one another. Family therapy allows us to see in a vivid way how the family contributes to perpetuate psychopathological interactions; it may also be of service to the individual therapist in sorting out what is intrapsychic and what is interpersonal.

Finally, I would like to address myself to the question of the patient's need to learn the language of the therapist in order to produce a good result. The patient in my presentation was the daughter of professional parents, so that the terminology that emerged in the treatment came from them and not from me. My own practice and advice would be to use the simplest words and to eschew jargon of any sort.

Dr. Worland:

I only encourage parents to learn terminology with regard to concepts that are really novel for them. I have heard it said that there is no reason to use a term such as "positive reinforcement," but the reason that I do so myself is that the term often has, paradoxically enough, the negative connotation with schoolteachers and parents. Criticism by a teacher may act as a positive reinforcer for good behavior in the child, but it also looks like punishment. By explaining the concept, the parents are able to separate the notion of the ward from that of positive reinforcement and to see them as separate issues.

Mrs. Kornblum:

I think that I should also try and answer the question about the language of therapy, since transactional analysis has often been accused of being jargonized and simplistic. What I do with my clients at the beginning is to give them a little book that explains the treatment and the language that is used, and this fairly simple language then becomes the tool for communication. There is, of course, danger that it might be misused to intellectualize to avoid problems, to persecute other people and to practice one-upmanship.

Dr. Kernberg:

An interesting question has to do with whether the child patient learns a sort of psychodynamic theory from the therapist and if this contributes to his improvement. Heinicke made a comparison between children undergoing four-times-a-week [therapy] versus [those in] twice-a-week psychoanalytic psychotherapy, where the therapist was kept constant so that the quality of the training did not confound the investigation. What he found was that children learn better when they come more frequently. This was due to the identification with the analyst, not in terms of what he was, but [in terms of] of what he did in the treatment, such as [developing] the capacity for raising insightful questions, the use of introspection and reflectiveness, the ability to delay gratification to contain anxiety and to anticipate future developments.

With this kind of therapy, it has also been found that the I.Q. increases, possibly because cognition plays a central role in many of these functions, so that the process of thinking is constantly exercised. This better performance on tests of intelligence was found in the Menninger Foundation psychotherapy research project. It would therefore seem that the capacity to tolerate ambiguity and uncertainty that is learned from the therapist, together with the model he provides of a nonintrusive, nonauthoritative attitude, provides the maximum opportunity for the child to reach his fullest potential. You will see how complicated and difficult the analytic process is, so much so that at times I could almost wish to be a behavior therapist and simplify my life.

Dr. Gilpin:

I would like to discuss some therapeutic modalities for hysterical children and their families.

Having had the opportunity to consider the same case from differing therapeutic perspectives, as well as to consider the overall psychoanalytic perspective as presented by Dr. Kernberg, [I think] it is perhaps possible to develop some ways of approaching treatment planning for hysterical children that are both rational and emphatically in tune.

One can picture the little girl treated by Dr. Kernberg emerging from her analysis guiding her own destiny more than many children and secure about her identity and strengths. But we must note she must have possessed considerable strength to start with and a family that could sustain, financially and in terms of frequent sessions, a lengthy treatment program. Furthermore, the parents have to have had the strength to sustain this while receiving essentially no feedback or help with child management—in short, while receiving a silent message that their participation is needed strictly on a material level. It would seem we could steer few children and families to this in-depth therapeutic endeavor.

The other possible therapies have much to offer, as we've seen, and clearly become most of what must be chosen among for most of the hysterical children seen by mental health professionals. We have, of course, not covered the entire gamut of treatment possiblities. Psychoeducation modalities do not usually come into the picture, as by and large these girls are not in academic trouble, but those with an Adlerian background or group therapy advocates or perhaps others may have had contributions to make to our understanding of therapeutic choices.

Part of the decision-making seems to need to be in relation to the perceived stress in the family members and their ability to invest in doing something about this stress. Thus, the main stress both girl and mother (as well as others in the family) are complaining of may be continual disciplinary arguments. The professionals may recognize this is on a female rivalrous basis, but they may also recognize a family that is labile emotionally, that can only make shallow and short-term investments in receiving help, that has a healthy wish to avoid dependency and an equally healthy wish to cope by themselves. A course in techniques of child management as outlined by Dr. Worland could well be the treatment of choice under those circumstances. It should be noted these techniques leave the child still free to choose to comply or not comply and to be her inner self. They can be carried out in such a way that the child is an active participant in choosing target behaviors and consequences, not a passive pawn. In fact, at her age, these techniques should be carried out in that way to be most effective.

One of the difficulties in choosing among therapeutic procedures is in knowing how to decide whether this or that good will outweigh this or that harm. For instance, with child analysis and its freeing up of the child's inner world, what are the reverberations on the outer world, and what is the growth-enhancing or growth-inhibiting feedback it in turn gives? For a child to become so self-aware is not part of "normal" growing up; does he from then on grow in "abnormal" ways, in terms of family feelings, perhaps, or in other ways? What are the consequences in family attachments? I'm not sure what is known of this.

Equally, if a mental health professional chooses to do parent training in child management, what are the consequences in terms of family members having some feeling through the years that this therapy didn't really reach them as total human beings? ("Mental health people don't really understand.")

We also need to bring into focus some of the problems inherent in deciding between individual or family therapy. Some of the previous discussion applies to this concern. Again, part of the reason for choosing one or the other may be put in terms of, Where is the perceived stress, in family interaction or in self? But there are dangers. Where individual family members are very narcissistic and needy, they may not be able to tolerate family therapy. One also needs to think, What are the consequences for a child who starts in individual therapy, finds this is what she's been looking for, and [is pulled out of her] treatment prematurely [by her parents], a frequent occurrence in clinics? Would dropping out of family therapy have been less of a trauma because of a diluted attachment to the therapist? In any case it points clearly to the need to choose a therapy that parents can ally themselves with or to begin by working with parents and/or family to help them move in the direction of being able to ally with a suitable therapy. Hysterical mothers who are themselves experiencing help should better understand and support thier daughters' therapeutic experience.

Empirically, at our clinic combined family and individual therapy have been most successful of all our attempts. The therapists are not the same people, as the changing stance between individual and family therapy can be confusing for a child. There is a risk in this combination that the child may be reinforced in blaming interactions in the family situation and therefore not encouraged to examine herself in the individual therapy. Collaboration needs to be thorough around such issues.

When the choice has been made to see mothers separately from daughters, much of the transactional-analysis point of view may be helpful to incorporate in an understanding of the parent. In the Doe case, the mother's worker was working on some of the issues and "scripts" that have been pinpointed by Ms. Kornblum, but with caution in relation to how needy and without self-regard mother was and with regard to keeping a positive transference. Knowledge of the T.A. kind of analysis does not always give clear guidelines as to how to use it therapeutically, with awareness of developmental and transferential issues, and with the awareness of the vicissitudes of an alliance, which sometimes must be for the mother's needs to be a good mother and sometimes for the mother's needs for other things.

Overall, it would seem one chooses a therapy, together with parents and child, that respects where people are in resources and limitations and respects where freedom for growth can be achieved.

Chapter 6

Summing Up on "The Hysterical Child"

E. JAMES ANTHONY

It would seem, from these various presentations, that the hysterical child is alive and kicking (in the absence of paresis!), at least in St. Louis. Using a developmental-dynamic set of criteria, the child psychiatrists at the Washington University Child Guidance Clinic have found both her and him, but in relatively uncommon amounts, in its clinic population; and using a checklist on a descriptive-empirical approach, the so-called Renard psychiatry has even measured the amount in a sample that it collected. It is a scientific pity that divergent philosophies did not permit the simultaneous study of both sides of a shared sample and that the opportunity for studying complementarity was missed. In any system of "two cultures," many such golden opportunities are lost. As always, there are pros and cons on both sides.

The first approach has been castigated in the first place for basing its diagnosis on higher-order theoretical constructs that are so complex that their recognition becomes a function of the clinician's knowledge, experience, and theoretical bias. For example, classical psychoanalysts may restrict the criteria to the presence of phallic-oedipal conflicts, summarizing the struggle between incestuous wishes and the relatively mature defenses, such as repression, against them. There is no doubt that Freud always saw the Oedipus complex as the nucleus of hysteria, with the conflict remaining around genital sexual wishes and unconscious fantasies, and with symptoms reflecting the conflict. This dynamic-developmental theory is still incomplete although it has considerable explanatory power in the assessment of individual patients. I will say something about the incompleteness a little later, but at the present time it would be sufficient to say that we are not too clear about the nature of the hysterical ego and superego. We are not too

121

sure to what extent the preoedipal development contributes to the genesis of
hysteria. We do not know in what way and to what degree the hysterical
personality interrelates with the hysterical symptomatology. We are clinically conscious of aggressive impulses in the hysteric (when we are not being
seduced by his charm), but we have as yet to find a specific role for it in the
metapsychology of development. We may appreciate the "false self" that
confronts us in these patients, but then again, we do not have a coherent
account of its evolution. And finally, we have no convincing idea of how
specific parents with specific child-rearing philosophies create a pathology of
this nature. The dynamic world of hysteria, therefore, is full of unanswered
or inadequately answered questions.

The descriptive-empirical approach is in no healthier state. The checklists
apparently demonstrate a stable, definable clinical syndrome called hysteria
(distinct from conversion reactions), but symptoms provide a fleeting and
rickety base upon which to build a diagnosis of hysteria. There is no good
rationale (since there is a complete absence of theory) as to what is included
and what is left out, so that we get a mishmash of symptoms, traits, somatic
complaints, mood disturbances, etc. When the patient's behavior strikes the
clinician as "naïve," "childish," or "self-dramatizing" (whatever these may
mean to different clinicians), the tendency to diagnose hysteria is strongly
reinforced. Guze (1967) suggested that for the diagnosis to be valid, the
patient should be suffering from the same illness on follow-up and that other
members of his family should manifest the same condition. Unfortunately,
Guze's own studies have been severely criticized. Krohn (1978) has pointed
to the "rampant methodological and inferential fallacies . . . that make it
useless," yet on the positive side this approach allows for the greater clarity
of definition so that both reliability and validity studies can be pursued by
other workers.

As Dr. Kernberg points out in her presentation, the hysterical ego
demonstrates not only a marked tendency toward repressing ideational
content—a distortion of reality by wishful thinking—but also a particular
type of cognitive style that tends toward the vague, the global, the impressionistic and the intuitive. The hysteric's thinking is inclined to be illogical,
largely dissociated, and "fogged" by internal and external experience. The
hysteric's ego appears to be potentially adequate, but at the same time
chronically overtaxed by conflict.

It is not possible in the children's sample to isolate the four types of
hysterics described by Zetzel (1968). "Good hysterics" and "potentially good
hysterics" are said to have experienced a true "triangular conflict" and have
been able to retain significant object relationships to both parents. They can
recognize and tolerate internal reality, its wishes and conflicts, and are at the
same time capable of distinguishing it from external reality. Effectively, they

are able to sustain anxiety and repression. The so-called good hysterics and hysterical character disorders (or hysteroids) cannot make meaningful distinctions between internal and external reality and are incapable of tolerating a genuine triangular situation. Their egos are conflict-ridden, and their tolerance for anxiety and depression is poor. Her major point is that hysterical symptoms by themselves are not good indicators of treatment potential, and this, I think, would be true also of the hysterical child. Briefly stated, the "good hysteric," whether adult or child, has a good ego, but one that is characterized by good reality testing, consensual logic, and well-developed defenses. The not-so-good hysteric, who may verge on "borderline," has a shaky ego and poor reality testing.

The hysterical superego, as compared to the obsessional superego, is relatively mild and responds to the pressures of acceptance, praise, and love from others. The morality is flexible: What is right is what will bring support from important objects.

The child hysteric is very much a personality in the making, and so we see transient manifestations of hysteria more frequently. There is no doubt that in order to make fresh discoveries in psychopathology, one will need to carry out careful longitudinal studies on a sample of children and to plot the natural history of the condition. I would imagine that many of the children diagnosed as hysteric might not be diagnosed as such in adult life because there are certain qualities that children have that could be labeled "hysteroid." Hysterics have been less studied in recent years since the major studies initiated by Freud and Breuer, and the reason for this may be either that there are fewer hysterics around to study or that character disorders have come to dominate the clinical horizon. Krohn (1978) has said: "The study of hysteria is so interwoven with the early development of psychoanalytic theory that it has even been suggested that the course of psychoanalysis might have been different if Freud's initial patients had not been hysterics. And yet Freud's own comments on the syndrome are 'scattered, unsystematic, strangely late or non-existent' (Wisdom, 1961)."

And finally, in order to absolve ourselves from any guilt at not solving the mystery of hysteria, we should quote Veith (1965): "Hysteria is an extraordinarily interesting disease, and a strange one. It is encountered in the earliest pages of recorded medicine and is dealt with in current psychiatric literature. Throughout all the intervening years it has been known and accepted as though it were a readily recognizable entity. And yet, except for the fact that it is a functional disorder, without concomitant organic pathological change, it defies any attempt to portray it concretely. Like a globule of mercury, it escapes the grasp."

We began these presentations portraying hysterical children through Freud's eyes as the beautiful double flowers of mankind, and we now end with a picture of them as globules of mercury. It is this attractive but elusive quality that continues to haunt the clinician.

REFERENCES

Guze, S. (1967) The diagnosis of hysteria: what are we trying to do? *Am. J. Psychiatry*, 124:491.
Krohn, A. (1978) *Hysteria: The Elusive Neurosis.* New York: International Universities Press.
Veith, I. (1965) *Hysteria.* University of Chicago Press.
Zetzel, E. (1968) The so-called good hysteric. *Int. J. Psycho-Anal.*, 49:256.

PART II: THE ANXIOUS CHILD

Chapter 7

The Phenomenon of Anxiousness

E. JAMES ANTHONY

In the GAP classification of childhood disorders (1976), the psychoneurotic group of disorders in which anxiety was the essential element was separated out. Characteristically, they made their appearance only after the beginning of latency, when the child's development was sufficiently advanced to permit the operation of conscience, the development of a structural neurotic conflict, the internalization of that conflict, and the action of various defense mechanisms resulting in symbolic symptom formation. This represents the usual course of events, but under certain circumstances the psychoneurosis may begin differently and end differently. In the first instance, a reactive disorder occurring in otherwise healthy children as a result of stress, trauma, or crisis may undergo internalization and structuralization if unresolved or aggravated by unhealthy parental responses.

In the second instance, for reasons that are not quite clear at the present time, the symptoms may not develop, but instead the entire personality of the child may become affected by neurotic conflict and give rise to a neurotic personality disorder. There are five pathognomonic symptoms and signs characteristic of these anxious personalities: They are chronically tense and highly strung, apprehensive in new situations, given to extremely vivid fantasies, and inclined to see the environment in general as threatening. In spite of these, they remain intellectually and socially competent. They are different from children with anxiety neurosis in not being crippled by anxiety; from children with massive inhibitions in that very little restriction of the personality is present and they are able to deal adequately with new situations following initial anxiety; and from children with developmental deviations in that stage-appropriate capacities are unaffected.

Let us look a little more closely at the apprehensiveness with which these anxious children approach new situations and the way in which they perceive the world around them as dangerous and threatening. Their parents tend to refer to them as "nervous and high-strung," meaning by this that they become tense, fearful, and restless when exposed to change or novelty. The parents are well aware that they need careful preparation for such encounters, but that even this may not relieve their agitation.

What makes for such persistent and pervasive anxiousness, and why is it so difficult to relieve with reassurance?

The GAP report referred to earlier drew attention to the fact that *for reasons that were not completely clear*, anxiety was handled differently by the psychoneurotic child and by the child with an anxious personality disorder. With the former, the anxiety was maintained below the level of disruption by the operation of a variety of defense mechanisms and by the production of symptoms; in the latter, the internalized conflict pervades the whole person, making them chronically tense and apprehensive, as if they are constantly anticipating dangers around the corner, especially the unexpected corner, and are constantly elaborating disturbing fantasies in connection with this. In some ways, the fantasies take the place of symptoms.

Let us see if we can put together, for heuristic purposes, an etiological schema that might help us to understand why some children exposed to an overload of anxiety develop psychoneurosis, why other children first respond with a reactive disorder that is subsequently internalized and transformed into a psychoneurosis, and why a third group is able to internalize the conflict but then bind it to the personality as a whole rather than make use of the psychoneurotic devices. To carry out this task, we must set about it ontogenetically.

Let us first admit that anxiety is an existential phenomenon with a psychobiological basis in the individual.* The role of norepinephrine and other hormonal and neurotransmitter substances in the elaboration of anxiety has not yet been clearly determined, but recent talk would seem to suggest that Freud's first anxiety theory, based on a physiological-energic-organismic set of mechanisms, may not be as outdated as we once thought. From observations of the neonate, there is some support for the notion of an inborn predisposition to undue anxiety furthered when internal and external

---

*Phylogenetically, Uexkull (1921) described the *Umwelt* in which animals live as being more or less the same for the members of a species and as instinct-bound. Human beings are also embedded in an *Umwelt*, which is not only more differentiated, but also largely cultural and not instinct-bound. However, from time to time, the human being is able to transcend these *Umwelten* of home, job, neighbors, friends, community, language, culture, task, country, etc., and to explore new aspects of the world. The discoveries are then assimilated by the culture, institutionalized, and made part of the *Umwelt* so that the ordinary people, as opposed to the conquistadors, may experience them without fear or apprehension.

stimuli evoke too great an anxiety response, all because the tolerance threshold for anxiety is set too high and the organism overresponds to a normal range of stimuli. Some investigators have found that a traumatic birth experience may render children significantly more prone to manifestations of anxiety than those whose births have been judged to be normal.

During the first year of life, the infant may offer many indications of increased anxiety output, starting from the experience of helpless global discomfort as a result of separation from his intrauterine womb. As Freud emphasized, there is, in spite of the "impressive caesura of birth," considerable continuity between intrauterine life and earliest infancy (1949). The continuity consists in the replacement of womb by preoccupied care of the mother; this cannot, in the nature of things, be complete, and although the baby soon learns that its cry or restlessness has the power of making the mother reappear to comfort it and to take care of its needs, there are inevitable delays, so that growing tensions from hunger or discomfort may continue for a while to harass the helpless child. Mothers vary considerably in their capacity to meet the needs of the distressed baby, but good enough management will generally keep the tension within limits.

This brings us to consider the mother's role in the ontogenesis of undue anxiety in the child. First of all, the mother may be incompetent, unloving and even rejecting, so that the infant is actually neglected and is allowed to develop intolerable degrees of tension before he cries himself into apathy or has his needs grudgingly met. Another contribution may come from mother's own anxiety: She may become unduly anxious because she is unable to pacify or gratify the demanding infant, or her own chronic anxiety may be in some way transmitted to the baby. Sullivan (1953) has assumed that there is an empathic induction of anxiety from the child by the mother's anxiety, and Escalona (1953) spoke of the "contagious" manner in which anxiety is passed from mother to infant. There is no doubt that an anxious mother can put distance between herself and her offspring and so further aggravate normal separation anxieties. The overprotective mother, like the rejecting mother, may impose another load of anxiety on the developing infant. Her own unresolved separation-individuation problems may make it difficult for her to tolerate separateness from her baby and thus add to its problems of separating from her. Overprotectiveness exercised over time may act as a powerful suggestion to the child that the environment is intrinsically dangerous and that it is best avoided. The mother's attitude and behavior, depending on her own level of anxiety, may orient the child's outlook on his environment in two opposing directions: In the first, the outlook is open toward the environment and leads to increasing contact with it through numerous encounters stimulated by the child's exploratory drive and avid curiosity about the unknown (Portmann [1951] has referred to this as *Weltoffenheit*); and in the second, the child is "embedded" (to use Schachtel's term [1959]) in its familiar home environment and is reluctant and fearful to venture beyond the symbiotic boundaries with the mother. It is interesting and lends further support to the point of view being put forward that Balint (1955) spoke of two kinds of children: those who were *ocnophilic*, were afraid to explore the space around them and clung to the geocenter of their world, the mother; and those who were *philobatic*, were ever ready to explore the unknown and to venture into the wide-open spaces away from home. The *ocnophilic* child is anxious, as Heidegger (1949) would say, about being-in-the world without protection and separated from embeddedness. It has none of the world-openness, the *Weltoffenheit* of the *philobatic* child. The one may hide behind its mother's skirt upon seeing a stranger and may hesitate to taste a new, unfamiliar dish, while the other will greet the stranger with pleasure and engage immediately in the new association.

With these polar types in mind, we may speculate that the anxious child is the embedded child with a predisposition to undue anxiety, whose signal anxiety, as Freud would put it (1949), rapidly becomes disruptive anxiety under minimal internal or external stress. With the environment-open child, not only has the world outside become well-differentiated but so have internal structures. The anxiety signals never reach disruptive proportions, and when confronted with an internal conflict, it makes use of relatively mature defenses to deal with them. The symptoms, like phobias, generally remain circumscribed, and no anxiety spreads to the personality. It also deals with objective anxiety efficiently.

The transmission of anxiousness and undue anxiety reactions to stress seems to run in families, so that one sometimes sees an intergenerational "anxious constellation" (the equivalent of Benedek's [1956] depressive constellation), in which transactions that once existed between grandmother and mother in the latter's infancy become reactivated when the mother has to deal with her own infant. The increased ambivalence and the increased anxiety can be observed in both partners. When maternal management is adequate, the child is able to develop an accurate sense of reality and see the environment as it is before the frightening fantasies have been projected onto it. When this is the case, the child can cope with anxiety-inducing situations and keep its own reactions within bounds.

The clinical picture of the anxious child is not difficult to recognize, especially if one looks at it developmentally and in depth. There is a long history of apprehensiveness and overreaction to almost every unexpected environmental stimulus; this in association with a combination of a lowered stimulus threshold, a tendency to generalized responses, and a lability of affect causes the child to reverberate for long periods after a disturbing experience. We learn from the parents that he has *always* been timid, hesitant and ready to withdraw at the smallest appearance of novelty or danger. He has *always* been afraid of everything and everyone, having been overwhelmed throughout his early development by separation anxieties, stranger reactions, obsessional fears, dread of going to school and an apprehension of social contact outside the immediate family. There are no specific attacks of any kind, no specific objects of fear and no specific frightening situations (Anthony, 1975). Way back in the last century, Ciambal referred to this condition as *lebensfeigheit*, which roughly means "a cowardice about living."

A nine-year-old girl, the daughter of an extremely anxious woman, had been "a worrier since birth." She worried about everything that one could possibly worry about. During the day she was anxiously preoccupied about getting sick, about dying, about her parents dying, about the dog next door, about ghosts, about going to school and about going upstairs to bed at night. She was afraid of the dark and suffered from severe nightmares. She was described as having a "super-sensitive alarm" easily provoking bouts of panic. Her signal anxiety was grossly overused, and the anxiety soon became disruptive. At such times her face would flush, her pupils would dilate, her heart would beat faster, her hands would tremble and her body would break out in a sweat. Although anxious from infancy, the extreme apprehensiveness had developed after the death of her maternal grandmother, an event that had left her own mother deeply depressed. At about the same time she had undergone a tonsillectomy, and this exacerbated her fearfulness. During therapy she disclosed intense shame and guilt around masturbation, particularly with fantasies that focused on a man who had lodged with the family and had attempted on one occasion to manipulate her genitals. The girl thought that if her mother found out about these sexual activities, she would have her "put away."

This case demonstrates the complex interplay of constitutional, familial, traumatic and intrapsychic factors that operated together to maintain a level of constant anxiousness. The constitutional predisposition, together with the exposure to the mother's anxiety, prevented the emergence of the usual psychological mechanisms for binding anxiety in a psychoneurotic form.

Another clinical type of chronically anxious child is the hypochondriacal one, and a great many different factors contribute to the genesis of this disorder: an identification with ill parents or siblings, the adoption of familial somatization and techniques for dealing with anxiety, self-mothering in the absence of parental figures, attention-seeking aimed at obtaining greater acceptance and approval within the family, flight into sickness to avoid threatening situations or pressures, a reactivation of the sickness role that once obtained for the child a moratorium from his everyday stresses as well as the loving solicitude of his parents, the compensation for social and educational failures linked to a lessening of self-esteem, a need to ward off indefinite and formless anxiety by the use of a definite form of illness, and finally, the atonement of guilt feelings with regard to hostile and sexual impulses. The nature of the somatic transformation is determined by naive, infantile theories of disease, and may be as unconvincing as hysterical conversions. Like other syndromes of anxiousness, hypochondriasis is a family affair in which the other members appear to have an unconscious understanding of the anxious child's need to have somatic complaints and may thus help to maintain and even exaggerate the condition.

In 1893, Freud discussed the "modern nervousness" brought about in large part, he thought at that time, by the rat-race life in which "all is hurry and agitation: night is used for travel, day for business; even 'holiday trips' keep the nervous system on the rack; important political, industrial, financial crises carry excitement into far wider circles than formerly . . . Life in large cities is constantly becoming more elaborate and more restless . . . Modern literature is concerned predominantly with the most questionable problems, those which stir all the passions . . . Our ears are excited and overstimulated by large doses of insistent and noisy music. The theaters captivate all the senses with their exciting modes of presentation; the creative arts turn also by preference to the repellent, ugly and suggestive, and do not hesitate to set before us in revolting realism the ugliest aspect offered by actuality." This was the picture of "modern nervousness" in 1893 and not, curiously enough, in 1980. Although we are often told that we are presently living in an "age of anxiety" typified by an almost perpetual bombardment of the senses on the outside, it is clear that a sensitive observer like Freud had a similar view of the previous century. His colleague, Binswanger, felt that anxiousness was essentially an American disorder, which was not surprising, since it was in the United States that the greatest accelerations of living due to technology had occurred. For most people, according to Freud, there was a limit beyond which their constitution would not comply with the demands of the environment, and so excessive tension and nervousness resulted.

We have tried, in this opening presentation, to indicate what complex forms and origins psychopathology in the child can take. The anxious child is not simply the logical product of anxious parents living in an anxious age. He is a composite of intergenerational, constitutional, developmental and environmental experiences of living, and the expression of his disorder is shaped by intraspsychic and interpersonal factors as well as by such external considerations as social class and ethnic status. All these are seldom unraveled in a particular case, and such encompassing etiologies are given short shrift in clinics, which feel, justifiably, that one cannot wait for total knowledge about cause before treating the effects in the child.

REFERENCES

Anthony, E.J. (1975) Neurotic disorders. In *Comprehensive Textbook of Psychiatry*, Vol. 2, A.M. Freedman, H.I. Kaplen, and B.J. Sadock, eds. Baltimore: Williams and Wilkins.

Balint, M. (1955) Friendly expenses—horrid empty spaces. *Int. J. Psycho-Anal.*, 36:225.

Benedek, T.B. (1956) Toward the biology of the depressive constellation. *J. Amer. Psychoanal. Assoc.*, 4:389.

Escalona, S. (1953) Emotional development in the first year of life. In *Transactions of the Sixth Conference on Problems of Infancy and Childhood*, M. Senn, ed. New York: Josiah Macy Foundation.

Freud, S. (1893) Modern nervousness. Standard Edition. London, Hogarth Press, 1966.

———— (1949) *Inhibitions, Symptoms and Anxiety*. London: Hogarth Press. Group for the Advancement of Psychiatry (1976) *Psychopathological Disorders in Childhood*, E.J. Anthony, pref. New York: Aronson.

Heidegger, M. (1949) *Sein und Leit*. Tuebinger: Neomarins Verleg.

Portmann, A. (1951) *Biologische Fragmente zu einer dehrer vom Menschen*. Basel: Benno Schwabe.

Schachtel, E.G. (1959) *Metamorphosis*. New York, Basic Books.

Sullivan, H.S. (1953) *The Interpersonel Theory of Psychiatry*. New York: Norton.

Ueckull, J. (1921) *Umwelt und Innenwelt der Tiere*. Berlin: Quoted by Schachtel, E.G. (1959) *Metamorphosis*. New York, Basic Books.

Chapter 8

Anxiety in Childhood: Developmental and Psychopathological Considerations

ANNEMARIE P. WEIL

In this paper I shall examine first the developmental and then the clinical aspects of anxiety. I want to start with a statement by Benjamin (1961): "We think that there is *felt* anxiety in the four- and five-month-old, but that it is of a different quality than is *experienced* later in the first year because of the stage of development of ego functions, drive organizations and object relations [p. 664]." I would like to add that still later, in the third or fourth year, the child develops a mental representation and conscious awareness of his anxiety.

DEVELOPMENTAL ASPECTS OF ANXIETY

Anxiety is part and parcel of growth and development. At times, it is hard to separate the purely developmental aspects of anxiety and its special landmarks from variations and even deviations.

When and how does anxiety start? What are its forerunners in the neonate and very young infant? Early investigators have described failure to achieve homeostatic equilibrium. Mahler (1967) speaks of organismic distress. Greenacre (1941) discusses preanxiety, an organic tension stemming from fetal life which may be augmented by subsequent early distress in painful or uncomfortable situations. She states that sometimes "an infantile predisposition to anxiety is great due to an overload of potential in the prenatal, natal, or immediate postnatal experience or the combination of this with constitutional factors [pp. 50–51]."

It is remarkable that Greenacre said this in 1941, when we knew much less about neonatal functioning. Her statement is still valid. Recent infant, especially neonatal, research teaches us more specifically that the earliest threshold levels and the initial capacity to deal with stimuli—in other words, the rudimentary integrative function—are decisive in determining a particular child's proclivity or resilience to preanxiety. We know now that even neonates search for new stimuli. Familiarity, sameness, becomes boring and brings about a lessening of alertness. The unfamiliarity, the newness that the infant welcomes, however, must be of an intermediate variety. If a stimulus is too new, it brings tension. Here one finds considerable individual variation, and much depends on the mother's attunement to her individual child's needs.

Within this constellation of stimulus need and stimulus integration, the *four-week period* stands out as a critical one. We learn from Benjamin (1961) that at four weeks there is a maturationally determined, rather sudden lowering of the threshold, which exposes the infant to a greater onslaught of stimuli and often results in increased distress and irritability. Without special maternal shielding, this may leave a stamp of lowered resilience on the infant's subsequent development. Benjamin also speaks of a "predisposition to anxiety."

These early weeks determine how the infant will experience the symbiotic phase and how he will emerge from it. It is at the end of the symbiotic phase, around four months, that the infant moves from organismic distress and diffuse affectomotor reactions to felt distress, with gradually more distinct states of felt anxiety, i.e., of felt helplessness.

The *fourth month* represents a special landmark in the developmental sequence of anxiety. It is at this time that the infant becomes capable of increased perceptual discrimination. This greater perceptual discrimination brings not only increased pleasure, for instance, at the sight of mother (expressed in an especially bright smile), but also increased displeasure when, for instance, mother is not there or when she leaves the room. In general, the four-month-old infant shows a greater awareness of, and reaction to, any noticeable change of gestalt. We find a gamut of varying reactivity in different children.

At this time, there is also increased expressiveness. I mentioned the smile. Similarly, distress tension is now less often released purely somatically (i.e., through variations in skin color, changed rhythms of physiological functioning, etc.) or is released only through crying. It is now revealed through unmistakable physiognomic expressions. If one has ever seen a four-month-old infant fearfully look (and cry out) when his own mother appears with her hair in rollers, one will not doubt the presence of Benjamin's "felt anxiety." The infant's reaction indicates not only the greater expressiveness at this age, but also the infant's improved, though still faulty, discrimination. Perceptual awareness thus may enhance anxiety, especially in the sensitive infant, who needs less to trigger tension and anxiety and whose reactions often are stronger.

It is interesting that during, or soon after, this period of more clearly felt—and also more expressed—anxiety, the infant may begin to form a special attachment to a transitional object (Winnicott, 1953). According to Tolpin (1971), this attachment reflects the infant's attempt to outgrow the anxiety experience of helplessness by playfully dosing and controlling it himself.

By *eight months*, there is not only considerably more precise discrimination, but also greater libidinal investment of the more clearly formed images. As the formation of inner memory images begins to establish object permanence, it is no longer a change in mother, but rather the stranger, the not-mother, who brings various degrees of initial unpleasure and anxiety—until the stranger, too, becomes familiar. From now on, the change in gestalt, the not-just-right degree of novelty, recedes in importance as a stimulus for anxiety, while object-related anxiety comes to predominate in the healthy infant. This is also the time when *felt* anxiety becomes more *experienced* anxiety (cf. Benjamin's statement quoted on page 1 of this chapter) owing to a somewhat greater state of awareness.

The introjection of a maternal image, with its libidinal, as well as probable aggressive, investment (Benjamin, 1961), sets the stage for separation anxiety at the *end of the first year*. At this time, not only anxiety but also defenses become more conspicuous. Infants have various ways of dealing with anxiety which can be seen as precursors of defense mechanisms. Looking away in the stranger situation, for example, represents avoidance. Selecting a transitional object to practice separation and dose anxiety is a displacement mechanism. Infants also have adaptational means of dealing with anxiety. In one infant test, the "diaper test" (Buehler and Hetzer, 1935), the examiner places a diaper on the head of a sitting infant. Most infants with adequate adaptation mechanisms pull the diaper away; others—the tense, preanxious ones—may freeze or cry, although they are well able to grasp and pull in other situations. Benjamin et al. (1962) have termed such aspects of nonadaptation versus adaptation "passive acceptance vs. active mastery."

There may be a certain decline in anxiety levels in the beginning of the *second year*, during the practicing period. At this time, the child is at the height of pleasure in his own functioning; he is overwhelmingly curious and needs to explore everything. However, the daring too far away from mother or daring into risky situations without her being nearby ushers in renewed concern about her, and thus leads to the rapprochement period, in the second half of the second year.

Separation anxiety now reaches a peak and is associated with all the difficulties of that period, which are, needless to say, more prominent in the hypersensitive toddler. Difficulties around separation from mother, implying object loss and the state of helplessness, are frequently associated with anxiety around falling asleep.

Here it seems important to note that many steps in the development of object relation, with the increase in object cathexes, are associated with passing experiences of unpleasure and anxiety. Mild, transitory stranger anxiety and transitory sleep difficulties may thus actually be positive signs with regard to the child's capacity for object relationship and his ego development (Weil, 1956). The next step in development, however, usually brings relief. The infant learns that his mother will be there, behind the stranger, and that the stranger may bring pleasure too. The toddler learns that the separation at night is followed by a reunion in the morning. (Poor handling of such a symptom as a sleep difficulty, which usually passes, can make for a developmental disturbance, which may then become the forerunner of a neurotic symptom.)

Due to a crowding of maturational and developmental advances, the end of the second year is fraught with anxiety constellations. Most in the fore is the emergence of evocative memory—that is, the ability to evoke inner images and also to interconnect them, and the ability for representational symbolic thinking. This step includes connecting the present to the past, and above all, to the future. The latter development especially has considerable impact on the anxiety situation: Danger situations can now be anticipated. The toddler moves from being automatically overwhelmed by a sense of helplessness to experiencing anxiety as a signal of danger that threatens to come—a most decisive developmental achievement.

But this is not the only significant change. Due to the new capacity to introject, to love, and to think, the fear of loss of love acquires momentum. Moreover, this fear is compounded by an emerging awareness of sex differences, associated with castration anxiety. In addition, with the beginning introjection of parental demands, we see the precursors of superego anxiety (e.g., in relation to toilet training).

Thus, during the rapprochement period at the end of the second year, all kinds of anxieties come together. It is a difficult period indeed. The toddler not only senses himself as separate from his mother and cedes omnipotence to her, but he also tries to defend himself against his longing for fusion, strengthening his sense of self by negativism. Torn between the two tendencies, he wishes for, and yet is afraid of, re-engulfment; he is full of ambitendencies and ambivalence. The increasing organization of aggressive energies may interact with anxiety in a spiraling way. All this makes the toddler difficult and apparently regressed in his behavior until further development toward object constancy and a more stable representation of self and mother even things out.

In the *third and fourth year*, as representational thinking continues to develop, each child acquires his idiosyncratic, very specific symbols. The variety of associations, displacements, fantasies, and connected anxieties are thus diversified and numerous. From now on, each child has his own inner psychic world of symbols, fantasies, conflicts, and fears.* Moreover, he knows that he is afraid, and has reached the third stage, namely anxiety awareness, which I mentioned earlier.

There are archaic and animistic fears similar to those found in primitive men. They include fears of outside objects and events that are not wholly understood—especially those of a sudden, unpredictable nature (thunder, darkness, etc.). These fears may have started preverbally, but they can now be expressed. Some are associated with the child's increasing capacity to fantasy and with individually varying degrees of aggressive strivings.

Fears of monsters, ghosts, etc., are almost universal and have a philogenetic (in the history of cultures) as well as ontogenetic (special to each child) history. They may express projections of early distress (Greenacre, personal communication) amalgamated with later fantasies, or projections of strong excitations, as those associated with primal-scene exposure. Or they may represent projections of good or bad introjects (the engulfing mother, the mother of separation) or of the child's instinctual needs, as well as of his defenses. The monster's character may range from scary fiend to helpful, protective friend. Furthermore, each child may produce his own monsters or borrow them from his exposure to other children's monsters, to stories, and to TV. (In particular, children with a great deal of basic anxiety tend to externalize anxious excitation in monster fears and monster games.)

From about three years on, with the attainment of various degrees of object constancy, the child increasingly moves into the oedipal period with its load of conflicting feelings and fantasies, wishes, and fears. These are reflected in the ubiquitous infantile neurosis or they may develop into a structured neurosis as the child enters *latency*. Fixations, regressive proclivites, and defenses determine the character of the ubiquitous infantile neurosis, or of the structured neurosis, if such eventuates.

Let me remind you of the "classical etiological formula" for the development of a neurosis, which Anna Freud (1965) so clearly stated: ". . . initial developmental progress to a comparatively high level of drive and ego development (i.e., for the child to the phallic-oedipal level . . .); an intolerable increase of anxiety or frustration in this position (for the child of castration anxiety within the oedipus complex); regression from the age-adequate drive position to pregenital fixation points; emergence of infantile pregenital sexual-aggressive impulses, wishes, and fantasies; anxiety and

---

*Because the child now has his own inner world, it is harder to generalize about this period. On the other hand, the anxieties which occur from the third year on are clinically better known since they relate predominantly to the verbal period.

guilt with regard to these, mobilizing defensive reactions on the part of the
ego under the influence of the superego; defense activity leading to compromise formations; resulting character disorders or neurotic symptoms . . . [p.
150]." Hence, there is anxiety in the beginning (deriving from the oedipus
complex and castration fear), and then anxiety again because of the
regressive wishes.

The compromise formations, the symptoms, are determined by the
predominant psychosexual level and the predominant defenses used, while
the individually varying content relates to each child's unique inner world,
especially the rejected impulses and fantasies.

Most frequently, particularly in young children, we find phobias, which
are both built on anxiety and re-create anxiety with conscious awareness of
anxiety and fear. Phobias are based on the predominant defense mechanisms of projection, displacement, and avoidance. In contrast, compulsive
developments (such as habits, rituals, obsessions) are based on regression to
the anal-sadistic level, with reaction formation, undoing, denial, and isolation as specific defenses. Many times the clinical picture is a mixed one, since
various neurotic solutions may overlap. Some children still readily somatize; hypochondriacal symptoms may be partly somatized, and may be
partly of a (more advanced) hysterical nature, i.e., one associated with
unconscious elaborations.

In latency, the fortunate child finds a solution in which the infantile
neurosis is only a potential. The ego has been strong enough to master
conflicts and, with the increasing capacity for neutralization, to channel
drive energies into many newly opened-up areas of competence and into
socialization with peers. Residual anxieties are dealt with via defenses,
predominantly in the form of character traits. Some of these residual
anxieties are clinically quite conspicuous and transparent, as, for example,
in the physically overcautious boy, who still betrays his castration anxiety,
or in the constantly envious girl, who is overconcerned with differences,
hurts, or losses, and expresses chronic feelings of being short-changed.

In tracing the development of anxiety, I have touched on some potential
for neurotic development. It seems that potential neurotic development is
inescapable whenever the child has reached sufficient ego structuring and
superego formation and has lived through an oedipal triangle. We all know
the importance of this triangle for the burdensome, but also enriching and
organizing, oedipal experience (Harley, 1961). If potential neurotic development associated with more or less defended-against anxiety is ubiquitous in
children who have had sufficient ego and superego development and in
whom (given the oedipal situation) inter- and intra-systemic conflicts arise—
what other causes of anxiety do we look for?

It seems that in many children we see a combination of various aspects
determining the symptomatology. In the clinical part of this paper, I shall

address myself to anxieties that aggravate, intertwine, and often continue to intertwine with each child's potential neurotic development, as well as to factors that may preclude anxiety.

DEVIATIONAL DEVELOPMENT AND ANXIETY

As indicated in my description of the developmental aspects of anxiety, there are considerable constitutional variations in children's threshold levels and their capacity to deal with, and integrate, stimuli. My experience with infants and young children has led me to conclude that in certain infants, postnatal distress is not only associated with but is actually due to a prenatal—namely inborn, constitutional—heightened tension proclivity. It seems that some infants are born with a very low threshold and an imbalance between hypersensitivity and tension discharge as part of an early lack of integration in their patterning and functioning (Weil, 1956). The findings of Sander and his coworkers (1970) are a case in point. They describe hypersensitive neonates in whom there is a lack of self-synchrony—that is, a lack of integration of subsystems in various rhythms of their physiological functioning. This lack of integration often precludes the development of an initial fit (a "regulatory synchrony") with the mothering person, even if she is devoted and empathic. (An initial fit will, of course, be even more difficult if the mother is perplexed or easily anxious herself.)

In a previous paper (1970), I pointed out how in each patient we actually have to deal with a spectrum of ego functioning—a basic core or fundamental layer that ranges from harmony to imbalance. I also indicated the importance of the earliest interaction with the mother. Only if the innate imbalance and organic tension are so extreme that they preclude any fit, and thus preclude the experience of being well mothered (Escalona, 1965), will persistent, organismic distress prevail. In some hypersensitive infants, even a mother's extremely empathic response is not enough to avert distress and preanxiety. Sometimes, however, this interaction can overcome the infant's initial vulnerability; and an originally hypersensitive, tense, potentially preanxious infant, whose capacity for integrating stimuli with ease is limited, may thrive if this mother succeeds in cueing, in offering just the right kind and degree of stimulation, and in toning down tension.* The empathic mother of a tense infant will avoid being too intrusive; her handling thus differs from that of the mother of a child who can easily and eagerly deal with stimuli. Regulating stimulation is, of course, most important during periods of rather sudden threshold changes, when the vulnerable infant reacts more easily with distress, which is often severe and prolonged.

---

*This also relates to the gaze exchange (Stern, 1971).

It is thus not surprising that, at the end of the first year and into the second, the vulnerable, deviational child, with an overload of innate tension, often displays a continuous anxious response to the not-maternal environment, evidenced by excessive clinging to the mother, and has a severe and lasting sleep disturbance. The tension proclivity and basic anxiety will then aggravate the rapprochement crisis, which in turn is often marked and prolonged in these children, and ego structuring will proceed less than adequately. No wonder that Mahler (1971) points out the connection between this state of affairs and borderline pathology.

In children with the deviational basic core, in whom aggressive tendencies are sometimes also overly strong—or have become overly strong in the second year, especially during the rapprochement period—fears may be very marked. Often these fears and anxieties are connected with the original hypersensitivity to light and sound phenomena: The vacuum cleaner or shadows may be fear-arousing. Conflicts and symptoms around toilet training, associated with castration fear, may be more marked and more persistent than those transitorily encountered in many children of this age.

I have recently (1978) described observations of toddlers with perceptual hypersensitivity and integrative difficulties—hence, with an excessive proclivity to tension and anxiety:

There are those who continue to react with fright to anything which is either unpredicted or unpredictable: a new child or adult in the room, a new activity, or a different room. For example, even a different seat at the lunch table may result in frozen immobility or an affectomotor explosion, best described as a panic-rage. It is understandable that some of these children revert to innumerable rituals as a protection against such eventualities.

Others avoid excitation by vigilant control of themselves and their surroundings. Like little child-adults, and with a narcissistically oriented emotional distance, they survey more than participate, ever on the alert lest they be confronted with disturbed anticipations. Occasionally, we may observe breakthroughs of a more genuine self, as far as it could develop, or a complete collapse. Not rarely, such hyperanxious toddlers may find relief by joining in, or themselves instigating, chaos. It is as if they are turning passive into active by projecting inner turmoil onto the outside. They libidinize their anxiety. Their excited games sometimes have a sexual tinge. Such children are drawn to, or even promote, seductively sexual . . . excitations from others.

No doubt, a need for control in itself increases perceptivity, so that in some this may serve an extreme acquisitiveness for factual knowledge, deriving possibly from the preconceptual notion: 'The more I know, the less I can be surprised and overwhelmed.' Some of this unneutralized, ritualistic collecting of encyclopedic facts may later provide acceptable outlets for conflictual themes; sometimes, it may fuse with more neutralized learning; and/or sometimes it may be elaborated in obsessive ruminations.

A constant, relatively high level of anxiety readiness may in certain cases worsen matters by precluding the development of signal anxiety. This anxiety readiness precedes and intensifies phase-specific conflicts. Further . . . the basic amorphous tension is also frequently associated with a relatively high level of aggressive potential. This then contributes not only to phase-adequate channelizations, but to conflict and conflict proneness . . . and, consequently, to secondary anxiety [pp. 469–471].

Some such children, especially with therapeutic help, may improve considerably. In others, however, primary narcissism, the persistence of omnipotence, and the lack of development of the integrative function, in association with the overload of anxiety, distort the oedipal experience and hinder a satisfactory solution. Neurotic development may then intertwine with a great deal of basic anxiety and continued anxiety manifestation. The more archaic, automatic anxiety of helplessness outweighs signal anxiety and the anxiety of loss of love. Castration anxiety is extreme and continues to be expressed in thinly veiled fears similar to those of a much younger child. The child, for example, may be afraid of a person with a cast or even with a Band-Aid. Such fears are far removed from the complicated unconscious defenses and displacements of a true phobia.

In latency, the overload of tension and anxiety is sometimes expressed diffusely in driven restlessness, sleeplessness, or inability to concentrate. Again, due to continuing hypersensitivity in these spheres, there may still be fears connected with sound and light phenomena (also the hark response,* Greenacre, 1941). In some children, anxiety in relation to change continues to dominate the picture. In others, the overload of anxiety has been channeled into sequences of fears, phobias, compulsive habits, rituals, mannerisms, obsessional preoccupations. The abundance of anxiety manifestations, as well as the sudden appearance, disappearance, and interchangeability of symptoms, is characteristic and distinguishes them from truly neurotic symptomatology (Weil, 1953).

To summarize: We find a gamut of pathological deviational developments—a spectrum within the spectrum of basic cores. On the one end, there are the children just described whose manifestations are abundant and extreme. In these children the automatic anxiety of helplessness juxtaposed with omnipotent needs and expectations may spiral into panic-rages.† On the other end, there are the children who are only mildly ego-disturbed and in whom manifestations of the basic anxiety are more clearly intertwined with neurotic anxiety and symptomatology. As a matter of fact, with some such children the mild degree of perplexity and the anxious, slightly clinging quality of their eye contact make them quite appealing, and one reaches out to them.

---

*Reaction to accidental noises, such as hissing of the radiator.

†Mahler (1958) describes panic tantrums in young children with autistic-symbiotic psychosis.

The more experience we gain, the more we come to recognize these milder versions of the basic disturbance in development. Our conceptualization and diagnosis of such children has extended from Bender's (1947) category of childhood schizophrenia to categories of the preschizophrenic, the borderline, the ego-disturbed, and the deviational child, and to general considerations of the basic core. We have also learned to recognize shadings of pathology at younger and younger ages. Lack of integration in functioning and patterning, anxiety readiness, and poor object-directedness are already distinctly recognizable in infancy and toddlerhood.

EXPERIENTIAL FACTORS IN THE DEVELOPMENT OF ANXIETY

Before discussing further the pathological aspects of anxiety, I wish to review briefly the role and the importance of the mother in relation to the child's anxiety potential.

From the very beginning, by bringing about an initial fit, even with a hypersensitive infant, the mother may soften initial imbalances and facilitate a more harmonious basic core and a good symbiotic phase. This lays the groundwork for trust and a later feeling of well-being, and softens the tension and anxiety potential—if the infant's constitutional endowment allows him to experience sufficiently this good mothering (Escalona, 1965).

To elaborate: This development of trust has a mollifying influence on the proclivity to anxiety and allows a good-mother introject. All through infancy, the mother's ability to create an atmosphere of warmth and calm, as well as stimulation, her dosing of novelty and anxiety experiences to just the right degree for her child, as well as her later tolerance for, and help with, rapprochement difficulties, are significant for the infant's ego and drive development. A relaxed, warm, libidinally infusing and gently limiting mother may tone down even markedly aggressive tendencies and, in consequence, soften the potential aggressive tinge of ego and superego, thus diminishing the later potential superego anxiety.

An anxious mother increases the child's anxiety potential not only because she may lack the aforementioned capacities, but also because the infant tends to mirror (through "a kind of centripetal empathy," according to Greenacre, 1941) the moods of those around him. The consciously or unconsciously ambivalent, aggressive mother increases the child's aggressive tendency, and with it anxiety levels. A disturbed mother with catastrophic expectations is, of course, deleterious. She raises the child's general anxiety level considerably, frequently with repercussions in his psychosexual development and increased castration anxiety.

I want to turn now briefly to the opposite of what I have talked about so far: the inappropriately nonanxious child. With so much mutual resounding as a prerequisite for optimal development, it is no wonder that without maternal investment there is not enough appropriate anxiety and fear with regard to real danger situations.

How much of a mother's care and caution are introjected becomes convincing when we hear a child repeat mother's words while doing something a little risky for the first time. One source of accident proneness is in fact associated with insufficient libidinal investment of his self by the mother so that in consequence, the child does not libidinally cathect and protect that self (Frankl, 1963, 1965). (Granted, this is not the sole reason for accident-proneness.)

More conspicuous even is the *lack* of development of anxiety in the extremely emotionally deprived child, the child growing up without one steady caretaking person, such as children growing up in institutions or institutionlike circumstances.* Bender (1945) has drawn attention to this symptom picture and coined the term "psychopathic personality" for such children. She has noted that these children will later show no attachment, no aim, no anxiety; ego and superego development are stunted; impulsiveness prevails. There is diffuse drivenness akin to an organic tension. (And, in fact, more recent knowledge teaches us that maternal stimulation furthers structuring in the neurophysiological sense, in addition to the metapsychological one.)

Besides anxiety (or lack of anxiety) related to the kind of mother-child interaction, various kinds of reactive anxieties occur in relation to situations that are too new, too sudden, revive old anxiety of object loss or loss of love, or demand significant reorientation. These situations include separation or divorce of the parents, illness, impending or actual death, remarriage with the associated loyalty conflicts, major financial or geographical changes, etc. These are events frequently associated with at least one parent being anxious or depressed, so that parental cathexis-withdrawal and identification with an anxious, upset parent may also come into play. Needless to say, such reactive anxieties intertwine with or aggravate anxieties from other sources.

The child's age and stage of development are always factors in his reactions. Of particular importance is the level reached with regard to separation-individuation and object constancy, i.e., the level of his identification—primitive or secondary—and his psychosexual level, which colors his fantasies.

One situation deserves special mention: a child's anxiety reaction to his own illness. This may amalgamate with the preceding psychic constellation, his fantasies, conflicts, and defenses. Accidents may have a special meaning because they lend themselves to the thought of self-infliction.

---

* We find the same kind of disturbance at the other end of the socioeconomic ladder: children left to everchanging nurses in infancy and early childhood.

Most important, of course, is always the parents' and in particular the mother's attitude. This also applies to outside catastrophic events, especially in young children. A. Freud and D. Burlingham (1943), for instance, have described how during the London blitz the child's reacting with more or less anxiety depended largely on his mother's reaction.

Another situation that should be mentioned is mental illness of a parent. Anthony has conducted intensive studies of such families (1969, 1972, 1976). The children show rather varied reactions. Some may identify with the sick parent and his/her symptoms; others may show greater or lesser anxiety reactions; but some appear to be surprisingly invulnerable. The gamut of reactions seems to depend on the age of the child, the duration and intensity of the parental illness, the degree of contagiousness, the kind of outside support, and last but not least, his/her hereditary genetic anlage, which determines the resilience or proclivity to anxiety or the basic capacity to cope.

ANXIETIES RELATED TO NEUROPHYSIOLOGICAL DYSFUNCTION

Finally, I shall give a short survey of the anxieties of children with neurophysiological weaknesses. The anxiety reactions of children with Minimal Brain Dysfunction (MBD) take several forms. To disentangle them enables us to make decisions for therapeutic planning (Weil, 1973a). Six considerations should be mentioned:

First, in some MBD children we find a basic neurophysiological "driven-ness of brainstem origin" (Kahn and Cohn, 1943) with the potential for "catastrophic reactions" (Goldstein, 1954), i.e., overreacting and falling apart on mild frustration.

Second, there are diffuse anxiety reactions experienced by children with maturational lags because of the confusion and perplexity the maturational lag may entail. This pertains especially to lags in the language sphere or weakness in the capacity to organize diverse experiences visually, through hearing, and conceptually (due to a foreground/background disturbance). These deficits may lead to increased and prolonged dependence on the mother, often symbiotic in appearance.

Third, we encounter the experienced, more or less conscious, anxiety of the child who is aware of not measuring up to his peers in the acquisition of motor and cognitive skills, including reading. In fact, the child may be just as intelligent as his peers.

Fourth, we find a proclivity to superego anxiety in the MBD child, who has introjected parental expectations and has developed his own standards, but cannot live up to them due to his neurophysiologically determined inability to restrain himself and to inhibit his impulses. This failure then adds to a bad self-image and low self-esteem, and evokes fear of loss of love.

Fifth, in addition to the neurophysiological impairment, the child may have had from the beginning a certain proclivity to anxiety because, within the spectrum of basic cores, he belongs to the more imbalanced, hypersensitive kind.

Moreover, sixth, all of these anxieties are intertwined with anxieties derived from the oedipal constellation and the castration complex, as described earlier.

To summarize: All the anxieties specifically caused by MBD are also intertwined with neurotic and experiential features, as well as with the child's basic makeup. To arrive at a complete clinical picture of the child, we always have to ask, What would this child have been like without the neurophysiological damage or without the maturational lag?

THERAPEUTIC CONSIDERATIONS

Our therapeutic and prophylactic approach will be determined according to the various sources of anxiety. Predominantly neurotic anxiety calls for psychoanalysis or psychoanalytically oriented therapy. A deviational child, especially if very young, may respond to therapeutic educational help; ego strengthening (Weil, 1973b) may be achieved, sometimes with the help of a special teacher. Benefits are gained from a warm, predictable, libidinally infusing relationship, from structure and verbalization, as well as by carefully dosing new, changed, and anxiety-burdened experiences. MBD children often respond to the same technique; in addition, they need considerable tuning down of stimuli and diminishing of expectations in periods of fatigue and lowered ego resilience. More importantly, they need special help in the spheres of their neurophysiological weakness. Both environmental and psychotherapeutic help are indicated for a child's reactive anxieties, the more so since they are usually amalgamated with his neurotic potential.

As I have stressed previously, the importance of any kind of ego-strengthening work lies in the help it gives the child in directing his energies into neutralization. MBD children need to find areas of pleasure and pride. In some deviational children, their unusual sensitivity and perceptivity sometimes evolve into special gifts. In others, the unusually high intelligence (apparatus endowment vs. ego development), with the associated frequently irrepressible memory (Mahler and Elkisch, 1953), allows them to reach a high level in scholastic achievement. In this context, we might note that two of Anna Freud's (1965) criteria of ego strength are resilience, associated with the ability to deal with anxiety, and the capacity for neutralization.

It must be stressed that anxiety, with its pain and displeasures, is an essential component of growth and development. Anxiety is engendered by development, and anxiety in turn fosters development.

REFERENCES

Anthony, E.J. (1969) The mutative impact on family life of serious mental and physical illness in a parent. *Can. Psychiat. Assn. J.*, 14 (5):433–453.

—— (1972) The contagious subculture of psychosis. In *Progress in Group and Family Therapy*, Sager, and Kaplan, eds. New York: Brunner/Mazel, pp. 636–657.

—— (1976) How children cope in families with a psychotic parent. In *Infant Psychiatry: A New Synthesis*, E.N. Rexford, L.W. Sander, and T. Shapiro, eds. New Haven: Yale University Press, pp. 239–247.

Bender, L. (1945) Infants reared in institutions permanently handicapped. *Bull. Child Welfare League of America*, 24:1–4.

—— (1947) Childhood schizophrenia. *Am. J. Orthopsychiatry*, 17:40–56.

Benjamin, J.D. (1961) Some developmental observations relating to the theory of anxiety. *J. Am. Psychoanal. Assn.*, 9:652–668.

——, et al. (1962) Panel discussion. *J. Am. Acad. Child Psychiatry*, 1:59–66.

Buehler, C., and Hetzer, H. (1935) *Testing Children's Development from Birth to School Age*. New York: Farrar and Rinehart (1932).

Escalona, S.K. (1965) Some determinants of individual differences. *Transactions N.Y. Acad. Sci.*, Series II, 27:802–816.

Frankl, L. (1963) Self-preservation and the development of accident proneness in children and adolescents. *The Psychoanalytic Study of the Child*, 18:464–483. New York: International Universities Press.

—— (1965) Susceptibility to accidents: A developmental study. *Br. J. Med. Psychol.*, 38:289–297.

Freud, A. (1965) *Normality and Pathology in Childhood: The Writings of Anna Freud Vol. 6.* New York: International Universities Press.

—— (1971) The infantile neurosis: Genetic and dynamic considerations. *The Psychoanalytic Study of the Child*, 26:79–90. New York: Quadrangle.

——, and Burlingham, D. (1943) *War and Children*. New York: Medical War Books.

Goldstein, K. (1954) The brain-injured child. In *Pediatric Problems in Clinical Practice*, H. Michael-Smith, ed. New York: Grune and Stratton, pp. 97–120.

Greenacre, P. (1941) The predisposition to anxiety. In *Trauma, Growth and Personality*. New York: International Universities Press (1969), p. 27–82.

Harley, M. (1961) Masturbation conflicts. In *Adolescents: Psychoanalytic Approach to Problems and Therapy*, S. Lorand and H.I. Schneer, eds. New York: Hoeber.

Kahn, E., and Cohn, L. (1943) Organic drivenness: A brain stem syndrome and an experience. *N. Eng. J. Med.*, 210:748, 752.

Mahler, M.S. (1958) Autism and symbiosis: Two extreme disturbances of identity. *Int. J. Psycho-Anal.*, 39:77–83.

—— (1967) On human symbiosis and the vicissitudes of individuation. *J. Am. Psychoanal. Assn.*, 15:740–763.

—— (1971) A study of the separation-individuation process: And its possible application to borderline phenomena in the psychoanalytic situation. *The Psychoanalytic Study of the Child*, 26:403–424. New York: Quadrangle.

————, and Elkisch, P. (1953) Some observations on disturbances of the ego in a case of infantile psychosis. *The Psychoanalytic Study of the Child*, 8:252–261. New York: International Universities Press.

Sander, L.W., Stechler, G., Burns, P., and Julia, H. (1970) Early mother-infant interaction and 24-hour patterns of activity and sleep. *J. Am. Acad. Child Psychiatry*, 9:103–123.

Stern, D.N. (1971) A micro-analysis of the mother-infant interaction. *J. Am. Acad. Child Psychiatry*, 10:501–517.

Tolpin, M. (1971) On the beginning of a cohesive self. *The Psychoanalytic Study of the Child*, 26:316–352. New York: Quadrangle.

Weil, A.P. (1953) Clinical data and dynamic considerations in certain cases of childhood schizophrenia. *Am. J. Orthopsychiatry*, 28:518–529.

———— (1956) Some evidences of deviational development in infancy and early childhood. *The Psychoanalytic Study of the Child*, 11:292–299. New York: International Universities Press.

———— (1970) The basic core. *The Psychoanalytic Study of the Child*, 25:442–460. New York: International Universities Press.

———— (1973a) Children with minimal brain dysfunction: Diagnostic, dynamic and therapeutic considerations. In *Children with Learning Problems: A Developmental Interaction Approach*, S.G. Sapir and A.C. Nitzburg, eds. New York: Brunner/Mazel, pp. 551–568.

———— (1973b) Ego strengthening prior to analysis. *The Psychoanalytic Study of the Child*, 28:287–301. New Haven: Yale University Press.

———— (1978) Maturational variations and genetic-dynamic issues. *J. Am. Psychoanal. Assn.*, 26:461–491.

Winnicott, D.W. (1953) Transitional objects and transitional phenomena: A study of the first not-me possession. *Int. J. Psycho-Anal.*, 34:89–97.

Chapter 9

A Descriptive Study of Children with the Diagnoses of Anxious Personality and Anxiety Neurosis

DAVID T. WELLS

INTRODUCTION

This study represents the culmination of a one-year seminar that had addressed the topic of anxious personality disorders in children. There was concern as to whether such a classification as "anxious personality" as proposed by the Group for Advancement of Psychiatry was indeed a specific clinical type that could be distinguished from other disorders, especially with specific reference to anxiety neurosis. A major concern of this study was to investigate the similarities and differences that occurred in two groups of children diagnosed as anxious personality and anxiety neurosis as compared to a random control group within the clinic. As a result, it was hoped that a better understanding of the anxious personality would result with specific suggestions for further study of this group.

Subjects

The subjects of this study were twenty-one children who were seen at the Washington University Child Guidance Clinic from July 1, 1968, to July 1, 1975, and who proceeded from intake through the postdiagnostic interview. The twenty-one children represented three groups of seven ($n=7$). The first group represented all of the children diagnosed as anxious personality according to the Group for Advancement of Psychiatry (GAP) classification criteria during this seven-year period. The second group were those children diagnosed as anxiety neurosis, while the third group was a control group selected at random. The control group represented children within the clinic population and not a "normal" control group. Both the anxiety neuroses and the control group were matched on sex, race, and age to the anxious personality group.

Apparatus

The primary instrument used in the study was a checklist comprised of 217 variables. The variables comprising this checklist contained both hard and soft data, derived from a survey of the anxious personality group by the seminar participants during the initial period of study. The hard data included the presenting problems, developmental history, and psychosocial history. This information was gained through the use of symptom checklists, school reports, developmental checklists, and the psychosocial history respectively. The questions and method of presentation were identical across all children.

The soft data included the reports from the psychologist and child psychiatrist who conducted the evaluation of each child. Only the testing and psychiatric interviewing that were completed in the clinic were included in the study.

The variables on the checklist were rated on their presence or absence as determined by the material found in each individual chart. The absence of reporting represented either a "not present," "don't know," or a "data omission from the chart"; therefore, not just a "no" response.

Procedure

All of the children diagnosed as anxious personality (AP), according to GAP criteria from July 1, 1968, to July 1, 1975, and that had proceeded through the post diagnostic interview were used for the first group ($n=7$). The second group selected were seven children diagnosed as anxiety neurosis (AN), also according to the GAP criteria, and were matched as to sex, race, and age. A total of fifty children were seen with the diagnosis of anxiety neurosis during the seven-year period, from which a sample of seven were selected. After initial matching on the three variables, there were multiple cases for each age group. The final seven were selected using a table of random numbers. The random control group (C) was then selected from the cases admitted immediately following the population group of anxious personality children, as determined by the case assignment number, and were also matched as to sex, race, and age.

Following the selection of the twenty-one cases, a survey was conducted by the seminar members to determine those checklist items appropriate for a more detailed investigation. Following the completion of the checklist, a thorough investigation of each variable was conducted by the investigator for each individual chart.

Statistics

Due to the small number of cases within each call, a Fisher's Exact Probabilities Test was used to determine if there were any significant differences between the three groups on each of the 217 variables. Three separate tests were conducted for each variable (AP vs. AN, AN vs. C, AP vs. C). A t-test was used to determine if any significant differences existed between the means of the three groups on family income, I.Q. or Beery Developmental Quotient.

Limitations of the Study

The population group is conspicuously small and is highly subject to the type 1 error, finding a difference between the groups when a difference does not exist. Generalization of results are limited due to the small N and the fact that the same investigator rated all subjects. The reliability of reporting the soft data should be taken into consideration due to both the nature of the testing matter and the differences in approach of the professionals involved. Also, as noted previously, the absence of data on the checklist lends itself to several interpretations, e.g., omission of data in the chart, don't know response, or not present. As with any type of retrospective study, much discretion should be used in the interpretation and inferences derived from the data.

Results

During the seven-year period of the study, a total of seven children were given the diagnosis of anxious personality (AP). All seven of these children were males; six of them were white and one black. This is in part a contrast to the clinic population as a whole, where over one third of the population is female and one third is black. The average income for the families of the AP children was about $8,000, with a range from $1,750 to $13,000. This was the lowest of the three groups studied, and also a figure that represents about 11% of the child guidance clinic as a whole. The most frequently occurring family size for the AP group as well as for the others (anxiety neurosis, control) was a family of four. The most frequently occurring age was seven, and most frequently the identified patient for the AP and other groups was the oldest child. All of these variables are consistent with the clinic as a whole. The most common referrals were schools (33%) and physicians (33%), both also in congruence with the clinic as being the most common referral sources.

The AP child under study appeared to be a white seven-year-old male living in a family of four. The family may have an income around $8,000, and the referral source was probably either the school or a physician.

As an initial starting point, the presenting problems were inspected first. The most frequently occurring presenting problems, such as failing in school, somatic complaints, eating or sleeping habits, friendlessness, or clinging, were some of the areas under consideration. No clear cluster of presenting symptoms appeared, and none of the symptoms were significantly different from either of the other two groups. A notable trend was for the neurotic children to be more hyperactive than the control group ($p=.10$). It was also interesting to note that more neurotic children were presented as "tense or nervous" (57%) than in either of the other groups.

The symptom checklist obtained from the school also found no significant differences between the three groups on behavioral difficulties at school (see Table 1). Five of the ten most frequently reported characteristics occurred in all three groups. However, the ranking of the items on the checklist was interesting. Difficulty in concentrating and restlessness appeared to occur the

Table 1. School Symptoms Reported in Order of Frequency for Anxious Personality, Anxiety Neurosis, and Control Group

Anxious Personality	Anxiety Neurosis	Control
1. Daydreaming	1. Difficulty concentrating	1. Difficulty concentrating
2. Difficulty concentrating	2. Restless	2. Disobedient
3. Fails to get along with other children	3. Daydreaming	3. Restless
4. Nail biting	4. Lying	4. Fails to get along with other children
5. Restless	5. Slow in learning to do things	5. Resistant to authority
6. Slow in learning to do things	6. Boastful	6. Temper display
7. Lying	7. Depressed	7. Daydreaming
8. Physical complaints	8. Disobedient	8. Fighting
9. Resistant to authority	9. Fails to get along with other children	9. Lying
10. Unusual fears	10. Fighting	10. Depressed

most frequently in all three groups. In contrast, daydreaming appeared to be higher on the list of the AN and AP than of the control group. In both the AP children and the control group, failing to get along with other children was noted more frequently than in the AN group. It should also be noted that the control group had the most reported symptoms for all children, with an average of 8 per child; the AP children were next with 5 per child; and the AN children were least with an average of 3 per child. In the narrative section of the school reports, the teachers most frequently commented about the AN children as having difficulty in starting and completing their assignments. For example:

> S. appears to be a capable child who learns easily, thrives and requires praise and attention. He has great difficulty keeping at a task until it is finished. He is constantly shifting position in his chair, plays with his pencil, paper or anything that is available. Much of the time he seems inattentive, however, he is usually aware of what is going on in the classroom.

The subject listed most frequently as being the most difficult for all children was arithmetic.

From the presenting problems, no measurable differences were noted between the three groups. However, most of the children were having academic difficulties at school. The teachers attributed part of this problem in both groups of AP and AN children to their being daydreamers having difficulties in starting and completing their work, perhaps as a defense from the intense anxiety they were experiencing.

The next area that was investigated was that of the developmental history of the child. Of the identified patients for all groups, 43% were raised by both natural parents, a figure somewhat higher than the clinic as a whole (39%) but consistent in being the most frequent category. There was a trend for the AP children to have a much higher percentage of being raised by adoptive parents (43%), as compared to the AN or control groups, in which none were reported. This is also much higher than the 3% found in the clinic as a whole. The AP children were also shown to have been administered significantly more consistent discipline ($p=.05$) than the other two groups.

The AP children, while not differing significantly in number of problems listed in the developmental history, nonetheless appeared to have suffered more severely in degree during their early development. For example:

> S. was product of unwanted pregnancy. Mother ran around on father when child was in early infancy. Parents were divorced when S. was about three years old and was awarded to mother. The child was taken from mother at age four when mother was barmaid taking child along and also entertaining boyfriends in bed while S. slept on floor. Mother was frequently absent serving time in jail for harboring stolen goods. S. has witnessed paternal grandfather beating father and grandmother with belt. S. is presently center of court

custody battle, being torn between mother and stepmother questioning him as to whom he owes his most love.

The numerical data in this section may not accurately represent a qualitative difference of apparent additional severity the AP child suffered over the other groups of children.

As in the previous categories the data obtained in the parental histories revealed few differences among the three groups. However, one significant difference did appear to be found in the AP group in that the mothers of the AP children were reported as having been more "anxious or nervous" as adults than the control group mothers. The fathers of the AP group were also reported as more "anxious or nervous" as adults, but this time in comparison to the AN group. In general, both parents of the AP group appeared to be more anxious as adults than the parents of the other two groups. Another interesting finding was that there were significantly fewer depressed mothers of the AP children ($p=.05$) than of the AN group. In six of seven cases (86%), there was either a depressed mother or a depressed father present in the home of the anxiety neurosis child. The more consistent discipline and lack of depressed mothers may have helped the AP child from becoming depressed and hyperactive and as acting-out as the AN children were, noted in the referral symptoms earlier.

The data in the psychological reports indicated that the AP children were significantly less cooperative during interviews ($p=.01$) than the control group. The AP group also showed more underlying feelings of unmet dependency needs. For example:

> The overall personality pattern S. manifests is one of passive dependency with concern over rejection, failure, and frustration in not having basic needs satisfied . . . his fantasy deals mainly with a family relationship in which he is deprived of something so that his family can have what they need . . .

The AP group was also more significantly fixated at the oral level ($p=.01$), with more oral aggression present ($p=.05$) than in the control group. The AP group also showed significantly poorer ego boundaries ($p=.03$). All significant differences were between the AP and control group, and not with the AN group.

As reported by psychologists and psychiatrists, there was a trend for the highest level of psychosexual development to be the phallic level for the AP group. Psychologists reported the most common cause of anxiety was fear of attack and bodily harm for all three groups, but they did not differ significantly (see Table 2). The defenses most commonly used by the AP group were projection, fantasy, denial, and intellectualization. Fantasy was used more than any other type of defense. No significant differences were reported for level of superego development.

Table 2. Fears as Reported by Psychologist for Three Clinical Groups in Order of Frequency

Anxious Personality	Anxiety Neurosis	Control
Attack, harm	Attack, harm	Attack, harm
Destruction	Impulse control	Castration fears
Impulse control	Loss of love	Loss of support
Oral engulfment	Rejection	Aggression
Dark	Loss of support	
Abandonment	Oedipal fears	
Castration fears		
Rejection		

The Intelligence Quotient and Beery Developmental Quotient obtained from the psychologist's report indicated that none of the groups differed significantly from the other. However, the AP children did have the lowest average full-scale I.Q. (98) and verbal I.Q. (95), with the performance I.Q. of 102 falling between the AN and control groups (see Table 3). The AP group also had the lowest average Beery Developmental Quotient, 83 (see Table 4). Both the AP and AN groups had lower scores than the control group, giving the impression that an anxiety factor may have contributed to a lower performance. This would certainly be consistent with the history of the influence of anxiety upon visual motor performance.

The psychiatrists' reports indicated fewer significant discriminations present than in the psychologists' reports. The AP children tended to be less cooperative during interviews than the other two groups, just as they were for the psychologists. There was a trend for the AP group to have poorer ego boundaries, a poorer identification with the same sex, and less guilt over aggression than in the control group. Both the AP and AN children had better frustration tolerance than the control group, with the AN group having the best ($p=.03$). The highest psychosexual level reached more frequently for the AN group was the oedipal. Again, there were no significant differences between the AP and the AN children. All major

Table 3. Average Level of Intelligence on Wechsler Intelligence Scale for Children—Revised for the Anxious Personality, Anxiety Neurosis, and Control Groups under Study

	Anxious Personality	Anxiety Neurosis	Control
Average verbal I.Q.	95	104	96
Average performance I.Q.	102	101	103
Average full-scale I.Q.	98	104	104

Table 4. Average Beery Developmental Quotient for the Anxious Personality, Anxiety Neurosis, and Control Groups under Study

	Anxious Personality	Anxiety Neurosis	Control
Average Beery D.Q.	83	88	98

differences were between the two groups (AN and AP) and the control group.

Both the AP and AN groups had more children identified as "anxious or nervous" than the control group. The fear of physical harm was reported by psychiatrists as the most common cause of anxiety among the three groups, as it was in the psychological reports, although many types of fears were given (see Table 5). The most common defenses for the AP were aggression as a counterphobic defense, identification with the aggressor, isolation, denial, reaction formation, distancing and regression. The psychiatrists in the study reported the AP children as having more defenses than was observed by the psychologists.

The area of treatment was also investigated. It was found that more AP children ($p=.05$) were brought into treatment than in the control group. Also, there were more AP and AN children treated by clinic staff rather than by trainees than the control group. There were also more successful treatments reported with both the AP and AN groups than the control, but not significantly.

The final area investigated was the Group for Advancement of Psychiatry (GAP) diagnostic criteria for the diagnosis of anxious personality. The trend that approached significance ($p=.10$) was the AP children being able to deal more adequately with new situations after the initial anxiety. However, none of the groups differed significantly from one another on any of the criteria.

Table 5. Fears as Reported by Psychiatrist for Three Clinical Groups in Order of Frequency

Anxious Personality	Anxiety Neurosis	Control
Harm	Harm	Harm
Oral incorporation	Castration fears	Rejection
Agressive impulses	Rejection	Abandonment
Punishment	Separation	Castration fears
Rejection	Inadequacy	Loss of love
Abandonment	Unmet needs	Unresolved ambivalence
	Loss of love	Oedipal fears
		Loss of control

SUMMARY AND CONCLUSIONS

The differences observed among the three groups included in this study appear to be between the two anxious groups and the control group. The anxious personality and the anxiety neurosis groups seemed to differ from the control group by the following: (1) The anxious children seemed to daydream more often than those in the control group. (2) The mothers of the AP and AN were reported more "anxious or nervous" than those of the control group. (3) The AP and AN groups were fixated more at the oral psychological level than the control group. (4) Both of the anxious children groups had a better frustration tolerance. (5) Both anxious groups had poor ego boundaries, poor identification with the same sex, and less guilt over aggression.

Some differences did exist between the anxious personality and the anxiety neurosis group and are summarized as follows: (1) Anxious personality children were raised significantly more by adoptive parents. (2) Anxious personality children were reported as having more consistent discipline than the anxiety neurosis group. (3) The fathers of the anxious personality group were more "anxious or nervous" than in the other two groups. (4) The mothers of anxious personality children were related as "less depressed" than the anxiety neurosis group. The parents of the anxiety neurosis children were significantly more depressed than in the other two groups, depression occurring in six out of seven families studied.

There were no significant differences noted in the intellectual level or visual motor abilities among any of the three groups. However, the anxious personality children did demonstrate a trend of having the lowest I.Q. and visual motor developmental level. The GAP criterion that seemed to distinguish between anxious personality and anxiety neurosis children was that the anxious personality children were better able to deal more adequately with the new situations after the initial anxiety ($p=.10$).

The other criteria for diagnosing anxious personality children did not seem to clearly discriminate between AP versus AN populations; however, they did discriminate quite well versus the control group under study. The "anxious" children seemed to clearly represent a distinct group as determined by this study.

The charts of children diagnosed as anxious personality, with an additional misclassified child (n = 8), were subsequently checked for the 17 profile items of the "true fluid" borderline, and were also checked against the "true fluid" diagnostic tree. The results are shown in Table 6. The average number of items was 9. Only one child met the "true fluid" diagnostic tree requirements. The one who met the tree requirement had 11 of the profile items. Two anxious personality children had more items on the profile, 13 and 14 respectively.

Table 6. Characteristics of Anxious Personality Children

	Yes	No	?
1. Father in home	6	2	
2. Temper	4	3	1
3. Temper and/or panic	4	3	1
4. Impulsive	5	2	1
5. Lacks friends	4	1	3
6. Ego state shifts	3	2	3
7. Disturb reality test	6	2	
8. Disturb reality or logic	6	2	
9. Three levels (x)	6	2	
10. Death themes	4	2	2
11. Pleasure principle (x)	2	1	5
12. Depression (x)	2	3	3
13. Projection	4	1	3
14. Aggression turned outward (x)	6	1	1
15. Unneutralized aggression (x)	4	1	3
16. Lack insight	1	1	6
17. Capacity for basic trust or ready for relationship	4		4

Note: x = significant item

This would seem to suggest that the category of anxious personality is not synonymous with the category of borderline psychotic, as had been postulated at times.

It was noted by further review of the anxious children under investigation that an additional three cases could have been diagnosed as anxious personality had the diagnostician followed the GAP criteria more closely. This certainly represents a clear need for a consistent and thorough use of diagnostic criteria as set forth by the GAP classification system.

Should future studies be carried out on the same variables as in the study, it would be important to include a thorough investigation of the developmental history, school reports, and psychosocial history in addition to the clinical interviews, as these areas appear to offer much in attempting to make a distinction between the anxious child and other clinical groups as a whole.

Chapter 10

The Anxious Child in the Smith Family

10.1 THE PSYCHIATRIC EVALUATION OF THE ANXIOUS CHILD: CASE RECORD SUMMARIZED FROM THE CLINIC RECORDS

E. JAMES ANTHONY

John Smith is a nine-year-old white boy who lives at home with his mother, two older sisters, ages thirteen and eleven, and a younger brother, age three. He is in the fourth grade at school and is having problems learning and getting along with peers. He also appears to be very concerned about the divorce of his parents.

His early development was far from being average or expectable. The pregnancy was unplanned and was a source of much pain, both mental and physical, to his mother. When she announced that she was pregnant, her husband at once informed her that he no longer cared for her and wanted no more children by her. In the first trimester, he beat her severely and openly hoped that this would bring about a miscarriage. Mrs. Smith was hospitalized for three weeks, but the pregnancy continued, although marked by severe nausea, vomiting and gain in weight. She had had two Rh babies previous to John, and so there was some question of concern regarding his birth. The parents separated during the pregnancy, but the fighting between them increased. Mrs. Smith had experienced depression after each birth, but with John she was very depressed during the entire pregnancy. She was by herself most of the time, away from relatives, and also had to work. Delivery was normal and the baby was full term. The first year of life was unhappy for both mother and child. John was a colicky baby with a serious feeding problem. He was sickly and would cry continuously every night. Mother was distressed by the marital conflict and tired with the care of John. After nine months, the father left the home and served in Vietnam the next two and a half years. Throughout John's early development, mother worked and left the children with babysitters, so that a good deal of inconsistent management resulted. John's anxiety was manifest from the beginning. He had a panic reaction whenever a stranger appeared and would cling desperately to his mother. The bowel and bladder training was accompanied by almost uncontrollable temper tantrums on his part, so that his mother found him even more burdensome as a toddler than as an infant. She admitted that she had rejected him since conception and blamed him for being the cause of her losing her husband. She would beat him almost nightly on the slightest provocation and began to hate him so much that she had murderous impulses toward him. She felt that he resembled his father in many ways, and that when she was feeling angry and depressed he became the natural target for her abuse. As she put it, she just felt resentful toward males, whether men or children.

THE MOTHER'S BACKGROUND

Mrs. Smith spent the first five years of her life with her grandmother, but then joined her mother when she remarried. She saw very little of her natural father and described him as an alcoholic. Her grandfather committed suicide by slitting his throat with a razor, and her younger brother, who was said to have had "a red streak on the brain," hanged himself in jail. When she was 13, she had an illegitimate pregnancy and was aborted by a midwife. A large number of her aunts and uncles were also alcoholics. She had liked her stepfather until he approached her sexually, and then she took an instant dislike to him. She described her mother as cold, unable to express feelings, and unable to give of herself. She still remained very angry over this rejection.

THE FATHER'S BACKGROUND

Both Mr. Smith's grandparents were alcoholic and his natural parents were divorced. He grew up mainly in foster homes, and all his siblings had had difficult and stormy marriages that have ended in divorce. In line with the family pathology, Mr. Smith began to drink heavily and to gamble, so that the family was soon in dire financial straits. During his wife's pregnancy with John and for the year after, Mr. Smith became interested in what his wife described as "weird sexual practices," especially wishing to watch her have sex with more than one man or to engage in group practice. At first mother refused to participate but eventually acquiesced. While the father was in Vietnam, he encouraged her by letter to engage in sex with others, which she did, whereupon she felt disgusted with herself.

THE EXTENDED SMITH FAMILY

The mother remains in constant conflict with the maternal grandmother but is also ambivalently dependent on her. The house is often in a turmoil, with the stepgrandfather threatening to kill the maternal grandmother with a shotgun. Mother has lived in a state of constant anxiety, and her physical health at the time of referral was poor. She is soon to have a hysterectomy. She constantly complains of the poor life that she has had and how misused she has been. She has no confidence in herself as a woman, as a wife or as a mother. She feels very needy herself and angry that her needs have never been taken care of. A psychiatrist described her as a very masochistic woman who set herself up unconsciously for disappointment and suffering and appeared to be racked with neurotic anxiety. Her opinion of herself was poor and she manifested a host of psychosomatic complaints. The impression she gave was of being constantly in conflict with herself and the world around her. Her husband was no better. Mrs. Smith sees herself as a potential child abuser because of her uncontrollable rages and anxieties, and she has used tranquilizers to help her calm down. The atmosphere of violence in the home has not been improved by the presence, on visitation, of Mr. Smith. On one occasion, while he still lived with the family, he beat John so severely that he was hospitalized and required a lot of stitching up. The impression he gave the psychiatrist was of an irresponsible, psychopathic individual, verging at times on the psychotic. His course in the army had been chaotic, and he was eventually court-martialed for theft. Of the other siblings, the older girl was described as quiet, chronically sad and keeping her feelings to herself. The second girl was viewed by mother as "bottling up her fears and anxieties," especially since she learned of the suicide of her uncle. The "baby" was difficult to discipline, especially as mother was reluctant to do so. His aggressive reactions would immobilize her.

JOHN'S PRESENTING PROBLEMS

Mother felt that both she and John ought to be constantly on tranquilizers because both of them were so anxious and fearful. Like his mother, John had a very low opinion of himself and his abilities, saw himself as a victim, felt neglected by everyone and found it difficult to cope with the "scary things" inside himself. His main problem had to do with the numerous fears that he had and the panic attacks that overtook him from time to time. He was afraid of the dark, of ghosts, of monsters, of being abandoned, of being alone, of strangers, of war, of guns, of knives, of loud noises, and of snakes. In fact he seemed to live in a world of fear and constantly anticipated being afraid. Like his mother, he had not only a strong sense of persecution, but also a low boiling point, so that fear and rage were his two major affects. Like his mother again, he had many psychosomatic complaints involving his bladder, his bowels, his kidneys, his intestines and his blood. (He was said to have a chronic iron deficiency.) He also suffered from insomnia and would not or could not go to sleep until his mother did, which was usually around one or two in the morning, since she also had difficulties in falling asleep. He was also afraid to sleep alone or to sleep without a light, and regularly wet and soiled himself. He was often afraid but could not say why and was also fearful of contact with others.

PSYCHIATRIC INTERVIEW

John was described as a cute, slim, healthy-looking boy who stood or sat very close to the interviewer. He said that he lived at home with his mother, two sisters and a younger brother, and that his mother and father were divorced. "Dad doesn't give us any money—he doesn't care for us—we are poor and have no money and we don't get much food." He then started relating an incident that occurred several years ago when his father threw him against the wall and cut his head open so that he had to go to the hospital to have it sewn up. He said that his mother was trying hard to find a way to make money, and he wished that he could work and get food for her. He would also like to become a doctor so that he could help injured people. When asked about dreams, he said that these were very scary. Recently he had a dream about a big round ball on a chain which at first was sitting on a chair and then got into a fight with a man; the man killed it. He also told of another dream in which a big wind was blowing; it blew everything over, things were flying around in the air, and he was very frightened. At times during the interview, he appeared to experience feelings of anxiety and fear, especially when talking about incidents relating to his father. At such times, his thoughts were quite disjointed and lacked continuity. He appeared to react to danger situations with apprehension and avoidance. He was also very concerned with getting supplies, being preoccupied with money and food. He was also anxious about being hurt. His defenses did not seem strong enough to handle his anxiety, so that they spilled over constantly. In an overall way, he impressed the interviewer with his anxiousness, which appeared to be almost part of his personality.

PSYCHOLOGICAL EVALUATION

Throughout the sessions John expressed fear about being hurt in regard to some of the projective materials, and was "scared" when the phone in my office range or when I came up behind him in the waiting room. Nevertheless, he did relate to the psychologist well, maintained eye contact, attempted to engage him in play and expressed a wish to return for further sessions. On the WISC, he had a Full Scale I.Q. of 96, but there was a 17-point discrepancy between the verbal and performance figures. This was regarded as significant and suggested prehaps an additional visual motor problem. On the personality side, the most prominent aspect about him was his intense fearfulness of personal harm and destruction plus repeated expressions of deprivation of his needs. Throughout the test material, the prevalent theme was one of unfulfilled wants and a desire to be protected and cared for. However, this was not obtainable from women, who were viewed as ungiving and "dry." He also seemed to be fearful of losing control of his aggressive impulses. Religion was a frequent theme (the family attended the Assembly of God Church). He said that his worst fear was of touching the stove, and that he must keep everyone else from doing this. If he did not succeed, the whole house would burn down and so would all the food. He then listed the many different foods that he liked. When the TAT cards were being administered, he was frequently overwhelmed with anxiety. He rejected one card (a surgical scene) because it reminded him of his uncle, who hanged himself in jail. He was very frightened when discussing this and said that he tried not to think about it. After completing the test, he continued to appear upset and then began writing something and drawing boxes around it, talking rather incoherently, in such sentences as "I stand on my brain." (It seems that when anxiety is acute in this boy, his reality testing becomes a little shaky.) However, he was able to recover quickly and to be aware of his transient confusion, remarking that he "got mixed up sometimes." His main defense mechanisms of denial, projection, reaction formation and undoing were clearly not working successfully, so that he was often flooded with primary feelings. Oedipal struggles were also very evident, and castration anxiety was part of his general fear of bodily harm. The two major concerns were of losing supplies and being hurt.

Both psychiatrist and psychologist independently diagnosed him as an anxious personality.

COMMENT

In this vivid and yet not unusual case, we can learn something of the dark forces that breed such constant anxiety in the developing child that it eventually takes possession of his total personality, pervading every part of it with anxiousness. As we study the case from its inception in previous generations, we can observe the condition in the making, from the disastrous relationship of the parents with their parents to the present predicament of all the children, with John as the major casualty to date. We can catalog the stresses that afflict him as they accumulate over time in ways that seem inevitable and unavoidable. Even his very existence in the womb is attacked; he is unwanted and his father attempts murderously to get rid of him. His infancy is a torment both for him and for his mother, and she, too, at times has thoughts of getting rid of him. He is enveloped in an atmosphere of despair and desperation created by the generations before him that drive the older members of the family relentlessly to alcoholism, violence and suicide. The unpredictable and fear-provoking environment can in no way be relieved by the anxiety-ridden mother, whose extreme neediness makes her unable to meet the needs of her children, who are ever in danger of bodily harm at the hands of their uncontrolled, psychopathic father. There would seem to be no one around to hold any of these children and facilitate their path through childhood.

We are surprised that John is still alive and well, but we cannot be surprised that he is a fearful, anxious, and apprehensive child. There may be genetic and constitutional factors predisposing him to undue anxiety, but do we need to weight the etiology further when there already appears to be a plethora of causes? Perhaps the hypothalamic tuning and the ergotropic-trophotropic balance may have been hereditarily upset, but if these are present, may they not be effects rather than causes? The path of anxiety is probably strewn with epiphenomena of all sorts.

What can we do therapeutically for such a child coming from such bleak circumstances? He would seem to be in need of a primary mothering and fathering experience, but overworked clinics can rarely provide such basic essentials. They can, however, offer counseling for parents who know nothing of parenthood and who have become parents in spite of themselves. They can also offer some degree of protection by monitoring the dangerous environment and ensuring that it is reasonably safe and secure. And they can offer a therapist for John so that he can *begin* now to trust an adult who is emotionally consistent, available at times of threat, capable of responding to anxiety without anxiety and to aggression without aggression, and empathically in touch with the monstrous fears that beset small children. It is not possible to meet all the unmet needs of the past, but it is possible to give this type of child something of a second chance within a warm and accepting therapeutic relationship.

Now, a final word about the diagnosis: In dealing with childhood, Freud (1909) makes the following four points that provide us with a sound basis for further nosological considerations:

1. Anxiety hysteria may be combined with conversion hysteria in any proportion, so that somatization becomes a variable part of the clinical picture.

2. Anxiety hysteria is the *commonest* of psychoneurotic disorders, the *earliest* to appear, and the neurosis *par excellence* of childhood. ("When a mother uses such phrases as that her child's 'nerves' are in a bad state, we can be certain that *in nine cases out of ten*, the child is suffering from some kind of anxiety or *from many kinds of anxiety* [author's italics]."

3. Anxiety hysteria tends to develop into a phobia or phobias, and in the end the patient may have got rid of all his anxiety, but only at the price of all kinds of inhibitions and constrictions.

4. The aggressive propensities (hostility against the father and sadism against the mother) are very evident in anxiety hysteria.

Today, with our greater clinical experience, our direct studies of children, and our observations during child analysis, we are in a better position to detect the ramifications and elaborations of anxiety in different levels of development, in different situations, and in different forms. We are able to see the oral anxiety of the deprived, the separation and stranger anxiety of the dependent, the castration anxiety of the oedipal child, the moral anxiety of latency, the social anxiety associated with the emerging self, the existential anxiety that comes with the fuller knowledge of death, the depressive anxiety that comes with the threat of loss, and the pervasive persecutory anxiety that stems from both the internal and the external dangers. The interrelationship of anxiety and aggression is a close one, so that much of the symptomatic content (overactivity, impulsivity, immaturity, oppositionality) is drenched with both anxiety and aggression.

The transformation of anxiety hysteria into the anxious personality implies the shift from neurosis into neurotic character disorder. This involves time, trauma and threat in unrelenting sequence, or put differently, an anxiety-provoking mileu (from neglect and abuse), an anxiety-exuding parent (especially the mother), and an anxiety-disposed child (as a result of neurophysiological deficits or dysfunctions). The vulnerability or resilience to this pathogenesis is derived from both genetic and environmental sources.

REFERENCE

Freud, S. (1909). Case history of Little Hans. Standard Ed., No. X. London: Hogarth Press (1955).

10.2 PSYCHOTHERAPY OF THE ANXIOUS CHILD

DORIS C. GILPIN

Since children diagnosed as anxious personalities do not seem to be a homogenous group with regard to the roots of their anxiety, there certainly cannot be just one way to proceed in psychotherapy with them. In fact, the only generalizations we can make about them as a group with any degree of conviction are that they fit into no other diagnostic category, manifest at times a poor reality sense, and display massive anxiety over prolonged periods of time. Anxiety itself operates so widely in all mental disorders that its presence cannot be used as a single criterion for classifying an illness. In the field of mental health, workers are constantly engaged in observing it, understanding it, empathizing with it, dealing with defenses set up against it, and trying to relieve it; and although such core experiences help in the treatment of the anxious child, they do not by themselves provide specific diagnostic indicators. In treatment, two main possibilities are open to us: We can accept it as a motivating force in those patients who can tolerate its presence, or we can resort to measures aimed at diminishing anxiety in those who are unable to do so. This dichotomy derives mainly from therapists working with adults. In children the need for one or the other approach is not so clear-cut, since certain clinical types may fluctuate widely along this tolerance scale. However, the same principle applies to both adults and children: Given adequate ego strength, the therapeutic aim would be to free the patient from the early anxiety signals and to indicate when to explore and when to support. When the ego strength is inadequate, therapeutic management focuses more on anxiety stemming from the here-and-now, and tries to reduce it and improve the reality testing of the child. This mode of work is optimally slow and gradual, with no expectation of rapid change.

The term "anxious personality" may be something of a misnomer, since personality disorders are defined in terms of fixed characterologic defense structures, adaptations that are ego-syntonic, and anxiety that is well bound; but these cases show much free-floating anxiety and apprehension, a good deal of which spills over into the treatment situation.

The process of therapy in a nine-year-old boy will help to illustrate the therapeutic management of the anxious child. The patient had been a battered child for whom residential treatment had been initially suggested because of extreme anxiety amounting to panic at times, motor restlessness, double incontinence, insomnia, aggressiveness with siblings, temper tantrums and learning problems. In short, he was a fairly severe behavior disorder *but* associated with anxiousness and anxiety attacks. No residential placement could be arranged, and he was placed in a special school for the emotionally disturbed for one year. Treatment on an outpatient basis was given a trial. With his first therapist the child was initially disorganized, preoccupied with his strength and power, and unable to discuss his feelings at all until the second six months. He then began to accept some limits.

In treatment with the present therapist he manifested many sources of anxiety. He feared that if he entered the relationship, it would be used to exploit him, but then on the other hand, he felt guilty if he resisted this development. He felt as responsible as an adult for his siblings and their needs, yet feared his helplessness and rage about this. He felt he had to sacrifice his life to save others, yet feared the torments of his conscience and the punishment in the hereafter. He felt he would not get supplies, would run out of them, or that they would be stolen or poisoned; yet at the same time, he feared that if he had adequate supplies, his family and his own conscience would reject him. He would like to express himself honestly, but he was afraid of retaliation and further loss of supplies. In every conceivable way he feared hurt, damage and death from a dangerous and nonprotective world, one made worse by his own provocations. There were many hazards in the way of getting attention or having his needs satisfied. Most of all he shrank from his own death wishes. Altogether, he was so pervaded with a fearful anxiety that he almost seemed to seek out danger in a fascinated but horrified way.

The following are excerpts from my first session with him:

> He asked if he could have a model. I asked if he had had models a lot with his previous therapist, and he said he had. I said that I would have to think about it because I wasn't sure I would be able to help him with what he needed to be helped with if he was working on models. He looked extremely downcast, and I said, "It looks like you're feeling some disappointment." He just barely nodded his head a few times in a very disappointed way. I said that it was a shame he was that disappointed, and I certainly didn't want our sessions to be disappointments to him. I did hope that there would be fun or some pleasantness in the sessions. I said that what I could do was to get a model this time and see if I would be able to help him, and then we would know more. He perked up at this.
>
> When we were coming up the steps to get the model he had said that he sometimes played like Frankenstein when he walked up steps. I said that I'd bet he felt like being like Frankenstein when he thought he wasn't going to get a model.

He immediately went to work on the model without looking at the instructions at all. I commented that he seemed to figure out without looking at the pictures. He said that the instructions usually were wrong.

He said his mother doesn't let him make models at home because the glue gets all over everything and he has too many other things to do. I said, "So if you hadn't gotten the model to work on here, or if I just gave you a model to take home, you wouldn't have had a chance to use it." He agreed that that was right.

He explained that he liked airplanes with a pointed front better than the ones with the flat front. The reason was that the ones with a pointed front, if they nose-dived into the ground, had enough stuff inside before the pilot that he wouldn't get injured. I said that was a safer type of plane and that safety was what he liked best. He agreed.

He said that he had left his model out on a table once at the clinic, and the maintenance people had damaged it. He said, "Guess where we found it." I said I didn't know. He said they found it in the wastebasket. I asked if it was broken and he said it was. I said that it was too bad that he had had a bad experience with the clinic. He wanted to take his model home, even though it wasn't done, and bring it back the next week to finish up, because if he left it at the clinic it would get damaged. He said that even when he left it in his box, the box jiggled and the airplane was damaged. I said that he really had had a bad experience. I asked if he thought his model was really safe at home, and he thought it was. I said I wouldn't want him to have another bad experience, but I thought that I could put his box someplace where it wouldn't get jiggled. I could lock it up in a cabinet. I asked if he would give the clinic another chance, and he said he would, once. I said that I'd bet he really would feel like being Frankenstein if it did get damaged again. He sort of laughed. He said that if we tried to fly the plane it would all break up, and said, "Wouldn't it?" I said I thought if we tried to fly it, it really wouldn't fly, but would break up. There was an airplane passing overhead at that time, to which he called my attention and said, "Well, we can't ask him. We can't fly up there and ask him."

He noted that the door didn't have a mechanism to slow up its shutting and said it sometimes caught you when you didn't expect it. When the time was about up, I told him how much time we had left. He felt he ought to try and finish the model in the remaining time, but this was not possible. He did place it very carefully in its box and then put it inside his therapy box. He was really reluctant for me to have it, apparently feeling I would be more awkward than he. He carried the box up to the office himself, and I explained to him that I was going to take it on up to a cabinet where I could lock it up. At some point during the session I said that we were able to talk together fairly well, and maybe I would be able to help him as he worked on models.

Much of this session could have made any therapist, and not just the child, anxious. Very near the beginning, a decision was needed about getting a model. A therapist does not want to buy an alliance, nor does a therapist want to wreck the possibility of an alliance by being too frustrating. Also, model making is not very conductive to meaningful dialogue and thus can be antitherapeutic. I elected to be as giving as the previous therapist, but to put it clearly on an experimental basis. The giving of the model permitted a glimpse of his frustration anxiety and rage. He was able to joke about Frankenstein and was not left to be overwhelmed by the monstrous force of his feeling.

Another anxiety-provoking moment for the therapist had to do with his working on the model without attention to instructions. He was also quite awkward, sloppy, and seemingly unaware of possibly messy consequences of his movements. A therapist could well get anxious about the disorganization of the model and whether the environment would remain intact. It would be easy to get ping-ponging anxiety reverberating and escalating between this boy and concerned adults.

The episode in which the boy wanted to take his model home was another possible occasion for therapist anxiety, and once again a decision needed to be made that kept in mind the formation of the therapeutic alliance. Could I really assure the safety of the plane? How disappointed would he be if he was frustrated at this point? Would he see the therapist as more frustrating or more protecting? Would I be infantilizing him by not letting him protect his own creation? I concluded that he needed an external ego to protect his property and to demonstrate to him trustworthiness. I was also concerned that remembering to bring the model back was too great a responsibility for him. I was trying to reduce his anxiety about me.

Safety was certainly a theme for the boy, and I clearly needed to be able to keep the therapy safe in the face of complex interactions.

One week later he demonstrated the risks he took in direct contrast to his wish for safety:

He asked me to hold the front wheel of a model plane in place. I held it for a very short time while he watched my watch, and then he decided I didn't need to hold it any more, although in fact it was still rather loose. He held the airplane up in the air to see if the wheel would drop out and kept predicting that it would. I said that it seemed sort of contradictory—if he felt it really was going to drop out, he was certainly running that risk. As he was coming down the stairs from getting his next model, he walked with his back bent way backwards and his eyes almost on the ceiling. He missed a couple of steps that way, and he commented on it. I said he'd talked a lot about being safe, but he sure wasn't really doing something that was keeping him safe. He didn't comment.

So far, the therapist's interventions have been merely to call attention to what was happening in the session and to point to any lack of logic in the boy's statements in order to promote awareness and curiosity about the way his mind worked.

Two weeks later we came up against another aspect of his anxiety—that other people could make mistakes that could be dangerous to him, and he could get paid back for being dangerous to others:

He was making bombing noises . . . *k-boom*. He pointed out in the picture where there was a bomb and there was a rocket. He told some tales of how a bomber on the ground might drop its bomb and then the bomb would blow up the whole airplane. He thought these were atomic bombs or pretty close to it. He talked of something he had seen either on TV or in the movies, where the pilots were supposed to look before they let go of the bomb, but they didn't, and let it go at an airport instead of at the target. He put a pilot in the model with his feet up in the air. He laughed about it and said that instead of working the gas pedal he would work the bomb pedal and accidentally bomb the wrong thing. Referring to the show again, he related that after the pilots blew up the airport they had no place to land. They shot some other planes that were trying to shoot them and finally got to another airport, where there was a German jeep. They had some paint along and painted the jeep in American colors and got away. I talked of how people who were trying to be dangerous to other people and bombing other people often found they were in danger themselves, like in the story. He thought that was very true. On the model box cover he pointed out the helicopters and said that he would like to have one of those things that goes straight up. He asked, "You know where it will get to if it keeps going straight up?" I asked, "Where do you mean?" He said, "Heaven." I asked if that is where he wanted to go, and he thought he did. He said, "You can only go there if you don't have any sin." I said that it seemed like he thought it was going to be pretty hard to get there. He wasn't sure. At some point there was a siren in the street, and he said, "Danger." I commented on the fact that we had been talking about dangerous things.

The following week his anxiety over supplies and other people's promises to supply was illuminated:

He immediately wanted to get another model and said something about having a model every time. I said that I felt he really was very eager to get something every time. He agreed. As we went up the stairs, he was saying that his mother had promised they would have a banana split the day before, and then later she had said she would get it today, but he was not sure she would. I said, "She doesn't always keep her promises, huh?" He agreed. He picked a battleship. This helped keep the therapist alert to how he would tend to think of her.

In the next session he made a stronger issue about supplies. He looked in his box, wanted the clay, but could find only Play-Doh. We went back up again to the toy room. We could not find clay, but did find a chess set and some toy money, which he took without asking. He said he now would have plenty to do. I said that I would see if the clinic couldn't get some clay. We went back down again, and he busied himself punching out the play coins, which were in cardboard. He wanted to know if he could take them home. He could do a lot with them at home. I said that it sounded like he thought he didn't have enough to do at home. He agreed. I said that was important, and we needed to talk about it. I also told him what my general rule was about taking things home. I explained that things which were all finished and couldn't be used again, like the play models, could go home, but the things that could be used over and over, like the play money, should stay here so that they could be used many times. He said that his former therapist had let him take play money home. I said that we would need to discuss that some more too. The time was up, but he kept punching out. I asked him why he wasn't stopping. He said he just wanted to get these punched out. He thought his mother wouldn't be ready anyhow. He said that he didn't have anything else to do. Then he looked up quickly and said, "Maybe you have to see somebody else." I said that that was one of his thoughts. It looked like he felt it was more important for him to finish his punching out than for me to see whoever he thought I was supposed to be seeing. At this point, he asked if he could take the coins home. I asked what he had heard about taking things home. He then put them inside the box.

Again the therapist needed to be a secure protector of the boy's supplies in therapy even at the risk of being seen as depriving him of supplies for his life outside of therapy. A number of other points in this session need to be stressed: The therapist needs to feel secure in relation to the previous therapist and not to attempt to undermine the image created in the child. The therapist should not overpromise supplies; presumably this might allay the boy's anxiety about draining the therapist with his needs, but would not alleviate the anxieties he seems to be expressing about sufficient supplies in the rest of his world.

The following week I faced a new challenge—whether to play a win-lose game with the boy:

He got out the chess set. The board that came with it was very lightweight and was bent, so it didn't lie flat. He decided to use the board from the checker set. He asked me if I wanted to play, and I said that I usually did not want to play a game where there was one side against the other with someone that I was supposed to help. It was so easy for the person I was supposed to help to see me as someone who was fighting him rather than helping him. He teasingly said, "You just put an idea in my head." I said that what he could do was play both sides and then we could see how he *thought* I would play and how he would play against me. He did this with no further protest. As he set up the pieces, he said that his sister had a chess set, but she had lost several pieces, so they couldn't play any more. She had also lost her board. He wanted to take the board that didn't lie flat home to his sister because he didn't need it since his checkerboard would serve both games. I asked if he remembered what we had said about taking things home. He didn't reply. I said it seemed that he would have some feelings about having two boards when he only needed one and his sister did not have any. He said that was right. He played a game with very idiosyncratic rules. He talked about the fighting and made some *pow-pow* noises. I asked if he thought he and I were fighting about the checkerboard that he wanted to take home to his sister. He didn't think so. At one point my king was in danger from a pawn of his, and he moved the pawn away. Immediately after this he got very excitable, saying, "What if only the king and queen were left on each side . . . boy, what a battle there would be!" He had captured most of my pieces. He then had my queen move over next to his king, and he said she was in danger. He had my king go to rescue her. In actual fact the king did not rescue her because his king captured both my queen and my king. He said that the game was over and he had won. I said he sure did. He said the king shouldn't have tried to rescue the queen because he just got caught himself. I said yes, I supposed there were times when one had to think of saving one's self and not another person. He said he couldn't save her anyway. He said the whole game was lost anyway because most of my pieces were taken. I said perhaps so; in that case I thought that the king should at least have tried to save himself. He thought so too. I said that when he talked about his mother telling him that he should just look out for himself and manage his own life it sounded like she wouldn't rescue him. He said nothing. I asked if there had been times in his life when he had had to sort of save himself even though he couldn't save others or didn't save others. He said there had been. He wouldn't say any more when I asked when these times had been. I said that actually in the game the queen was supposed to save the king. I reminded him that he had explained that the object of the game was to get at the king, so the queen's job was supposedly to save the king. He didn't comment on this either.

I was trying, in the metaphor, to relieve his anxiety as to who I was there for—him and not me.

By now he was working with the money, punching more coins out. He wanted to take the money home to his five-year-old brother. I asked why. He said that his brother didn't have anything to do, so he would go into the kitchen and bother his father. Then his father would whip him, and his screams would get to the boy; he didn't want to hear his brother scream. I asked if that meant there wasn't anything else at home for his brother to do. He said there wasn't. I asked why not, and he said that they didn't have enough money. Now he was cleaning out his box, and he asked me if I wanted some of the paper. He said, "You can have it." I said that he was sure trying to do things for other people. He was trying to get things for them . . . the checkerboard for his sister, and the money for his brother, and now the paper for me. I said that it looked to me like he was the king trying to rescue people—the queen, Dr. Gilpin—and maybe he was putting himself in danger that way. I asked if he would be in any kind of danger or trouble if he did take the things home to his brother or sister. He didn't think that he would be because his father would be glad that his brother had something to do to keep him from bothering father. I asked if his brother and sister had some feelings about him having the things here that they didn't have. He didn't answer that. I said it looked like he had some things here that they didn't have. Again he didn't answer. I said I was here to be *his* doctor and not here for his brother or sister, but I could understand that I was supposed to help him feel better and that he might feel better if his brother didn't scream. I said I still didn't think I could let things go for someone at home which *he* needed to play with here. I said what I could do was talk with the man who talks with his mother and maybe help her figure out a way to get something for his brother and sister so that they wouldn't get in trouble and then wouldn't be whipped and scream. I asked if that would be okay, and he didn't answer. I said I guess it was not quite fair to ask if that would be okay, but that was the way I felt it would have to be for now. I asked if there was some other reason why he felt that he had to take home something for his brother. It turned out he had promised to take something home to his brother. I said that I knew how he felt about promises . . . that he really felt that it was important to keep them. I said that what we did have here that he could take for his brother and sister were the suckers; he could take those and that way he would have kept his promise. I said that I didn't think that I could let him take the things that he would need to play with here. He had been very reluctant to put his box of coins inside of his box, but eventually he did. He left looking thoughtful and possibly a bit depressed.

We see that the decision not to join in the game was not taken as frustration and permitted some very revealing fantasies to emerge. It might, in fact, have relieved the anxiety about us becoming opponents. Here we see him putting himself in danger in order to help others, but he was unable to keep himself safe, either as the king in the game or as the brother of needy siblings. The therapist was trying to encourage him to feel all right for wanting safety and getting help for it. The picture of home as lacking in play materials was unfortunately true and again could be a source of anxiety for the therapist. How could her weekly therapy remedy the daily trauma at home? It was also becoming an obstacle to a therapeutic alliance, but no solution seemed immediately practical.

The next excerpt is from three weeks later, and here we get a clearer look at his anxiety about his aggression:

He wondered if I was going to watch "Rudolph the Red-Nosed Reindeer." I said that it sounded as if he was wondering if I watched things like that, and I wondered if he did. He said he did and had watched it before. I said that must mean that he liked it. He agreed. I asked what part of it he liked. He said, "The part where the world gets foggy." He said that before that part there was singing and dancing, and then it gets foggy. I asked what it was about getting foggy that he liked. He said that after that they liked Rudolph. I asked, "Then it was not really the fogginess; it was the fact that Rudolph got to be liked?", and he agreed. I said that he must think that it was something pretty important to be liked. He said it was. He said that Jesus had liked everybody. I said that must mean that Jesus would have liked Rudolph even before the fog, before Rudolph helped. He agreed. I asked him, "How are you about liking?" He felt that he liked everybody. I said, "Just like Jesus." He agreed. He said that he thought he liked everybody . . . blacks, Germans, Japanese . . . they really were all right. He thought you should like everybody. He then began talking about Hitler, it seemed. He spoke of some man who built dungeons and told people that they were going to be taking showers; when the nozzles were turned on, stuff came out that looked like water, but it was really gasoline. It gassed them and killed them. He said that they wanted to do it to the Americans, but the Americans wouldn't let them. So there was a war. He also said that he had seen pictures of the war starting. The Germans had a lot of planes that had flown over France. Nobody else had any airplanes. So the French had to shoot down a lot of German planes to get enough money so that they could get some airplanes of their own. He thought that the Germans weren't fair and asked if I thought it was fair. I said that it certainly didn't sound like it, the way he was putting it. He decided that what you should do with murderers, instead of locking them up, was to have them join the army and go shoot the Germans. You couldn't like the Germans anyway. I said that it sounded like he had some conflict there, because he had been talking about how you should like everybody and here he was saying that it was okay for the murderers not to like the Germans. He sort of didn't hear me and kept talking about how murderers want to kill. Therefore, they should have somebody to kill that it would be all right to kill. I said something about helping the murderers to change so that they didn't want to murder. He thought they couldn't change. He again felt that it was all right to kill the Germans and not like them. I said that he must have a conflict because at one point he was telling me that you should like everybody and here he was saying that you don't. He still didn't discuss this point and insisted that the murderers should be let out to kill the Germans. By this time, he had completed his clay thing and announced that it was a Civil War soldier. He began throwing a clay ball at it and then got out his dart gun. He really began shooting at it, earnestly trying to destroy it. He got more and more worked up and talked more and more angrily about how frustrating it was, his efforts to break it up. He would loosen its parts, and then it would come apart easily. Then he would tighten its parts, and it wouldn't come apart easily. I talked about how part of him wanted it to be easily destroyed and part of him wanted it to be hard to destroy.

My attempt to alleviate anxiety about aggression by suggesting change possibly did not help. He was now unanxious enough with me to begin to demonstrate anger in my presence, presumably feeling that I would accept such affect.

At the following session we began dealing with the anxiety of too much responsibility again and the consequences to the alliance if there was not assistance to the boy in this area:

He had gotten out the play money and said proudly that he remembered to talk about it first thing. I said I knew that he often brought it up at the end of the hour, and I would say that we needed to talk about it. He said that he remembered this time. I said, "Okay, let's talk about it." He asked if he could take it home. I said that that was what he wanted, and he had said that before; I said that we had to decide whether it would be really helpful for him to do that. He said that he really wanted to keep his brother out of trouble. I said that he had said that too, but it was usually the parents who tried to do this. I said that it sounded like he was trying to be a parent, and he answered, "Well, you might put it that way." He said that his brother went with him everywhere except to school and here. I said, "So you are a parent a lot of the time," and he agreed. I said that it was a really big job to be a parent when you were not even grown up, and I expected that he had some feelings about it. He indicated that sometimes it was a bother. I said that if he were bothered, that meant that he got mad sometimes. He said that it was worse at bedtime, because he didn't like the dark, and the door had to be closed when he went to bed, so it was dark. Then he would ask for his brother to come with him. I said that it seemed as if his brother was like his parent, taking care of him, and he agreed. I said that we had been talking about his getting mad when he was bothered, and now he was talking about being scared, and I guessed that when he got bothered he was also scared. That made sense, since it must be scary to have to be a parent when you were not grown up yet. I asked how it struck him that his parents were having him be a parent, and he said, "They don't care." What did he think about their not caring? He said he didn't know. I said that it looked to me like there would be some feelings or thoughts about a parent that didn't care about that. I said that maybe it was one of those times when he really didn't want to notice those feelings because they would be so bad or awful if he did notice them. He said that his mother was too tired with doing dishes and all that; his father was always drunk. He asked me if I noticed his clothes. I said that I hadn't and that that was a shame, because I had tried to remember to notice his clothes after the day I hadn't noticed his shoes. I said that I could see his shirt and his shoes, and they both looked very nice. He said he had only worn them twice. His parents hadn't bought these; someone had given them to him because they didn't fit her son. I asked if he wanted to be that kind of giving person to his brother, and he wasn't sure. I said that his thought about his mother and father not caring about all the parenting he was having to do was that they just weren't able to care. I wondered what his thought was about me when I wasn't giving him the money to take home. He stared at me a long time and said that he didn't know. I said that it looked like he had thought about it a long time, and maybe he had had some thoughts about it, even though he didn't know. He didn't reply. I said that maybe this was another time when he had some kind of feeling that would be so bad and awful that he really didn't want to look at it. He asked if he could take the money home and bring it back next week. I said that I had talked with his mother's worker about maybe finding some way to help his mother plan something so that his brother wouldn't be in trouble. I said apparently that hadn't worked, from what he was saying. He said that it hadn't. I said Christmas was coming pretty soon, and it might be possible for the clinic to give him and his brother a present that would take care of the situation. I asked what he thought would be a present that would help his brother stay out of trouble. He thought a *putt-putt* train would do. I asked him what he wanted for himself, and he said he wanted a racetrack. I asked him if he thought that this would help his situation in regard to his brother. He thought it would.

The therapist's decision was again not an easy one to make. Would the therapist be getting into escalating demands that she be Santa Claus all year round to the entire family? What was she introducing into the family when she was seemingly going beyond the patient's needs to his mother's needs (although in her own mind, she was doing it for the patient's needs)? Was the alliance really so fragile that this parameter was required to be introduced? Was she helping with real anxieties that he was unable to tolerate?

One month later, after several missed sessions, the boy was more openly aggressive and tried to frighten me, indicating one of his ways of trying to handle his fears:

When he saw me go into our room, he burst in through the other door and tried to scare me. He said that he liked to scare people. I asked if he knew what it was that he liked about it. He said that he liked to see them jump, that it was fun. He said, "Why don't you try it sometime and see why you like it?" He said that he often tried to scare the guard and that sometimes he jumped. I asked him to help me understand why it was fun. He said that people laughed after they jumped and that it was fun to get people to laugh. I wondered about it being fun for the person who was scared, but that maybe if you thought something was scary for a second and then found out that it was nothing at all, you could laugh at yourself.

He was turning a passive experience of fear into an active experience of causing fear, but it was fear modified by the relief of finding out there was no real danger. This is what he would like to find out about all his fears.

We had to miss two weeks, and in the session that followed he was able to demonstrate his anger at me more directly:

He got out the dart guns and the clay figure he had made and set it up so that in shooting at it he would really be shooting at me. I pointed out to him that I was right behind it. I said maybe this showed some of his feeling about me and the change in his appointments, and that he was feeling pretty mad at me. He then went slightly to the side and shot at the figure. One dart glanced off the box and hit me. I commented that he had still hit me. He still continued to shoot from that angle, and I commented on that. I said even when he knew there was a risk of hitting me, he was still shooting from that angle. He then placed the box between the clay figure and me, but in fast-draw shooting he shot right over the box and hit me with quite a sting. I said he sure was mad. He then came around to a safer position, shooting more or less from my direction at the clay figure, but still at an angle. He called the figure a man. I asked, "How come you call it a man, when it is clear that what you want to shoot is a woman, me?" He said that a man could take the shots. I said it was sort of unfair to have that man taking the shots when it really was me he was mad at. He pointed the gun sort of threateningly at me and laughed. He then did call the clay figure Dr. Gilpin, and shot off its head. I said, "You sure got my head that time. You really were mad."

Here anxiety about showing his anger at me was obviously relieved, as I clearly accepted it and facilitated symbolic, but not real, destruction.

While he was painting a model three weeks later, we were able to talk about supplies in a more in-depth way, trying to understand, rather than just concretely be, supplier and "supplyee." He was more secure that not all would be lost if supplies were rationed out, and more confident that the next supply would come.

I almost winced at the way he used the paint thinner. He would take a full brush of paint and dunk the whole thing into the paint thinner without wiping the brush clean first. He pointed out that the paint thinner first had looked green and now it looked black and was almost impossible to tell from the black paint. He wanted to know if I could get a whole can of thinner. I said that I thought I could see the problem, that the thinner was getting dirty pretty quick. I said that certainly I could get more thinner, but I didn't know if I could keep getting a whole lot. I didn't know whether I could get a whole can. I wondered if there wasn't some way that we could make the paint thinner go farther. I said maybe I could bring a rag so he could wipe off the brush better before he put it in the thinner. I said that maybe he could wipe it dry first. He said that if it was dry it wouldn't need thinner, and I said that I meant not really dry but not with so much paint on it; then the thinner could get it off without getting so colored up itself. He decided that he was through painting and wanted another model, so we went upstairs. He chose two things. I said, "Remember that you can have one model each time." He put one thing back, and we went back downstairs. I said I was noticing how much he wanted to have supplies ahead so as to be sure that he didn't run out. He had wanted the glue at least three times before it did run out. It hadn't even quite run out today. He had wanted the extra paint thinner right away, and he had wanted an extra model today. I said that I could see that it really bothered him to think of maybe not having the things that he wanted and needed. He agreed. I said that he must have had times when he did not have the things that he wanted or needed at the right time, so he had learned to plan ahead. He said that was right. He started telling about how his brother had some money and played a game and won a prize. He himself didn't. His brother got there first and won it. I asked him how he felt, and he said that he felt pretty mad at his brother. I said that it must be maddening not to get the thing that you wanted and needed, and that probably he'd been mad at me when I hadn't let him take the second model; maybe he had been more mad at thinking that some other guy would get it before he could have it. He agreed with that; then he would have been really mad. He said, "But I could have had other models." I said that it sounded like it was difficult for him to let me know how mad he was at me; it was really difficult for him to let me know about his being mad at me. I wasn't sure why. I knew he had all this concern about supplies. Did he think that if he let me know how mad he was, he wouldn't ever get any more supplies? He didn't think that was it. There was some further conversation about him trying to say things would be all right instead of really letting himself know how angry he was. He put another piece on the model even after I had said that there really wasn't going to be time to glue any more. I said it looked like he was also concerned about supplies of time, and that he felt that he really didn't get enough supply of time to get done all that he wanted to do. At some point he said that on the way here he had been thinking and wondering if he could paint over his box. I said that it sounded like he planned ahead about what we would do here even before he came, and that perhaps he planned ahead for a lot of things in the same way. He agreed.

Planning was obviously one way in which he tried to organize himself and his world to avoid the anxiety of neediness or uncertainty. I supported his planning as well as his disclosure of anger and the revelation of extra tension when someone else got what he wanted. I was trying to relieve the anxiety of the reprimand from his conscience.

A small vignette the next week showed him beginning to connect therapy with growing out of infantile dependency. He was beginning to glue myriads of accessories and parts on the basic model of a battleship.

He said, "The battleship when it's started is a baby, and now it is getting grown up." I said, "You mean the more parts it gets, the more grown up it is?" He said, "Yes. It's fun turning the baby into a grown-up." I asked if he felt his growing up was like that, with more parts being added, but he thought not.

I wondered to myself if he also felt I was to be helping the baby in him grow up. Was he getting some relief from the continually gnawing anxiety of infantile neediness?

One week later another therapeutic dilemma occurred with regard to the use of medicine:

His mother stopped me and said that her son had broken his two front teeth today, and they would not be able to be fixed until summer. She said that she had noticed his hand was shaking so much when he was painting that she wondered if he needed some medicine for his nerves. I said I would talk to him and see. I went downstairs. He had been hiding and jumped out at me. He asked if I got the thinner, and I told him that it hadn't come yet. After a silence, I said that his mother had asked about medicine for his nervousness, and I asked if he had noticed he was nervous. He said he had. I asked if he could talk about it. After quite a silence, during which he had his head down and looked really miserable, he shook his head and said that he could not. I said that was okay. I imagined it was hard to talk about losing part of a tooth. It was like losing a piece of oneself, even if it was going to be fixed later in the summer. I imagined it was a pretty awful feeling, maybe sort of like feeling sick. He said he did feel sick, and that he couldn't eat steaks and things like that. I said, "How awful, not to be able to eat what you want." I would have thought he might be able to bite off something with his side teeth. He said the doctor said he couldn't eat except for stuff like hamburgers. I said I could see that that could really be awful too. He said his sister had had her teeth broken off too, but she got them fixed right away. I said that maybe she knew how he had felt then. He said she laughed at him. I said, "Oh boy, that would make it even worse." I wondered how she got hers fixed right away. He said it was because she was a teenager, but for his teeth it was somehow better to wait. I then returned to the question of his shaking hands and asked if he'd had this kind of nervousness before. He said it was worse than it had ever been. He wasn't able to sleep very well. What feelings did he have with it? He thought "mad." I explained to him that I was trying to figure out whether it would be a good idea to give him medicine, as his mother had asked. I asked how he would feel about it. He said he didn't know. I explained that the medicine wasn't something he had to have, like penicillin when you had a bad infection, but it was possible that the medicine could help him feel better. After a silence, he asked me if I was still wondering about giving him the medicine, and I said yes. He said he thought he did want some.

I gave him a few days' supply of 5 mg Librium b.i.d. It seemed to me a needed parameter for him to perceive me as someone who tried to help with anxiety in a variety of ways. I did not, however, want to give him a self-image of helplessness without the crutch of medicine.

After some more sessions on clarifying the limits to supplies that were inevitable in therapy, there came a most dramatic session with a reenactment of the child abuse he had once suffered from his father. This was five weeks after the previous session.

He used the brush with such a flourish that the paint flew off and hit the radiator. He laughed a lot sort of hysterically. I tried to wipe the paint off. He then began pretending to slop paint on me with his brush and would get the brush very close to my face. I would blink and startle, and he would laugh. He said he was really scaring me. I said that he seemed to be really enjoying trying to scare me.

When the time for painting was through, he washed up the brush. We cleaned up the place as well as possible, and he threw out the trash. He began to clown around, and I commented that he was clowning. He was pretending that someone was knocking him around.

I said, "Boy, you're really getting knocked around." He then lay on the floor behind some chairs. Then he popped up and said, looking at me, "Oh, aren't you gone, isn't he gone?" I said, "Oh, I'm a he, am I? Boy, I'm a pretty mean man to be knocking you around so much." He kept laughing and getting wilder and wilder, throwing himself all around as if he was getting innumerable blows. I said, "Oh gosh, I really am a mean man to just hit and hit and hit." He then sat as if he were a little baby. I said, "Oh, it looks like you're a baby now. And I'm the kind of mean man that hits babies?" He said, "Yes." Then he continued as the baby, throwing himself all around. I would talk about what a mean man I was to be doing this. At one point the baby tried to hide himself behind some chairs, but somehow the man got in there. I said, "Oh my gosh, the baby tries to hide and can't even get away then." Then he lay very motionless. I said, "Oh my gosh, the baby's unconscious." He said, "Didn't you know? The baby's dead." I said, "Oh my gosh, what a disgusting mean man I am."

He then flopped over another chair and sort of hit the edge of the table, and said he'd hurt himself. I said "Oh, that's too bad." He said that the baby sort of wanted to hit the mean man back. I said I could imagine so. Then the baby would try to hit back, and the baby would just get smashed harder. I said, "My gosh, the baby is just so powerless when the mean man is trying to smash him." Then he grabbed his soda bottle and pretended to swing it around. I said, "The baby wants to pay the man back so much that he would even use a weapon if he had to get enough power." He pretended several times that he was trying to leave the room. I would talk about the baby trying so hard to get away from the mean man and just finding no way.

Through all of this the mood had gotten more and more serious instead of full of the laughter it had begun with. Sometimes the baby also acted terribly scared. I talked about how awfully frightened the baby had felt. Then he began saying, "Why did you hit me?" I said the baby couldn't even understand why the mean man would hit him. He then opened the door and with a sweep of one arm suggested that I go out the door. I said, "You've timed it exactly right because our time is up and it is time to go up." I picked up the box and carried it up.

All the way up the stairs as well as through the door he would say, "Ladies first." I would say, "Well, I'm the mean man, and that doesn't mean me first." Then he would say, "Men first," and I would go first. Then he would say, "Men first," and he would go first. Next he was doing "ladies with men first." At this he would go ahead of me and then he would stand back and wait for me to go ahead of him. Finally, the last four steps up he said, "Let's go up together." So we walked up the last four steps side by side.

The finish of that session with the ascent together was a poignant signal that we indeed were allied in moving on through therapy. At the following session he tried to play chess with no piece getting "killed"—i.e., captured—on either side. The "beating up" reenactment had enabled him to share one of the more anxiety-provoking events of his life with some emotional catharsis and some reworking and mastery in the transference of the originally overwhelming trauma.

In another two weeks we were able to talk directly about how it excited him to be in danger.

He has now been seen for an additional nine months, during which he made a not very convincing suicide gesture when angry at mother. He has talked more openly of not being liked and of wishing his family talked problems over like we do. He has begun to want to take care of wild animals, including ferocious ones, when he grows up, and rarely talks of war anymore. He also has brought in conflicts with stepfather. He has begun to trust instructions, and feels some confidence that he will be supplied.

There were many sessions in which "nothing" seemed to be happening therapeutically. It seemed that he needed time to peacefully pursue age-appropriate interests and explorations and to achieve some age-appropriate successes without the distracting and anxiety-provoking stimuli of home or school. Such "nonproductive" sessions may well be anxiety-provoking for a therapist.

During the course of this therapy, he had also moved from his desperate efforts to try to be a stereotype of a normal boy via a well-nigh compulsive preoccupation with models and racing cars. He has begun to have real "fun" being creative and imaginative. Here is a recent session.

He got out his airplane to work on. As he sat to work, he said, "Well, how was your week? Did you have any problems?" He laughed and said, "You see, I am the doctor today." I said, "Well, hello, Dr. G." He laughed some more. I asked, "How were things for you?" He said okay. He looked in his box and said, "I'm rich." He was talking about how many things he had in his box. I said he was feeling like something today; he was feeling like a doctor, and rich. He was working very carefully, and he would ask me things, such as, "Is there anything I should put in first?" He made sure that he used all the parts. He announced, "I feel like an ordinary, everyday, normal boy." I said that it sounded like he felt really good. He repeated to himself, "I feel like an ordinary, everyday, normal boy." I said, "How great." I asked how long he had been feeling that way. He said, "Well, for maybe three months." He wasn't sure what had happened to make him feel that way. When he finished, he said he thought it looked good. Then he said, "There, what do you think?" I said I thought it was the best he had ever done. He said, "See? There is no glue showing. I glued on the edge instead of around it." I said, "Yes." He also said that he put in every piece and didn't leave out anything. I said, "Yes, there is nothing left over, and you used to leave things over." I said, "It is really neat." He said, "I used to work too fast." I said, "Yes, you used to be in a real hurry, and you've now slowed, and you are more careful and don't seem to have to get finished so quick." He said, "Well, I still like to get it done." He then said, "Oh, there is one thing left out—the decal." This was a decal of the instrument panel. He didn't think there was any way to get the airplane unglued except for maybe turpentine, and then he thought, "Oh, no, it would melt the plastic." He remembered a time when he experimented, and how the plastic had melted. I said, "Well, one teeny thing left out when all the rest was absolutely perfect, that was pretty doggone good." He began flying the airplane, and it bombed me. I said, "When we started this session, you jumped up and scared me, and now you are bombing me. There must be something on your mind about me." He said that there was something on his mind about girls. There was more teasing aggression, and I said, "Well, are you doing this to me because it is me or because I am a girl?" He didn't really answer. He kept teasing me, and I said, "I know boys do get mad at girls sometimes when girls give boys excited feelings." He said, "Yeah, when they are in love." I said, "Yes, love can be awful scary, and so the boys get mad." He said, "I'll say." I said I was sorry if I had excited or scared him in any way. He said, "Not you." I said, "Have you been in love?" He said, "Yes." I said, "Did you like it?" He made a face that showed really mixed feelings.

In therapy I had tried to demonstrate I would not exploit him. I served his needs, but tried not to let him exploit me for wishes. We had dealt somewhat with his conscience in relation to sacrificing himself, and I had not permitted him to sacrifice his therapy supplies. He had gradually begun to feel more secure. He could be angry without retaliating physically or through the withholding of supplies. He had found a piece of the world to be protective and nondangerous. He has been able to move past the most primitive anxieties to a phallic-oedipal anxiety.

Many of his symptoms have been alleviated. He was no longer enuretic and encopretic. He was more manageable at home, and slept better. His academic performance was still below average, but he was making an occasional A on papers. His behavior was not a problem in the classroom. In his latest school report he was said to have lots of friends and not to get into fights.

In summary, it would seem that these children need a therapist who has many resources to deal with anxiety and the ability to face anxiety. The therapist needs to have an understanding of and "feel" for the child's ego capacity in relation to his specific or general anxieties so as to know when to reduce anxiety by some supportive intervention and when to help the child look at and be curious about his anxiety.

The case material demonstrates fairly clearly some of the therapeutic hazards in the psychotherapy of an anxious child, and also illustrates how beneficial such therapy can be.

Chapter 11

Summing Up on "The Anxious Child"

E. JAMES ANTHONY

What sort of feelings does the anxious child experience? He is unable to tell us himself, not only because of the limitations of language, but also because what worries him is a feeling complex that is hard to disentangle into its separate components. When the philosopher Ryle (1949) attempted to define feelings, he wrote that what he had in mind were the sort of things that people describe as "twinges, pangs, throbs, wrenches, itches, prickings, chills, glows, loads, qualms, hankerings, curdlings, sinkings, tensions, gnawings and shocks." The anxious child probably runs the gamut of all these, for which anxiety merely represents an abstraction. Embedded in this chaotic stream of feelings are also ideas that we ordinarily call moods, feelings and emotions, but which are, as Kaufmann (1961) points out, nine-tenths thoughts. When one speaks of separation anxiety, stranger anxiety, castration anxiety, death anxiety, social anxiety, and so forth, one is, to a large extent, including ideas that mesh with the "wrenches, itches and prickings."

Prior to the work of Freud (1936), the clinician would have been content to speak of anxiety as a unitary phenomenon appearing mysteriously out of the psychosomatic entity that constitutes the human individual. What Freud offered instead was a theory, or rather a sequence of theories, that opened up the process of theorizing in this area. Freud was not right in his first anxiety theory and certainly not complete in his subsequent anxiety theory; but as Gide (1952) said, "The importance of . . . a new explanation of certain phenomena is not gauged only by its accuracy, but also, and above all, by the impetus it gives to the mind . . . by the new vistas it opens." Freud's work on anxiety undoubtedly opened up "new vistas" to the clinician, so that we can now think of it not only physiologically but also psychologically. He laid the foundation not only for a new approach to anxiety but also for a cognitive theory of the emotions. His clinical work led him to a series of important conclusions: that individuals differ in their perception and appraisal of the dangerousness of the world about them; that signal anxiety, or the anxiety of anticipation, has an adaptive function that alerts the individual to the possibility of danger and prepares him to deal with it or avoid it; that when his capacities to cope are inadequate or limited, his anxieties increase to the point of becoming disrupting, disorganizing, and maladaptive; that a realistic appraisal leads to ordinary or objective anxiety, whereas unrealistic appraisal may conduce the development of neurotic anxiety.

The infant is in no position to evaluate the outside situation with any degree of accurancy, and so his attachment and separation promote something very akin to fear that contains an amalgam of clinging, jealousy, possessiveness, greediness, immaturity, and overdependence. Bowlby (1973) uses the term "anxious attachment," making it clear that "the heart of the condition is apprehension lest attachment figures be inaccessible and/or unresponsive." He also links the emotion of anger to the *anxious attachment complex*. The anxious child may therefore be defined as one who has failed to resolve or maintain within normal limits this anxious attachment complex.

Izard (1977) speaks of various forms of anxiety made up from combinations of affects, such as fear-distress-anger or fear-shame-guilt, with fear as the dominant emotion in the pattern if the pattern is to be considered a form of anxiety. According to her, therefore, anxiety is a general, imprecise term which may refer to different interactive combinations of fear with other affects, and which contains certain cognitive orientations.

Since in our sequence of presentations we have referred to the psychological, the psychodynamic, and the phenomenological, I would like, in this summing up, to remind our readers of the neurophysiological substrate to any consideration of anxiety. In the biochemical context, it has been assumed that intense fear is *trophotropic*, while mild to moderate fear is *ergotropic*. These terms were used by Gellhorn (1965, 1967) to support his theory of anxiety as characterized by the simultaneous and antagonistic functioning of both the ergotropic and the trophotropic systems, or in neurophysiological terms, the sympathetic and parasympathetic nervous systems. This would lead to a wide range of differentiated feelings that could be summarized under the generic term of "anxiety." Let me try and summarize his work briefly:

1. According to Gellhorn, the trophotropic syndrome prevails in acute fear, during which EEG potentials are slowed, parasympathetic activity increases, and muscle tone, heart rate and blood pressure decrease. The

ergotropic influence that is also present at the same time uses pupillary dilatation, sweating, and increased blood flow through the muscles.

2. Under conditions of anxiousness (chronic fear), simultaneous upward discharges of ergotropic and trophotropic systems take place, leading to a breakdown in the reciprocity of the two systems and a dysfunctional outcome. The anxious child may therefore show two different patterns of response: an ergotropic dominant reaction, characterized by restlessness, hyperactivity, dilatation of the pupils, sweating, and other sympathetic responses associated with fear-anger feelings; and second, a trophotropic dominant reaction, characterized by hypoactivity, slowing of the heart rate, increase in blood pressure and other parasympathetic responses, associated with fear-distress feelings.

3. Biological hereditary predispositions may effect hypothalamic tuning and the ergotropic-trophotropic balance, but there may be other individual differences that influence the patterns of somatic symptoms in anxiety.

4. Anxiety may also be associated with an increase in epinephrine and a concomitant decrease in the norepinephrine-epinephrine ratio together with a shift in the ergotropic-trophotropic balance to the trophotropic side. At the phenomenological level, this biochemical change may be experienced as acute fear or distress, with a decrease in anger and aggressiveness.

5. Funkenstein (1955) found that individuals who could be angry at others for causing them stress had a mild response to a parasympathomimetic agent, whereas those who became angry at themselves and blamed themselves, showing anxiety and depression, had a strong reaction. The reactions of those manifesting outer-directed anger were very similar to reactions induced by the injection of norepinephrine, whereas those individuals who reacted with anxiety-fear had responses similar to those induced by injections of epinephrine.

6. Increased steroid levels can also be found during anxiety and have been interpreted as evidence of strong ergotrophic discharges.

These pharmacological studies would support the thesis that fundamental emotions, such as anxiety and anger, have specific and distinct hormonal and autonomic patterns, that both trophotropic and ergotropic systems are involved, and that fear and anger can combine to constitute one form of anxiety. These views would not be at variance with the clinical findings described in the previous chapters.

One should also add, from the point of view of learning theory, that there are both innate and learned causes for anxiety. The thresholds of response may be influenced by biologically based individual differences, by idiosyncratic experiences, and by the sociocultural context. The innate releasers of anxiety include being alone, being confronted by strangers, unfamiliar situations, or being exposed to sudden changes of stimulation or sudden approaches.

In the case reported of John Smith, one can note what a large number of fears and anxieties he has accumulated. The case demonstrates very well the range of fear from apprehension to terror, and also shows that regularly repeated exposures to such conditions lead inevitably to uncertainty, insecurity and the sense of imminent danger. The individual feels not only a high degree of tension but also a high degree of impulsiveness. The adult's own apprehensions stemming from his own childhood may significantly influence the level and persistence of anxiety in his children, and this is also manifest in the case of John Smith. The parents may transmit fear not only through their own fearfulness but also through their own fearsome attitudes and behavior. Such parents show little concern about the fearfulness of their children but complain about their poor academic performances, their nightmares and sleep disturbances, and their clinging behavior. The interplay of anxiety between parent and child is one of the critical factors in the genesis of the anxious child; the exposure, in therapy, to a nonanxious adult itself has a remarkably mitigating effect. The reduction of anxiety may occur during insight psychotherapy, but it may also be reduced by the techniques of habituation, desensitization, flooding, and modeling.

Successful treatment may or may not require understanding on the part of the therapist or patient. It cannot therefore be used as a test of theory.

REFERENCES

Bowlby, J. (1973) *Attachment and Loss, Vol II: Separation, Anxiety and Anger.* New York: Basic Books.

Freud, S. (1936) *Inhibitions, Symptoms and Anxiety*, Standard Ed., Vol. 20. London: Hogarth Press (1955).

Funkenstein, D.H. (1955) The Physiology of Fear and Anger. *Scientific American* 192:74–80.

Gellhorn, E. (1965) The neurophysiological basis of anxiety: A hypothesis. *Perspectives in Biology and Medicine* 8:488–515.

———. (1967) The tuning of the nervous system. *Perspectives in Biology and Medicine* 10:559–591.

Gide, A. (1952) *Corydon: Four Socratic Dialogues*, P.B., trans. London: Secker and Warburg.

Izard, C.E. (1977) *Human Emotions.* New York: Plenum Press.

Kaufmann, W. (1961) *Critique of Religion and Philosophy.* New York: Anchor Books.

Ryle, G. (1949) *The Concept of Mind.* London: Hutchinson's Universal Library.

PART III: THE BORDERLINE CHILD

Chapter 12

Betwixt and Between: The Psychopathology of Intermediacy

E. JAMES ANTHONY

Prior to the theory of evolution, taxonomists were mainly preoccupied with the systematic arrangement of organisms and species, genera, families, orders, etc., as in the quinary system of MacLeay, with the ultimate purpose of finding a discrete niche for every living creature. In 1832, Darwin, still voyaging on *The Beagle*, wrote to his teacher Henslow as follows: "There is a poor specimen of a bird which to my unornithological eyes appears to be a happy mixture of lark, pigeon and snipe. Mr. MacLeay himself never imagined such an inosculating creature." This was his first use of the word "inosculate," defined by the dictionary as having characteristics intermediate between those of two similar or related taxonomic groups. The word acquired historical importance since it dates for us the beginnings of the evolutionary idea in Darwin's mind. Since then, taxonomists in all fields have been alert to the continuum between groups and to the importance of the inosculate as a bridge between groups. The inosculate is generally a "poor specimen" incorporating a mixture of elements from different sources.

It is not historically clear when the term "borderline" was first used to describe conditions lying between neurosis and psychosis. In 1884, Hughes wrote of borderline psychiatric records and of prodromal symptoms of physical impairment. Six years later, Rosse produced clinical evidence of the existence of "borderline insanity." In all this earlier work, the term "borderline" was used to indicate the transitional phase of disorder on its way to becoming a clear-cut psychosis.

This concept of a transitional state became less acceptable with increased clinical experience. The borderline case seemed to maintain a curious identity of its own. It was not easily classifiable into neurotic or psychotic,

193

but had characteristics intermediate between the two, like Darwin's inosculate. Like the latter, it is generally a "poor specimen" in terms of behavior and adjustment, and clinicians prior to 1884 certainly did not recognize or define such an inosculating creature. On looking back, it became evident that borderline characteristics existed both in adolescence and in childhood, manifesting the same oscillations between the neurotic and psychotic and, although frequently verging on a break with reality, managing to maintain this curious "stable instability" (Schmideberg, 1959). There is at no stage in the life cycle a characteristic pattern of symptoms, and every case displays its own blend of normality, neurosis, psychosis, and psychopathy. As Grinker (1975) puts it, "the borderline personality is a life-style of vacillating eccentricity" that sometimes appears overtly as the borderline syndrome, and sometimes, for reasons still unknown, remits into near normality. At no time do the cases show thought disorder and at no time do they develop frank schizophrenia.

The families are frequently negative and rejecting and offer little support and protection during the early period of ego development and differentiation (Pavenstedt, 1964).

Child and adolescent patients show poor object relations, impaired ego functions, unstable identities because of conflictual identifications, low tolerance for anxiety, an excessive development of aggressive drives with frequent angry explosions, and a lack of primary autonomy (Grinker et al., 1968; Kernberg, 1967). The general impression of most clinicians who have followed these cases through childhood, adolescence, and early adult life is that the syndrome represents a developmental defect.

Pine (1974) has helped us diagnostically by looking at the disorder in terms of a spatial metaphor, and he maps out phenomena belonging to the "upper" border, the intermediate area, and the "lower" border.

At the "upper" border, there may be what looks like a neurotic conflict between drive and defense; but in addition there is obvious ego malfunctioning (with a disturbance in the reality sense and a failure in signal anxiety, so that the child becomes extremely prone to panic) as well as abnormal object relations (characterized by shifting levels, too great dependence on contact, and regression to primary identification). All these are primary developmental failures rather than secondary regressions, but the line between the two is not always clear.

In the intermediate area, the phenomena are variable and may be subsumed under the rubric of chronic ego deviance. Thus, they retain their primary omnipotence, their magical thinking, and their governance by the pleasure principle, and fail to develop age-adequate defenses and synthetic function (Weil, 1953). Because they lack these basic stabilizers, they are unable to respond reliably and predictably to internal and external events.

One of the most dramatic aspects of the syndrome in fact is the shifting levels of ego organization based on the fluidity of the ego structure (Ekstein and Wallerstein, 1954). The oscillations are from reality to fantasy, from near-autistic unrelatedness or symbiosis to true object-relations, and from the earliest level to the latest levels of personality development, all seen in kaleidescopic succession. Basically, these children seem to have failed in establishing a solid hierarchy in their ego states and functions, in their object relations, and in their drive organization.

While Schmideberg (1964) refers to them as "stably unstable," Pine sees them as "predictably unpredictable." As he says, these children "are often children from homes where child neglect or abuse, violence, psychosis, prostitution, addiction, and the like, usually in combination, are the setting of daily life." Because they often make such rapid gains when hospitalized, he feels that the grossest forms of their pathology are reactive—massive stress reactions, explosive releases of tension, or despairing withdrawals. Thus it would seem that an appreciable part of the internal disorganization is a response to the external disorganization of the environment, and this has been my observation as well in relation to the impact of psychosis on the developing child (Anthony, 1969, 1970). Related to this is the incomplete internalization of psychosis where the love object is a psychotic parent. All these "intermediate" factors lead to a marked stunting of development associated with the severe ego limitation. There is a limitation in thinking, in learning, in feeling, and even in perceiving, so that the children are often unresponsive, withdrawn, isolated and completely lacking in curiosity and exploratory drive. Many of them become chronically suspicious, mistrustful, and even "paranoid."

On the "lower" border the phenomena are often very close to the psychotic with the use of quite primitive ego mechanisms, poor reality testing, and very peculiar behavior.

Like other clinicians, I am often left bewildered by the borderliner's facile ability to slide up and down the scale of reality. The moment we think that we have put salt on its neurotic tail and caught it, it suddenly eludes us and becomes strangely alien and psychotiform in its characteristics; the moment we are ready to make a psychotic diagnosis with conviction, we are confronted by an almost normal or neurotic child who, however, as we learn from bitter experience, continues to remain "stably unstable" and "predictably unpredictable." This is the certain uncertainty that the clinician must live with. It is confusing and disconcerting, but also compelling and challenging.

When one hears the language of the borderline child, one is sometimes haunted by its archaic quality, which resonates into the very unconscious aspects of our own lives. It is not enough to say that it is primary process thinking or prelogical activity, and that since we meet with it in mythology and since we should all be good mythologists as part of our professional lives, the arcaneness should not surprise us. Let me remind you, for example, of a myth—an Eskimo one—coming from the Bering Strait and dealing with cosmological problems. This is how it is told:

> Long ago, a man and his wife lived in a village on the coast. They had two children, a boy and a girl. When the children grew up, the boy fell in love with his sister. He pursued her unceasingly with his attentions, so she finally took refuge in the sky, where she became the moon. Ever since then the boy has never stopped pursuing her in the form of the sun. Sometimes he catches up with her and manages to embrace her, thus causing an eclipse of the moon.
>
> The sister in her anger deprived her brother of food and offered him instead her severed breast. "You wanted me last night, so I have given you my breast. If you desire me, eat me!" But the boy refused. The woman rose into the sky where she became the sun. He changed into the moon and pursued her but was never able to catch her. The moon, being without food, waned slowly away through starvation until it was quite lost from sight. So the sun reached out and fed it from the dish in which the girl had placed her breast.
>
> After the moon is fed and gradually brought to the full, it is then permitted to starve again, so producing the waxing and waning every month.

Not only does this myth establish links between incest, cannibalism, oral sadism, and animism, but the eloquent metaphors of the myth speak at all levels—unconscious, preconscious, and conscious. Mythic thought draws its raw material from the world outside and the world inside, and there is a participation between the two experiences. As we become sophisticated and logical and synthetic in our formulations, we begin to maintain an adequate distance between the internal personal myth and its various multiplicity of levels and the corrective and collective experiences from the outside. Once the myth remains internalized, personal, idiosyncratic, and privately formulated, it is hard for anyone to penetrate the semantics of meaning; only then can we fit it into some figurative interpretation and attempt to claim an explanatory role for it.

Thanks to our understanding of myths, we have discovered that metaphors are based on an intuitive sense of logical relationships between one realm and another, and that the metaphor reintegrates the first realm with the totality of the others in spite of the fact that reflective thought struggles constantly to separate them. Metaphor, therefore, far from being a decoration that is added to language, purifies it and restores it to its original nature. It may sound hyperbolic and rhetorical, but when taken in its entirety within the life space of the person, it seems curiously isomorphic with him.

As a great mythologist, Freud intuitively understood the new language of psychiatry that he introduced to the world. He realized that these divided patients were communicating facts of inner life that often constituted a matrix of meanings, which in part were generated by the minds of the patients involved and in part reflected an inner image of the world already inherent in the structure of the mind. Freud reminded us, as did Levi-Strauss, that in dealing with primitive phenomena and production, we must first examine the raw material from nature, before we prepare to "cook" it, always realizing that "cooking" transforms the natural ingredients and makes them artificial.

I have concentrated on language because Ekstein, whose chapters follow, is not only a student of language and trained by some of the greatest linguists on the continent, but he also tends to use metaphor and mythology in presenting his intricately contrived thought. To understand what the patient is trying to tell us in his own idiomatic form is the first duty of the clinician. Thus, bringing the primitive and modern worlds together in these communications does help us make sense of what was once regarded as lunatic nonsense. In all this, we must keep in mind Freud's dictum that there are no final scientific truths and that the scientific mind does not so much provide the right answers as ask the right questions. Furthermore, not all the solutions we put forward in these presentations will have equal value, but our aim is toward a better knowledge of the thought processes and mechanisms involved. So what can one say about a child who is never the same child; who goes his own peculiar way irrespective of circumstance; who lags behind in some ways and seems forward in others; whose behavior is marked by fluctuations; who does not know how to deal with people either inside or outside him; and who apparently experiences the universe in a Pascalian-Kierkegaardian manner, as remote, terrifying, and inexplicable?

To understand his strange idiosyncrasy, one must try and understand him developmentally, in terms of a vulnerable infant being reared unhelpfully, inconsistently, and disturbingly by those around him. To achieve autonomy from external stimulation, a baby must learn, in an ambience of relative security, the attributes of his environment and the changes to be expected from it in the way of unfamiliar demands and displays. With adequate support, he can then cope with an increasingly wider range of novel experiences. To achieve autonomy from internal stimulation (drive tensions and distress in general), he must learn to develop a pattern of reciprocal relations with care-taking people and thereby develop internal mechanisms for controlling these inner pressures. Thus, he can be overwhelmed in two ways: by too much from the outside or by too much from the inside. When he is faced with too much from the outside—stimuli that are too strong or too strange for him to assimilate—he withdraws and gradually learns to respond by avoidance. He turns into himself. When faced with internal distresses that rise above the limits of his threshold of tolerance, he develops what Winnicott has termed unnameable, "unthinkable anxiety"—the feeling that one is falling to pieces, losing one's supports, lacking direction, and unable to relate to oneself, one's body, or others. The average concerned mother can do a great deal to diminish these feelings, but often they seem to overpower her as well, especially when she has been unable to deal with them in herself. Her only recourse, then, seems to be to identify projectively with the infant and thereby to impede the process of differentiation. As a final result, the child does not develop an outer sense of safety and an inner sense of security, an outer feeling of an ever caring presence and an inner feeling of having his needs met when they arise. Without these inner and outer assurances, the child emerges with a peculiar state of "skinlessness" that makes him a constant prey to the perpetual internal and external stresses to which he is subjected.

It is at some early point along these developmental lines that the borderline propensity must begin, but we do not as yet know what are the specific responsible factors. We are also ignorant of the practices conducing to healthy development since we have learned that there are children who seem to thrive on adversity and become precociously self-sufficient where other children succumb. A definition of a good enough mother is one who is flexible enough to learn that there may be different prescriptions for different babies and who acts accordingly. Chess et al. (1965) have suggested that there may also be a constitutional mismatching between mother and child that leads to exaggerated tension states with which neither can cope. Under such conditions, both mother and baby lose confidence in her mothering, and a mutual dissatisfaction and expectation of disappointment is engendered, so that a core of ambivalence is set up within both partners. The borderline condition may be one outcome when this happens.

We have spoken of borderline phenomena that run the gamut from overwhelming rage to a loss of relatedness, loss of identity, and isolation. The mechanisms to deal with these are so limited and so primitive—splitting, massive denial, acting out, projection and introjection, withdrawal and regression—that very little self and object constancy can evolve. What does the child experience under such conditions? What is the phenomenology of the borderline state? It would take a borderline genius to describe the subjective aspect of this disorder adequately. One such genius, Virginia Woolf, gives us some notion of what the borderline child and adolescent has to endure. Her anxiety over discontinuity and fragmentation was matched by her attempts to depict unity. She spoke of having "never been able to become part of life, as if the world was complete and I was outside of it being blown forever outside the loop of time. Other people seemed to live in a real world but I often fell down into nothingness. I have to bang my head against some hard door to call myself back to the body." (Bell, 1972.)

The patients in *The Divided Self* (Laing, 1970) describe less articulately the feelings of merging with or being engulfed by the outside world. The oneness would result in a strange terror at the loss of identity and fusion of self. Yet what was dreaded most was also most longed for. One patient described how if she stared long enough at the environment, she would blend with it and disappear, while another explained that she had to die to keep from dying.

These are the paradoxes of this betwixt and between world, the pulls from the upper and lower borders, one way drawing the patient toward normality, conflict, and identity, and the other way leading toward madness. What better term is there to describe the borderline case than Darwin's "inosculate"?

I talked at the beginning of the first use of the term "borderline," and now I want to say something about what must be the first account of a borderline child in the psychiatric literature. By this time, we have ceased to be surprised by Freud's clinical acumen, his range of clinical experience, and his anticipation of later clinical developments. In the course of analyzing the case of the Wolf Man between the years 1910–14, he furnished us, according to Blum (1974), with a dramatic and vivid account of this strange diagnostic condition. In proposing this thesis, Blum makes a number of telling points:

1. The Wolf Man's borderline childhood evolved into a borderline adolescence and adulthood, emphasizing the continuity in psychopathology.

2. The Wolf Man's borderline childhood was the basis of his subsequent vulnerability to uncontrolled regression.

3. The Wolf Man's "childhood paranoia" would now, in its essentials, be appraised as a borderline condition, so that one would anticipate in this case, correctly, that there would be a paranoid core to the adult borderline state. (The persecutory anxieties were very much in evidence throughout childhood and adolescence.) After his nightmare at the age of four, he could not bear to be looked at and would scream if he felt a fixed stare. "Why do you stare at me like that?" he would cry. (Later he was erythrophobic and obsessed hypersensitively with his nose and skin, and still later his social anxiety pushed him further into seclusion.)

4. The borderline constellation described by Freud during childhood included attacks of panic, fantasies of torture, screaming reactions, and uncontrolled, flooding rages, suggestive of an anlage of ego deviation (Weil, 1953). In adult life, the ego deficiency manifested itself in narcissistic sensitivity, detachment, disturbed object relations, affective impoverishment, poor impulse control, and a tendency to severe regressive response. At times, however, the neurotic elements appeared to be more prominent than the borderline ones, but there seems never to have been a period when he was totally asymptomatic.

5. Although Freud had been preoccupied with the significance of the primal scene and was making original discoveries about it, there was no

doubt that he was also aware of the Wolf Man's disturbed sense of reality in his childhood. Had he had all the clinical material that subsequently emerged in the later analysis, he might have seen this childhood state "as a template and model of the Wolf Man's adult paranoia" (Blum), and detected the "paradigmatic infantile prototype of paranoia" at three and a half to four years of age—"taking offense on every occasion, raging like a lunatic," with ideas of reference, distrust, and a merger of nightmare and reality. He would have seen how the preoedipal influence molded the oedipal conflicts of the borderline personality.

REFERENCES

Anthony, E.J. (1969) A clinical evaluation of children with psychotic parents. *Am. J. Psychiatry*, 126(2):177–186.

—— (1970) The influence of maternal psychosis on children—folie à deux. In *Parenthood*, E.J. Anthony and T. Benedek, eds. Boston: Little, Brown, pp. 571–598.

Bell, Quentin (1972) *Virginia Woolf*. New York: Harcourt Brace Jovanovich.

Blum, H.P. (1974) The borderline childhood of the Wolf Man. *J. Am. Psychoanal. Assn.*, 22(4):721–742.

Chess, S., Thomas, A., and Birch, H. (1965) *Your Child Is a Person*. New York: Viking Press.

Darwin, C. (1832) Letters to John Henslow, Nov. 24.

—— (1836) Notebooks.

Ekstein, R., and Wallerstein, J. (1954) Observations on the psychology of borderline and psychotic children. *The Psychoanalytic Study of the Child*, 9:344. New York: International Universities Press.

Grinker, R.S., Sr. (1975) Neurosis, psychosis and the borderline states. In *Comprehensive Textbook of Psychiatry*, Vol. 2. A.M. Friedman, H.I. Kaplan, and B.J. Sadock, eds. Baltimore: Williams and Wilkins.

——, Werble, B., and Drye, R.C. (1968) *The Borderline Syndrome*. New York: Basic Books.

Hughes, C. (1884) Borderline psychiatric records. *Alien & Neurol.*, 5:85.

Kernberg, O. (1967) Borderline personality organization. *J. Am. Psychoanal. Assn.*, 15:641.

Laing, R.D. (1970) *The Divided Self*. Baltimore: Penquin, p. 73.

Pine, F. (1974) On the concept of "borderline" in children. *The Psychoanalytic Study of the Child*, Vol. 29. New Haven: Yale University Press.

Rosse, J.C. (1890) Clinical evidence of borderline insanity. *J. Nerv. Ment. Dis.*, 17:669.

Schmideberg, M. (1967) The borderline patient. In *The American Handbook of Psychiatry*, S. Arieti, ed. New York: Basic Books, pp. 398–418.

Weil, A. (1953). Certain severe disturbances of ego development in childhood. *The Psychoanalytic Study of the Child*, 8:271–287. New York: International Universities Press.

Chapter 13

The Concept of Borderline: A Fresh Perspective

RUDOLF EKSTEIN

You must all take it for granted that as someone who has worked for many years with borderline children and adolescents, I know what the term "borderline" signifies. I should therefore start this chapter with a confession in the manner of St. Augustine four centuries ago. He was once asked to speak of the concept of time, and his answer carried all the scholastic subtlety that was so habitual with this great doctor of the Church: Whenever someone asked him what time was, he indeed knew, but when he was further invited to define time, he no longer knew. He was differentiating between the recognizable and the definable. I can recognize a borderline child as surely as any experienced clinician, and I can offer clinical reasons to justify my recognition, but when I am asked to define what I mean by "borderline," I become curiously uncertain. I am not alone in this attitude. There is a superabundance of literature about borderline cases that can make us rapidly familiar with the phenomenology presented by individuals so diagnosed, but the concept remains as elusive as ever, and I find myself able to approach it most helpfully through a series of similes.

The term "border" or "borderline" is one of those everyday words that have been borrowed by psychology and imbued with an esoteric nuance. In order to fully appreciate the psychological connotation, it is helpful to return to the original sense of the term. According to Webster's dictionary, "border" refers to the boundary or part adjacent to a limiting line; "edge" refers to the limiting line itself; and "margin," to the strip adjacent to the limiting line and more or less clearly defined by some distinguishing feature. "Borderline" is more specifically related to what is acceptable, valid, or normal, and hence has a questionable or indefinite status. According to the dictionary, one may speak of a "borderer" as someone occupying this marginal or borderline area. Geographically, we can therefore refer to the border between two countries, and politically, there are borders that can be crossed or not crossed, or crossed only with the sanction of passports or visas. Among the free nations, for example, one has the option of crossing at will, whereas crossing behind the "iron curtain" can be fraught with problems or difficulties.

Another border is that between sleeping and waking states, which people cross every day of their lives. Once again, however, there is a borderline state in which the individual is half awake and half asleep and may experience hypnogogic or hypnopompic hallucinations. Under such borderline conditions, thinking is dominated by primary process; the same is true when the mind comes under the influence of drugs, alcoholic, or traumatic experiences, when the generally easy transition between mental states may be interrupted as we linger in a borderline condition. Nevertheless, for most of us most of the time, there is an option to cross from the land of dreams, fantasy, and fairy tale into the land of everyday wakeful life. Those who cannot effect this crossing easily and comfortably and retain options of crossing back and forth can be identified as borderers, marginal people, or borderline personalities.

What I am suggesting here, therefore, is that we all have borderline experiences from time to time from which we "recover" completely, and it is these experiences that allow the clinician to identify borderline phenomena, to recognize borderline cases, to empathize with them during treatment, and thus to be in a position to help them. Being able to help them, however, does not guarantee that we can understand why they remain stuck in this type of adjustment, although a few of us who have had the misfortune to be borderers are in a better position to appreciate the problem of living in this mode, and it may not be entirely fortuitous that I myself have specialized in treating these cases.

When I go to Europe these days, I carry an American passport that allows me immediate access to my native country of Austria as well as immediate egress when I want to leave it and return to the United States. It was not always so. Forty years ago, in 1938, I had an Austrian passport that permitted me to leave the country but not to return. Before I left my native country I tried to learn as much English as I could, because the problem involved in crossing borders is that the language changes, and unless you learn the new language, the problems of adjustment become more difficult. This second language, however, never quite replaces the mother tongue, and there are many feelings, perhaps our deepest feelings, that one cannot express in the new language. There was one phrase that sank into my mind when I attempted to master idiomatic English, and this was "to sigh with relief." My friends, who had to stay behind, promised me that when I crossed the border from Germany into Belgium and became free and no longer persecuted, I would say out loud to myself, "I sigh with relief." When I came to the border, I completely forgot the phrase, and instead recalled in an obsessive way another that I had learned from the great German-Jewish poet Heine, who died in exile. The words that haunted me were, "The giant touched mother earth again and his strength grew anew." As I continued through Belgium, I realized not only that had I forgotten the phrase "I sigh with relief," but that I had not even felt like sighing with relief, for the reason that my thoughts were concerned not with going into exile but with returning home. Heine had smuggled himself from Paris back into Germany, where he was forbidden to be and where he was sure to be arrested, and yet he felt as if contact with his native soil gave him new strength. Like him I wanted, in the deepest part of myself, to go back, not to go forward, and to return to my mother tongue, the language of my parents, and not to speak the English language. I could not, therefore, sigh with relief, because I wanted to go back, but what did I want to go back to? To a state of chaos where a year later all my relatives were to be burned and killed. It appeared almost as if I wanted to go back to a psychotic state because there was spoken primarily the process language that I had learned as child. It was almost as if I was being asked to forget the early years of my life in the way that children are sometimes forbidden to read fairy tales because of the likelihood of becoming immersed in unreality.

For a few years, then, after crossing the border, I was an interesting borderline type (what Kurt Lewin referred to as a "marginal man" and Levi-Strauss called the "amputated man")—uprooted, disoriented, confused between my internal and my external loyalties, and unable to express myself. I could not talk German, because that was the language of the enemy, and yet that was also the language that I loved most, particularly in the form of the Viennese dialect of my childhood. It took twenty-five years before I stopped being a borderline case and once more carried a passport that allowed me to move freely between the country of my origin and the country of my adoption without apprehension or embarrassment. I lecture in both countries to the same kind of professional groups interested in families with the same kind of clinical difficulties, with one difference: In this country I talk English with a Viennese accent, and in Vienna I talk Viennese with American overtones and idioms.

I am offering the nonclinical illustration to give you some idea of how much work and pain is involved in trying to find a way forward or a way back, in trying to speak and express onself in two different languages, and to empathize with the predicament of those without a valid passport to cross and recross borders.

Let me offer you still another analogy from everyday nonclinical life: In Los Angeles I live in an area where there are many different kinds of people speaking many different native languages. In fact, there seem to be very few people who are actually born in Los Angeles and claim American English as their mother tongue. About a hundred miles to the south is the Mexican border with its own remarkable border traffic. As one crosses from one to the other, one moves from one culture to a completely different one, politically, socially, and economically. The "border-crossers" vary themselves considerably: Some are crossing for sightseeing, some for vacationing, some for legitimate business, and some for illegitimate business, those who lack immigration papers and are attempting to enter the United States to escape the unemployment and poverty and general misery of their country. So great is the pressure that sends them over the border that even when these illegal immigrants are caught and sent back, they return over and over again. These so-called wetbacks who cross "under the nets" are always in danger, as are the smugglers who traffic in drugs. They disguise themselves, they forge their papers, and they try and find unguarded areas where they can jump the border.

All these analogies should inform you by this time that the clinical borderline situation varies in its etiology, its phenomenology, its history, and its outcome. It is obviously not possible to describe a "typical" case or to give a concise definition, even though we are always in the position to recognize the borderline situation. The critical factor differentiating the groups lies in the options that are open to them. Some are free to cross and recross; some may cross but not recross, and some may not be able to cross at all. At this point, I would like to replace the social and political metaphors with a psychological one, and to think no longer of Austria and Belgium or Mexico and the United States but of the "countries" in our minds and of different states of mind. In the healthy individual, one can cross and recross the borders between different mental states as if one had an inner passport that allows us to think in terms of fantasy or reality at will. You will note that although I am a psychoanalyst, I am creating here a set of metaphors that in many respects I find more useful than the conventional language of psychoanalysis derived from structural theory, since it allows me greater flexibility in describing the fluctuating borderline states. The borders between the id, ego, and superego are not quite clearly established, and when borders themselves are shifting or indeterminate, one cannot be sure at any time where one is with respect to the borderline. Returning for a moment to our political metaphor, there were never any clear boundries during the American Civil War or during the war in Vietnam or during the Cold War apparently existing between Israel and Egypt; in these a "no man's land" came into being. Anyone who enters such an area finds himself neither on one side nor the other, and may in fact be struck by bullets from either side. I would like to suggest that in the inner mind of people with borderline disorders, there is no strict differentiation between the primary and secondary processes. When we are in this no man's land, the fantasy expressed may be delusional or a normal rehearsal for action; and the play one observes may be normal or psychotically determined.

You will notice that I have made the problem of border crossing more complicated by pointing out that the border may itself be variable and that borders themselves may be in a state of flux, as in the political world when border wars are being fought. Similarly the border between fantasy and reality may alter, and children may suffer from borderline conditions; in such children, the fairy tale may carry some danger in that it may conduce unpredictably to either regressive or progressive states. There do not seem to be the same options open to them as there are to the normal child who can move from reality into fantasy without the danger of becoming stuck. When interviewing the borderline child, one is never certain whether they are in the office with you or in Wonderland with Alice or in the Land of Oz with Dorothy. (Another version of this is contained in the clinical joke that normal people build castles in the air, neurotics furnish them, and psychotics live in them; one might perhaps add that the borderliners are guests in them from time to time?) With regard to passports, the situations described in the political metaphor correspond roughly to the conditions existing psychologically: Healthy people have "inner passports" that allow them to cross and recross different mental states; psychotics have passports which do not seem to be able to get them back, while borderline individuals have passports that do seem to get them back, but often with considerable difficulty.

In dealing with the treatment of borderline conditions, it is necessary for the therapist to develop skills to get the patient back once he has crossed the border into unreality. He has to recognize, in the first instance, that the issue of the "inner passport" in such cases is fraught with problems.

Let me bring you back again for a moment to the political metaphor: When I crossed the border from Germany into Belgium, I knew I could not go back, but I also knew that this was not because of something to do with me. My passport had been externally imposed upon me by an oppressive government. It took years for that government to lose the war and many more years for the new government to rebuild it and to make it possible for me to revisit it freely with my new passport. The problem of my passport was not my inner problem. Psychologically speaking, the borderline child has a passport that is an inner problem. He has an incomplete passport that does not seem to function adequately, as if there was a visa missing. In order to help him, we have to put a visa into that passport that allows him then to enter and return.

To accomplish this is by no means easy from a therapeutic point of view, since what may be a friendly overture to a neurotic child may be unbelievably anxiety arousing in the child who is borderline. I left Austria as a poor refugee who could not go back. Years later, it took not only an American passport but also a friendly overture from the Austrians to get me to go back. Clinically, one has to learn how to make a friendly overture with a borderline child that is acceptable and not intimidating. One has to learn about the correct approach behavior so that the child is sufficiently reassured to feel that he has a passport with a visa that allows him to come back. The therapist must learn not only what brings the child into contact with him but also what drives the child away into fantastic, obsessional, or psychotic behavior.

For some children, the inner passport would represent an accomplishment of finding an object to which they can relate again. Whether the object is experienced as positive or hateful is the crucial problem. For example, I recall a case of a thirteen-year-old who sometimes saw the therapist as the lost mother, sometimes as the dangerous father who should be killed, sometimes as a figure upon whom to project all his good and bad feelings, and sometimes as a real person with his own reality. All this was regardless of what the therapist said or did and was a function of what analysts refer to as "transference."

The same transferences, affecting attachment and separation behavior, occur to teachers. Some children become extremely frightened by the most innocuous teachers, and some teachers are treated by some children with lavish praise and affection, even though they themselves are aware of nothing that they have done to deserve all this.

In order to figure out the kind of inner passport possessed by a child, one needs to study the type of bonding that occurs. The opportunity for observation is available every day as the child separates himself from home and attaches himself to school and then later on repeats this in reverse order. For the normal child, the situation, after some common initial anxieties, comes naturally, but nothing seems to come naturally for borderline children. Such children often want to be left alone with their private fantasies, and this limits their contact with other people. Underlying this wish to be left alone is a terrible fear, more devastating than any fearfulness experienced by the normal child. The latter's social relationships may fluctuate: Sometimes he may be shy and sometimes brazen; sometimes he makes friends easily and sometimes keeps himself aloof; sometimes he is depressed and apathetic and disinclined for activity; and sometimes he is trusting, while at other times he may be suspicious. The past history of acceptances and rejections determines to a large extent how the child deals with approaches and separations.

With borderline children, on the other hand, the reactions are invariably unpredictable and extraordinary. A borderline child may crawl onto our laps one day and ask to be told a fairy tale, but the very next day he may be consumed with terror. In another instance, as soon as the child has attached himself to the therapist in an interview, he is able to talk realistically about himself and his problems, but when the moment of leave-taking comes, panic sets in and he becomes instantly delusional.

The movie *The Wizard of Oz* may be regarded as a remarkable metaphor about psychological treatment. As Dorothy follows along the Yellow Brick Road full of fear, hope, and wonder and accompanied by a variety of creatures, all afflicted with some basic complaint, she and they together search for the magic possessed by the wizard, only to find in the end that behind the mystery of the wizard is the quintessence of ordinariness, with solutions to problems that seem far from magical.

Treatment with the borderline child is full of magical expectations, and he can languish for long periods in the Land of Oz. Unlike the normal child, he never spells out the conditions of encounter, and it may take a great deal of tact and intuition on the part of those who work with him in the process of matching their approach to that of the child. One must not be overwhelming, and yet one must not remain too distant. Can one, for example, reach out and touch the hand of such a child, or would this be understood in terms of some horrendous fantasy?

Our problem, as therapists, is to find out the right conditions of approach so that, psychologically speaking, the touching becomes acceptable. When dealing with these patients, the therapist must be constantly aware of approach and separation behavior: How do I approach the child and how does he approach me? How do I leave the child and how does he leave me? Can I let him go and can he let me go?

During the hour, the most important question is how to maintain the optimal distance needed by the child. How does one discover the optimal distance? In this context, Freud was found of quoting Schopenhauer's account of the porcupines' dilemma: In order not to freeze to death, they moved closer together, but when they did this their quills caused them mutual pain, and so they would move apart only to be driven together by the cold. The presumption was that they found the optimal distance that allowed them to survive.

This is precisely the human condition: In every relationship, we must be close enough for warmth and affection and yet far enough away for identity and autonomy to be preserved. With borderline children, the dilemma is more agonizing and the optimal distance much more difficult to establish. I must remind you again that we need to know not only their conditions but our own conditions for contact, and we must learn to modify our own conditions within the service of the treatment.

The issue of optimal distance is basic to all treatment of children whether we are educational therapists or therapeutic educators. We have to learn how to bring about the necessary closeness so that the therapeutic influence can be exercised, and we also have to learn how to bring about the necessary separation so that termination can be orderly and acceptable. Each borderline child that comes to us is different because his inner passport is different, and with them, more than with any other patient, we have to know how to bring (the approach), to be in contact (the optimal distance), and how to end (the separation). Not only is every borderline child different in all these respects, but he himself is unpredictably different at different stages of the process.

One of the pioneer psychoanalysts, Simmel, once claimed that all we needed to do was to listen to our children and that they would tell us what is good for them. It may be true that we should listen to them very carefully, but on the other hand, we should never give up the position that as adults or therapists, we do know to an appreciable extent what is good for them. It may be true that sometimes we will learn from them, but we also want them to sometimes learn from us.

I like to think of therapy as a two-way process, a struggle between two people, both "porcupines" in many respects and both responsible for how they can get together. Keeping in mind this two-way process, one should speak not only of the borderline child but also of the borderline teacher or of the borderline therapist, because when it comes to this type of child, our techniques are just as "borderline" as is the child's mind. When we start, we do not know what is going on; we find out very slowly, and we adjust ourselves and our techniques to what we find out. Not only does the child sometimes need to borrow an inner passport from us, but we ourselves need an inner passport in order to reach out to him. Yet we may not even know what to put into the passport or where to apply for it, but we can try to find out. The best way to apply for a passport, if we want to reach these borderline children, is to listen to them, to learn from them, and to help them learn from us.

In fact, I think that we should give up thinking about the borderline child or adolescent, and consider instead the borderline process, which I have previously compared to an encounter between two porcupines. In the process, one may discover limitations on both sides: The therapist may not know how to reach the child or the child may not be able to be reached. There are therapists who cannot reach borderline children, and it is wise for them to find this out as early as possible and not waste their own precious time and that of the patient. The language of the borderline child is far too difficult to learn for those who have no talent for primary-process thinking for the reason that they abandoned it too completely in the process of growing up. In working with borderline children (as with children in general), one needs to be "bilingual," that is, one must be able to think in both secondary and primary-process modes, to speak through the medium of play and symbolism, and to understand the uses of "acting out." Many adults and adult therapists find this "bilingualism" an impossible task to master.

In the language that I have developed for this presentation, the problem that these very disturbed children present is that they have no inner passport and therefore no inner capacity to go from one language to another and from one emotional state to another and back. In this context, children without inner passports are children at risk. Therapists who can work with these children can be thought of as having "diplomatic passes," in that they can travel freely backward and forward without hindrance and the children they treat can share in this privilege. Can this "bilingualism" be taught? To some extent, yes. What must also be learned and tolerated are the endless disappointments that accompany treatment, the sudden and severe regressions that may occur at any time, and the very small therapeutic gains that seem to be made. Perhaps if the therapist is in supervision and has someone with whom he can discuss these setbacks, or if the therapist is in analysis himself and can learn to what extent he has contributed to the setbacks, it may help.

In ending this presentation, in which I have tried to define the many different meanings of the term "borderline," I would like to say a few words about the experience of treating a borderline child. In the play space created by the therapist and the child, they begin to communicate with each other in the language of play. One can think of the play space as a stage from which a drama is going to unfold. If the patient is neurotic, the drama tends to unfold in a meaningful sequential manner that is gradually understood more and more by both the patient and the therapist. When the patient is borderline, on the other hand, what happens is different but also very interesting. It is reminiscent of a development in the theater that has recently taken place, in which the actors enter the stage in front of an audience in search of their characters, and only then do they decide by a process of argument who should play what. In the course of doing this, the whole nature of the play undergoes a change. In the case of one particular borderline child, it was clear that he knew that in order to put on a play it required a cast of characters. In his therapeutic sessions covering many months, he would spend each hour establishing his cast of characters, but by the time the cast was established, the session would be over and no play or action would have ensued. As time went on, he turned his attention to the scenery and the accessories which he would need for the play. By the end of the year (and one can imagine how bored and impatient the audience would be by this time, and perhaps the therapist as well if he was inexperienced and new to the borderline game!), there was a cast of a king, queen, and their son, and the son had a knife, and the therapist was wondering whether the child had read *Oedipus Rex*! But the curtain falls, the session is over, the cast is all on stage, complete with accessories, and there is still no plot. It is beyond the capacity of this borderline boy to begin the action and unfold the plot. What he brings to us is a *tableau vivant*, the frozen portrait of the cast, an instant of the process, a dream image, the rest of which is beyond his reach and beyond his recall. He stops at the border. He has no passport for the borderguard. Can the therapist help him to obtain one?

Chapter 14

Play Space and the Borderline Child

RUDOLF EKSTEIN

When we work with children therapeutically, we need to ask ourselves before we begin whether the play space or play equipment is suitable for what we have to do. We find the need to alter them strategically according to the age of the child, the sex of the child and the disorder that provokes the referral for treatment. I will illustrate the changing play space and its contents during a disturbed development, and the adaptation of the therapeutic play space for the needs of the patient, by citing the case history of a fifteen-year-old adolescent boy whose referral itself constituted a further trauma in a much traumatized life.

I received a call from his father following an urgent message he had received from his wife—whom he had divorced a year previously and who had moved to California with her son and his younger sister—that the boy had begun to steal. His thefts were at first from his mother's purse, but then he took to robbing other people.

Divorce plays havoc with the play space of children, and not surprisingly, my patients for many years have been exclusively children of divorce. When the divorce is associated with battles over alimony and child support, the disruption is even greater; this was so with this family. Before the rupture, they had lived in the Midwest in very well-to-do circumstances. The father had been employed by his own extremely wealthy father and consequently shared in the general affluence. When the mother and the two children moved to Los Angeles, their standard of living sank to modest middle-class proportions. The mother had lost the court battle for larger amounts of support, since her ex-husband could prove that he received only a very modest salary from his father. She deeply resented this blatant legal maneuver to deprive her and her children of a life style to which they were entitled. As is usual, the children became pawns in the parental game, resulting in conflicts of loyalty. According to mother, their father was depriving, and according to father, the mother was indulgent and infantilizing. The father refused the demands of the children on the basis that he simply could not meet them, and pointed out to his son that he was now old enough to take a small job. In his opinion, the children would have been better off in every way living with him.

Following the stealing episodes, the mother found a psychotherapist for her son and now pressured the father to support the cost of treatment. The therapist understood the boy's symptoms as a reaction to the deprivation imposed by the father, and he in turn put pressure on the father to increase the boy's allowance substantially so that he could associate with his wealthy peers in Beverly Hills without shame. As a preliminary, he suggested that the father buy his son an expensive car, in keeping with the boy's social status. Unless he could function on a level with the others, he could not go out to parties, on dates, etc. The therapist's suggestion was so much at variance with standard therapeutic procedures that I thought that the most fruitful contribution I could make would be to work with him, help him to resolve his identification with the mother, and perhaps try to build a therapeutic bridge between him and his patient. At this particular time, he appeared to be functioning as an extension of the mother in her determination to force the father to increase supplies. Neither of them saw that the boy's real problem lay in separating from both parents and moving toward an identity of his own at this stage of his development.

Before I could implement these good intentions of seeing the boy and consulting with the therapist, the latter had written an angry letter to the father that provoked him to stop payment for the treatment and thus to stop the treatment. On the day that I was scheduled to meet with the patient, the phone rang very early in the morning; the mother informed me her son had been arrested during the night for breaking into the music room of their high school and stealing a great deal of equipment. The boy was in jail, and since this was his second or third break-in, the police would consent to let him go only for the purpose of consultation. I advised the mother to discuss the legal questions with a lawyer and to bring her son to see me at his appointed time.

Let us now discuss all these developments in terms of my overall concept of play space and its potential culmination in the therapeutic space to be established by me. His play space included Beverly Hills and its particular cultural significance, a high school for an elite group of children, the many musical groups that flourished in the neighborhood, a need for physical instruments to establish his own particular niche in this particular world, an associate to help him, his objectives, and a car. All this quite suddenly shrank to a room in the jail house and the almost complete deprivation of objects. Both parents had failed him, and so he had no one to whom he could turn.

What was to be my role? I was required to enter the situation now and to take the place of his parents, the therapist he had lost, the car that he could not afford and the musical environment that he had been trying to create for himself. It was also possible that they may have removed him from school and treated him as a felon. The question was, Could I transform this trauma of deprivation and failure therapeutically into an opportunity for growth? It required a new play space that was an acceptable substitute in the boy's mind for the one from which he came. Society was beginning to react negatively to his aspirations for conquering the musical world by whatever means he could obtain, including theft. Could I turn society's reaction into a professional response? Could I respond in such a way that a new play space would be created? Could I take the whole traumatic life sequence—the marital conflict, the breakup of the family, the struggles over custody, alimony, and child support, the move from the Midwest to California, from a starlit Midwestern community to a seductive and glamourous Western one, the continuing battle between the parents, the struggle for the loyalty of the children, the wish to find a place for himself in his new world, the delinquent act, the confrontation with the police, and finally jail—could I turn this now ingrained expectation of rejection into an experience of acceptance? How would he receive me; how would I receive him? Would he come defiantly, remorsefully, quietly, resistantly, or silently? Would he come at all?

My mind was full of uncertainty, as it always is with borderline cases. There is so little written to help one, even of what I had written myself, because each borderline child becomes a world unto himself where generalizations cease to apply. With each case one has to begin from the beginning.

Under such unusual circumstances, the therapeutic play space can quite easily become a battle space where one may wonder when one leaps whether one will come back alive. Could I alter this space to allow for a new kind of play between him and me, and a new kind of play conceived in his mind? Finally, could I bring about a radical shift in the language of his space so that he no longer needed to express himself in action (acting out), but in words, associations for discussion? One has to remember that the classical therapeutic play space is a well-defined situation appropriate for certain well-defined conditions that provoke certain well-defined interactions. In this case, I did not know as yet whether all this would apply: Whether play spaces previously used for burglary could give place to play space for therapy. If the previously dangerous play space persisted, the police would enter the case again and stop the treatment. Ruminations of this kind are part of the preconscious ideas that flit through a therapist's mind and orient him diagnostically before he makes even his first contact with the patient.

Now with the reality of the encounter: The patient came in, looking a little guilty, and slumped down in his chair with very little to say for himself. Gradually I was able to extract some sort of story from him about the theft of the musical equipment. What I realized at once was that both he and his associate were relative tyros of crime and totally incompetent in how they went about it.* If he had attended the school of Fagin, as portrayed by Dickens in *Oliver Twist*, he would undoubtedly have been a dropout! I wondered how my old teacher Aichhorn, who was an expert on deliquent acting out, would have gone about the task of making this child treatable by "neuroticizing" his delinquency and converting the thieving activity into anxiety. In my terms, the strategy would have been to turn deliquent play space into neurotic play space.

With this in mind, I asked my patient as sternly as I could why he did not come to see me before the break-in, since he knew that we had an appointment scheduled. From my point of view, he certainly had no need to demonstrate that he was in need of help, and so I let him know, with a touch of reproachfulness, that I saw no purpose for the deliquency as a cry for rescue. (Readers will note that here I was not behaving in the classical analytical style of accepting with objectivity and neutrality everything that is told. In a way I was counter-acting out purposefully as an initial therapeutic move.)

The boy clearly understood what I wanted to convey to him: that if he had seen me before the break-in, there would have been no need for a break-in. He said with some share of remorse, "I guess I should have come to see you." Furthermore, if he had come to see me before the break-in, he might even have done a better job at it without being caught, since the way he and his friend had gone about it was utterly incompetent. All this was said with great seriousness on my part since I was in no way trying to tease him. He saw that he was under enormous pressure, and I knew that in this case I had to play for all or nothing. Either I would draw him into a therapeutic orbit or I would fail him. At this moment, my internal support came from Aichhorn, whom I had internalized for many years previously.†

I then said to him that stealing was not one of his accomplishments and that perhaps there were other things that he could do much better. He then

----

*Aichhorn, who had some early delinquent experiences of his own to fall back upon, not infrequently confronted young delinquents with their ineptness. They were no good being bad!

†There were other inner figures out of the past who might have caused me to hesitate. Anna Freud endorsed Aichhorn's special skills with delinquent children and approved of what he tried to do with them. Her own classical posture, equidistant between the ego, the superego, and the id, was heuristically and technically correct for the neurotic phase. My patient clearly required a different analytic posture with regard to the opening gambit, one that was far more precarious in operation.

went on to tell me that he was a good vaulter and that he had been on the school team. This immediately rang a bell in my memory, and I suddenly remembered a newspaper cutting on my desk that I had treasured, recording that my son had won his high school competition for vaulting. Again I did something that broke all the classical rules, and once again I must ask you to remember that I was under great pressure with this case: I called my patient's attention to the cutting and asked him if he knew why this particular boy found it quite unnecessary to steal. He shook his head, and so I told him that this boy, my son, wanted to be number one in vaulting and earn a gold medal for himself. Would he like something like that for himself?

So this is how we started this crucial interview. I began by identifying with the thief in him, criticizing him for his lack of skill but not scolding him for the crime. He in turn was then able to identify with my son, the gold-medal winner for vaulting, and to succeed in the same way. Thus, the precarious working alliance was established by provoking a remote transference longing of a rejected and rejecting boy who had given up the search for an understanding parent and had concluded that love must be stolen rather than earned. The therapeutic contract insisted on the understanding that I would not intervene with his parents or with the police, but that I had enough confidence that he would settle things for himself. I would not be asking his father for a car for him, nor his mother for a key to allow him to stay out at night; nor would I protect him from the consequences of the law. All I was willing to do and able to do was to treat him, provided he wanted a psychotherapeutic experience with me. When I made this clear to him and to those concerned with him, he was put on probation and we started the treatment.

The probationary situation, the mother's anger, and the father's criticism all forced him into generating and occupying this new therapeutic play space. It was not easy to keep the parents out of this space. They forbade him to see the friend with whom he had been involved in the theft, and so he had no place to go but his own room. They also put pressure on me to be *their* surrogate. This is true for all borderline cases. The parents invariably intrude on the therapeutic play space and thus interfere with the resolution of intrapsychic conflicts. I do my best to limit this intrusion and to refrain altogether from entering their play space. I declined to intervene in their relationship with the child in this case until they explicitly asked for advice and the mother wanted to speak to me; I listened to her. I learned that the boy had hardly any contact with her or his sister. After meals, taken in silence, he would return to his room. She wondered about his isolation and what he did by himself. "What does a fifteen-year-old boy do when he locks himself in his room?" she asked, and I pondered about this but did not give her an answer, since I was not sure that I knew. I thanked her for not being intrusive; I had tried myself not to be intrusive. Thus I did not pursue the secret, since the experienced psychotherapist knows that such secrets are eventually revealed to him without his asking for them. I merely told the boy that his mother intended to find out what he did in his room. I also let him know this was his own business, just as it was his own business whether he told me anything or not.

In a few weeks, a picture of the delinquent boy causing the external upheaval had actually faded away, and a different aspect of his life, his inner life, made its appearance. He asked me whether I thought what he did by himself in his room was dangerous. He then revealed that he spent his time watching television; that a few weeks earlier (mentioning a specific date), he had fallen in love with a particular actress appearing on the screen and had become completely preoccupied with her. She filled his thoughts so completely, both at home and at school, that he even became afraid that he might go insane. Did I think, he asked me, whether it was all right to have such intense daydreams? He knew, of course, that his mother wanted him to spend time with her and his sister, but he preferred to have the love affair with the girl on the screen than to be with his mother, who constantly coerced him to write to his father for more money. This seemed to me like the American version of the Oedipus story, written in dollars. The patient eschewed the maternal pressure and instead found for himself the transitional fantasized object. He had found for himself a woman never to be met who served the purpose of helping him work out his crucial problem: How to get away from his very intrusive mother. It represented a first step in bringing this about. The television had now entered the therapeutic play space, and so he permitted me to get to know his loved one—the heroine of a spaceship adventure—and brought me photographs of her, which he himself snapped while the show was on. On one side he saw her as a wonderful woman with a lovely body and beautiful breasts, but on the other side she represented danger—an unreal being, dressed in military uniform and employed on computers. She took command when the captain left the spaceship. The puzzling aspect to her dangerousness was that she might lead him to become insane. What lay behind this anxiety? She was certainly not the kind of transitional fantasy object that an average adolescent might have chosen, but there was no doubt about the intensity of his interest, as evident in the dialogue that he created for the little shows that he put on for me and the slides that he projected upon my walls and for which I provided a projector.

In all these ways, he brought right into the therapeutic play space a touching, though concrete, simile of the therapeutic process. In the classical situation, the analyist becomes the catalytic agent for the projection of internal images, but in this special instance technology is brought in to facilitate the externalization.

As with every analyst, my interest also lay in his choice in fantasized objects and in the stereotypes with which he embellished her. For example, she gave no sign, no smile of direct encouragement, and went about her quasi-military duties in space without reference to him. Adolescents need very little external nutriment to feed their fantasies, but nevertheless, it must be hard to fall so passionately in love with a complete abstraction.

As the treatment progressed, the scripts that he developed were increasingly produced for the benefit of the analyst. Furthermore, in order to encompass his internal needs, he split his own image in the fantasy into two: In one role, he was the commander of the spaceship, and so occasionally dined and danced with his loved one; but unknown to her, he was also the lead singer in a small band that entertained the crew in its off hours at a Hollywood-type nightclub built into the spaceship. The splitting of the internal image had been programmed by him with the unconscious intention of working through his inner predicament, which involved a test of love. Was it my therapeutic task to find a way out for him in this quandary, to allow him to retain his self-esteem sufficiently for him to fall in love with himself again as a development of secondary narcissism? Could she, the fantasized lady, love him as the commander of the spaceship with an expert knowledge of computers—the professional goal that his father had in mind for him—or would she love him as a musical star—the acme of his teenage counterculture? It is usual for adolescents to carry such multiple roles in fantasy, but this particular script bordered so closely on reality that as the covert struggle continued within him, I needed to make manifest for him the intense anxiety mounting to panic that he felt at the thought of being discovered as the embodiment of both characters and that he was at the same time pretending and confessing. In one sense, he was a pretender to his father's "throne," fearful of the possibility of acceptance and rejection. The other aspect held as much anxiety: Could she love him as the thief if he confessed to her about this, now that the acting out had been transformed into therapeutic playing out?

Where were we now with this case? The play space of the delinquent boy had been gradually transformed into the fantasy space of a strange child who had no real contact with me and was apparently unable to enter into any kind of interpersonal relationship. Psychoanalysis has suggested to us that thought is experimental action; so I was able to follow the patient's thinking through the sequences of behavior and through her over and over again, but could not quite succeed in representing the essence of her reality as he conceived it. For example, he was unable to elicit even a faint smile (even a Mona Lisa smile) even though through fantasy they had become the closest of friends and she spent hours listening to him singing or dancing with him. The process, as with all transference involvements, moved slowly toward a more realistic involvement. The pains of adolescence, which all of us somewhere remember, had to do with this encroachment of reality and fantasy. The "magnificent obsession" was gently and tactfully and very slowly interpreted to him within the therapeutic play space. He remained anxious that she might discover the two parts of him and thus reject him. Her enlightenment had to proceed step by step: He furnished her with all the necessary cues until there was little doubt that she knew of his secret, but she still wanted him. This gradual process threw light on the nature and necessity of the transitional object and the accompanying transitional self. The boy was in the stage of losing his childhood objects and his childhood self and of gaining or attempting to gain new objects and a new self. We began with an angry boy who attacked his father with deprivation and desertion, who stole in order to satisfy his mother, and who now tried to involve his therapist in his actual space. He had to come to terms with these inner demands, and in order to do so he had to invent a specific fantasy as a transitional device, clothing her in dress instead of slacks, making her look more feminine, and trying to elicit a smile on her face. This was the adolescent Pygmalion at work attempting to bring life to fantasy. At the same time, he was also experimenting with different versions of his self, the acceptance of that self in therapy, and the consequent enhancement of his self-esteem.

He became increasingly spontaneous in his therapeutic play space once the issue of self-acceptance was settled and the trauma of self-rejection resolved. On one red-letter day he said to me quite unexpectedly, "I'm through with the show; I'm not going to watch it any longer!" A little later, he was able to ask me why he was so shy in school and so socially anxious that he could hardly talk to a girl. His development was continuing. He had moved away from his real mother to a closed room where he lived with a fantasized television woman; he gradually discarded the plots supplied by the medium, fabricated his own scenario, and redrew his own version of the woman to fit his needs. Now he was in the act of considering a real relationship with the girls in his school. The play space was in the state of dynamic flux. The earlier play space offered by his mother was too dangerously seductive; the transitional play space generated by treatment became eventually too unrealistic; and so he now went in search of a real play space with real flesh-and-blood girls. At this point, he made his first real date and a real person entered his life.

The concomitant external developments were in keeping with the inner changes. He was doing much better at school, and his vaulting had improved so much that he was likely to become the school champion. His real girlfriend attended his performances and admired his successes. He took a part-time job so that it was no longer necessary for him to take money from his father.

It was not surprising to me that his mother turned up at the office to pose a new problem: How could I allow him to take a part-time job when his college acceptance was at stake? His father ought to continue to pay and so allow him to concentrate on his schoolwork. I was reminded here of how flimsy the therapeutic play space actually is and how easily and frequently it can be sabotaged by the parents. For the mother, the old battle was still going on, even though her son had developed beyond that. The situation for the adolescent in the process of emancipating himself was still fraught with danger, and the therapist could by no means claim final success. The boy took a job in one of the music stores, where some other employees succeeded in getting him involved in drugs. This is a risk for all adolescents today—to enter the play space of the world governed by such uncertain and conflicting rules and values.

Although the situation is improving, the potentially traumatizing incidents do not end; the seductions, the oppressions, and the pressures continue, but what had in the past led toward pathology was now motivating toward change and mastery. He did win the school's gold medal for vaulting, and they did want him for the university team; he was offered scholarships; and he did have a job. However, the mother would still prefer him to study than to work, and the father is proud that his philosophy of the work ethic had not fallen on deaf ears. The boy is not sure whether the father is proud of him because of his needing to give less money to the mother or whether the mother was proud of him because she was demonstrating to the father how well she could do with her children without him around. There was no doubt that the boy's self-esteem, as well as his self-confidence in his competence, had risen considerably.

The work came to an end when he graduated and went on to college. Living away from home, he was free from the ill pressures while facing new challenges. It seemed the most convenient point at which to interrupt the therapy, although no adolescent therapy is ever completed to the satisfaction of all parties concerned. Better conditions, however, had been created for the second individuation, for the separation from home, for the transition from high school to college, for the changing play spaces, and for the availability of new and exciting opportunities. In the context of the play space, the analyst functioned as a transitional object and worked with a transitional self in the child to help him to reach the next stage in his development. One may wonder whether the patient made as much use of the transitional therapeutic figure as of the transitional fantasy figure; in a sense, she was another component of the transference and mirrored its vicissitudes.

At various points in this essay we have been referring implicitly to the positive aspects of trauma, of anxiety-arousing events, such as separation in the termination of treatment. If termination is well worked through, well prepared for and well understood, it will act as a growth trauma and lead to genuine individuation; if it occurs prematurely, it may very well provoke new regressions. The most positive trauma of the therapeutic experience is the belief of the therapist in his patient—in his capacity to grow, to reverse projection, to come to terms with his rage against his parent, to dissipate the acquired façade of delinquency, and to direct his thought and feelings inwardly. How permanent would one expect such changes to be? To what extent would the residual trauma prepare the psyche toward further growth and development or toward regression?

As with many serious cases at adolescence, this patient, it would seem, has been given a second chance and is preparing to leap forward once more. He has become a much esteemed vaulter who can soar into the air, come back to earth, and stand upon his own two feet; he can also fall from time to time, but get up again. Metaphorically, the same holds true: He is on his way forward and has lost the urge to retreat or mindlessly tear down all that is established. If one follows his playfulness through life, one can follow the ups and downs as he turns from his early play to a play that takes risks, to the play of delinquency and to the play of treatment. In a sense, he lost the capacity to play when he fell from grace and became delinquent. Treatment showed him the options he had and helped to restore his capacity for play. This emphasis on play (and the same point has been made by Winnicott and Erikson) can best be understood as a life activity, permeated not only by playfulness but also by seriousness. Play is the child's form of psychic work, and it is through play that one learns how to work and eventually how to make a living through work. The first play of this patient was a total risk; one could not predict whether any good would come of it or whether he would leap in such a way that he would be unable to make a life of it. He risked his life and emerged with the confidence to be truly playful again.

When I speak about the capacity to play, I speak about the kind of work that is joyful. In our profession, we need to maintain an attitude that allows our work to be at once serious and playful. Only those who work playfully will be able on rare occasions to make a new leap to teach us more about our work. I would like, in fact, to leave you with the idea that our work remains forever a serious type of play, a joyful leap, as Plato described it, and a safe return to stable ground. One sees in it the Eriksonian synthesis of "toys and reason, the fruits of two seasons."

Chapter 15

The Borderline Spectrum in Children

JULIO MORALES

THE BORDERLINE STATE

The absence of specific symptoms and signs makes it difficult to diagnose the borderline state with confidence, but paradoxically, this very pleomorphism has itself become a diagnostic criterion. Furthermore, although the symptoms of psychosis, neurosis, and psychopathy may also occur in borderline cases, there are indications that a specific type of borderline presonality may exist and may even be recognized as such by clinicians of different theoretical persuasions.

Modell (1961), for example, has laid emphasis on a relationship based on identification, on a strained sense of identity, on subtle disorders of the reality sense, on the presence of destructive fantasies, and on transient and limited regressions. Knight (1962) conceptualized the condition as primarily a disorder of ego function with impairments in thinking, planning, maintaining relationships, defending against inner impulses, and adapting to the environment. These deeper difficulties may be glossed over by a show of superficial adjustments and shallow relationships. The personality profile presented by Kernberg (1967) also stresses ego weakness with concomitant difficulties in controlling impulses, tolerating frustrations, neutralizing aggresions, sustaining relationships, and making use of adequate and mature defenses to prevent dangerous regressions.

Generally speaking, in psychoanalytic terms, there is a striking absence of phase-specific pathology, so that internal conflicts appear to arise from almost every psychosexual stage of development.

Lately, since the concept of the self has come into focus as an important nonclinical and clinical entity, the pathology of the borderline state has been reinterpreted in terms of a pathology of the self. This new profile views the borderline self as feeling abandoned, rejected, unloved, and inundated with feelings of hopelessness and helplessness—defended on the one side with compensatory feelings of grandiosity and omnipotence, and huge destructive capacities on the other, the one set of feelings fluctuating with the other and thus leaving the borderline self fragmented, poorly integrated, unstable, and constantly shifting.

The reasons given for such ego and self deficiences have been attributed to constitutional factors, early traumatic experiences, and developmental arrests and fixations of unknown etiology.

THE CONCEPT OF A BORDERLINE SPECTRUM

Modern nosology is still grappling with the complexity and heterogeneity of the psychopathologies that plague the human condition. Rather than speak of single disorders or reactions, the present-day tendency is to look at illnesses such as schizophrenia or manic-depression in terms of a spectrum of subtypes, varying qualitatively and quantitatively along the continuum. A basic premise is that all the subtypes belonging to the spectrum share a core pathology to which are then added degrees of intensity and secondary attributes. In the first section of this presentation, the core pathology of the borderline spectrum has already been discussed in terms of the different levels of ego and self organization with corresponding problems in object relations, adaptive capacities, levels of fixation, and tendencies toward regression. In the second section of this paper the borderline spectrum will be described as it covers a continuum of subgroups extending from the border of psychosis to the border of narcissistic personality disorders. Table 1 shows some factors that could help to explain the differences among the subgroups of the borderline spectrum.

SUBGROUPS OF THE BORDERLINE SPECTRUM

Subgroup 1: Proneness to Sudden and Severe Regression

When children belonging to this subgroup are exposed to frustration, loss of supplies, and stress, a precipitous regression takes place to the point of complete disorganization of the ego and self, loss of controls, and release of intense and diffuse aggression. Little or no attempt is made to master the traumatic situation. During the period of regression, many display strong paranoid feelings associated with general suspiciousness and mistrustfulness, retaliatory fears regarding their aggressiveness and destructiveness, and

TABLE 1. The Borderline Spectrum in Relation to Ego and Self Organization

Psychotic End	Signal Function of Anxiety	Regression	Active/Passive Mastering of Traumatic Situation	Integration of Self
Subgroup 1 Borderline child who collapses	Absent	Precipitous	Passively experiencing	Fragmented self
Subgroup 2 The angry borderline child	Absent	Episodic	Actively destroying	Fragmented self
Subgroup 3 The borderline child who clings	Absent	Less precipitous	Actively clinging	Low self-esteem predominates
Subgroup 4 The borderline child who presents separation anxiety	Present	Shift between regression and recovery	Actively manipulating	Self fragmentation during regression. Otherwise brittle integration
Subgroup 5 The stable borderline with narcissistic veneer	Present	Resistant	Try actively to adapt	More integrated self
Narcissistic Personality Disorder End				

feelings of helplessness that are compensated for by fantasies and ideas of omnipotence and grandiosity. They seem to live on the very edge of psychosis, but for some mysterious reason they do not pass the border, and may maintain a precarious adjustment under conditions of a holding and facilitating environment. In many cases these children have been exposed to parents who have physically or sexually abused them or grossly neglected them.

John was a thirteen-year-old white boy who was admitted to a psychiatric facility for setting fires. He was first seen at the age of six, when he was diagnosed as hyperkinetic and placed on Ritalin. A year later, another, more careful evaluation took into account the presence of a psychotic mother, and a diagnosis of borderline state was made. From time to time, his behavior would improve and then deteriorate, sometimes appearing to depend on the psychotic state of the mother. At the age of eleven, he "accidentally" took an overdose of Ritalin and was admitted to a mental hospital in a state of marked disorganization. He recovered rapidly from this, but his behavior deteriorated again when his parents divorced and he began living with his father and stepmother. It was at this time that he started setting fires.

Upon examination he was stiff, awkward, and unsmiling, extremely fearful that something was going to be done to him and very constricted in both affect and speech. During his sessions he rarely mentioned people, but when he did he saw them as mostly cold and uncaring. His suspiciousness was difficult to overcome and interfered with the establishment of a therapeutic alliance. There was never any evidence of thought disorder or a frank break with reality. His developmental problems had been lifelong, and he had had adjustment difficulties since infancy. Every stage of development was replete with conflicts and symptoms. A genetic factor had also to be considered, since his mother's twin sister had also had a psychotic episode and had eventually killed her husband. His father tried to be helpful but was largely ineffectual.

At the present time, John is in a state of partial remission: His anger is still indiscriminate and uncontrollable, and the aggressiveness alternates with regressive behavior, in which he smears feces and masturbates openly. His present self has little substance and his self-esteem is at a low ebb, so that he sees himself as insignificant, worthless, and unlovable. His two siblings would also be classified as borderline, but their pathology is less severe, perhaps because there is less "organicity" in their make-up.

Subgroup 2: Proneness to Unpredictable, Impulsive, and Murderous Rages

With this subgroup of children, the major difficulty is not in controlling their regressions but in containing their aggressions. The more frightened they get, the more aggression they experience, the more they let loose a deluge of unneutralized aggressiveness. Not only have they had extremely violent and brutal parents, but the entire family history is characterized by uncontrolled brutality, criminality, and murder. In subgroup 1, the proneness to regression generated a wide range of infantile behavior; in this subgroup, the proneness to uncontrolled aggression generates a wide variety of hostile behavior coupled with a fragmentation of the self as part of the clinical picture. This extreme sensitivity to hostility once again makes the formation of the viable therapeutic alliance difficult to maintain.

Greg was an eleven-year-old black boy who had been in psychiatric facilities since he was eight. He was first seen at the age of five because of hyperactivity, enuresis, and very severe temper tantrums. By the age of six, he had become so aggressive that he had to be suspended from school in the first grade. He was not only aggressive but cruel and even sadistic. He was caught on several occasions committing vandalism. His father was aggressive, antisocial, and alcoholic, spending many years in prison and finally dying there. The mother had also been sociopathic since adolescence, and there was a strong history of alcoholism and psychopathy in her family. Greg's older brother had been committed to a correctional center because of his antisocial and violent behavior.

Upon examination Greg expressed open hostility toward his parents and all adults. There seemed to be a great deal of anxiety underlying his hostility, and it was this reservoir of hostility that seemed to provoke most of his affective storms. His defences (projection, introjection, splitting, and denial) were primitive and ineffectual. He showed little capacity to control his impulses or to postpone gratification. His vision of the world was of a threatening and dangerous place, and his own response was therefore threatening and dangerous in return. He had no concerns whatsoever about hurting other people and showed no remorse of doing any injury that he had inflicted. His gender identity was also confused: He liked to parade in the nude in front of other children, to dress up as a girl, and on occasion to have homosexual interactions with other boys.

With the use of psychotropic drugs, his hostility became more manageable and psychotherapy more possible. The underlying neediness then became much more apparent, and as treatment progressed, his wild, chaotic aggressiveness gradually abated.

Subgroup 3: Proneness to Extreme but Nondiscriminating Dependency

Children in this subgroup seem desperately to search for attachment and bonding, and cling to every person that they meet, refusing to be brushed aside and persisting in their attempts to keep in contact. There is a very pathetic quality to their craving more contact and attention; they seem almost to want to devour the adults around them.

Once again, they seem to have no stable ego or self-organization, no capacity to delay gratification, and no ability to control their moods. As with other borderline children, their self-esteem is chronically low. In their early histories, they have suffered from almost complete emotional deprivation with no one-to-one satisfactory and continuous relationship. They have often had to compete with other children in institutions or in crowded foster families. Their progress in treatment is slow, and they appear to need to repeat their whole infantile experience, but this time with a loving and constant object. In most instances, it is difficult to meet the extent of their neediness, the urgency of their demands, and the insatiable character of their orality. A continued therapeutic relationship with one member of the staff who singles the patient out as special and more or less "adopts" him during his stay in the facility may set development going in a more progressive direction.

Jeff was a twelve-year-old boy who was admitted to a psychiatric facility because of serious problems of adjustment to his foster home. He constantly sought attention from his foster parents, who found it difficult and exasperating to meet all his demands. He would compete constantly and intensively with the other foster children, and when he failed to make physical contact with the foster parents, he would try, clearly out of his neediness, to involve the other foster children in sexual practices that mostly involved close bodily contact. His mother had deserted him after his birth. She had been a chronic schizophrenic woman whose ten children had been placed in different foster homes. His father was a chronic alcoholic with no interest in his children. Jeff had had to spend the first five years of his life in the hospital because he required surgery for an imperforate anus, and while in hospital during this stage, he became very much a case of Spitzian "hospitalism."

Upon examination he was seen as immature, needy, clinging, indiscriminately searching for attachments, but not knowing what to do with the object of attachment except to fasten himself to it like a limpet. He seemed to be suffering from inordinate affect hunger. There was evidence of very strong and very permanent oral and anal fixations with no evidence of any further psychosexual development. As with other borderline children, his reality testing was at times impaired, his impulse control poor, his defenses primitive, immature, and inadequate, and his superego was still not internalized, so that fears of concrete retaliation for wrongdoing were constantly present. His self was characterized by feelings of deprivation, rejection, and low esteem. He saw himself very much as a victim of fate. When thwarted in his indiscriminate clinging to people, he would either persist, turn to the next person who was available, or behave in some extraordinary way to gain attention. On one occasion, when rejected by a person, he swallowed a penny and voraciously ate a pencil in front of her!

Subgroup 4: Proneness to Extreme Separation Anxiety

These children are different from the previous group in being more discriminating in their attachments, and their behavior is typified by intense anaclitic tendencies. In their everyday life, they experience chronic fears of abandonment, chronic fears of separation from their attachments, and a display of marked disorganization when the bond is ruptured. They seem to have a defective time sense, so that the solace of eventual reunion does not appear to enter their thoughts. The child generally comes from a family with close kinship ties, and the mother has as much difficulty in separating from the child as the child has in leaving the mother. The mother's unresolved symbiotic relationship to the maternal grandmother is repeated again in the case of her child.

What separates subgroup 4 from the previous three subgroups is the appearance, for the first time in the spectrum of the signal function of anxiety, a capacity for the ego to recover more quickly from regression and the ability of the ego to overcome traumatic situations. These children are altogether better put together, have had less traumatic histories, relate better to people, and when they enter treatment, are more able to establish a workable alliance.

Fred was a ten-year-old boy, an only child of an intensely possessive mother who felt that no one else could hold or handle her child apart from herself. She even excluded the father from any close contact with the boy, and this led to some degree of estrangement between the parents, with the father drifting into a relationship outside the home. The mother breast-fed her baby for almost three years, and then gave this up very reluctantly on medical advice. Since the father had moved into another room, the boy slept in the same bed as his mother, and generally slept in a fetal position in close contact with the mother's abdomen. Since he showed a marked disinclination to go to school or to play with any other children, his mother decided to tutor him herself; this led to the educational authorities becoming involved and pressure being put on the mother to allow her child to attend the local school. She resisted this for a long time, but under threat of the court, eventually gave in; she would accompany him to the door of his classroom, where they separated daily with much embracing and mutual crying. The class teacher was understandably scandalized and repeatedly attempted to get the mother to refrain from such dramatic separation scenes. When the boy was eight, the mother underwent a severe depression and had to be hospitalized. The maternal grandmother came to live with the family, but the boy was disconsolate and seemed to undergo a Bowlby-type separation response. After a turbulent period of protest, he became depressed, despairing and, as the weeks went by, remote and detached. On examination he seemed to be almost out of touch, made no affective response to the interviewer, and seemed "far away" and wrapped up in his own thoughts. He was admitted to a psychiatric facility for observation, where a diagnosis of borderline state was made, which seemed justified because his ego and self began to disorganize. The mother finally returned from hospital, the two were reunited, and his general condition at once improved. At this point, the mother was persuaded to enter treatment for herself and to allow the boy to continue with outpatient treatment.

At the present time, both seem to be doing much better, although the boy is still regarded as a "mild" borderline case.

Subgroup 5: The Intensely Narcissistic Variety

The children belonging to this subgroup seem extremely self-centered, aloof, and cold. Their relationships with people are superficial, and their choice of relationship is purely narcissistic: They idealize those who gratify them and devalue those who disappoint them. On the surface, they seem to lead reasonably well adjusted lives until a blow to their self-esteem breaks down this superficial and fragile adaptation. They then clinically resemble the other subgroups of borderline children. Symptomatically, they appear as loners with no close friends at all, preferring to be by themselves. They are often bright and intellectualize their situation, using it as a means to isolate themselves even further from others. They are given to hypochondriacal complaints, and on closer examination a chronic depression can be detected. They have been generally rejected by their families for various reasons and have been used as scapegoats in family conflicts. At least one of the parents, frequently the mother, is a narcissistic personality disorder with a marginal psychological adjustment. In some ways, the narcissistic child appears to model himself on the narcissism of the mother.

As with the children in subgroup 4, these cases operate on a higher level of adjustment than the first three subgroups, responding to the signal function of anxiety, coping with stressful situations, resisting ego and self-regressions. In the therapeutic alliance, the major difficulty has to do with the tendency of the children to shift from idealization to devaluation at the slightest hint of disappointment.

Bob was a thirteen-year-old boy, the oldest of three children whose parents were divorced two years previous to the psychiatric referral. Bob lived with his father, who remarried, and a conflict began between him and his stepmother. She regarded him as totally unmanageable and prevailed on the father to have him hospitalized. The boy's memory of his childhood was dismal. He recalled being always unhappy and described his biological mother as vicious and out to get him. She used to beat him when he was only a baby, and with great bitterness he referred to her as "an alcoholic lesbian."

He seemed to have no concern for anyone else but himself and to be incapable of meaningful relationships. He preferred to read than to mix with other children. He wanted very much to be the leader of any group and to have others look up to him and respond to his authority. He also wanted to maintain the good image of himself in the eyes of adults and to feel appreciated by them. His self-centeredness, egocentric attitudes, however, had the opposite effect, and so his narcissism was repeatedly injured.

The borderline quality was especially evident on projectives in which he saw himself very much alone in the world and preoccupied with death. Sadistic fantasies were rampant, with males strangling females to death at the height of sexual relations. His reality testing was also tenous, and his superego poorly developed and depend on fears of external punishment. The narcissism was so extreme that a therapeutic alliance was never truly established. He spent many sessions with headphones on, listening to a pocket radio, thus effectively shutting off the therapist. At other times he would read magazines during the session or light small fires in the ashtray.

CONCLUSIONS

The subgroups are not dissimilar from those described by Grinker et al. (1968) with respect to adult borderline patients. Here we have an example of an interesting juxtaposition of clinical art and science. Grinker et al. used cluster analysis to obtain four groups: those bordering on psychosis (similar to the subgroups 1 and 2 described here), those bordering on neurosis (similar to the subgroup 3 in this presentation), the core borderline syndrome (which would correspond with subgroup 4 here), and the adaptive, affectless, "as if" character (roughly comparable to the subgroup 5).

A second factor of great interest is the persistence of the groupings from childhood into adult life, speaking once again to the stability of the borderline structure, in spite of its kaleidescopic clinical manifestations.

The subgroups employed by Pine (1974), culled from different descriptions in the literature and from the diagnostic categories furnished by the APA and GAP manuals of classification, describe four borderline types and also some others that would be more appropriately placed in a psychotic category. His most clear-cut group is one that he describes as having "shifting levels of ego organization"; this corresponds to what Grinker et al. refer to as a core borderline syndrome and label in this paper "severe separation anxiety." Pine's subgroup of "internal disorganization in response to external disorganization" is fairly similar to Grinker et al.'s group 1 and the second subgroup described here (see Table 2).

The group referred to by Pine as "incomplete internalization of psychosis" is one in which he describes an interesting psychodynamic mechanism of partial internalization of a psychotic love object—a mechanism previously described by Anthony (1970) in his cases of *folie à deux* and by Anna Freud

TABLE 2. The Borderline Spectrum

Subgroups Presented Here	Groups Described by Grinker	Groups Described by Pine
Subgroup 1 Severe regression with collapse	Group 1 Bordering on psychosis	—
Subgroup 2 Severe aggression	Group 1 Bordering on psychosis	Internal disorganization in response to external disorganization
Subgroup 3 Severe clinging	Group 4 Bordering on neurosis	—
Subgroup 4 Severe separation anxiety	Group 2 Core borderline syndrome	Shifting levels of ego organization
Subgroup 5 Stable narcissistic borderline with a narcissistic veneer	Group 3 The defended, adaptive, affectless, "as if" character	—

in *Depressed Children with Depressed Mothers*. The author prefers to regard this as a special variant of psychosis. His other group indicating "chronic ego deviance" corresponds to the description given by Rosenfeld and Sprince (1963), as well as by Weil (1953), of borderline children in general, and it is therefore not useful to call it a subgroup.

REFERENCES

Anthony, E.J. (1970) The influence of maternal psychosis on children—*folie à deux*. In *Parenthood*, E.J. Anthony and T. Benedek, eds. Boston: Little, Brown.

Grinker, R.S., Sr., Werble, B., and Drye, R.C. (1968) *The Borderline Syndrome*. New York: Basic Books.

Kernberg, O. (1967) Borderline personality organization. *J. Am. Psychoanal. Assn.* 15:641.

Knight, R.P. (1962) Borderline states. *In Psychoanalytic Psychiatry and Psychology*. R.P. Knight and G.R. Friedman, eds. New York: International Universities Press.

Modell, A. (1961) Denial and the sense of separateness. *J. Am. Psychoanal. Assn.* 9:536–545.

Pine, F. (1974) On the concept of "borderline" in children. *The Psychoanalytic Study of the Child*, Vol. 29. New Haven: Yale University Press.

Rosenfeld, S.K., and Sprince, M.P. (1963) An attempt to formulate a meaning of the concept "borderline." *The Psychoanalytic Study of the Child*, Vol. 18. New Haven: Yale University Press.

Weil, A.P. (1953) Certain severe disturbances of ego development in childhood. *The Psychoanalytic Study of the Child*, Vol. 8. New Haven: Yale University Press.

Chapter 16

Research on the Concept of the "Borderline" Psychotic Child

DORIS C. GILPIN
SANDRA SEXSON
CAROL WALD

INTRODUCTION

There is considerable confusion about the use of the term "borderline psychotic" in children. It does not exist as a diagnosis in the *Diagnostic and Statistical Manual II*. The Group for the Advancement of Psychiatry manual *Psychopathological Disorders in Childhood* suggests the use of the diagnosis of personality disorder with the addition of the symptoms of the ego defects. However, much of the literature seems to refer to a more clearly distinguishable group that yet has no clear-cut personality-disorder diagnosis; it is in fact rather vague about this. A series of studies are being undertaken to more carefully delineate the existence and boundaries of the syndrome or syndromes. This paper presents some of the early findings.

RESEARCH FOR PROFILE

Initially the literature was searched for suggestions as to important items of history, symptoms, or findings, and a comprehensive list of these items was compiled. Diagnostic material in the charts of children whose diagnosis suggested a "borderline" condition was studied for the existence of these "characteristic" items. This material included a developmental form, a symptom list, school report, social history, psychological testing report, and psychiatric evaluation. These were from all kinds of "borderline" psychotic

conditions. There were no criteria for inclusion other than the attachment of
a suggestive label at the time of the diagnostic conference. Eighty-one items
were used, which were defined as operationally as possible, and a manual
was made. Raters rated the same charts using the manual until interrater
agreement was met. There were forty-nine charts of children not so severely
out of touch with reality as to be floridly psychotic, but with some reason to
be considered as possibly psychotic, at least at times. These were cases since
July 1968. Thirty of these could be considered to deserve a GAP manual
diagnosis of personality disorder, such as obsessive-compulsive personality
disorder or tension-discharge personality disorder, with a qualifying phrase
delineating the presence of some ego weaknesses, such as illogical thought or
poor reality testing.

Nineteen seemed to fall into a group which could not be given a clear-cut
personality-pattern diagnosis and which we came to call "fluid borderlines."
These had been diagnosed as borderline at the time of diagnostic, and one of
us agreed with the diagnosis on reviewing the chart.

Table 1 shows the age, sex, and position in family distribution of the two
groups of borderline children, and also a comparison with floridly psychotic
children. The fluid borderline children were all in the latency-age range.

The mean I.Q. of the fluid borderlines was 107.44, while for nonfluid it

Table 1. Age, Sex, and Ordinal Distribution

	Fluid Borderline	Nonfluid Borderline	Psychotic
4			1
5		2	
6		6	
7	5	4	
8	4	2	1
9	5	4	2
10	3	4	1
11	2	1	
12		4	1
13		2	
14		1	
TOTAL	19	30	6
F	2	8	2
M	17	22	4
Only	3	4	1
Oldest	10	13	1
Middle	3	7	3
Youngest	3	5	1
Unknown		1	

was 100.37. This is not statistically significant. For overt psychotics, of whom we had only six, there was a mean I.Q. of 89. There is statistically a trend for fluid borderlines to have a higher I.Q. than psychotics.

In the group of 30 nonfluid personality-disorder borderlines, there were divisions into many subgroups. These divisions are shown in Table 2. No group contained more than 5 children. The last two subgroups (organic brain and deprived) are not personality-disorder diagnoses, of course, but seem to be logically separable from the fluid borderlines. Thus the nonfluid personality-disorder borderline children had ego weaknesses in reality testing or illogical thought, but presented a relatively fixed, recognizable personality pattern. The fluid borderlines had similar ego weaknesses, but did not have a fixed, recognizable personality pattern by GAP manual standards. They tended to shift and swing through various kinds of adjustments and organizations. They moved from oral stage material through anal to oedipal and back, often in a confusing way.

We then examined the charts of the 19 fluid borderlines. Of the 81 items, 20 were not noted on the charts repeatedly enough to draw conclusions about this, although there were no instances where there was a "no" on the chart about any of these 20 items.

Table 3 lists these items and the number of charts where these were present. We do not know if these were not recorded on the remaining charts because of failure to enquire or to record, or because they were in fact not present. A prospective study is needed to see if any of these items are significant.

Forty-four items did not seem to provide useful data, as they were not found to be characteristic for these children.

Table 2. Nonfluid Borderline Diagnosis by Gap Manual

Obsessive-compulsive	2
Isolated	2
Combination obsessive-compulsive and isolated	2
Oppositional	3
Overly dependent	2
Mistrustful	2
Overly inhibited	1
Tension-discharge, impulse-ridden	5
Tension-discharge, neurotic	3
Anxious	1
Depressed	2
Hysterical	1
Organic brain	3
Deprived	1
TOTAL	30

Table 3. May Be on Borderline Profile—Not Enough
Evidence but No "No's"

Double bind M	6
Tests constantly	4
Too many stimuli perceived	9
Can't differentiate past and present	2
Can't keep track of time and space	6
Remembers too much too vividly	4
Judgment discrepancy	0
Uses symbolism	8
Words felt to have magic power	3
Anxiety over separation-disintegration	9
Feels empty and dead	1
Ego splits	3
Concrete objects important	2
Aggression inward	9
Fuses aggression and sexuality	2
Total personality lacks harmony	4
Structure of school soothing	1
Mother transference	2
Possessions seen as self-extensions	0
Progress if understood	1

There were 17 items marked "yes" on 14 or more charts of the 19 "fluid" borderlines, as shown in Table 4.

On only 3 of these items were there any "no's" at all. These 17 items tend to give a profile of these children. Three items were positive for all 19 of the children: These were that father was in the home, the children were depressed, and there was unneutralized aggression. None of the 19 charts had less than 12 of the 17 items marked "yes."

Let us illustrate some of the items: Let us take ego-state shifts. We quote from the chart of one boy: "Performance on structured tests was good. On the less structured tests his entire demeanor became more wild and bizarre. He spoke in different voices and giggled inappropriately." Here is an illustration of temper: "He wanted to leave the office. He started throwing things around the room, such as the wastebasket, throwing chairs on the desk and yelling." Here is an illustration of poor reality testing: "He expressed a great deal of fear that the third floor would crash through on us." Here is an illustration of how all three levels of early psychosexual development were seen on projective tests: "Women are sexually appealing, but have the face of a devouring wolf." He saw volcanoes and rockets and bombs.

Looking now at the personality-disorder non-fluid group, only 2 of the 30 had this profile. One of these had a diagnosis of isolated and obsessive-compulsive personality; she was age 13. One boy, age 8, had a diagnosis of

Table 4. Items with 14 or More Yes's in Fluid Borderlines

1. Father in home   significant
2. Temper
3. Impulsive
4. Ego-state shifts
5. Lack of friends
6. Impairment of reality testing
7. Themes from all three early
   levels of psychosexual development*   significant
8. Death themes
9. Uses pleasure principle primarily   significant
10. Depressed   significant
11. Projective identification
12. Aggression directed outward   significant
13. Unneutralized aggression   significant
14. Temper or panics
15. Illogical thought or poor reality testing
16. Basic trust or ready for relationships*
17. Lacks insight*

*Only items with any no's at all.

isolated personality. So the profile of all the fluid group fit only 7% of the non-fluid group.

We next tried to see which items, if any, distinguished this group from the children most like them—namely, the other 30 children who were, by other labeling, "borderline," but who we are calling personality disorder with some ego weaknesses that put them close to or in and out of psychosis; in other words, the group that we labeled non-fluid borderline. We found 6 items were significant in differentiating the two groups.

We need to say something about the calculations of significance: First, on such a large number of items looked at—that is, a total of 252 ways of looking at the items—chance alone could account for 12 to be significant. We found 16. Chi Squares were computed on most, using Yates' correction. Where the n was small, Fisher's exact was used. It may seem a contradiction to write first of 6 items being significant and now of 16. Let us explain: Of the 6 items, some were significant in more than one way. Thus there were two calculations on themes from first three levels of development and on outward aggression, as you can see. Also, some items that did not have 14 or more "yes's"—i.e., were not part of the profile—still distinguished between the two groups. These were two calculations of separation difficulties; two calculations of visual-motor defects, remembers too much too vividly, and worries over oral engulfment; and two calculations of difficulties with developmental tasks. We then took profiles of psychotic children for comparison.

FATHER IN HOME

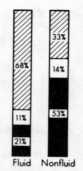

SEPARATION DIFFICULTIES
Trend yes vs. all else
Sign in being mentioned
at all

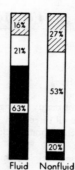

V-M DEFECTS
Yes vs. all else
Yes vs. no

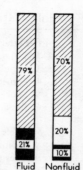

**REMEMBERS TOO MUCH
TOO VIVIDLY**
Yes vs. no

☒ Not mentioned in chart
☐ No
■ Yes

**THEMES FROM
FIRST THREE STAGES**
Yes vs. all else
Yes vs. no

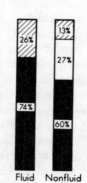

**USES
PLEASURE PRINCIPLE**
Yes vs. no

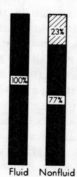

DEPRESSED
Yes vs. all else
Being mentioned vs.
not being mentioned

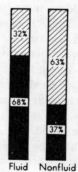

**WORRIES OVER
ORAL ENGULFMENT**
Trend yes vs. all else
Trend mentioned vs.
not mentioned

☒ Not mentioned in chart
☐ No
■ Yes

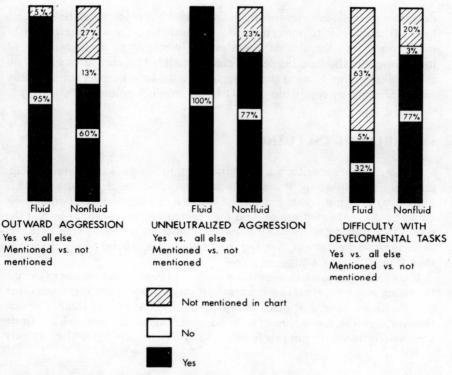

Figures 1, 2, and 3. Differentiating items.

There were only 6 psychotic children, which makes the *n* too small for meaningful statistical handling. No psychotics had a fluid borderline profile. Striking differences are seen in themes from all three levels, and in severeness of illogic and poor reality testing.

RESEARCH WITH CONTROLS

We then compared 10 new fluid borderlines not of this original group of 19, pulled from charts before 1968 (which, unfortunately, did not always have as much material on them), and compared those with 10 charts in the file matched for age and sex and with sufficient information in them—that is, we were comparing them with the clinic population. These borderlines were, again, not chosen to fit any specific criteria except that of being judged borderline at the time of the diagnostic conference and possibly fluid borderline by one of us. Two raters rated these charts. One rater used our manual with no other instructions on rating items. He was able to use our definition reliably, even though the items were often psychoanalytic concepts held to be difficult to operationalize. Nevertheless, the average of the 17 items found on control charts was only 6, whereas the average of the 17 items found on the fluid borderline charts was 13. This compares with 17 on the original group. Nine of the 17 items were the least number found in any one borderline, as compared with 11 in the original group.

CRITERIA FOR INCLUSION

Can we, then, set criteria for the inclusion in the fluid borderline group, and is it useful to do so? It seemed to us it would be useful, because this 19 is quite a large group compared to that where a definite personality diagnosis could be made. In that group, you may remember, there would be 5 at the most in a particular category. Can we construct a logical tree that will delineate these children? Are some findings more crucial to the diagnosis than others? Figure 4 suggests a tree.

It seemed to us to make sense for purposes of comparing groups to use the following items to separate out a clear group of fluid borderlines from other classifications: There should be poor reality testing or some illogical thought, but it should not be of severe degree. This would establish a definite separation from all nonpsychotics and a separation from the severely

Figure 4.
DIAGNOSTIC TREE

psychotic. If those criteria had been used, two of the second "fluid" borderline group (who, incidentally, did not have items from the three early levels of psychosexual development) would have been dropped from the list and placed in the clearly psychotic group.

The second thing that could be done would be to separate out those who could be given a GAP diagnosis of personality disorder of a particular type or some other label—the nonfluid ones. We included gross organic brain syndrome in this group, as before. As we mentioned before, only 2 of 30 with a personality-disorder diagnosis have a fluid profile. These 2 have been isolated or obsessive-compulsive or both. In other words, they are the only nonfluid borderlines with a fluid borderline profile, but they would now be excluded from "fluid" by virtue of being able to make a personality label.

The third and fourth things would be to have ego-state shifts and to have all three early levels of psychosexual development present thematically to separate the true fluid from other miscellaneous fluid borderlines. This produces quite a homogeneous group. If this criterion has been used, there would have been 3 additional cases dropped from the true fluid group, leaving 14. All of these 14 cases, in addition, have capacity for basic trust or are open and ready for relationships, and have some evidence of superego. We think these items are important. It tends to show that the group is more homogeneous in regard to treatability, and probably also as to outcome. These are not, however, needed as criteria. This group of true fluid borderlines is probably on a continuum with other conditions, but for purposes of communication and research, boundaries are useful.

The following list shows the suggested criteria for a relatively homogeneous group of true fluid borderlines with the same potential treatability and prognosis:

1. Some illogical thought or poor reality testing, though not severe
2. No clear-cut diagnostic label on personality or organicity or deprivation
3. Themes from all three early levels of psychosexual development
4. Ego-state shifts through these levels of development

On using these criteria on the second group of 10 fluids and 10 controls, 4 fluids and 1 control met the criteria. It turned out that this control was a true fluid borderline. Thus the criteria developed in this exploratory study identified only true fluid borderlines, even though it excluded some originally selected. In other words, no other types of children fit these criteria; there are no overlaps, and these criteria do exclude the isolated and obsessives that overlapped before. This suggests that this method might be highly useful for research. This group continues to have a recognizable profile, clearly distinguishable from psychotics and from the nonfluid borderlines.

TREATMENT

Now a word about treatment and outcome. The treatment of 13 of the true fluid borderlines was checked. Table 5 shows some treatment results.

Three sets of parents refused therapy. Five children were seen for less than a year and terminated because of lack of parental commitment and many failed appointments. (Parents usually were the ones pulling out after considerable discussion about commitment.) The number of sessions were 7, 12, 22, 25 (which is an estimate), and 50 (which is an estimate). Four were seen two or three times a week for at least three years, three having two therapists, one having one therapist. Outcome at the time of termination on these seemed very good. Follow-up on three of these for as long as ten years is also good. One additional case is still in therapy after two years. Thus these turn out to be relatively long-term cases, and much of the success of therapy hinges on finding ways to help parents become involved and stay involved.

One hundred percent of those with long-term therapy at our clinic seem to do well, but only 38% get this treatment. The information on treatment does not confirm or deny that this is a homogeneous group in regard to prognosis.

DISCUSSION

These 19 fluid borderlines were akin to those children Pine termed "borderline with shifting levels of ego organization" or possibly "chronic ego deviants" in his article in the 1974 *Psychoanalytic Study of the Child.* Aarkrog's "mixed maturity" type seems similar, too.

Table 5. Treated Fluid Borderlines

Refused therapy	3
Seen less than year and terinated without commitment to treatment	5
Seen 2-3x/week for at least three years and terminated much improved	4
Still in therapy after two years	1

	Ten-year follow-up of all kinds		
	Borderline	Neurotic	Character
S.A.	13.67	11.05	12.13

The child listed as "deprived" Pine would probably call the child with "ego limitation." None of these seem to correspond with Pine's internal-disorganization type, and it is possible that type would be found in reactive disorders, as diagnosed at our clinic. (We tend to diagnose children under age five as reactive disorder rather than borderline, as it seems early to label them with the implication of a fixed state.)

Certainly the profile we found is consistent with many discussions about borderline children. Striking, though, is the prevalence of the depression in these children. We were not aware of attention being called to this so forcefully before. One wonders if some of this depression is the kind that is the normal accompaniment of Mahler's rapprochement phase, which is the stage when the child is mourning his loss of symbiosis and omnipotence. Is it perhaps related to how poorly these children retain objects inside themselves? That is, are these children in mourning repeatedly at experiencing over and over symbiosis and loss of symbiosis?

The six differentiating items in the profile make considerable sense, with two exceptions, which at first are not clear. There is no particular reason why the two groups should differ on illogical thought or poor reality testing. Temper or panics, impulsivity, basic trust, lack of friends, and the use of projective identification need not distinguish them, either. But we had postulated the ego-state shifts would be found more in the fluid borderlines; this was not found. We now postulate that the impact of the ego-state shifts is more dramatic when the swings are through several levels of ego development than when they are just in and out of psychosis. Therefore, such children give the impression of more fluidity. In other words, the children with a fairly fixed personality pattern, even if they regress, tend to shift at the most to a psychosexual level just below where they were fixated and often just in and out of psychosis. The fluid borderlines shifted through three levels. Ego-state shifts in and out of psychosis would be characteristic of both groups. If we had been more careful to define a certain type of ego-state shift—i.e., through psychosexual levels—we might have different results.

In the 16 significant items, one not-easily-accounted-for difference is the fact that all the fluid borderlines had father in the home. The father's presence may have been a force that aided these children in progressing as far as they did developmentally.

The visual-motor-defects finding is somewhat surprising; it may suggest an organic or constitutional substrate. At first the relative lack of separation difficulty in the fluid borderlines also seemed surprising. However, these children may well, in their worry over oral engulfment, find it safer to overtly separate than others do. The greater difficulty of the larger group of nonfluid borderlines in developmental tasks fits with their lessened achievement of developmental stages.

DYNAMIC DESCRIPTION

Dynamically, we can describe the true fluid borderline children as unhappy children with much difficulty in development, particularly in regard to development of stable and helpful introjects; yet they have not been arrested in the first three psychosexual stages. Such a child often seems to have particular trouble with fears of symbiosis and tends to have shifting levels of ego organization fluctuating through the first three levels of psychosexual development. He experiences periods of being out of touch with reality or of using illogical thought, but not of a severe type. He has, however, developed some trustingness and at least a partial internalization of superego. This description seems compatible with the majority of the clinical literature and is quite compatible with Pine's classificatory system.

SUMMARY

To summarize, at this point we have found at a child guidance clinic a population of children with some ego defects of poor reality testing and some illogical thought, but no florid psychosis. These have been subdivided into non-fluid, true-fluid, and miscellaneous fluid borderline psychosis on the basis of criteria that arose out of the study of their characteristic profiles. Clear-cut criteria are suggested especially for the true fluid borderline psychotic children. The criteria are compatible with much of the clinical literature, with dynamic considerations, with treatability, and possibly with prognosis.

This classification has been compared with Pine's previously suggested classification of borderlines, and is, in some points, comparable. It is suggested that these criteria be used in research and communication to enhance meaningful understanding.

Chapter 17

The Borderline Child in the Jones Family: Collaborative Therapy with a Borderline Child

LILLIAN WEGER
DORIS C. GILPIN
JULIO MORALES

Collaborative therapy in which one person works with the parents and one person works with the child is extremely difficult and extremely important in cases of childhood borderline psychosis. The enormity of the needs of both parents and child almost demands two therapists, and having two therapists makes issues of symbiosis and transference easier to deal with. The strains of such a collaborative effect, however, are manifold.

Let us look at the parents of borderline children to try to understand what the parents face in child management and what they face in their inner resources, and from this, gain some picture of what their therapist will need.

At our clinic the mothers of the "true fluid borderline children" were found in all cases to be stuck developmentally. Some were narcissistic and some were passive-dependent. They were often also borderline, or nearly so, themselves. Many of the mothers (eight of sixteen) came from broken homes, and for five there had been a psychiatrically ill maternal parent.

This information tends to mean, from what we notice clinically, that the mothers must sustain a very high investment in themselves. Their investment in the child becomes an extension of this investment in themselves. They find it difficult to nurture the child's self-directedness, often have had limited examples of successful mothering and are both unknowing and unable in the task of actively assisting the child with controls.

Thus, we are met with mothers who have limited parenting skills and meager emotional resources to use what information they might cognitively acquire. They arrive at the clinic harassed, confused, and seeking help in handling their children, but can use little educative assistance before they've received adequate attention to their own growth needs. Sometimes, it is necessary to recommend psychotherapy independent of a therapeutic focus on themselves as parents.

The parent's therapist is faced with a dilemma. There is compelling reality in the mother's demands for help in child management, a reality to be elaborated on later, but there is an equally compelling reality to the mother's being unready to function in any better way with the child for a very long time.

There are problems in the marriage and in the father, too. Although there was always a father in the home of the true fluid borderline child, in nine cases there was chronic open marital discord. The parents are invested in keeping their marriage together, but the child can be a focus of marital conflict. We have also noticed clinically that a large proportion of the fathers need to deny that their children are disturbed. They may be blind to what is obviously bizarre behavior.

We cannot ignore what parents face in trying to get along with a borderline child. The child's reasoning is unreliable, so how can a parent "get through" to him rationally? The temper tantrums and impulsivity in public or in private can render the parent helpless and/or enraged and acutely aware of "what will the neighbors think?" The unpredictable shifts from baby to precocious adult make no one guideline to management safe and no one method of handling "work."

For anyone, parents too, constant exposure to raw and primitive id and affect is very stimulating to the "beast" in oneself, and one becomes vulnerable to behaving in ways that hold oneself together, that can be "crazy" in relation to the child's needs. Therapists experience this stimulation and vulnerability in the few hours a week they see the child. Think what it must be like to live with such a child and try to be parent to one.

We begin to see why the severest challenge to a collaborating team of therapists is in the task of engaging the borderline child and his parents in a therapeutic relationship, and then in responding adequately to the needs of each participant in the changing process so as to enable them to manage the predictable periods of accelerated anxiety and the awesome sadness that accompanies their disengagement from archaically anchored relationships.

The parent's therapist needs to be secure in understanding the child-management problems and in how they can eventually be resolved. The child therapist needs to have confidence in this understanding. At the same time both therapists need to know that parents' management cannot be moved on until much groundwork is laid. The child's therapist may be dismayed by certain interactions at home and want instant change in the growth-impairing family system. He/she needs to handle his/her own feelings and not pressure the parent's therapist to act prematurely. Some child therapists in these circumstances may plan with the parent's therapist to meet with both parents and clearly set forth what the parents must or must not do with their child. This then lets the parent therapist stay out of an authoritarian role, and he/she can help the parent work toward those behaviors as the parent is able. When the parent cannot comply with the child therapist's guidelines, the therapist is there helping to look at why, empathizing with the difficulty in compliance, and yet clear in his own mind about ultimate goals.

The need for trust in the child's therapist needs to be strong too. Parents can put considerable pressure on their therapists to mistrust their colleagues' work. "Johnny is no better. Isn't anything happening?" "Johnny says Dr. X uses dirty words." "Why can't Dr. X give him medicine?" "Dr. X won't talk to me."

Another potential source of distrust is the mother's need to intrude on the child's therapy. Mothers often try to bypass their therapists (who may feel denigrated) and make sure their children's therapists hear them directly. They try to find out exactly what is happening in the developing intimacy of the therapy, for it is threatening to the mother and she may be very frightened of it. The child's therapy needs the support of mother, and both therapists need to be secure that the child's therapist will be firm about untherapeutic intrusiveness without punitiveness or rejection of mother. Occasional meetings of the parent with both therapists may be indicated in order to maintain or develop an alliance for the child's therapy.

Especially important for the maintenance of the therapeutic gestalt is the effort of the mother's therapist to prepare the mother for the closeness of the relationship between the child and his therapist. Even before therapy begins, mothers need to be alerted to the fact that they may, at some point, wish to terminate their children's treatment abruptly, and they need to be helped to see the importance of being willing to discuss this impulse rather than act on it. In our experience, the most frequent cause of failure in therapy of borderline children is the "surprise" termination of the case by mother just as the child has really entered a trusting therapeutic alliance. Serious consideration needs to be given as to whether the parent's therapy needs to be begun before the child's so that mother will have developed a sustaining relationship of her own before the child develops his.

This problem, of child having something parent doesn't have, occurs later in therapy, too, in a different way. The child may, because of youth and flexibility, pass up the parents in his development. This is both threatening and depressing for the parents.

Both parents and children may have characteristics that are uncomfortable for the collaborators. Often the overwhelming anger of a parent is hard to identify with or empathize with. Collaborators may unwittingly fall in the trap of splitting off and projecting their own angry countertransference in an effort to deal with their discomfort. They start to fault each other for lack of empathy or understanding.

For both therapists there can be discouragement at the lengthy therapy with frequent sessions and the relative lack of movement. "If only you'd get parents to change, then Johnny could." "If only you'd get Johnny to change, then parents could."

There are often specific management difficulties, such as family secrets not divulged until after several years of work or the refusal of parents to let there be communication with the school. Again, mutual collaborative trust that all are heading toward the same goal allows for the patience needed to assist in movement toward that goal and not a breakdown of therapy.

With regard to the child's school, the collaborators need to discuss which of them will act as liaison. Many hours may need to be spent in this area of the child's environment.

Dealing with father's tendency to deny the existence of his child's problems or his participation in them may be another collaborative problem. Should one continue to see the child if father, at some point, refuses to be involved? There is no easy answer to the question, and perhaps it needs to be settled on an individual basis, taking into account the stage of the child's therapy. One needs to know if father will try to take mother and child out of treatment with him.

In general, the forces tending to disrupt the smooth working-together of parent therapist and child therapist are stronger in the cases of borderline children than in any other kind of case ordinarily seen in an outpatient clinic.

Follow-through on a recommendation for long-term treatment of a child who presents with borderline pathology requires the participation of parents who can claim at least a beginning understanding of the therapist's goals and the capacity for rudimentary support of the program. Marked ambivalence about treatment can be anticipated at the time recommendations are made, and it is only when the team can interact with unfailing efforts to communicate with each other clearly, sympathetically, and with high regard that a family can begin to take the risks it needs to take to establish the outlines for a new direction in living.

Excerpts from the process of such a case will illustrate some of these difficulties.

The family we will focus our discussion upon for the remainder of this chapter, whom we shall call the Jones family, struggled with their ambivalence for three months before they could make a first treatment appointment following a diagnostic evaluation and the sharing of clinical impressions and recommendations.

The initial treatment team included a Fellow in child psychiatry and a student from a graduate school of social work. The treating physician was able to sustain a treatment commitment to the Joneses and their son John over a period of several years, and to serve as an advocate for parents as well as child during periods when they were in transition—that is, moving from one therapist to another—or when their relationship with the parent therapist to whom they were assigned was peculiarly weak.

John and mother's mistrust of their assigned therapists was initially massive. Mother requested details of the interaction between John and his therapist and supported father's refusal to actively participate in the therapeutic plan. Mother's willingness to work with her social worker derived from her wish to understand what the experience between John and his therapist was like and to maintain some sense of closeness to it. After four months of working with her social worker to better define John's needs and problems as they related to family interaction, mother recognized that John was beginning to ally himself with his therapist in a way she was unable to do with her own. She experienced a sense of discomfort comparable to that which preceded her first treatment visit and withdrew John from treatment, as she would do many times again when unable to cope with the threat of a real intrusion on the nature of the bond between her and her son. Fears were experienced as a need to share more fully in John's treatment by more frequent contacts of her own with his therapist, and a need for more detailed reporting of the content of their treatment sessions. Mother's expanded sense of fear and helplessness found expression in increased acting-out behaviors on the part of John and an urgency on the part of mother to secure therapist's assistance in better controlling his behavior through medication.

Mother was unable to use the support available from her social worker, a young male who reminded her of a younger brother for whom she had acted as a parent surrogate. Mother's mounting concerns were expressed in angry, critical behaviors, which stimulated negative and distancing responses not only from the social worker, but from the nonclinical staff with whom she was sometimes required to interact. Mother's demands for greater control over clinical goals and process and her growing sense of alienation from clinic representatives could not be successfully managed by mother's social worker despite vigorous effects in collaboration on the part of the treatment team around understanding her needs, wishes, and observations. It became necessary for John's therapist to actively engage with mother and to place John on medication to preserve treatment.

Following mother's interview with John's therapist and a better sense on

her part of having been heard and allowed to retain a measure of control in
her relationship with John, mother was able to allow her son to reinvest in
treatment, and also to return for regular appointments with her social
worker. This relationship never became one in which mother could experience trust or explore feelings, but the intensity of her dependency-
independency conflicts, and their infusion in the transference to her social
worker, was temporarily alleviated when she became pregnant just six
months following the onset of John's treatment. This unplanned pregnancy
introduced as many problems as it answered.

John, age seven, was an adopted first child whose introduction into the
Jones family within a few days after his birth precipitated a pregnancy,
despite mother's understanding that she and her husband would not be able
to conceive. The Jones' first natural child, Steve, was delivered less than one
year following John's placement in their home. There had been no further
pregnancies until the onset of John's treatment.

Awareness of mother's pregnancy provoked intense feelings of loss in
John and deep regressive movements and symbiotic merging with the
therapist. Mother struggled with fears that she might damage the expected
baby as she felt she had damaged John. Despite increased feelings of
depression and a wish for greater control over John via higher doses of
medication, mother resisted investment in a therapeutic relationship of her
own and found it increasingly difficult to support John's treatment, cancell-
ing appointments at the clinic with destructive frequency. John's fear of
losing his therapist was symbolically expressed in a spectrum of ways and
can be seen in the content of a session from this period.

John talked of a trip into space (his therapy), and said that the spacecraft
might crash because the pull of gravity was so great (the intensity of his
symbiotic merger with mother). Someone had died already on this trip
(mother's therapy), and a child was frozen and near death. John then
pretended to float in space and started falling under the influence of gravity.
Suddenly he exclaimed, "The gravity will pull the child out."

John's therapist again intervened directly with mother in behalf of John's
need for continuing help. Collaboration between parent and child therapist
(i.e., social worker and Fellow) became increasingly stressful as the social
worker's frustrated efforts to engage mother began to be experienced in
personal terms. Both therapists felt a part of their self-esteem tied into the
family's continuing treatment, and the successes and failures of their efforts
began to intrude on their capacity to communicate in an open, mutually
supportive way. The painful conflict between mother and social worker soon
affected mother's relationship with others at the clinic, and personnel
struggled with their identification with John's appeal for care and their
countertransference to mother. Mother was transferred to a senior staff
social worker upon the termination of her first social worker's commitment

to the clinic. There was reasonable concern that any therapist who was already a part of the clinic system might be burdened with feelings toward both mother and her child's therapist which would be derived from the first social worker's sense of failure and his defenses against mother's critical, demanding posture.

Mother herself was fearful of a second failure and of the manifold changes the clinic represented in her life, and brought an even greater degree of mistrust, anger, and resistance into her relationship with the new therapist.

Medication was discontinued by the child's therapist, but mother handled her rage and sense of helplessness by securing a prescription from her pediatrician and administering it without the knowledge of the clinic. John's progress in treatment was marked by continued symbiotic attachment to the therapist, self-fragmentation, and the emergence of aggressive and sexual impulses. Mother defended against the threat to John's interconnectedness with her with increased anger and hostility toward him and anyone representing this increased individuation.

Collaboration between parent and child therapist was marred by mutual defensiveness and projected anger relevant to a fear of failing this child. The birth of the new baby, a third male child, Frank, became a rationalization for both parents to reinforce one another in a decision to discontinue John's treatment. The parent therapist experienced their resistance as unworkable and the child therapist's reluctance to let go as unrealistic. It was again necessary for interventive efforts on the part of John's therapist, who succeeded in securing a commitment from father to support the treatment process by bringing John in on a regular basis. He also secured the first positive report from John's world outside of the therapy hours. There were signs of change. Father shared at this time that John was developing the capacity to delay the satisfaction of his wishes, that he was less fearful, less turbulent, less demanding and less pugnacious. It was agreed that father would not be required to meet with a parent therapist, an exception to clinic policy, and mother had several months reprieve due to her need to remain at home with the new baby.

John was able to utilize the three-month period of mother's absence from the clinic to work further on his intense fear of losing his therapist and his rage toward the new sibling and others in his family, and at the same time he allowed himself further regression and fragmentation.

Mother returned to the clinic following this three-month period as a result of concern and encouragement on the part of John's therapist. Tension between parent and child therapist was high and characterized by mutual distrust of each other's goals and skills. The level of exchange was locked into the giving and taking of details as opposed to a communion of purpose and a cohesiveness of program.

John's first clear steps toward separation-individuation provoked mother's need to again intrude on John's relationship with his therapist. She went beyond interrupting his sessions to more direct challenges to his therapeutic effectiveness by continuing use of the pediatrician to medicate John and by arranging for John to be seen by a school counselor on a regular basis. Despite his mother's feelings of alienation from the clinic and antagonism toward both parent and child therapists, John continued to make significant gains in treatment. He had been in treatment for eighteen months when a spurt of rapid growth took place, which included the development of ego controls, a capacity to resist regression, advances in psychosexual development, and the beginning of internalization of the superego.

John had completed two years in treatment at the clinic when his therapist's commitment to the clinic reached an end, and the uncertainty of his continued availability to the family precipitated a new crisis. John's anxiety and despair were exacerbated by mother's rejection of her own therapist, with whom she had not been able to develop an alliance, and her decision to again discontinue John's treatment. The decision of John's therapist to remain with the clinic and his efforts to preserve John's therapy were experienced by the parent therapist as diminishing and intrusive. John's therapist succeeded in communicating to mother his understanding of her loneliness and his acceptance of her fears to a degree which enabled her to try again with a third therapist, who was new to the family was well as to the clinic and hopefully unprejudiced by a history in which she had no role.

John's need for additional time to extend, consolidate, and sustain gains within a secure therapeutic relationship could not be met effectively unless mother could experience the clinic as a strong and dependable advocate for her own needs and aspirations. The drama of change in this family needed to include mother and others as well. Mother, too, needed a relationship in which she could slowly test and try out possibilities within clearly defined boundaries where the encouragement of growth impulses was paramount.

Building a therapeutic alliance with mother was a gradual process necessitating maximum flexibility on the part of the therapist, a more experienced social worker with several children of her own.

Mother's ambivalence about participating in the treatment relationship available to her was the focus of her sessions over several months. The first three interviews with her new social worker were held in the waiting room and hallway, exploring whether angry feelings toward both John and the clinic could be accepted and understood, and whether her need to control the direction of her interviews would be allowed. The choice to continue appointments rested entirely with mother, whose perception of the clinic was one of "waste" (loss), "stress" (fear), and "inconvenience" (asking what was too difficult to give). Mother's sense of helplessness, inadequacy, and failure in managing John's behavior at home was responded to with appreciation of the realities of her pain and confusion.

There soon emerged a family picture in which the patient's behavior gave expression to all the things mother did not like about herself, including her concerns about her own fragile controls, while Steve, the oldest natural son, expressed all the attributes of mother's idealized self. The interactions with each older son, which reinforced one extreme pattern or the other, were not being called upon in her responses to the new child. Instead, it appeared that an attempt to modify the two extremes of good and evil was taking place in the parenting activity related to Frank. Mother's first requests for participation on the part of her new therapist were in relation to better understanding the needs of her preschooler and her wish to improve her skills in responding to them. It was possible to talk about behaviors in developmental terms in relation to her toddler, whereas it was not yet possible to think about behavior in these terms in relation to the older boys.

Mother continued to seek support and reinforcement of her strengths, projecting her sense of failure and inadequacy on her child's therapist and his school. She began to test her alliance with her social worker, first with intense criticism of John's therapist and subsequently by challenging his thinking and therapeutic efforts with the differing ideas of her child's pediatrician.

Both child and parent therapist now needed to exchange an increased amount of mutual support so as not to get caught up in mother's spiraling fears. Mother's difficulty in resolving the conflict between her own need to have John medicated and his therapist's strong opposition to this as an ongoing procedure required that the social worker find a way of sustaining her position of advocacy for mother without allying with her against the treatment plan. Mother was fearful of being dismissed from treatment, but more fearful of surrendering this much control to John's therapist. She first chose to continue the medication, cautioning both her son and her social worker to conceal this from his therapist.

Mother's therapist utilized both her empathy and her educational skills to help mother see and accept that the nature of John's relationship with his doctor was a contradiction to secrecy. John, through play, would remain loyal to both, while his therapist, through his knowledge of symbolic behavior and his commitment to helping, would become aware of the dilemma. John was in fact reacting to the threat to his treatment with even greater anxiety and symptomatic behavior than the clinic had seen in some time. Mother and John's therapist read the significance of John's medication in related play material (John having shared the pertinent content of his sessions spontaneously and directly with his mother) within the same week and in the same way. Subsequently, mother became more sensitive to the way in which a parent working as a partner in the treatment process shared information about events in the child's world, which enabled the therapist to better read the child's productions.

Following the sessions, which opened up the opportunity for both members of the therapeutic team to discuss the problem of John's medication with mother and with one another freely, tensions between child and parent therapist began to threaten the therapeutic process.

Mother's depression deepened, and she became preoccupied with fantasies of abandoning not only John, but her whole family. The threatened change in mother-child interdependency could only be experienced by mother as one of total loss and mutual abandonment. Her therapist keenly felt her need for adequate time to deal with her fear, pain, and rage. A mandate to discontinue medication immediately could threaten the still-tenuous alliance between mother and her therapist and precipitate an abrupt termination in John's treatment.

The social worker reported to mother, in an ongoing way, both the content and process of her collaborative sessions with John's therapist, and offered to participate in and advocate for her concerns and needs in any direct negotiations between them. The decision regarding how long John's therapist would continue to engage in treatment with John if medication was administered which was not prescribed by him was a decision only John's therapist could make. This reality—as well as the social worker's perception of John's therapist as struggling to preserve his relationship with John and effect an environment in which he could continue to grow without at the same time ignoring or diminishing mother—helped mother to allow time for a more relaxed and meaningful collaboration. Thus, neither mother nor child therapist needed to push the conflict to a self-defeating resolution.

Mother and child's awareness of the efforts of each member of the parent-child treatment team to understand, discuss, and resolve differences derived from their different perspectives served as a model for the resolution of lesser conflicts to come, not only within the clinic but in its relationships with outside agencies, with whom we were able to serve as spokesmen for the family. As each therapist was able to approach the task of conflict resolution with profound regard for one another's integrity and skill and an unflagging concern for the recipients of their service, the issue of winning or losing was dissipated, and the ensuing level of expanded trust enabled the child's therapist to allow mother more time to let go and enabled mother the increased sense of well-being that can afford the unfolding of a growth process.

Following mother's decision to discontinue John's medication, she began to explore her initial wish to place John in a residential treatment center as an all-or-nothing way of dealing with the dependency-independency conflict with a better-controlled and considered regard for their different and individual needs. She was appropriately aware that a special school environment could direct more attention to his inability to interact with peers in a way that was destructive neither to them nor to himself, and could help him begin the task of social participation.

Mother first considered a hospital environment where child's therapist was a staff doctor and might be visibly available as a surrogate parent. She needed to struggle again with John's readiness for greater independence than she could imagine assuming herself and was able to graduate to a position of encouraging his enrollment in a day program for emotionally impaired children who needed special attention to the problems they presented in the attempts they made to function as a member of a group.

Once committed to the school program recommended by the clinic, mother leaned heavily on the supportive help available to her in her negotiations with representatives of funding sources of the school of their choice. In a departure from the past, anxiety and vulnerability were handled with less projected anger and a new belief that others would respond to defined needs without coercion and control.

John's increased absence from his home following his acceptance into the day program precipitated a new crisis. Now, however, mother's increased awareness of John's role as spokesman for her own feelings enabled her to sort out his fears from her own and to face the consequences of his growing independence as an individual with responses unique to herself. Despite the unavailability of personnel to assist mother at the new school in more fully understanding their program, she was able to recover quickly from an initial panic and relate this experience to others in the past beclouded by merged egos. She remembered her own terror when sent to camp as a child, her discovery that it was she, not John, who dreaded holidays, that it was her discomfort with in-laws, not John's, that governed visits with paternal grandparents, and that it was she, not her son, who was so intimidated by the aggressive behaviors of others. Mother gained increasing perspective on her use of her children to express her own feelings and wants. The oldest of twelve children, she had always perceived herself as the link between child and authority, existing to interpret wants and facilitate exchanges regarding the requirements of others. There was little opportunity to become acquainted with rhythms and dreams of her own, and the concept of self-directedness was foreign and threatening. Her first affirmation of an independent self was the adoption of John, a decision strongly challenged and criticized by the community of grandparents. Mother could not feel whole without bringing to her marriage the balancing act of formative years. Thus, Mr. Jones was assigned the role of the all-powerful but distant parent, and mother continued in her role as both caretaker and spokesman for the young children in this new family.

John responded rapidly to his mother's changing attitudes and behaviors and began to struggle in therapy with issues relevant to his own amorphous identity. He spent many hours in therapy talking about the T.V. drama "Roots" and the former slave who traveled to Africa to seek information and understanding of his origins. He subsequently could talk about his beginning awareness of psychosexual insecurity and the pain he endured when referred to as a sissy by his peers. He was able to plant a seed in his therapist's office and involve himself in the growth of the seedling. His identification with his therapist became stronger and more evident.

This identification and enhanced internal cohesiveness was particularly apparent in his more acceptable and successful ways of dealing with stress. During his move and adaptation to a new school environment, he was able to express his fears without panic, entertain threatening fantasies without regression, and indulge in moods and feelings of anger without losing control of his impulses. Both John and the treating team had a renewed sense of his greater comfort and skill in dealing with his inner self when mother was required to be absent from the home for a considerable period to undergo major surgery. John's appreciation of his own internal changes was clearly demonstrated when he could say to his therapist, "I think I can handle it this time."

John recently celebrated his thirteenth birthday and could verbalize his wish to include his therapist in a ritual recognition of his first year as a teenager. Finally, he could introduce the idea of termination and say, "Doctor, very soon it will be four years that I have been coming to see you. I think I've learned what I needed to learn. I think we could end on Christmas Eve."

Mother, along with John, is learning to tolerate a separate sense of self, discovering and appreciating her own talents, and beginning to claim goals distinct from those of others in her family. Her enhanced sense of self-worth allows her to begin to enjoy John and to reward his positive behaviors in matter-of-fact ways. Father and Steve have responded to the more relaxed family system with increased contact and pleasure in each other's company. Steve is able to function in normal rather than ideal ways, claiming his own share of fears and failures.

Mother and John are now working on a new set of emerging conflicts, their ambivalence and tempered readiness to leave the clinic system. John vacillates between confidence and doubt about his readiness to end, and handles his fear and grief with even stronger internalization of his therapist's strengths and stability. Each participant in this new separation process, mother, child, child and parent therapist, is in touch with their whole personal inventory of earlier separation experiences. Bitter and sweet vary in quality and strength from one palate to another. The sounds of letting go are from four separate participants in the parent-child bonding, which had slowly expanded to include the therapeutic team and now allows it to fall away.

CONCLUSION

The Jones family demanded of its collaborative team the ability and willingness to grow in their partnership much as they would need to change and grow in their own right, both as individuals and as members of their family. The modeling of attention and focus directed away from the self, the diligent efforts to sustain and reinforce trust, the acknowledgment and examination of intra-team tensions, the consciousness of boundaries, and the commitment to inalienable rights, all were as intrinsic to the success of the therapeutic process as the unfettered work between therapist and child itself, the last of which has too often been seen as the ultimate goal of parent, parent-therapist participation.

Chapter 18

The True Fluid Borderline Child in Psychotherapy

DORIS C. GILPIN

The treatment of the "true fluid" borderline psychotic child is both extremely simple and extremely complicated. The simplicity is that if the therapist is being helpful, the child gives immediate feedback and makes an immediate gain, unlike the patient who does not reveal results of interventions readily. The complication is in knowing how to be and in being the kind of person who is helpful. In a previous paper, I have reviewed the literature on psychotherapy of these children and given a case example. In this paper I would like to examine what the profile shown in the research chapter tells us about how to understand this child in order to be helpful. The ego-state shifts, illogical thought, poor reality testing, and presence of themes from all three levels of psychosexual development delineate a very confused child, a child who is never the same and who experiences the world as confusing and shifting and unreliable. All these items, then, say to us, "Try to stabilize his world and help him to stabilize himself."

The world outside the treatment room may need to be adjusted in various ways to provide a more reliable structure. Thus, for example, a change of the school setting may be helpful. Many of these children need special school arrangements for clear-cut directions and goals and clear-cut consequences. They may need decreased stimulation. Often the structure of regular school is soothing enough and able to provide the child with sufficient consistency so that he can learn and progress.

The home environment is crucial. The parents need to be worked with to help them provide a setting that can be relied on, that is fixed and stable. This has been discussed more fully in Chapter 17.

The need for stability for the child implies the need for a stable therapist, a calm, unthreatened, unconfused person who stands for unwavering concern for the child's real needs, no matter how the child himself fluctuates. The therapist should try to be present as the representative of the needed object relation during the child's ego-state shifts. Thus, if the child is talking about phallic themes, but is manifesting neediness for supplies from the therapist, it is the latter to which the therapist responds. The pictures drawn may be penises, but the child is interacting by demanding more paper and crayons to draw with. The usual course as one follows the child is for the most primitive kinds of object relations to be worked out early, and then there will be a movement to progressively higher levels. Thus, at each stage, foundations of internalization of a stable and helpful object are laid.

The therapist should represent reality, not only the outside reality, but the reality of the possibility of an important other human to have inner stability, maturity, and lack of narcissistic investment in the child. The therapist, by implication, therefore, must have come to terms in a fairly healthy way with his own developmental stages, especially including his own attitudes toward symbiosis. He would need to have understanding of and empathy for the crucial functions of the important adult in a child's life at various stages of development. Thus, he would need to be comfortable in nurturing and handling issues of control, rivalry, or seduction, since these functions are crucial for the child to be able to internalize a positive, nondistorted view of himself, his lovability, his competency, his world. Such a child does not then need unreality and illogic. The therapist needs to be accepting and, in order to be accepting, to recognize that the child has inevitably had to become what he is, is miserable at what he is, but is powerless to change without dedicated, knowledgeable help.

It would also seem that once-a-week therapy is not enough to provide sufficient experience for adequate internalization. A well-furnished office in which the therapist is narcissistically invested may not be a suitable locale for the therapy, as the child's needs might become secondary to preserving the office. The child may need contacts with the therapist, at least by phone, at unscheduled times in order to experience the helpful other at times of crisis. Therapist absences need to be carefully prepared for well in advance, as such children have few inner resources to deal with separation from the helpful outside ego until near the end of therapy. The child may need to be scheduled at a time when the therapist is fresh and comfortable and therefore capable of the full and sensitive investment needed. The patient needs a therapist who will be around long enough for the child to integrate the therapist's introject inside him solidly in relation to all the child's conflict areas and as-yet-incompletely-worked-through developmental internal crises.

In general, interventions are not interpretations, although they may superficially sound so. They are statements about the organization and logic of the primary process world. These statements to the child mean, "At last, someone understands." The child's defenses do not keep the child from being in touch with his inner world, so an "interpretation" is not giving him a glimpse of inner world, as in a neurotic. He knows his inner world, but can't make sense of it and is terrified by it. The therapist's statements are a means of translating primary process into secondary process, and therefore of reducing the horrifying alien quality of it; they also let the child know he is not alone, is not strange and impossible to accept, but that he is human. When the therapist's statement is "right on," the child shows instant relief and a reduction in regression. It seems to be felt as a soothing balm.

There are some problems about knowing what statement needs to be made, of course. The children give unclear messages, half-revealing and half-concealing. If one gives several possible meanings, the child may be confused. A careful collecting of clues, including one's inner responses, may need to be made before one can be fairly confident about an intervention. Reviewing the process at a later time may bring enlightenment, or one may need a consultation about a particularly knotty communication. Often, however, interventions are needed urgently, and one steps in as best one can.

We now have a beginning picture of the therapy: Structure and stabilize the environment by working with school and parents. Be consistent in therapy. Be the auxiliary secure ego needed for each shifting state of the child.

Let us take some more items from the profile and examine their implications for therapy. The presence of temper, aggression directed outward, and unneutralized aggression is very pertinent to the conduct of therapy. The rage and destructiveness of these children can be enormous. Sooner or later these children may need to be held gently and calmly in order to prevent injury or too much damage to the environment. The holding is usually felt by the child in two different ways: It is comforting that they are not left lonely and helpless, fearing the fantasized, frightening consequences of their overwhelming anger nor the terrible primitive punishment from the super-ego. Nevertheless, in being held, they may be overstimulated by the closeness, fearing engulfment or seduction. An arm's-length kind of holding is therefore less threatening. The therapist welcomes the child's aiming the whole burden of hate at him. For, as the child experiences the therapist as still accepting him as a human being and not a monster, and as he observes the therapist still concerned about him and not moved to negative affects by the power of the child's hate, he begins to be able to take some of the benign, controlling therapist into himself, creating his own internal benign control.

The joint presence of death themes and depression illuminates another aspect of the therapy that has been hinted at above—that is, the low self-worth these children feel. The death themes are not all aggression turned outward; some of them are suicidal in content. These children are very unhappy, not just about the world, but about themselves. With remnants of infantile omnipotence, they fear their power to send the environment fluctuating and storming, a fear confirmed often by parental reactions to their states. They fear the power of their death wishes. They need to know they are not overwhelmingly responsible for the feeling states of others, that death wishes for others are not magically going to come true. Again, this knowledge comes best from experiencing the therapist unchanged by the child's rage and destructive wishes.

Now a word about the impulsivity and the primary use of the pleasure principle, which demands instant gratification. At least early in therapy, the therapist needs therapy to be able to respond quickly and, often, givingly, perhaps introducing joint thinking about the request after it has been gratified. The child may ask the therapist if he lives nearby. The therapist might say, "Yes, but I expect your question means you are wondering if I am close to you at other times than during therapy," thus answering the question concretely and without introducing a delay, but moving on to express empathy for the underlying concerns. If a request can't be granted or is unwise to grant, the therapist may try to substitute a different gratification. The child may ask, "Do you have children?", and the therapist might answer, "I expect you have lots of thoughts and feelings about what it would be like to be my child."

The use of the defense of projection needs to be clarified. These children use for defense a great deal of projective identification, which means they tend to see all people as like themselves. Therefore, they don't really get rid of their hate by attributing it to other people, as in a pure projection; they are merely justifying it. Again, the therapist should be calm and warm in showing the child the falsity of the projective identification. "You feel I must be angry just as you are angry."

Naturally, every therapist will have some of his own feelings aroused by the confusion, rage, impulsivity, demandingness, and lack of understanding of the child, but he can still gear his actions to the child's needs, not to the discharge of his own affects.

I have not mentioned one considerable asset these children bring to therapy: They almost always have some basic trust or readiness for relationship. These children may be shy or cling to mother at first, but they are not withdrawn or nonengaging. They are able to test the therapist as a suitable other very early on.

Another asset is that their lack of insight is usually very transient. These children very quickly understand what is therapeutic and what isn't, and have ways of letting the therapist know which is which. They further sense any form of fakery or self-servingness. They are quick to expose when the therapist has yielded to immaturity or exploitation of the therapy, or made a mistake arising from his unconscious conflicts. They let the therapist know they've seen this by their explosions of affect and regression.

The lack of friends, as noted on the profile (Table 4, Chapter 16), is usually the result of the child being tied up with relationships with adults. It seems to me it need not usually directly affect how one does the therapy. Sometimes a parent will want the child to miss therapy to go to a party. "He never gets invited to parties," they may explain. Part of the therapist's thinking must be, "Is he ready to handle himself at a party, or will it be another disaster? Is his relationship with me at the point where it is more important to continue working on it, or is it time to begin to work on peer relations in the real world?"

As in any psychotherapy, one tries to stay with the patient, continuously assessing what he needs at that particular moment to free him to grow. As mentioned, these children usually are so much in touch with their unconscious that one is not so much actually making interpretations to them as letting them know the therapist sees their unconscious too, and finds it quite understandable. Near the end of therapy, when they are fairly well stabilized at a stage triadic or above, defense interpretations are sometimes appropriate, as in a neurotic case: "You used to be a messy baby here because you needed my help with your insides about mess. I think now you are being a messy baby because more grown-up things are very hard for you."

Treating these patients can be exhausting and confusing, but very rewarding. They blossom visibly through appropriate interventions and interactions, and move on toward maturity with increasing confidence and enjoyment.

The following case example, with excerpts from process, is of an eleven-year-old boy who had been transferred from a previous therapist with whom he had had a good experience, so that his initial testing of the new therapist, while fairly typical for these children, was not prolonged. He had been seen twice a week, but was now on a once-a-week schedule.

Here is some process from the second month of therapy:

He then had the therapist work out puzzles he had written. The puzzles were all problems of sequence; how was one sequence like another sequence? It could be size or interval or numbers. He would give her a check and a star after they were worked. Eventually he gave clues. The therapist said she'd been really dumb not figuring these out. She said she had come to the conclusion that he was pretty smart and that she thought possibly he was going to find out how smart she was.

He then did some scribbling on a pad that was for phone messages. There was a place at the bottom for name and number. He would just scribble something for "Name," but he would put real numbers for the "Number." On the pad labeled "Engagements," he put a lot of x's for different times, and then

at the bottom, where it said "birthdays," he put "his, hers, mine, their's." He
then wrote on a memo pad and gave it to the therapist. It said, "Jack great."
She said, "You are right, you are great."

She had been saving the papers he'd given her and was studying them. He
came over and picked them all up and tore them up. He threw them in the
wastebasket. She thanked him for putting them in the wastebasket, but said
she really wasn't thanking him for tearing them up. She commented that he'd
started tearing the things right when she had said he was great. He went to the
door, and it seemed as if he wanted to leave. She said there must have been
something uncomfortable about that, since now he wanted to leave. She said
that he had been sort of kidding, and maybe he felt he was just kidding about
"Jack Great"; she knew that too, but there were still great things about him. He
indicated that it was time to go. She said, "Maybe, somehow, when I said that,
I got too close."

The amount of indirect and not clearly verbal material is still large, and there
is not a solid therapeutic alliance.

A session two weeks later illustrates the necessity for the therapist to
expose himself or herself in order for the child to develop trust, as well as the
rapid-fire types of interventions that are often called for. The boy clearly was
challenging any insecurities the therapist might have.

He came back into the room and began to use his left hand like a puppet.
The therapist said it still wasn't clear to her why he felt like communicating
without words so often. He then demonstrated that it was sort of fun, which
the therapist verbalized and he agreed with. The puppet would knock at the
door, and she would say, "Come in," and the puppet would come in and would
ask such things as "What's your name?" The therapist would say. He then
asked how old she was, when she was born, and where was she born. He
figured out from when she was born how old she was. He then asked why she
was born. At this the therapist replied, "That has a lot of answers," and he said,
"Well, forget it, then."

He then had the puppet pretend to be people who were coming to the office.
One puppet said he had a problem. The therapist asked, "Well, what's the
problem?" He said that he wanted a girl to go out with him and she wouldn't.
The therapist's reply was, "I still don't know what the problem is. Is the
problem that you want to quit *wanting* her to do that, or is the problem that
you want her to change?" He said that he wanted her to change.

"Well, I'm sorry, but that's the kind of problem I can't deal with. I can only
deal with you, and not somebody else," responded the therapist. He immediately left, and another puppet came in who was dancing and who was asked
what the problem was. The puppet said, "I dance all the time."

The therapist asked, "What's the problem about that?"

The puppet stopped dancing and said, "Thank you, you've solved my
problem." "I don't solve anybody's problem. Sometimes I help someone solve
his problem."

Another puppet came in, crawling on the floor and whispering, and asked the therapist to whisper, which she did. It turned out he was running away from the police because he'd stolen a million dollars. He wanted to be told the quickest way out of town. He was going to shoot the therapist, who said, "Well, I've got to think about that, because I certainly don't want to die."

Then the other "puppet" hand, which was a policeman, came in. The policeman asked if this child had been seen. The therapist asked the policeman why. The policeman said he had robbed a bank. The therapist asked if he had a warrant for his arrest. He said he did, so she told the policeman that the child was there. The child robber shot the policeman. The child robber then threatened to kill the therapist if she didn't tell him what was the quickest way out of town. She said, "What if I don't even *know* the quickest way out of town?" The sheriff came in and shot the child robber, to which the therapist commented, "Oh, boy, the policeman shot and a child shot."

The puppet then asked if there was someone who was twenty-three around, and the therapist said, "Not that I know of."

He said, "Well, someone born in 1923 would do." This was the therapist's birth year, as the boy knew. The puppet wanted her to go steal a million dollars and bring it to him. She said, "I need to understand about that. Why do you need a million dollars?" He said he wanted to buy a lot of stuff.

She asked, "What do you really need it for?" A policeman came in which was the other "puppet," and asked her if she had seen a person whom he described as an eighteen-year-old young man. In the meantime, that particular puppet was supposedly hiding and had asked her not to tell where he was hidden. She asked the policeman why he needed to know, and he said, "Well, he is going around trying to get people to rob a bank." She said, "Well that's no crime." The hand then became another puppet, who asked why all these people were coming to see the therapist. Was I famous? At this the therapist laughed and said, "I doubt that." He made an okay sign with his fingers. When there were two minutes left, he said he was going to leave. The therapist said, "Well, two minutes sure don't make much difference." He handed her the pot of artificial flowers as if he was giving her a bouquet, and quickly left.

After another two-week interval, the following session occurred where the boy was revealing and sharing, though still very symbolically, his awareness about some of his feelings of nurturance aroused.

He knocked. The therapist said, "Come in." An empty bottle was pushed in as a puppet. It said it was sad because it was empty, but it would go to be recycled and it would get filled up again. It really hated to be on the street and get broken under a car wheel or thrown by somebody. She said, "That would be pretty awful for you, I guess." It asked if the therapist could refill it. Then it decided it would go to the soda place and get refilled since this wasn't the real place for that. He then knocked again, and the bottle came in and asked if she had seen the other bottle that was empty. Quickly that one left, and there was another knock. An empty bottle came in and was whining. It said it was empty because its mother had taken all of its insides. It was asked why she had done that, and it didn't know why. It quickly left. There was another knock. The

mother bottle came in and wanted to know if the therapist had seen the little
girl. She was asked why she wanted to know. She said that she wanted to
apologize for taking all the insides. She quickly left.

The therapist then said that this reminded her of last time, when there had
certainly been something going on that was very uncomfortable between him
and his mother and maybe something between him and the therapist. He
indicated that he was king, and asked who the therapist was. She said, "I'm Dr.
Gilpin." He asked whether she wasn't a whole lot of fairy tale characters, which
he named. One was Little Red Riding Hood, one was the grandma of Red
Riding Hood, one was the big bad wolf, one was the mother of Red Riding
Hood, one was the wicked witch. He then said he must have gotten into the
wrong fairy tale, and the therapist said, "I guess so if you think I'm in a fairy
tale with you. I'm for real, and you're for real. Is there someone you would
want me to be?" He didn't reply. He wondered again who she was, and named
some more things. He asked if she was his mother. Then he said, "No, not my
mother, she's downstairs. No, she's home. No, she's dead. What am I saying?"
She acknowledged, "You're saying a wish that you have sometimes."

He was feeling closer, and in some subsequent sessions demonstrated that
this frightened him. He talked of feeling as if he was ready to terminate but,
as the following process shows, could recognize the inappropriateness of
this.

He made his hands into two animals that looked like wolves or foxes, and had
them biting at the therapist. She wondered if he thought her words were biting
at him. He didn't think so. She wondered if her words had made him feel like
biting at her. At that point, he began having the animals give the words to him.
He was putting them in his mouth and eating them. She said, "You are
thinking maybe I ought to be eating my words?" He said, "No." She said, "Are
you thinking you are going to have to eat your words about termination?" He
said, "Well, maybe."

This was two months after the previous excerpt.

Through the next several months, there were several occasions in which
the therapist could treat him as a more neurotic and "reasonable" person, as
the following material shows:

The therapist asked the boy what kind of report card he'd have given himself
if he had been writing a report card. He didn't know. "There is a lot about
yourself you don't know, especially how you function in the world," said the
therapist. "You and I both know that you have some unusual ways of
functioning that you can sometimes use and sometimes not use. I wonder if
you have made any decisions about how much you want to be the kind of
person that a lot of society expects people to be, and how much you want to be
unusual. Unusualness can be a real asset to have. It does involve some
choices." He really didn't know what his choice was. He said he wanted to be
better. He wasn't quite sure how.

He was asked if he liked himself. He said, "I don't know." The therapist commented, "Gee, that really is something that I would think would need to be done before I would feel you should be getting along without a therapist because I think it is real important for you to like yourself." He said that he was really being asked a lot of tough questions. The therapist replied, "That's right. I really am. They don't really all have to be answered before you're grown up, but I think we need to look at some of them. Even the ability to stay in there with tough questions is one thing that one needs to get along in the world. You've been doing a good job today really trying to talk about the answers and give them a good thought."

Some seven months later, it became clear that his fears regarding oral engulfment had moved on to a fear of being his mother's phallus and, of course, the therapist's.

At the following session, he was demonstrating symbolically all his warring, loving, not totally integrated parts:

He had brought several small rubber animals. By gestures, he indicated that one creature and the therapist were either the same or very much alike. Then he definitely showed that the cat, who was the therapist or was like her, was doing magic by making things appear and disappear. The therapist asked for confirmation: "Me and that whatever-it-is do magic?" He nodded "yes." He then put on a show using the pot of flowers as a curtain. The cat introduced the other animals. The shark was first, and it would stand up on its tail and leap up on the flowers. Then the alligator did more or less the same thing, only having to climb more heavily, and it had a hard time getting to the top. Next was the rhinoceros, who came out and boasted that he would be much better than anyone else, but in actual fact never even got up to the flowers. The boy said the moral of this is, don't say you can do things when you can't.

Then the vulture appeared and flew around and said it had a bee that apparently was getting honey from the flower. The boy then showed that all of these creatures were together in his hand and demonstrated that none of them could really get away. He had each one in turn kiss the cat, after which the next one would attack the one that had kissed the cat. The therapist observed aloud that it looked like if they loved that creature, then they got attacked. He kissed them himself, and showed that they were all together. The therapist said that it looked like he loved even the biting, hurting ones as well as the other ones. He said that he loved his mommy, his daddy, his sister, and his brother. The therapist followed this with the statement, "That must mean that you love yourself too and all your parts, some of which are biting and devouring other parts." He showed very clearly that the parts didn't all love each other. The therapist said, "They still sort of look like a penis to me when they went in that show and were standing up straight." He shook his head "no" and in fact had each creature shake "no" except that when he got to the rhinoceros, it nodded "yes." He asked, "What?" and all the other creatures were trying to tell it "no." The therapist pointed out that it looked like the others didn't want to recognize that the penis is part of it.

He spit out the wadded-up stem of his sucker at this point, to which the therapist's statement was, "We can see that there are parts of you that aren't all biting and devouring; sometimes there is a part that squirts things out." He picked up his spitball and put it in the ashtray. He lay on the couch and did a sit-up, and then acted like he was very very weak and falling off the couch. "Strong and weak," commented the therapist. He then showed he could do something and then he showed that he was totally helpless, and again the therapist commented, "Accomplishing and failing."

The session ended with him demonstrating taking in the therapist's things and using them, sometimes in an irritating way.

In this session he was certainly demonstrating the rise and fall of the penis and of its waxing and waning power in connection with his feelings of not being a unity.

In the following session, he again is demonstrating phallic concerns about power and is talking more communicatively.

He was being really silly, and the therapist said, "The comic part of you that you showed me last time and that you thought was the lovable part really is lovable." He was asked if he really thought the other parts weren't lovable. He indicated "no."

He got out the padded bat and hit the therapist hard enough to bring tears to her eyes, and she talked about the power that he admired and that he had with the padded bat. He played a game of baseball, playing the batter and some of the other parts. The team he was playing had three outs with the boy at bat last. The therapist was talking about how he liked the power of baseball, and then said, "It looks to me [that] also in playing all these parts, you're showing me that you can be lots of different people and still stay together." He said, "No, I'm showing you there are a lot more people in the world than you." "Yes," agreed the therapist, indeed there certainly were—there are your mother, your father, your sister and your brother. He agreed. She added, "There are a lot more people in the world than you," and he agreed again.

At some point, he brought out a toy phone and told the therapist her mother was on the phone and that she was mad at the therapist; he tried to get her to talk on the phone. She commented about his thinking about his mother being mad at him and that he had shown he really liked power and probably admired his mother's power. He agreed. He eventually got the phone working right again and left it alone. The therapist said, "You didn't have to straighten out the messes you made today, but you did." He asked, "What messes?", and she pointed out a spill with some soda and the mess with the phone. She said that she knew there really were kind parts to him.

There does at this point seem to be some cause for concern about his admiration of powerful, sadistic aggressivity relatively unmodified by warmth and tenderness, and one wonders if he may be solidifying into a character disorder.

Three sessions later, where therapy is currently, there can be talk about his defenses against closeness and the implied warmth and tenderness involved, so that characterologic sadistic coldness seems a less likely outcome.

He thought he would look for an ending date on a calendar. The therapist said, "It really is a good sign that you are planning ahead for an ending date. That's a sign that you probably will be able to do it at some time because you've met other goals for yourself and you may very well meet this one." He said that he really had nothing to say. The therapist responded, "Well, then, you won't make that goal because it's going to take some talking to get to it." He said, "I can't think of anything that needs to be said." She pointed out that "then you really won't make that goal, because we know from the outside world that there are things happening. If you're blind to those, then you really need some help. You're really not going to make that goal if you're going to stay blind to that."

He made a good eye contact, which had some warmth to it at that point. Then he shifted uneasily away and began clowning with his tongue. The therapist pointed out, "You know, just a minute ago it looked like we were fairly close, and now you're doing all this clowning. It looks like the clowning is some way of getting away from closeness." He agreed and added, "What's wrong with that?" "There is nothing particularly wrong with it," the therapist said. "People do need ways to get away from closeness, but sometimes you get in trouble with this particular way. Your clowning annoys people sometimes, and they take it out on you in ways that mean you can't succeed at things you want to succeed in. It does take care of the closeness, but it causes other problems. What we'd like to do in therapy is give people more choices, so if they want to keep away from closeness, they have other ways of dealing with it."

He went over to the desk for a minute and was clowning around some more. All of a sudden he said, "I can't think of other things to do besides clowning." The therapist thought aloud about telling him what other kids do, but that might not really be him. He thought he agreed with that. The therapist asked what would happen if he just told somebody, "Hey, I think I'm feeling like I'm getting too close to you and I want to get away for a while or do something else"? He thought for a while and said, "Well, that's not me." She agreed and called it a dumb idea. At some point, he was also asking about what was closeness.

He began clowning again at one point, and the therapist asked, "What's so scary about closeness, anyway?" He said, "Well, it's something about saying things that you can only say to your family." "You mean things like 'I hate you' or 'I love you'?" she asked. He thought something sort of like that.

The excerpts from process of a borderline boy do illustrate the complexities of the communications, the considerable stress on the therapist's stability and maturity, and yet the tremendous gains that can be made through the psychotherapy of these children.

Chapter 19

Early Object Loss and Borderline Pathology

BERNARD FEINBERG

The patient is a thirteen-year-old white boy who lives with his father. The mother has been dead for nine years. There is a married sister much older than John. He has been in a day treatment program that stresses educational therapy for the past eight months, and I have been treating him in twice-weekly psychotherapy for the past seven months.

REASON FOR REFERRAL AND FATHER'S DESCRIPTION OF THE CHILD

John was fearful, according to his father, of doctors, injections, the dark, storms, noises, and dogs when they barked. At the time of the referral John had just completed his second year at a public elementary school. His schoolwork had fallen off during his second year. The neighbors were not letting their children play with him, and they were complaining that he was making too much noise when his father was not at home.

The father explained that he would generally make primitive noises when he was disappointed, the chief overt disappointments consisting in father's inability to provide John with material possessions that John admired in other peoples' homes. His primitive noises consisted for the most part of barking. Mr. Smith was concerned that their new landlord would not tolerate the noise and would force them to leave. John was also screeching like the "Wicked Witch of the West," a symptom that had begun when he saw the "Wizard of Oz" at age five. For the past two years he had dressed as a witch on Halloween. He had been involved with some independent

269

activities since age five, but had recently given them up in favor of seriously pursuing activities associated with his mother.

Mr. Smith was also concerned that John "might be a transsexual case." He partially explained this by saying that John was aware that "the guys look at him kind of funny." In particular, there had been another boy in school who kissed John and stimulated himself by rubbing against him. John and his father had talked about masturbation, with the agreement that John would not do it and would instead save it until he was married.

Along with the noises that he made when his father could not provide him with material things, John had also threatened his father with a knife. On one occasion when he was actually touching his father with a knife the father's response was to say "kill me," at which point John dropped the knife and cried. There had been an episode within the year in which John put a plastic bag over his dog's head and then over his own, presumably to draw attention to his suicidal feelings. He stopped when father intervened and the father and he hugged each other. On yet another occasion, he inquired of the father whether St. Joseph's aspirin would kill him. The father treated this question by responding that it would make him sick and by removing the aspirin. On several occasions John had asked for pills with which to kill himself and had told his father, "I'm dumb, I have no friends, and I'm crazy."

Mr. Smith feels that John resembles his mother, and in that sense is prettier than his sister, who does not resemble the mother as much. Mr. Smith had attempted to court a lady, to which John responded with protests and crying such that father had to give it up. He is an obese boy whose intentional overeating began at age eight as a way of getting even with his father when the latter disappointed him. This pattern has continued to the present. At the same time he expects to be rewarded with a hug from his father when he does well in school.

DEVELOPMENTAL INFORMATION

The father is a college-educated, not very successful businessman who grew up in a large family and later changed his religious affiliation. At an advanced age he married a woman of another faith who was much younger than he and who was fond of dogs. It was not until after they were married that Mr. Smith noticed that her legs were asymmetric, a fact that disturbed him, and which she explained resulted from a fall from a horse.

Their daughter was born after two years of marriage, and John was born eleven years later. John's mother was fond of dogs. Prior to John's birth, his mother had been ill for many years, and because of this Mr. Smith did not want to have a second child, but gave into his wife's wishes for another baby.

Mr. Smith's description of his marriage consists mainly of discussions of his wife's physical illnesses, the great sums of money which he spent to keep her alive, to "save her," and a series of now-dead doctors to whom he took her who frequently could not make up their minds whether or not to operate. She had severe disc pains and took several aspirins a day, along with Equinal, Seconal, and sometimes codeine. She was also on cortisone. She was obese and regarded herself as a "fat slob." During the seventeen-year marriage there were many surgical procedures. Mrs. Smith had a growing dependence on drugs, and on one occasion Mr. Smith provided her with codeine in the hospital when she was recovering from surgery. (It may be that this recollection has more to do with the way Mr. Smith recalls and represents his wife than it actually reflects her drug dependence.)

During her pregnancy with John, Mrs. Smith said that her baby was dead on several occasions, but Mr. Smith reassured her that a baby was sometimes inactive. However, he experienced this reassurance as a "fib." Right after John's birth father thought that John was experiencing withdrawal symptoms as a result of his mother's drug dependence, but the doctors did not concur, which left Mr. Smith with a lasting impression that they had been putting him on.

In describing John's early development the father seemed to stress its ordinariness, and did not really seem to be acquainted with the details of John's infancy and childhood. He did describe him as having been cuddly and affectionate during his first six months. There were no feeding difficulties or illnesses in his first year. Developmental milestones were normal.

Mother was John's caretaker, but she often had to remain in bed. It is not clear how much her illnesses limited her availability to John, but there was one suicide attempt prior to her death from an overdose of Seconal, which occurred when John was four and a half years old. John was home when his mother's body was removed from the house, and he exclaimed, "I ain't got no more mommy." He was told by his father that his mother was "burnt like leaves," that her spirit was all around and that she could see him and watch what he did. Later on, seeing pictures of his mother, he would ask if that was heaven. The nursery school he attended shortly after her death described him as a sad, quiet child who didn't sing along with the other children when his father visited during an open house.

He did not want to be separated from his father and was worried that his father would "stop being his daddy." (This was also an actively voiced concern at the time of his present referral.) Father felt he was clinging too much. At age five, when he saw "The Wizard of Oz" and would then go about screaming like the Wicked Witch, he was laughed at by other children. In nursery school he followed instructions mechanically, and he would not go to another activity unless physically moved along by the teacher.

On the basis of these symptoms he was referred for psychological testing, and was then placed in a residential treatment program from his sixth birthday until he was eight years old. The psychologist who tested him prior to his placement in residential treatment noted that "the self which he has managed to develop is unusual in terms of the body consciousness, particularly rather primitive anal preoccupations. Also this is permeated with tremendous phobic concerns. He is unsure of the stability of any part of his environment, [and] all of it is threatening in some fashion, even to the point of representing perceptual confusion or inconstancy . . ." He scored in the borderline range, as measured by the Wechsler Pre-School and Primary Scale of Intelligence, but this did not seem to the psychologist to reflect his true potential, as he was in the high-average range in the Similarities Sub-Test.

After his two years in residential treatment, he attended a private school, but was withdrawn after two years when his father could no longer afford the tuition. The feeling of the school, based on his relationships with his peers, was that he would be "butchered" in a public-school setting. Nevertheless, he was placed in a public school for two years prior to the present placement. A note from that school describes him as having been submissive, cooperative, and demanding of attention. Along with the boy mentioned above who kissed John, there were other boys who called him on the phone to tease him.

PRIOR THERAPY EXPERIENCE

John was seen in twice-weekly therapy for approximately twenty months while in residential treatment. John's therapist observed about the father that he was "a very anxious man who tended to talk incessantly. His associations were quite fluid and he provided much stimulus for John's fearfulness and disorganized throught processes. Mr. Smith talked frequently about communicating with his dead wife; about her presence all around, etc."

At the beginning of his time in residential treatment, John was fearful of loud noises, especially of vacuum cleaners. It was felt his fear "related to his feeling that his mother was all around him and was in danger of being sucked into the vacuum cleaner." He showed little spontaneous fun at first and appeared quite infantile and awkward in his movements. Along with that, he seemed to be obsessed by storms and tornadoes. The therapist pictured John tiptoeing through his early years to keep from destroying his sick mother. In therapy he was quite involved with his "omnipotent fantasies of killing his mother, and defending against his anger with much denial. The child's fearfulness about his own identity and the safety of his world was also pervasive. He expressed phobic concerns and reality testing was extremely tenuous with fluid associations."

Approximately ten months into treatment the therapist stated "John is still testing out his aggressiveness in various ways and increasingly with direct, loud, physical attacks on me. At times he gets anxious about his expression of anger, peers into the hall to see if he is safe; at other times he wards off some of the intensity of his angry behavior with humor or by play-acting the part of a witch or a storm so he can project the meanness elsewhere. Many of his appointments are now spent demonstrating his new-found knowledge, writing words, reading; he gets obvious pleasure in mastery. His readiness to accept responsibility for his own thoughts and actions is increasing, but still is somewhat tentative and spotty. He generally seems more able to accept himself as a boy, though his body concept seems poorly integrated."

Just over a year into treatment, his therapist noted: "John has moved away from his dependent stance with me again. He often comes to appointments and wants to demonstrate what he knows. Physically he does not look as infantile as previously. There is very little posturing of his hands at this point. Occasionally he still plays out his aggressive roles, but there does not seem to be the extreme anxieties shown earlier with this. John is still a very fearful youngster, though there is still some attempt to indicate that he is brave while others are afraid. He is more able to accept his angry feelings as his at this point and to recognize the limits of his powers. He still talks as if he has a good deal of power to manipulate his father and is not totally comfortable with this." Despite some overall improvement, he behaved like a "helpless infant" in his father's presence, the father sometimes lingering after returning John at the end of the weekend to help him undress for bed.

At the time of his discharge from residential treatment, a few months before his eighth birthday, he was characterized as still being a fearful child, but it was added that his reality testing had improved considerably and he was no longer immobilized by his fearfulness. Toward the end of his stay in residential treatment he was seen in consultation and spontaneously brought up to the interviewer his masturbatory practices with another boy, which he felt was a bad thing to do. The decision for John to leave residential treatment was partly determined by the financial difficulties it was creating for his father; but also there was an incident that greatly disturbed the father, in which an older girl tried to have sex with John. The girl's father, on finding out about this, tried to choke John.

THERAPY

In describing therapy, I am going to present four process notes, including our first meeting and three more recent hours. The process material reveals my security operations and not just John's defenses, etc.

Interview 1

I went to John's class to get him. He was drawing a picture and asked if he could bring it with him.

He told me his father feels he doesn't stick up for himself enough. He said that he was in therapy with another therapist over the summer, and that with him he would imitate and take the role of a girl who used to call him Fatso and tell him to get out of her way. He said that in imitating her he was making fun of her. He told me how he had stood up for himself this morning when somebody hit him on the head: He hit them back harder.

He wanted to know what kind of doctor I was—one who gives shots? Or would I give somebody a shot if they needed it? I wondered when he thought somebody might need a shot, and also told him that I supposed I would give somebody a shot if I really felt they needed it. I asked, "For what, do you think, might somebody need a shot?" He said that he got out of control once. There was a fight in the classroom and he had to be put in the quiet room.

He talked about the friends he had and about another boy's parents, who he felt acted in a superior way. His father said people like that think they are better than anybody else. John told me his religion and then asked personal questions about me, especially about my religion. I told him I wasn't sure how to answer this question, whether it would make him worry less if I answered it or if I should just let him find out for himself what kind of person I was. He tried to reassure himself that, being a doctor, I wouldn't have a superior attitude, but that didn't work for him. For reasons best known to myself I answered his questions factually. I then found myself hedging about additional information he easily inferred, and told him that maybe I had made a mistake in telling him that about me, but I could see he might want to make himself more comfortable by fixing in his mind what kind of person I was. I said that he wouldn't really know that until he had known me for a while.

He went on to talk about his mother: He told me that she died when he was four and that his one memory of her was when she spanked him. He believed in reincarnation and feels that his mother might just as well be sitting next to him. He feels he has a special ability to tell important things that are going to happen: There was a hijacking in Japan; he was able to say what the hijacker would do, and his father thought that was remarkable.

His father wants him to grow up and be normal and have a lot of money. I asked him about "normal," and he told me it means happy. He would also like to be a musician and play in a room for a lot of people.

He was then curious as to whether I was married and whether my wife was religious. I told him that I could understand his questions as a way of making himself more comfortable. He then said he wanted to talk to the therapist he met with over the summer and that that person had a toy dog in his office which reminded John of his own dog at home. John wanted to finish drawing the picture of the castle that he had been working on in class and said that we weren't getting anywhere. I told him that I agreed in a way, that I noticed we were talking and then seemed to have difficulties. Did he think it was on account of my answering his questions? He didn't know.

As he drew his picture of the castle he said he would like to live in a castle. I asked, "Be King John?" He agreed and then said he would like to be a man witch and fly around and scare everyone. He would like a moat around the castle for protection and a castle under the one he was drawing. I asked, "So you could be well protected?" He agreed, and I tried to tie this to the fact that he wouldn't then have to protect himself or stand up for himself, that people would simply be too afraid to bother him. He again wanted to talk to the other person.

Interview 18

John came in and told me he didn't feel safe with me. I asked, "How come?" He began to talk about his resentment of lower-class people. They are poor and they steal. They should go to a home for parents.

He said he was angry at a note another boy had left him, a child I also see, which downgraded John's religion. He talked about his religious observances, and I asked if it was out of obedience. He agreed.

He went over to the radiator and turned up the heat. When it gurgled he stood on a chair and said he was scared of a mouse. I asked an externalizing question as to whether it had to do with the lack of soundproofing in the office. He agreed and sat down.

He talked about how rich he was, that his father had $500,000 in the bank, but it is a secret, as people would steal it if they knew. I asked about this, and John noticed my incredulity and accused me of having my own problems about money. He said I was poor and needed to work that out myself. He went and stood outside the door and asked if I had taken care of that yet. I said that obviously I had my own worries about being poor, but he also thought that having wealth was something he needed to maintain.

He came in and sat down, and said that I was trying to kill his father. I agreed that being with me threatened his picture or his hold on his father. He scowled and called his father on the phone, complaining about my not believing how much money he had. On hanging up he said he would see me just for his father, that he preferred to have Dr. X for his therapist. He looked teary-eyed, but wouldn't talk.

I moved slightly in my chair and he said not to come closer, that he was a cobra. He hissed and sprayed and threw a pencil over my head. He threatened to kick me if I moved. I asked how he expected me to act: Did he think I would let him kick me, or was he asking me to close the gap? Throughout most of this he was smiling. I found it contagious and started laughing. I said that I thought we were both noticing something that we couldn't name and that was coming out in our laughing. The time was up, he told me that I wouldn't have to throw him out, and he left. (In a previous hour he had insisted on staying forever and had left only when I told him that I would throw him out.)

Interview 20

John came up holding a picture book of dogs. He couldn't decide whether or not to come in. I told him that I could see him trying to decide and said that if he came in we could talk. He came in, threw a metal ashtray, and then the cover to a dough pot, which cracked. I told him I could see he was angry and also that I was going to put the things on my desk off-limits.

He told me he had ripped up his bus pass that morning out of anger at his father. The father had gotten him something, but it was the wrong thing. He felt I was laughing at him when he said it was connected with a possession of his mother's. He still doesn't have the original item she owned, though his father knows someone who might be able to get him the original. He is jealous of his neighbor who has one. The thing his father bought doesn't match the item his mother used to own and that now belongs to him.

He took off his watch and stomped it to let his father know how angry he was. He said something to the effect that it represented his mother, and that he always had damaged stuff. I said he was deprived of a mother. He said that he would clean up the mess (the watch). I said I wasn't worried about that as much as helping him to put his feelings in words.

He got out the picture book and found a picture of a Chihuahua; that was me. When his mother died he was given his dog to make up for it. I said that that wasn't the same as a mother.

He said that I am supposed to tell his father that if he doesn't get him the right thing, I (the therapist) will take him (John) out and kill him. He said he was going to pull a knife on his father if he didn't get those things. He picked up a chair and threatened to smash me with it. I took a firm hold of it and said I couldn't meet with him today if I was going to be frightened by him. He put the chair down and said he needed to call his father. I wanted to know why at that point. He didn't answer, but proceeded to call father and told him that he hated him. He wanted me to talk to his father and pushed the phone at me. I sat with my outstretched arm pushing up on the receiver with John leaning down on it. I didn't talk to the father.

He complained after hanging up that I never helped him. He then said that

I was too stupid to help him. He said he would run away again, slammed the dog book on the desk, and threw it down. I said that "there may well be something I need to tell your father that you can't, but I am just not sure yet what it is." (I thought, after the hour, that it was that he can't placate John.)

In another part of the hour John had the fantasy of taking ten sleeping pills and joining mother in heaven. People would cry about his having died, and he would live with his mother in a white castle and have lots of friends.

Interview 24

He came in with a large sheet of paper on which he had drawn pictures of appliances and vacuum cleaners. He hid behind his drawings and looked out at me sheepishly from the side.

He didn't say anything, and I asked him what he was thinking. He didn't answer and I told him that I was still struck by our conversation on the phone the night before. At first it seemed as if he wanted to rip his father to pieces, but at the end of the talk he not only had a reconciliation with his father, but they were very loving. I asked him how that had happened. He told me that I was stupid and that I had insulted him. He walked out of the office. I walked out with him and told him that apparently I had insulted him, but that he ought to come back in so we could find out how.

He came in and started drawing vacuum cleaners. He complained that my breath and the office smelled from coffee. I responded that smell and memory are often connected (and immediately felt that this was a hostile, knife-twisting remark on my part). He vocalized but made no words, and he stuck his tongue out at me.

I said it seemed to me that he wanted to stay at least tongue's distance away, that maybe he was also trying to show me something from inside of him. He looked interested in this. He kept drawing and making his sounds, and I asked him if he was telling me about a time when he watched his mother use a vacuum cleaner, but before he was talking. He turned his back to me and sat facing away. I asked him if he saw any significance in showing me his back. With that he got up and left the office for the second time and went down to his classroom.

I went down after him and into one classroom with him. He left and went into another room, and I told him that I didn't think we had the luxury of spending our time like this. I said I thought we needed to be together. He told me he was going home, and walked out of the building.

I walked after him. He started walking toward the bus stop, and I caught up with him. He wanted to know if I was going to stop him. I said that I didn't think he should leave, but I wasn't going to physically stop him.

He had found a pine bough and started waving it at me and barking like a dog. He asked what would happen if he left. I said that we would call his father to let him know where he was. He told me I couldn't come home with him, that his house was too clean. I asked him if he felt I would be invading his world too much. He thought so. He waved the branch in my face and I told him if he did it again I would take it from him.

He walked ahead of me on the way to the bus stop. He was ahead of me on the sidewalk, and there was heavy traffic going by. I had the fantasy of his stepping in front of it and being hit and then bleeding; and of my then holding his limp body and having to explain it to his father. When the traffic cleared he did step out and said he was going to commit suicide. I asked him how come, what was happening between us?

He came back to the sidewalk and said that I was bad for him. I said that there were probably parts of me that were bad for him, but that he needed to tell me about them so that I could see it myself and try to get rid of it. He told me that he was going to phone his father, who was going to punish me for letting him go home and for not being helpful to him.

It was half-past the hour, and I suggested that we start walking back. At one point he paused, telling me how the swishing bough was the tail of a huge dog and indicating how the dog was taller than he. He told me it was going to come back and do something destructive to my office. I said that it could leave a huge pile of shit. (I think I was still angrily reacting at that point to his telling me earlier in the hour how smelly I was and that my office smelled of coffee.) He was barking at me on the way back when he saw some college students walking by and seemed to be embarrassed; he stopped, but then began barking at them.

He stood on a grating as we walked, and whimpered that he was going to fall in. In the parking lot he wanted to know which car was mine so that he could scratch it with the branch. I told him that since he wanted to scratch it, I was darned if I was going to tell him. We then passed a small yellow car, and he announced that it was mine and began hitting it with the branch. I said it wasn't mine, but that in any event he ought to stop. He insisted that that was my car, as he always saw me coming by with that dinky yellow thing in the morning.

He came in the building and was in the office with me until the hour was up. He didn't want to leave, but instead went into the record room next door and started tugging at the drawers, asking me if his records were in there. I told him they were and that apparently he was having feelings about our having records on him. I suggested that we talk about that the next time.

I told him that I wanted to stop with him at that point, and walked down the hall to get coffee. I thought he had gone, but he knocked on my door after a few minutes to ask me if I would go down to his class with him. I went with him to his class, and I was then dictating in my office when he came in again.

He was waving his branch and barking like a dog. He said he was sad and wanted to talk with me. I said I could see him for a few minutes. He came in and went to the window. He wanted to know what I had been doing. I answered and asked him if his sadness had to do with our keeping notes on him. The gist of his feelings was that he wanted to see what was in them, but that he was also afraid to see. There was an interruption, and he left soon after that.

Interview 30

John had called me the evening before, and when I returned the call he was already sleeping. He came in and told me that he called because his sister had invited him out to eat on a day he was celebrating a religious observance. He complained that she didn't even realize that that would be a day on which they are having a lot of people over—a special day. He felt she would say, "Oh! Just have your celebration another day," so that he was afraid to tell her his reason for not going out with her. She wanted to go to a movie with him, but then it would be late and he would be grumpy in the morning and that's when he uses a knife on his father.

I had already told him in the hour that I would be able to meet with him elsewhere the following week (during a school break). He said it was a vacation for him, too.

He went on to tell me that his father tells him terrible things about me— for example, "That Feinberg gets you all mad." He said his father didn't trust me. He told me that he was going to see a certain fairy-tale movie Friday evening with his dad, and told me to please not ask him a question like, "How do you feel about seeing that movie with your father?" He said it was because there was nothing to do and that it was boring to stay home.

He recalled a beautiful home he used to visit and how he used to compare it to his own, with the feeling that he lived like a lower-class person. His sister used to blare her stereo, and his father smelled the house up with cigar smoke, in comparison to this other boy whose grandfather smoked a nice pipe and who had a mother to cook for him. He said, "Whoever heard of a boy sewing for his father? It's like being his mother."

He said something further about the father not trusting me and about my getting him (John) stirred up. I commented that the father felt like I was his enemy. He agreed with that, and went on to tell me how his father has been promising him to make a lot of money, and that he will be able to get him a big house.

He said he hates his father, as he always promises him things that never happen. The person who owns this particular beautiful house is even younger than his father, and he was able to become rich. His father told him he could have been a professional, but God's will was that it should not happen. He said he hates his father, but just then he wanted to call him. I urged that instead we try to look further at his feelings. Even if we didn't understand them we could experience them together.

He said I had better do something to help him or he was going to go crazy. In an effort to "do something," I said that I thought his sister's invitation to go out was very insulting to him, as it took away the small amount of good feelings he had about himself around his religious observances. He agreed and complained that his father didn't even know how to celebrate.

He then shouted out the window and was noticed by children outside. I told him that I saw that as a way of being admired for the moment. He went on to say that he could feel himself going crazy, and that he will wind up in a hospital; especially if his father dies he'll go crazy.

Again there was the idea of his father not trusting me, and I said that there were two ways to deal with it: One, I would want to talk with his father about not promising him things he can't provide. John said he would really go crazy if the father socked him in the jaw like I said. I told him I had meant that the father shouldn't worsen the situations in which John threatened him with a knife by making him feel more guilty, but needed instead to take a firm position to protect himself. He said that his father tells him, "Go ahead and kill me."

He had gone on at length earlier about his fascination with a material thing that this other admired family had. It was old but was still beautiful. He brought it up again and wanted to know what I could do to help him. I told him that as a person grew up they got filled with more experiences and had more good feelings inside themselves, and it looked like his problem was that he was stuck on the same things over and over again. When his sister had invited him out it was an insult to him, as it suggested to him that what he already had wasn't complete. He reminded me at that point about having to leave to get the bus, and I asked him how it came up then. He said he wanted to listen to me, but was worried about getting home.

COURSE OF THERAPY AND A WORKING UNDERSTANDING OF THE CASE

In my relationship with John, he very early on acquainted me with significant events of his life and the characteristic ways in which he related to his objects. He sees his father as a hyper-talented, potentially wealthy person who admires his sewing and other productions. At other times the father is seen as a fraud and someone who killed his mother instead of trying to preserve her. He is either a buffer between John and me or someone who stands in the way of the therapy. The sister is generally pictured as derisive and jealous of him for his closer physical resemblance to their mother, but also as an ally against his father's intrusiveness. His dog, which he feels he received as compensation for his mother's loss, is sometimes the only one who can understand him and at other times the target of his hate, whom he wants to suffocate along with himself. His teachers are seen as self-centered and insensitive, but also, at times at least, as helpful.

His self-representation includes the idea of his mother's death leaving him injured forever, that he's crazy, will wind up in a psychiatric hospital if his father dies, and that he is without anything good or substantial inside of himself. However, it also includes the idea that he is very talented; conscientious and superior in his religious observances; a good seamstress like his mother, and that he is soon to be highly wealthy and the envy of everyone.

His objects are largely, but not entirely, either admiring or derisive. He feels vulnerable and is easily insulted. The relatively narrow range of his attachments doesn't provide a potential outlet for his sexual feelings, and this leaves him feeling even more isolated and vulnerable.

In the beginning of treatment I was represented as the "Feinberg monster," a joint production of John and another boy whose mother died, in which I'm a ghoulish figure who tortures kids in therapy while ludicrously asking, "What does that mean to you?" This representation of me was helpful to me in seeing how I was approaching them. There have been hours in which he has demanded that I bring back his mother, and/or within which he has stated that he's going to stay with me in my office all day, if not forever. After attempts to end hours like these when he refuses to leave with a volley of interpretations, I took the firm position that I would throw him out if need be. This seemed comforting to him and allowed him to be less anxious as the end of an hour approached. He has derided me for my inexperience, my poverty, my snoring, my bloody, steaming vomit, and my baldness, which makes him worry that I am aging too fast, like his father. He has also seen me as a friendly woman neighbor who gave him milk and cookies after his mother died, and in the same hour as a person with a disease who begs Christ to cure him.

I understand some of his symptoms, such as the primitive noises, his screeching like a witch, and his almost fetishistic involvement with material things associated with his mother, as a way of keeping his mother alive within him; as a way of keeping people at a distance and also eliciting some admiration from them; and as substitutes for ordinary accomplishments and relationships. The barking may also be a way of calling attention to the fact that he has been left with a dog instead of a mother.

As the Wicked Witch of the West, he is someone who is teased and envious. Somebody else has been given magical powers that should have been given to him. The poor witch in the "Wizard of Oz" really proves to be totally impotent when she melts away. She's only able to get revenge to the extent to which she can scream and terrify Dorothy. This identification with the witch comes out when he's jealous and frustrated.

His thoughts of suicide come from his own depression and his identification with his mother, and is an interpersonal technic with which he coerces his father. It may also be a way of keeping his mother alive.

This child is the product of a marriage in which the mother was highly absorbed in her own unhappiness and in which the father treated the mother like an object of clinical interest. His readiness to provide her with drugs probably represented a certain amount of hostility toward her, along with a caring attitude. The mother's ability to invest in this child was probably limited, and the father has provided a kind of parenting in which he has sought to keep the mother alive in John. This is seen in various ways: One example is his encouragement of John's feminine interests, particularly his interest in items that belonged to the mother prior to her death; another is seen in his ideas about the mother as an all-seeing spirit. Also, the father felt that he'd had to placate John's wishes so as to prevent him from committing suicide. He has nourished a sense of entitlement in John as a sort of compensation for the severity and sadness of his loss.

John is a boy who had early maternal loss and who has not been able to successfully mourn it. He is still very lonely, and despite certain flamboyant kinds of behavior, is still withdrawn. His feelings are raw, and he makes extensive use of projection to get rid of his mean, angry feelings and his envy. Envy is his most painful affect. When he is hurt he moves closer to his father for admiration. When he feels the limitations of that relationship he becomes furious. It is an unhappy, unstable symbiosis, but his sensitivity blocks him from having new experiences with peers, his sister, and even his father. At the same time he is clearly a talented young adolescent. He is basically masculine in appearance, has a capacity for humor, and is creative artistically and musically.

ADDENDUM

Therapy came to an end one month after this material was presented, at which time John's father removed him from the center. My offer to continue with John in my new private practice was declined. After about one year, I received a cluster of calls from Mr. Smith in which he asked my help in dealing with the therapists at a center to which he had taken John for treatment. I did speak with a caseworker to convey my ideas on Mr. Smith. The father was not able to form an alliance with that center and treatment did not proceed.

Two years after I had last seen John he was brought to see me. He expressed anxiety over his awareness that he had homosexual interests. He confided that I had been right about this when he had been in treatment with me. Mr. Smith used this opportunity to let me know I was the most honest psychotherapist he had met, but did not accept my recommendation for further treatment. Through a mutual acquaintance I have learned that John subsequently had two additional brief-lived therapeutic experiences.

Three years after my work with John I feel I would now be less selfconscious in my technic, and more appreciative of his neediness. However, I question whether I would be any more able to reassure and soothe his father's worries. His father's anxiety has proved to be the chief obstacle to the formation of a therapeutic alliance and sustained treatment.

DISCUSSION

RUDOLF EKSTEIN

Dr. Ekstein opened the discussion dramatically by rolling a nickle on the table and asking people to describe it. Comments were that it was round, silver, flat, and money. He then pointed out that a case conference also represented a selection of clinical impressions that were predominate with some and not with others.

He asked around the room for impressions of the case. Some participants focused on the *hostility* shown by the child, and Dr. Ekstein wondered whether this meant, This is the first fact I will have to contend with; this may scare me; will I be able to handle it? He said that real hostility was not something that the therapist could let go or accept tolerantly. "If you step on my foot, I will step on yours" is a natural reaction.

The next participant was struck by the *emptiness* of the child, like a "empty container" that seemed to want to be filled, but there did not seem to be enough to fill it. For her the problem lay with emptiness and her ability to fill up the container, which seemed bottomless. How can I fill up the insatiable? Even the gods in their omnipotence (and according to Ernest Jones, all therapists unconsciously think they are gods) may give up in despair. We may have some of the megalomania of the gods, but we, too, oscillate between despair and hope—being unable to help and being able to help. All work with the borderline has this underlying quality of struggle between despairing and hoping.

Another participant drew attention to *the liaison with the therapist* and locked her fingers together to indicate symbolically the pull toward and away. It was a symbolic engagement. Can it keep people together or must they pull apart? *The liaison with the borderline child was full of shifting perceptions of the therapist, rapid changes in transference, and fluctuations in the total response.* The one predictable statement one could make about the borderline child was that he was wholly unpredictable.

Dr. Ekstein, over the years, was less inclined to predict. In the case presented it was especially difficult to predict. Within the triangle, the working space of therapy, the play space where so much went on and which was so implicitly understood after a while by the patient, the therapist was in the middle, with the father, on one end, not knowing whether he wanted his son, his dead wife, or a new wife. On the other point of the triangle was the ghost of the dead mother who was to be reincarnated and reunited with the son. The whole setting became a printing painted over and over, a print that was confusing as well as fusing, in which the father and son, mother and son, mother and father all melted into one another in fusion states that had a delusional quality. *The triangle was no longer the stable triangle of neurosis equidistant from ego, superego and id, as depicted by Anna Freud, but an unbalanced, shifting and precarious triangle in which there was war on all fronts* and where the problems changed from moment to moment—far from a peaceful equilibrium. The patient himself was at times enraged Cain, ready with his murderous knife, and at other times anxious and obedient Abel, ready to work with his problems.

Another participant dealt with the problem of countertransference and the reaction to the real human encounter provoked by this patient. Dr. Ekstein, like Redl, was quick to differentiate between realistic fears and unrealistic anxieties. Another participant raised the question of whether such a child could be treated except under very special residential circumstances. Could he be contained within the working and play spaces of the ordinary therapeutic environment?

Another participant focused on anxiety *resulting from traumatic losses* and separations, and Dr. Ekstein pointed out an example of this anxiety in early life. He himself recalled being lost as a child on a street corner and not remembering whether he was found or whether he found the others, and how difficult it was for the child to differentiate being found and finding.

We ended this interesting session wondering how to deal with reality testing, limit-setting, the extent of the support system, the establishment of a therapeutic liaison and a reasonable working space. Dr. Ekstein would do many things differently today than he did thirty years ago after he had been trained by a whole pantheon of supervisors.

We wonder about three things: First, how does a borderline, damaged, incomplete child deal with the problem of early loss, abandonment, and cumulative depression, especially when the child's activities are self-traumatizing? Second, how does a damaged, incomplete child with inadequate equipment deal with the delicate mechanisms of the regulation of self-esteem without becoming magically omnipotent or conceiving himself as hopeless? And finally, what are the reconstructive capacities for such a child with such an ego? Does he fall back on simple family romances to compensate for his own losses? Does he look for reunions and reincarnations? Does he find his mother swept across the winds of the world after her death? Does he in fact believe that she is dead?

Chapter 20

Borderline Psychopathology and Incest

EBRAHIM AMANAT

Widespread interest in the recognition and treatment of incest victims during the past several years lead to the formation by a group of twenty-six local mental health professionals of the Metropolitan St. Louis Sexual Abuse Committee. Referral sources have included the juvenile courts, police, social welfare agencies, child-care clinics, family services, community mental health centers, and child-abuse programs.

This presentation deals with the psychiatric evaluation of thirty-seven families in which incest has taken place and covers a period of seven years. Table 1 summarizes the essential demographic characteristics of the sample.

Since the taboo of incest is quite pervasive and universal, the reporting of its occurrence is naturally stigmatized and accompanied by shame and guilt, which makes it difficult to study epidemiologically. Furthermore, differential reporting at the various socioeconomic strata distorts the normal prevalence still further, since there is generally a tendency for all offenses to remain more covert the higher up one gets on the socioeconomic ladder. Our findings in Table 1 offer further proof of this bias. The studies of Guttmacher (1951) show significant correlations among poverty, poor hygiene, over-crowding, isolation (facultative incest), and social disorganization, all associated with a breakdown of incest barriers.

Factors promoting incest have been listed by Lustig et al. (1975) and include such dysfunctional family dynamics as the substitution of daughter for mother as the principal female figure of the household, actual incompatibility between the parents, unwillingness of the father to seek a partner outside the family so as not to lose standing in the community, feeling among the family members of impending disintegration of the family, and collusion by the mother. The anxiety that a family may break up is often prominent in incest families, as in a tendency toward "neurotic endog-

TABLE 1. Demographic Characteristics of Incest Families

Metropolitan area	City		Suburbs	
	16		21	

Age	<5	6–11	12–14	15–18
	1	11	21	4

Sex	Boys		Girls	
	5		32	

Ethnic group	Caucasian		Black	
	24		13	

Economic group	<$5,000	$5,000–10,000	$10,000–20,000	>20,000
	11	15	8	3

Relative involved	Natural parent	Step/adopted parent	Foster parent	Grand parent	Siblings
	18	8	1	2	1
	Other relative	Mother's boyfriend			
	4	3			

Religion	Protestant	Catholic	Other
	30	4	3

Parental education	Grade school	Junior/senior high	College	Special school
	20	8	5	4

Parental occupation	Unemployed	Unskilled labor	Skilled labor	Other
	13	13	9	2

Family size (no. children)	1	2	3	4	5+
	5	11	3	5	13

Inadequate housing	6
Social isolation	22
Family history of mental illness, alcolohism or retardation	25

Note: n = 37.

amy"—a term used to describe individuals who are unable to establish intimate relations outside the kinship group.

From Table 1 one might draw the conclusion that the child at high risk for an incestuous relationship is a white Caucasian Protestant girl in early adolescence coming from a family of poor socioeconomic status, with parents who are poorly educated, unemployed, or engaged in unskilled labor. In addition, the family is largely disaffiliated with the community and prone to mental illness, retardation, and alcoholism.

BORDERLINE AND INCEST PSYCHOPATHOLOGY

In the psychiatric evaluation of these thirty-seven incestuous families, a high incidence of borderline psychopathology was disclosed and raised the interesting question of whether the same conditions are likely to generate both types of deviations. The problems characteristic of borderline children and adolescents, such as ego malfunctioning, inadequate optic relations, undefined roles within the family, immature narcissistic strivings, and lack of structure coupled with inadequate boundaries, complicates the conditions of overcrowding, social isolation and alcoholism that further weakens the incest barrier.

In keeping with what others have found in borderline cases, in the majority of our families (86%) the psychopathology followed a multigenerational pattern, demonstrating cycles of deprivation, desertion, and disturbance. The fathers (in 32 of the families) and the mothers (in 29 of the families) had either abandoned, threatened desertion, or rejected the rest of the family, so that fears of disruption and further reduction of psychological supplies intensified the interdependency needs of the members. The grandparents (in 28 cases) gave a very similar history, so that each new generation had faced the same lack of nurturance. Severe developmental problems of childhood had been transmitted across generations, indicating a certain degree of psychological inbreeding, as if homogamous mating patterns predominated. Again, as with other cases of borderline pathology, the interference with normal development appeared to be present from birth onward.

According to Grinker (1975), the family type did not predict the type of borderline disturbance that would develop in a member. As he put it, "All families were overtly 'sick' but not in a specific way." In those borderline patients who occasionally decompensated, the families were poorly integrated and not at all protective. The mother's affect was frequently negative and rejecting. Kety et al. (1967) included the borderline states in the schizophrenic spectrum of disorders as a result of their studies of children of schizophrenic parents. This would suggest that the families containing a borderline patient may well have other members with spectrum disorders.

Another hypothetical reconstruction of the borderline family could make for a random dispersion of borderline pathology in the family, so that one member might show predominantly neurotic symptoms (phobias, obsessions, conversions, and dissociations); another might evince hypochondriacal and paranoid traits; a third might resort to infantile and impulsive behavior with a great deal of acting out, including the intake of alcohol and drugs (addictive personalities seem to have a borderline structure); the fourth may present as a typical narcissistic character disorder; and a fifth may demonstrate promiscuous and perverse sexuality, etc. All, however, could manifest chronic and diffuse anxiety, paranoid features, and depressive-masochistic tendencies with occasional outbursts of rage.

On examining the characteristics of our thirty-seven families of incest, the following characteristics were observed scattered throughout the families: a heavy emphasis on the survival of the family at any cost; the low tolerance for change; severe conflicts of loyalty; holdups in the development of separation-individuation, with a limited emergence of autonomy; the confusion and enmeshing of roles; chronic fears of abandonment, often associated with ritualistic and repetitive counterphobic devices; admixtures of primitive defenses in some members with precocious ego functioning in others; behavior that was often impassive, explosively aggressive, or indulgently and perversely sexual (nine of the fathers showed homosexual tendencies, either latently or overtly); problems around the development of intimacy with strong wishes associated with underlying threats; and sibling situations that reinforced incestuous relationships.

BORDERLINE AND INCESTUOUS PSYCHOPATHOLOGY IN RELATION TO INDIVIDUAL FAMILY MEMBERS

The fathers in our sample displayed a wide variety of pathological behaviors and personalities that could be described as immature, passive-dependent, rigidly authoritarian, inadequate, addicted, sexually deviant (homosexual, pedophilic, etc.), explosive, and borderline. The incestuous relationship appeared to be devoid of guilt feelings, and these were evoked only when there was a threat to the breakdown of the family. They often used a pseudo-heterosexual behavior to cover up their homosexual tendencies, and during the act of incest with their daughters, their pleasure was derived vicariously through a projective identification with the daughters. One of our fathers who was a homosexual child-molester before marriage underwent a disastrous marriage following imprisonment, producing several very emotionally disturbed children. With one of them, a tomboyish girl, he eventually began to have an oral-genital relationship.

These fathers regarded their own parents with marked ambivalence, describing their fathers as "brutal," their mothers as "unavailable," etc. One particular father began his incestuous career with his five-year-old sister and was severely punished for this "because he was too young to do such things." His psychiatric evaluation showed primitive defense mechanisms, poor reality testing, and poorly controlled hostile and destructive tendencies, suggesting the borderline adjustment. He was also alcoholic.

The mothers in our group were typical of those described in the literature. They had dependent, infantile personalities and showed a pathological degree of dependence on thier own mothers. They had little or no desire for sexuality with their husbands, and seemed to collude with them when the fathers turned toward the daughters. Twenty-six of the mothers in the sample denied having any knowledge of what was taking place in their homes but, paradoxically, experienced a certain amount of guilt when it was brought unequivocally to their attention. Because of the symbiotic ties to their own mothers, they also had difficulties with the separation-individuation processes, difficulties that became so pathological as to reach borderline proportions in some of the mothers. Close relationships became extremely threatening because of the possibilities of engulfment. A few of the mothers gave evidence of latent homosexual wishes, which would explain the lack of sexual interest in their husbands. One striking piece of inconsistency lay in the transformation of a protective and indulgent relationship with the daughter-victim during the first few years of her life into a hostile and negative attitude later on.

The daughters were not only at much higher risk for incest but were also more vulnerable to the development of a borderline psychopathology. Twenty-two of them had participated in incest in order to meet strong nongenital dependency and oral needs. Fourteen reported fantasies of sucking their father's penis preceding the sexual contact. These were, therefore, those whose whole development was predisposing them to the acceptance of the incestuous situation. Where the fathers were aggressive or violent, the daughters complied because of fear, but where the fathers were nonaggressive, the girls did not act hurt, injured, or guilty until the relationship was discovered. Borderline pathology, along with depression, withdrawal, confusion, and sometimes pseudo-maturity, was common in these incest victims. Most of them had a low tolerance for family tension associated with feras of desertion, and they clearly used the incestuous connection to reduce separation anxiety and to satisfy their dependency needs. In one instance, a fourteen-year-old schizoid girl had had a sexual relationship with her father two to three times a week since the age of ten with the knowledge and compliance of her mother, and she only became guilty when her boyfriend expressed serious concern for this situation. The mother, with borderline thinking, had regarded the father's behavior as "an expression of love," and even wanted the family to move away together to an isolated rural area so that the close family ties (of which the incest was only one aspect) would continue.

Where incest took place between son and mother, a borderline pathology was evident on both sides. In the case of one seven-year-old boy, the mother would take him into her bed because she needed someone to hold her when her husband was not available. She would masturbate him and press him to her while she made copulatury movements. It is not surprising that the boy, in addition to his borderline pathology, experienced severe nightmares, bed-wetting, and fears about making his mother pregnant. Several preadolescent and adolescent boys in the sample had been involved passively in homosexual incest with the father or other father-figures.

TREATMENT AND OUTCOME

Due to the prevalence of borderline pathology in our sample, we have used systematic family therapy in the hope of fostering greater separation-individuation among the children, working on the issues of basic trust, autonomy, triangulation, and the massive defense reactions of denial and projection. We have also tried to separate the nongenital needs for dependency and close attachment from the genital impulses leading to incest connections, attempting to get the child's basic needs for love and protection met by the family as a whole.

It is not surprising that the incest family, always fearing disruption, frequently resisted therapeutic influences that tried to bring about changes in the victim's response to her experience and therapeutic suggestions that the victim might be better away from the victimizer. As the individual in treatment developed more autonomy and individuality, the family's immediate response was one of panic at the possible loss of the pathological cohesion. Court pressure has been used to extend the period of family therapy for an average of at least eighteen months and to get all the family members to participate.

The incest therapist is expected to assume greater control than is usual in family therapy and, especially with the borderline cases, to represent a reality figure who attends to problems with patience and understanding. The areas of treatment include on one side, the discussion of guilt, shame, stigma, sexual misconception, and sexual fantasies, and on the other, the encouragement of any movement toward growth, individuation, autonomy, and greater social involvement outside the family, and the establishment of healthy relationships with nonfamilial individuals. Between these two are more subtle areas dealing with intrapsychic and intrafamilial conflicts, communications, and controls as they are used and misused to exploit and intrude on the privacy of the individual family member. These situations are better handled with a cotherapist since the two together could model desirable parental attitudes and behavior and relationships that are warm and close but nonsexual.

Although some investigators have reported favorable outcomes for the victims of incest, we have been more impressed by the radical and persistent pathology. Seventy-two percent of our sample of child-victims remained confused in their personal and sexual roles and continued to manifest problems with individuation and identity formation; 12% continued to show borderline psychopathology with occasional psychotic breaks (Grinker type I); 26% continued to be sexually promiscuous; 46% continued to have poor peer relations; 22% remained depressed; and 16% still resorted to delinquent acting out.

REFERENCES

Grinker, R.R., Sr. (1975) Neurosis, psychosis and the borderline states. In *Comprehensive Textbook of Psychiatry* Vol. 2. A.M. Freedman, H.I. Kaplan, and B.J. Sadock, eds. Baltimore: Williams and Wilkins.
Guttmacher, M.S. (1951) *Sex Offenses*. New York: Norton.
Kety, S.S. (1965) Theories of schizophrenia. *Int. J. Psychiatry*, 1:409–446.
Lustig, N., Dresser, J., Spellman, S., and Murray, T. (1966) Incest: A family group survival pattern. *Arch. Gen. Psychiatry*, 14:31–40.

Chapter 21

A Borderline Case in the Light of Piaget's Theory

JAMES H. GRUBBS

Extraordinary children have a way of calling forth extraordinary efforts from those who attempt to understand them. This paper will describe such an attempt to understand a borderline child by means of applying Piaget's theory and methods to the clinical assessment of the child. In doing so, the author was simply taking the advice of Anthony (1956), who long ago, and repeatedly over the years, has called for a complete integration of Piagetian concepts into clinical work, saying, "It is not sufficient to understand the dynamics of feelings; we must also understand the genetics of thinking, after which we may claim with greater truth that we really understand our patients. Our present understanding is too lop-sided."

THE APPLICATION OF PIAGET TO CLINICAL WORK WITH CHILDREN

In general, there are three types of works which have taken up the subject of Piaget's relationship to clinical phenomena: theoretical comparisons, experimental comparisons, and structural psychopathological investigations. Many of these works have direct relationships to clinical work with children, while others are only indirectly related.

The first two comparisons will be discussed only briefly, being relatively less clinically important than structural psychopathological investigations, of which the clinical material in this paper is an example and which is the actual application of Piagetian tests to patients. The works making theoretical comparisons of Piaget and clinical material using anecdotal cases or remaining purely theoretical have been written mostly by psychoanalysts, such as Odier (1947), Anthony (1956), Gould (1972), and Wolff (1960), with the exception of one very provocative but equally obscure paper by Piaget himself (1954). Each of these works, with the exception of Wolff's, which deals exclusively with the first year of life, takes advantage of the acknowledged similarity between the thinking of disturbed individuals and that of normal young children, especially of the preoperational age. Each of these papers tends to be reductionistic, emphasizing similarities of output without paying sufficient attention to the mechanisms of equilibration that produce the output, and therefore are of limited practical usefulness.

The second type of comparative approach has been more faithful to the Piagetian tradition than the psychoanalytic by attempting to find experimental validation for similar concepts in both theories. The studies of Therèsè Gouin Décarie (1962, 1973) are good examples of this type. Décarie and her collaborators sought to compare the Piagetian concept of object permanence to the psychoanalytic concept of object constancy, and to seek an experimental validation of the infant's reaction to strangers in comparison with Piagetian concepts of causality and object permanence, including person permanence. Her work strongly validated Piaget's findings and tended to validate psychoanalytic concepts as well, while pointing out some difficulties with them, as described.

The third type of study, the structural psychopathological investigations in which Piagetian tests have been given to individuals suffering from various types of psychological, developmental, or neurological deficits, are by far the least well known in this country. Simply put, patients have been made "epistemic subjects," as I have done with the subject of the case material to follow. Studies by several members of the Geneva School have been summarized by Schmid-Kitsikis (1973).

Bärbel Inhelder's *The Diagnosis of Reasoning in the Mentally Retarded* (1943) demonstrated certain analogies "between the reasoning of a group of retarded children (very heterogeneous in their repertory of reactions) and the egocentric mentality of younger children; the parallelism between the construction process and the interpretations of conservation notions in normal and abnormal children; the paranormal oscillations between different levels of construction and the effect of social interchange on the fragility of intellectual operations in mental retardation."

Inhelder maintains that the reasoning of the mentally retarded, some of whom attain stages that are comparable to those of "normal" preoperational children, is characterized by a "false equilibrium," in which elements of lower stages linger especially late in construction of higher stages. This is particularly so for the milder forms of retardation, which Inhelder defined as an "unfinished construction" of mental operations, as opposed to more severe forms, in which there is no construction at all.

A review article by Schmid-Kitsikis (1973), as well as an article by De Ribaupierre et al. (1976), reported that more recent research by the Geneva group has gone beyond establishing stage hierarchies for pathologically well defined groups to the examination of the transformations between stages and regulations within stages attained by the various groups. The outstanding work of the current genre is by Schmid-Kitsikis, *L'Examen des Operations de L'Intelligence* (1969), which focused on dysphasic, dyspraxic, mentally retarded, and psychotic children. Within the group of psychotic children are those which we would recognize as borderline (Schmid-Kitsikis, personal communication). She painstakingly compared the results of Piagetian testing with the results of traditional psychological testing and included a narrative vignette, although very brief, about each child's psychosocial history. This work took a step beyond Inhelder's toward clinical applications of Piaget's theory.

The work with psychotic and prepsychotic children is especially germane to this paper. The usual clinical characteristics of the psychotic children studied by Schmid-Kitsikis included inappropriate behavior, restricted use of objects, insufficient cognitive and affective investments, a fantasy life that was either improverished or filled with magical thinking and hallucinations. She found that the main difficulty was that the mental operations were not flexibly available to the child as situations changed. In tasks where physical transformation of objects was in question, as in conservation tasks, perceptual cues prevailed over the mental operations so that halfway stages were reached or there were oscillations between stages. Logical operations were relatively more stable.

The oscillation of psychotic children seems to be due to their inability to take their errors into account. The ability of normal children to do so allows for the decentrations that promote further construction of mental structures. Even in dyspraxic children who encounter perceptual obstacles, their awareness of errors stimulates an active attempt to overcome them by bringing other means to bear, such as verbalization or physical referents independent of a conflicted situation. This is not so of psychotics, in whom preoperational and operational schemes can exist in close proximity, sometimes in the same sentence. The procedures used by psychotic children tend toward avoiding conflicts even at the expense of transforming reality. The tendencies to avoid conflicts and transform reality are linked to the affective disturbances in the psychotic child, who has an affective need to annul too-obvious contradictions, thereby attaining a more stable affective equilibrium. These same tendencies are present in the prepsychotic children as well, but perhaps less intensely.

THE BORDERLINE SYNDROME IN CHILDREN AND ADOLESCENTS

The borderline syndrome in children and adolescents is much debated, and in some circles still denied, despite many attempts over the years to describe it precisely. There are several reviews of the borderline syndrome in the child psychiatric literature, those of Frijling-Schreuder (1969) and Pine (1974) being particularly noteworthy.

Frijling-Schreuder listed a number of parameters of comparison among childhood psychotics, borderlines, and neurotics. She described the borderline children as strange, hard to understand, lacking real phase dominance of drives, with poor modulation of aggression, a weak hold on reality, a tendency toward regression, use of primitive defense mechanisms, such as projection, identification, and pananxiety states, and a tendency to lapse into psychosis when under stress, but not under usual circumstances. Cognitive functioning as such is not described as being a differential diagnostic criterion. On the basis of clinical interviews and traditional psychometric testing, these children may score from the retarded to the bright range, although there is something distinctly odd about their thinking.

Pine (1974) has attempted to take the work of earlier writers, such as Frijling-Schreuder, further by describing subgroups within the borderline syndrome. Pine described several clinical subgroups, some of which are closer to the border of neurosis, others of which are closer to the border of psychosis. Among this latter group, he describes children with chronic ego deviance, into which group I believe the child to be discussed below would fall. There is also failure to establish phase dominance and drive development and a failure in the establishment of the signal function of anxiety, so that any anxiety rapidly escalates the panic. Even though thinking, the reality principle, and reality testing—as well as the synthetic function of the ego—are referred to, intelligence as such is not mentioned.

In turning now to the case material, I intend to examine the cognitive realm of a borderline child, which I feel could well be added to descriptions of the borderline syndrome and be complementary to other clinical descriptions.

CASE ILLUSTRATIONS

My "materials and methods" consisted primarily of my knowledge of Piaget, a set of concepts which I carry around with me and with which I assimilated by observations of the behavior of this boy. My conceptual thinking led me to the three episodes that I will describe, the first clearly a diagnostic maneuver, the second a diagnostic and therapeutic maneuver limited to the cognitive realm, and the third a diagnostic and therapeutic exercise that led to the elimination of a clinical symptom.

The Patient

L. was a thirteen-year-old white male who was the second of two children of an intact middle-class family. He was well known to special-education and mental health facilities in the area because of longstanding complaints about his behavior. His most recent referral was from his school, a highly specialized facility where he had been a student for four years but had made only limited progress. It was felt that his emotional difficulties were interfering. In particular he had tremendous difficulty using symbols and plagued his teachers with incessant questions. At times there was also severe anxiety manifested by grimacing or smiling, hand-clapping, toe-walking, stomping his feet, or pounding the table with his fist. These behaviors were much more severe at home and at times more bizarre even though no one felt that he was ever grossly psychotic.

Previous evaluations had revealed severe dysfunction in tactile and kinesthetic perception as well as in auditory discrimination, and marked dysfunction in form and space perception and in fine and gross motor skills. His language is behind by one or two years, his intelligence dull-normal, and his emotional difficulties significantly disturbing his performance.

Even though his home situation was relatively stable, it did not encourage emotional growth in this child. His mother was a tense, constricted, cold, hypochondriacal woman who was very demanding of others. His father, on the other hand, was a stout, pleasant man who was initially quite anxious but warmed up considerably and tried very hard to be appreciated as intelligent. The father, in particular, made considerable effort to understand his son and to be patient with him, but was not always successful.

Cognitive-Developmental Observations and Investigations

Immediately upon meeting this very unusual boy, I began to wonder about his cognitive skills and processes of equilibration of cognitive structures. Even though he was successful in some things he did, he always gave me the impression of having a peculiar way of going about things. And though there was very little of the overtly bizarre behavior in my presence, he would grimace, wring his hands, and pound on the table with his fist lightly when anxious or frustrated.

He would often come to me with problems to talk about from home or school, such as his mother's illnesses, difficulties he was having with peers, or some academic problem. His single biggest problem, which plagued him at home and at school and which brought him to the verge of tears more than once during a session, was his feeling "unsure" of things. This led to repetitive questioning in order to find out what was "right."

Because of the rigidity and one-sidedness of some of his thinking, I decided to investigate it more experimentally by administering a modified form of Piaget's well-known "sausage" task, in which the child is asked to compare two balls of Play-Doh, one of which is transformed before the child's eyes into different shapes with respect to mass, weight, and volume. One finds out whether the child believes that the variables have remained the same despite the change in shape or whether he thinks they have changed in concert with it.

L. found it very difficult to participate in such a task and was very reluctant to guess about things in general, experiencing considerable anxiety when asked to do so.

When one of the balls of Play-Doh was rolled into a sausage, L. said that it now contained less Play-Doh, weighed the same as before, and decreased in volume because it was long and thin. When I pinched the sausage into a number of small pieces, L. said there was more substance to the pieces than to the reference ball, but less weight, and less volume. When I re-formed the pieces into a ball again, L. reasserted his belief in the equality of all three variables.

With the exception of weight in the sausage part of the test, L. failed to conserve mass, weight or volume. Normal children conserve mass at about 8, weight at 9, and volume at 10. My conclusion was that L. was a nonconserver, and therefore preoperational in his thinking, with the exception of the one response which suggested an oscillation between conservation and nonconservation of weight. In other words, L. was more dependent upon the way things looked than on consistently held beliefs or concepts. By administering this test to L., I was able to confirm my clinical impression that he was experiencing a developmental delay in his overall level of operativity and that I would be well advised to think in terms of his depending on the cognitive skills of a much younger child.

In three-times-a-week therapy, L. showed limited but real progress. He was less anxious in situations that previously were anxiety-provoking. He was more willing to try new things and better able to generalize insights into his emotions.

He began to show interest in more complex board games, beginning with checkers. It took several sessions for L. to learn to set up the board, because "things didn't look right." The alternating symmetry of the checkerboard was very confusing for him. He was sure that something was wrong, but was not able to decide what.

His manner of play was quite striking. He tended to move one piece at a time, was not able to "take back" a move without becoming confused and losing track of a turn, and seemed to have no idea at all of what moves I might make. I began at this point to wonder to myself whether L. *could* make anticipatory images in his head; this led me to the second adaptation of Piagetian tests in order to clear up this question if I could.

I showed L. some pictures, asking him to anticipate how things would look if the orientation of the objects in space changed. These tasks made him anxious and he again had difficulty reaching an answer, but finally did so. The first picture I showed him was of a bottle, partially filled with a colored liquid, lying on its side. I asked him to tell me what the bottle would look like if it was stood upright. He correctly anticipated the horizontal level of the water of the liquid, but was not able to decide on how much of the liquid was present. The second picture I showed him was of a blue car upside down. I asked him to draw me a picture of what the car would look like right-side up, which he did correctly, but again with a great deal of obsessing over the details of the drawing as if they were as important as the other aspects of the solution.

The third picture I showed him was of a bottle partially filled with colored liquid, standing on its top. I asked him to tell me what the bottle would look like if it were turned right-side up. This time he indicated that the liquid would stay in the top half of the bottle even in an upright position. Oddly enough, he was relatively certain of this solution as compared to the others.

In the fourth picture, again a horizontal bottle, I asked him to anticipate how it would look if it were tipped on edge. Again he anticipated a horizontal level to the water, but was unable to decide on how much liquid was in the bottle, focusing only on one dimension of the liquid in the original picture.

L.'s responses to these tasks show the sort of variation that Schmid-Kitsikis has described in similar children—that is, L. sometimes got the right answer, sometimes the wrong answer, and sometimes the right answer for the wrong reasons or with great difficulty. All of his solutions remained closely tied to the initial perceptions of the pictures that I showed him, over which mental operations seemed to have had a weakened influence. Again I felt that I had learned something significant about this boy—his having particular difficulty with mental imagery, which shortly thereafter I was able to use in my effort to teach him.

After having gotten a rudimentary grasp of checkers, L. turned his interest toward chess. He was very insistent that I teach him how to play this game, mastery of which seemed to be very closely tied up with his self-esteem. Therefore, with some reluctance, I attempted to show him something about chess.

Setting up the pieces on the board, in particular the king and the queen, was a major hurdle for L. He progressed, over the course of four or five sessions, to the series of "rules" about how to set them up, necessitating a great deal of reassurance, interpretation of affects, and patience for me.

I initially set up the kings and queens and asked him to derive a rule about their placement. "Queens on their own color" meant nothing to him because that mnemonic depends on the ability to handle two independent variables simultaneously. As he sat behind the white pieces, he recalled his queen being on white and decided that "queens go on white squares" (rule 1). But this destroys the mirror symmetry of the pieces, which made it not "look right." He was unable to correct his error.

A session or two later, he stated rule 2, which preserved the symmetry of the pieces—queens are opposite, kings are opposite—but ignored the squares. I pointed out to him two "correct" solutions to his second rule: white queen on white or black square, and vice versa for the black queen. He realized that it did not "look right" again but could not correct this too general rule. In order to help him derive his next rule, I "trained" him with a class-inclusion task using eight black pawns and two white pawns, all made of plastic. I asked him whether there were more plastic pawns or black pawns. His initial response was "black pawns." After much obsessing over the two white pawns' not belonging, he finally was able to "decenter" his attention from the perceptually striking variable, the color differences, and to include the other relevant variable, their composition. He was able to then return to the kings and queens and decide that the white queen goes on a white square and the black queen goes on a black square. This rule allowed him to set up the board but is still not the most general form of the rule. In later sessions, he was able to state the general rule, always with considerable pride in his accomplishment. In this instance, I felt that I had used my cognitive-development conceptual framework to actually produce some therapeutic progress in this boy, whose self-esteem gained a great deal as the result.

Somewhat later I was able to shed some light on a particular symptom complex: a phobia of elevators. For several years, L. had been unable to ride elevators due to the panic that he would feel upon entering the elevator car. With my previously formed observations about his general level of operativity and his particular deficit in the use of mental imagery, I questioned him about his understanding of elevators. He told me that he had only recently begun to realize that there is one elevator in the shaft, even though there are five sets of doors, one for each floor of the building. He had previously been unable to construct, using mental operations where direct perception is not possible, the movement of the elevator from one floor to another, loading and unloading passengers. For him, the elevator was a box into which people stepped but from which they did not emerge. Or if there were people in the box when it reopened, they were not the same people as the ones before. For a child in whom the fear of loss of love object and annihilation is entirely too real, it was no wonder that he wanted to avoid such devilish contraptions at all cost.

During our discussions of elevators over the next several months, accompanied by his drawing some very poor diagrams of the elevator apparatus, his fear of elevators evolved into a fascination with the elevator's mechanical workings. Through this very laborious and tedious repetition of facts about elevators, he seems to have come to some sort of new cognitive and affective equilibrium with respect to how they operate and how safe they are for him to ride. Even though I do not claim to understand the process of equilibration which took place and which has eliminated the phobic symptoms, it did seem to me it was something other than making use of complex mental imagery, as is usually the case with normal children. That L.'s new equilibrium state is not altogether healthy is further suggested by his turning a phobia into an obsession. He decided he would become an elevator mechanic when he grows up.

In my work with L., I used aspects of both Freudian and Piagetian theory to guide me and to open up new possibilities. In some cases the therapeutic success consisted only in my feeling that I understood this boy better. In other cases I feel that it actually led me to therapeutic maneuvers which benefited the boy directly.

DISCUSSION

Even though I feel that my applications of Piagetian theory and techniques in my effort to understand this boy were worthwhile and fruitful, I entered into the undertakings truly experimentally. Clinicans must keep in mind that, at this point still, the application of Piagetian methods to the study of individual psychopathology is relatively uncharted. Schmid-Kitsikis (1976) has emphasized that the "epistemic" subject presents no concrete reality, since he is the result of an abstract construction (he represents, for instance, a child of seven to nine years of age or an adolescent from twelve to sixteen).

This hypothetical coherence at the structural level is not always noted in the normal concrete subject and even less so in the deviant subject who undergoes a series of tasks. We must emphasize the generality of Piaget's theoretical and experimental preoccupations: to study the dynamic processes of equilibrium in thinking, to discover general thought structures, and to demonstrate the structural isomorphism between the knower and what is known. Individual differences, the preoccupations of differential psychologists, are systematically ignored by Piaget.

A particular pitfall is the tendency toward reductionism in the use of Piagetian levels. While it is tempting, and perhaps clinically useful, to think of a child such as L. in terms of a normal younger child, it is making a broad generalization from limited data to do so. In fact, L. does not resemble a normal seven-, eight-, or nine-year-old very much at all, even though the productions of some of his thinking are similar to those of children of that age group. At the risk of creating a "weird psychological monster," which might be in danger of being lost therapeutically, as Anthony (1957) had cautioned, I must say that I do not understand much about the equilibration process of L.'s cognitive structures, but at the moment, I doubt that they are identical with those of normal children and must keep my mind open to alternative pathways. The study of the equilibration processes in disturbed children is a vast area of inquiry into which Piaget himself (1975) has, paradoxically and perhaps inadvertently, urged us. In his recent work on the process of equilibration, Piaget mentioned that this concept may provide the link between Freudian psychoanalytic psychology and his own genetic epistemology. Piaget suggests that the processes of equilibration are entirely general and should have correlates in the affective as well as the cognitive realms.

SUGGESTIONS FOR REFINEMENT OF THE BORDERLINE CONCEPT

Despite the many reservations that I have noted about the too direct or too facile application of Piagetian theory and techniques to psychopathology, I do feel on the basis of research already done in this area that a meaningful cognitive-developmental dimension can be added to the description of the borderline syndrome. According to Schmid-Kitsikis, and confirmed in some small way, perhaps, by my clinical presentation here, characteristic difficulties in the equilibration and modulation of certain cognitive structures are some of the characteristics of the borderline syndrome in children as described by Pine and others—chronic failures of object relationship, defensive organization, and reality testing. Analysis of the fluctuation of behaviors and of their cognitive content in borderline children suggests not an absence of constructions, but a fundamental difficulty in maintaining a definite logical structural level. The reasoning processes remain excessively linked to spatial and temporal considerations, and are formed by simultaneous construction rather than uniformly conserved over time, as in normal children. Each action seems to take on its own causality, which prevents the coordinations of the actions necessary for the logical structuring of thought.

Thus, carefully made cognitive-developmental observations can add to and complement preexisting knowledge about the extraordinary children with whom we deal.

REFERENCES

Anthony, E. (1956) The significance of Jean Piaget for child psychiatry. *Brit. J. Med. Psychol.*, 29(1):20–24.

—— (1957) The regression of the object concept in the psychotic child. *Congress Report of the IInd International Congress for Psychiatry, Vol. III.*

De Ribaupierre, A. (1976) Du sujet epistemique au sujet clinique. *Arch. Psychol.*, 44, 171:145–156.

Décarie, T.G. (1962) *Intelligence and Affectivity in Early Childhood.* New York: International Universities Press (1965).

—— (1973) *The Infant's Reaction to Strangers.* New York: International Universities Press (1974).

Frijling-Schreuder, E.C.M. (1969) Borderline states in children *The Psychoanalytic Study of the Child*, Vol. 24, pp. 307–327.

Gould, R. (1972) *Child Studies Through Fantasy.* New York: Quadrangle.

Inhelder, B. (1943) *The Diagnosis of Reasoning in the Mentally Retarded.* New York: Chandler (1968).

Odier, C. (1947) *Anxiety and Magical Thinking.* New York: International Unviersities Press (1956).

Piaget, J. (1954) Les relations entre l'intelligence et l'affectivité dans le developpement de l'enfant et de l'adolescent. *Bull. Psychol. (Paris)*, 7:143–150; 346–361; 523–535; 699–701.

—— (1975) *The Development of Thought: Equilibration of Cognitive Structures.* New York: Viking Press (1977).

Pine, F. (1974) On the concept of "borderline" in children. *The Psychoanalytic Study of the Child*, Vol. 29, pp. 341–368.

Schmid-Kitsikis, E. (1969) *L'Examen des Operations de L'Intelligence.* Neuchatel: Delachaux et Niestle.

—— (1973) Piagetian theory and its approach to psychopathology. *Am. J. Ment. Def.*, 77:694–705.

—— (1976) The cognitive mechanisms underlying problem-solving in psychotic and mentally retarded children. In *Piaget and His School*, B. Inhelder and H. Chipman, eds. New York: Springer-Verlag, pp. 234–255.

Wolff, P.H. (1960) *The Developmental Psychologies of Jean Piaget and Psychoanalysis.* Psychological Issues, Monograph 5. New York: International Universities Press.

Chapter 22

Summing Up the Borderline Child

E. JAMES ANTHONY

What can one say about a feast of experience and knowledge that has accumulated over the decades? I can only touch on some of the elements that need to be drawn together at this terminal point.

We have been, rightly, clinically preoccupied with the fragile and finicky "adaptive ego" of the borderline child and his adolescent counterpart. We have tried to describe him metatheoretically, phenomenologically, descriptively, but because we are still on the edges of knowledge, it is inadequate. (This is no criticism of our effort, since all our knowledge of one another remains in the end inadequate, inexact, and merely approximate.)

I recall a conversation that Erikson had with Paul Tillich, who also wondered about the clinician's preoccupation with the so-called adaptive ego and to what extent our hard technological approach drove us into the process of manufacturing human beings whose only purpose, or only main purpose, would be to adapt to what human circumstances brought to him. Tillich wondered about the ability to face "ultimate concerns" beyond adaptation, and to what makes a therapeutic streamlining of existence with the all and end-all of effort.

He was aware that we need to create some stability, some resolution of old neurotic resentments, some readjustments to present situations, but more than anything else, he felt that even if we were left with products that were not perfect—somewhat damaged—some feeling about the inward mind and the inward meaning of the world in which we live might play a part in the total rehabilitation of the patient (Evans, 1967).

At this point of termination, we can make at least a few important statements: It is not possible to terminate with a borderline child; one can bring proceedings to a halt; one can make other arrangements; one can create a progressive program; and one can monitor development over time.

But we need to follow our borderline child into borderline adolescence and into the borderline adult, and watch not only what therapy does for him, but what fate does for him, and also what he is eventually able to do for himself.

I want to say something, therefore, in addition to all that has been said already, about the therapeutic management as we have looked at it over these days. When the case is minimal and the prognosis brighter, we can do more, expect more, but our final therapeutic goals have to take cognizance of the therapeutic ceiling. It is sometimes disappointingly low, but yet high enough and good enough for what he (the borderline child) still has to do in life, which may be modest by normal expectations. With borderline patients especially, the therapist must keep his therapeutic expectation in check, just as the patient must get to know that his therapist has human limitations.

There are several models of care that have been suggested, and if I lean toward the one proposed by Dr. Ekstein, it is not only because his experience is so wide and intensive, but also because his therapeutic management makes so much sense.

What I appreciate most about such creative therapists as Ekstein and Bettelheim is their understanding and use of enchantment. It is almost as if we in this country had lost faith or belief in those "shadows of imagination," as Coleridge called them, that inhabit the inner world of the child and take on different guises as they emerge into the outer spaces. The transformation of fantasy into fiction as the fairy tale is formed becomes, under the aegis of "metaphoric" interpretation, a mutation of fantasy into psychic fact. With borderlines, transmogrifications occur that are deeply symbiotic or incorporative, with built-in dreads of annihilation and persecution. How can one enable the cannibalistic fantasy, for instance, with all its oral savagery and destructiveness, to moderate gradually to the point of identification with ordinary mothers and stepmothers? The wild borderline fantasy must be tamed before a manageable therapeutic relationship can operate. It can only be done delicately and sensitively, with an inward feeling for optimal distance. (Schopenhauer's porcupine dilemma: not too close for comfort, not too far for warmth.) Ekstein, like Wittgenstein, tells us not what to do, but only what he does, so that we can then choose to do what we ourselves can do, or wish to do. This is the definition of the perfect supervisor: to help the student catch the drift of the patient's unconscious and to put him in touch with it at any specific moment of treatment. The borderline patient struggles with the two polarities of neurotic and psychotic, between the cohesive and the chaotic, between the primary and secondary processes of thought, with the help of an inadequate sense of the world, an inadequate sense of the self, and an inadequate sense of how self differs from and relates to the world. The metaphor is there in the hands of a skillful therapist to bridge the gap between inner and outer and between fantasy and reality.

Such are the uses of enchantment. In the case of the Eskimo child* the same powerful cannibalistic fantasies are there; however, they are immersed in a subculture that does not leave him alone or alienated in his dread, but shares with him on the level of folklore and metaphoric understanding.

When Mme. Sechaye's (1951) young patient asks for the breast and is offered in place a "symbolic realization," an unconscious understanding occurs between the two: What I have to give I willingly give to you; it is only a metaphor, lacking in substance, but if you accept it, you will have something of me that will become part of you. How different this is from the report given by Bornstein (1953) of a little girl who had had a previous Kleinian analysis and remarked with professional glibness (a reflection of a great deal of Kleinian interpretation, presumably): "Please, Mrs. Bornstein, may I have a bit of your breast, I mean a piece of that nice cake."

What may seem so haphazard at the beginning of treatment—so full of random, disjointed associations, so full of nonsensical illusions—slowly begins to make what Jaspers (1963) called "meaningful connections" in the mind of the therapist. I recall an autistic, echolalic child with only a single phrase at his linguistic disposal, and this he would repeat over and over again: "Not tonight, darling." In it was contained, as the therapist came to understand, in multidetermined form, all the child knew about the relationship between his mother and father, all that he fantasized, disbelieved, dreaded, wished for with himself as substitute for one of the parents, and in summary, all the rejection and exclusion that he had experienced in his short and limited life. In the darkness of the night, he was confronted with some monstrous combination of these fears, fantasies, and wishes that seemed beyond reason, and he became fixated on its deadly secretiveness.

Other models for treating the borderline child seem comprehensive without being synthetic. The study at Yale, for example, by Lewis emphasizes the need for constant reassessment of the diagnostic profile because of its virtuoso quality, the availability of a stable object relationship, the importance of setting limits to acting-out and regressive behavior, the unlearning of old and inappropriate patterns of activity and the learning of more appropriate ways of being gratified. In the words of Alexander (1942), unlearning and relearning within the therapeutic context must proceed constantly. The only problem is that the level of anxiety is often so intense and massive that such cooperation can hardly be obtained. It often presupposes a level of socialization for which the child is quite unready, so that psychoeducational techniques focus on manipulation, modification, medication, before any semblance of inner controls have been established.

---

*See E.J. Anthony, Chapter 12, "Betwixt and Between: The Psychopathology of Intermediacy," in this volume.

The third type of model of management in treatment comes into play when the malignancy of the environment is so great that only residential treatment may suffice. Here the setting is more structured, more controlled, offers wider models of identification, and great opportunities to learn. The program presupposes coordination between the living experience, the staff, the group, and the treatment, so that what Lewis refers to as "an integrated pleuralistic approach" emerges. Before termination of the residential experience, the intense anxiety is likely to reappear, and preparation for placement or return has to be taken into very careful consideration. When the treatment is long, as it usually is, there is an adaptation to institutional care that carries its own malignant implications.

A fourth kind of model has been harnessed to the work of Mahler and has been described conceptually by Pine and used with adolescents by Masterson. Pine (1974) sets about "mapping" the upper and lower borders of the borderline spectrum—that is, the border that lies between neurosis and the border that lies on the other side toward psychosis—and he prefers to look at the picture not so much diagnostically as phenomenologically. On the lower end of the spectrum, we see that it looks almost like a neurosis with a focal drive conflcit in the setting of more or less normal ego and superego functioning and object relations and with some secondary regression from time to time. As we enter the spectrum, the picture changes—there are disturbances in ego functioning, the sense of reality, the development of signal anxiety, the disposition to panic, shifting object relations, regressions to primary identifications, and superego impairments by what seems to be an overall picture of arrested or aberrant development. At the upper end, the fluid ego organization is even more apparent. There is an oddity, an undifferentiation, a disorganization, a mechanization of gibberishness, and a paranoidlike suspiciousness, which is often mingled with confused primitive feelings of hunger, despair, fears and wishes for destruction.

Within the spectrum, I have described cases of folie à deux where the child has attempted to form a pathological attachment to a pathological mother; Anna Freud has also described a child of a depressed mother who tried to follow its mother into her own depression. Still within the spectrum, there is the inadequate, listless, lifeless child whose resources are meager and limited; there is the child with severe stunting of his learning capacities; there is the child with severe affect and stimulus hunger, behaving somewhat like an infant in an institution; there is the "frozen" child, the child bereft of primary mothering experiences. Yet we continue to keep them within the spectrum, edged on the one side by normality and neurosis and on the other by psychosis and autism. Perhaps like Ekstein we do pay attention to the "slight degree" of control that seems to distinguish them; that slight touch with reality that reappears every now and then; that slight degree to which they appear to be influenced by their environment; that lesser degree of fixity and rigidity. For this reason the idea of a continuum with no clear-cut demarcated diagnostic categories seems to be the most appropriate for clinical use.

Based on the Mahlerian idea, Masterson (1972) has described three phases of treatment using the separation-individuation paradigm. According to him, there is a faulty separation-individuation that leads logically to the depression of abandonment, to narcissistic-oral fixations, to primitive defense mechanisms of splitting, denial, acting out, and obsessiveness, to profound rages at parent figures, and to the persistence of object splitting and object inconstancy. He describes three phases in the treatment: The first is a treating-out or resistance phase, when he defends himself against the prospect of abandonment depression. During the second phase there is an attempt to work through this, leading to a consequent deepening of the depression and a great deal of abreactive recall of earlier separations and abandonments, accompanied by rage. A third phase is the termination phase, which reactivates the abandonment feelings and again precipitates much panic and anxiety. What Masterson tries to maintain is a "libidinal refueling station" so that the patient can, before he has completely mastered his separation-individuation anxieties, come back for more care at halfway houses.

For all of us who have labored with difficulty and some discouragement with a borderline case—we have had our partial successes, our partial failures and our complete failures—a remark by Masterson may help. He says that although the problems are severe and the therapeutic requirements high, *there is no reason for discouragement*, because, as he says, "We will have made it possible for him once again to harness the enormous power of his own inherent growth potential to his own ego development." I hear the same messages coming through from Dr. Ekstein, and it tells us once again what experience, dedication, understanding, and skill can do for patients. We always have to remember that when we are talking about treatable cases, we are also talking about the therapist who is treating them.

Now to two final problems: first, the familiar one of counter-transference. These children do not make sense to us at the beginning, and frustrate our omnipotence and omniscience very easily; they test us out to the full and beyond; they challenge our capacity for forming a stable alliance; if we are intolerant of regression or acting out, they can make us suffer; they can fill us with guilt for their emptiness and despair and hopelessness. They can make the long road to trust a hazardous one, but in the face of the steadiness and reliability of the therapist and his availability, a working, if erratic, partnership can be effected. The transference stages can oscillate among murderous and self-destructive impulses and wishes that occasionally frighten the therapist.

A second factor that interested me in the way that Masterson treats this kind of case is the fact that the patient seems to assimilate this plan and become part of it. For example, here is a girl talking of her treatment:

> I have gone through three stages here: first, it was really hard and everything was a drag. Second, then I went back to being a little kid, running to you and Mama. Third, now it is okay, I am growing up at last, I hope it will be more like a happy medium between the dependency I hated and the freedom I feared, like you have talked about for a long time now.

I cannot say that I myself have ever had any patients with such an overview of the treatment prospect that I had in mind, and I would begin to wonder about the modifications that I had brought about. There is something just a little glib about a patient who ends his treatment with a categorization of such a sort. I would prefer him to make some more general statements, such as, "I feel better," "I think I can manage now," "If I need help I know where to come," "It's been a long haul, but I really think that you have helped me a little to understand myself and what I've been through." But perhaps I am being unfair to Dr. Masterson here; perhaps for the unstructured patient it may be that the structured conceptualization of treatment is a crucial determinant.

I almost forgot about the parent of the borderline child. So often, they themselves have borderline syndromes and have suffered from gross parental neglect and poor mothering as children. Having never been mothered or fathered themselves, they see their children not as children but as peers, things, parents, or scapegoats. They do not know what to say to them, how to help them, how to comfort them so that they often have the same feelings. They are often as infantile as their children, clinging to them for symbiotic needs. Both child and family are vulnerable people who show an exaggerated tendency to respond overwhelmingly to internal and external persecutions.

Can we, in these days, when we are using so much technocracy to explore the world, make this kind of damaged, threatened child feel a little more secure? In the words of one author, Carson McCullers:

> The hearts of small children are delicate organs. A cruel beginning in this world can twist them into curious shapes. The heart of a child can shrink so that forever afterward it is hard and pitted as the seed of a peach. Or again the heart of such a child may fester and swell until it is a misery to carry within the body, easily chafed and hurt by the most ordinary things.

When your environment has not been average or expectable, you can be so easily chafed and hurt by the most ordinary things that your whole inner and outside world becomes twisted and distorted and shrunken and pitted and festering and a misery. This is what we therapists of the borderline have to keep constantly in mind.

REFERENCES

Alexander, F. (1942) *Proceedings of the Brief Psychotherapy Council.* Chicago: Institute for Psychoanalysis.

Bornstein, B. (1953) Fragment of an analysis of an obsessional child: The first six months of analysis. *The Psychoanalytic Study of the Child,* 8:313.

Evans, R.J. (1967) *Dialogue with Erik Erikson.* New York: Harper and Row, p. 117.

Jaspers, K. (1963) *General Psychopathology.* University of Chicago Press.

Lewis, M. (1978 *Residential Treatment of the Borderline Child.* Presented at the Institute, sponsored by the American Academy of Child Psychiatry.

Masterson, J.F. (1972) *Treatment of the Borderline Adolescent—A Developmental Approach.* New York: Wiley.

Pine, F. (1974) On the concept of "borderline" in children. *The Psychoanalytic Study of the Child,* Vol. 29. New Haven: Yale University Press.

Sechaye, M. (1951) *Symbolic Realization.* New York: International Universities Press.

In Defense of Diversity

E. JAMES ANTHONY

It is by no means an easy task to bring a book to its end and in a brief statement to try and mold together the different faces of childhood, delineated so richly by the participants, into a final impression. I could speak, of course, in more general terms of the intellectual and emotional enjoyment that stemmed from the sudden insights, the feelings of empathy, and the sometimes striking interpretations that have added new understanding to our clinical work. To call these occasions "workshops" is tantamount to calling a pearl an abnormal nacreous growth within an oyster, and hardly does justice to the experience.

As I sat and moderated these sessions (although moderation would have been the very last of my aims in chairing them), I was at times overwhelmed by the coruscating verbal flow, the breath of sympathy and wide range of ideas. It is quite invidious to choose for special mention any particular contributor. If I refer to Professor Ekstein, it is because he has been on the clinical scene longer than the others, teaches now with equal fare and distinction on two continents, and uses metaphors to tie together the ordinary and the extraordinary and thus carry his readership smoothly through difficult clinical shoals. He also makes use of the metaphor and the myth to elaborate the technique of therapeutic approach that is uniquely his own. One must have been born and bred an Ekstein to practice the Platonic leaps that he himself makes in his eruptions before a live audience. At such times one feels as Dr. Samuel Johnson felt about the great English orator Edmund Burke: "Yes, Sir; if a man were to go by chance at the same time with Burke under a shed, to shun a shower, he would say—'this is an extraordinary man.'"

Henry Copolillo, with his Italian heritage, brings a more Mediterranean type of exuberance into the lecture theater, although one still recognizes the fine scholarship and clinical acumen that underlies the fireworks. He grips his audience with the same intensity as Ekstein.

The women speakers offered a sharp contrast. Both Annemarie Weil and Paulina Kernberg are recognized authorities and speak authoritatively, but their demeanor is quiet and comfortable, although they are deeply concerned with what they are trying to put across to their listeners. Dr. Weil's contributions to the field of maturation are well recognized and highly appreciated. She seems to be equally at home on both sides of the mind-body relationship. On the one side, she can investigate and discuss metapsychology from the psychoanalytic point of view, and on the other side, maturation from the neurophysiological viewpoint. This range is unusual in the field today; it allows her to bring together factors relating to perception, motility, and language development and correlate them with clinical and dynamic thinking. Like Hartmann, she is deeply involved in "the organization of the organism" at various levels of functioning and development and from both physiological and psychological perspectives. Nor does she overlook the constitutional, or "given," factors in any particular case. I would like to give an example of her complex clinical approach in its dealing with the nature and function of sensitivity as it operates from the beginning life:

> From the very start of life, hypersensitivity shapes the environment and the infant's relation to world. I had occasion to observe identical twins. One, probably because of poorer intrauterine condition and more difficult birth experiences, was more immature, more hypersensitive, and required and received more care and attention. As a consequence, she became and remained more object related. This was evident even before the emergence of the smile. [1978]

In this brief comment, Dr. Weil brings together a host of interrelating factors—genetic, constitutional, reproductive, developmental, psychosexual and phenomenological. It is this density of context that has rendered her such a superb clinician.

Dr. Kernberg, who is both a child psychiatrist and a child analyst, is able to span the disciplines and draw from the one side to help the other. A comment from a member of the audience tells us something of her therapeutic skills. He said, while listening to her, that her empathy with the patient was so exquisitely used to further her understanding that he wished he could have been a child again to be analyzed by her. He added that he might have been a much improved adult. (These free-floating transferences do hover over an audience when a good therapist is on stage, but, unfortunately, they are often left unresolved as the people walk out nostalgically into the realities of everyday life.)

In clinical investigations of the type reported in this volume, one has to bear in mind two important epistemological considerations: The first is that the study of human behavior can never be an exact science; rigorous and controlled research may be essential for physics or biology, but knowledge of the psyche is unlike knowledge of insects or the movement of the stars. It is more like the imaginative understanding which makes us knowledgeable about the actions and reactions of people that we meet in our everyday life, as Karl Popper has insisted. If psychiatry was as deterministic as has been claimed, prediction and precision would both be integral aspects of it, but such a view would not be compatible with our clinical experience.

The second basic notion has to do with diagnosis. We provide labels that claim to capture the elusive flux of single human histories by reducing them to a word or a set of words that summarize individuals from the cradle to the time of a illness etiologically, diagnostically, and prognostically. The variety and plurality of life is suddenly reduced by a dreadful simplification, so that our need for organization and for perceiving the hidden likenesses in diversity are satisfied as we sit back comfortably with titles of "anxious," "hysterical," and "borderline."

Historians have informed us that at the time of the eighteenth century Enlightenment, the ancient belief that there was a single human nature, a single natural law, and a final solution to all problems, had reached its zenith, together with the dream of a comprehensive psychosocial science. It took the genius of Freud to restore complexity and diversity to its rightful role in human personality development. This meant not that there were not likenesses that characterized different clinical groups, but that the label was merely a stimulus to set in motion a host of associations, some of which might have relevance to the life history of a particular individual. Freud also assumed that human nature was not unalterable and that natural and therapeutic interventions could bring about decisive mutations in the course of individual lives. We are still, in our little art-science, struggling for final truths, for timeless natural laws, for encompassing psychological systems, although longitudinal and prospective studies are constantly reminding us that each individual has his own identity, with his own idiosyncratic values and goals, and that it is not possible to fit numbers of them into the same classificatory bed without a good deal of distortion and falsity.

Of one thing we can be sure: At the present state of our knowledge, we are in no position to endorse the final conglomeration of labels that in some mysterious way identify contending elements of nature and nurture and furnish us with predictable evolutions. Clinicians must bear in mind Kant's maxim that "out of the crooked timber of humanity no straight thing can ever be made." As these essays into clinical portrayal are published, the "crookedness" must be taken for granted. Our purpose has been to put together a wide and deep compendium of clinical experiences and to present views that not only differ but are dictated by single or multiple guiding principles. In a famous comment, Isiah Berlin contrasted the hedgehog, who knows one big thing, with the fox, who knows many little things. Readers will note that this book derives from both points of view and that our overall sympathies are not wholly with the hedgehog or with the fox. If the compiler is governed by one big thing, it is that there is no one big thing. In every clinical anthology, therefore, of this type, we need to combine the efforts of both hedgehogs and foxes so that we do not overlook the many little things that punctuate the course of development or the big thing that stamps its generic character, its sameness in spite of change, on the personality. Stephanie Doe may have the twenty or thirty checked items that stereotype hysteria, or she may give the overall impression or evidence of the nuclear underlying conflict suggesting hysteria, but to the therapist who sees her over time, she was, is, and will remain a memorable child with unique qualities and potentialities that combine to make her not what she is, but who she is.

In an article written by this author (1967), the child's capacity for diagnosing the elements in his environment is considered developmentally in terms of the Piagetian scheme. In infancy, the propensity for classification takes the form of differentiating between the searchable, the reachable, the observable, the prehensile, the malleable, the tearable, the audible, and so on. In the preschool years, sorting behavior is achieved not logically but intuitively, so that phenomena are classified by a figural criterion into the private, idiosyncratic, and nonshareable. At seven years and onward, things are put together on the basis of similarity of attributes, so that a hierarchy of classes and subclasses emerges, but the classifications are conceptually unstable and constantly in danger of turning into infralogical totalities. Categories are tied to the concrete and to what is perceivable, and it is only in the final stage of cognitive development that a "system" of classification comes into being that interrelates the various classifying operations and provides a new depth and sophistication to the codification of behavior. If one accepts this picture of the child's development as analogous to the efforts made over many years to classify the clinical disorders of childhood, one can note that many of the classifications put out appear to be "fixated" at some point within these stage developments. As the discipline grows, a synthesis of a sort begins to take place, although different points of view continue to push hard for the inclusion of their different points of view.

The world of child psychiatry, like the world of psychiatry, can be divided, like ancient Gaul, into three parts, the inhabitants of which live comparatively encapsulated lives, communicating little with those in the other parts because of the different traditions and beliefs. On one side there are "organic" child psychiatrists and these are much fewer in number than those in the equivalent part of the adult psychiatry world. At the other extreme are the "psychodynamic" child psychiatrists who boast an analytical frame of reference and pay special heed to "internal" processes. In between are a growing number who acknowledge constitutional, organic, psychological and social factors but who insist in dealing almost exclusively with observable behavior . . . the different groups tend, on the whole, to formulate their own classifications, since they find that the classifications of antithetical groups are generally useless to them, either in clinical or research work.

I also find occasion, in this same article, to regret the unhelpful and often antagonistic positions adopted by the antagonists who all look at the same clinical faces but through biased spectacles, and who can find little good to say for their opponents.

The organicists, for example, tend to see themselves as scientific, objective factual and realistic and are seen by the others as restricted, compulsive, concrete, simple-minded and shallow. The "internalists" see themselves as dynamic, deep, imaginative and complex and are seen in turn as mystical, nebulous, unscientific and subjective.

On this continuum of the organic-behavioral and psychodynamic, I placed myself somewhat on the right, but very ready to communicate and collaborate with those on the left. Clearly, this volume could have done more with the appraisal of some of the biological factors that predispose, precipitate, or perpetuate anxiety reactions, borderline shifts, or hysterical somatization, but the knowledge in this area is at best tenuous and uncertain. We believe that the account given in these pages reflects what we know about the present, with some intelligent guesses about the future.

To be a child has never been, at any time in history, an easy passage. There are growing pains at every stage and moments of acute depersonalization, derealization, and disorientation that occurs for almost every child in every culture. In addition, children are troubled by family problems, by cultural changes, by disintegrating social environments, when moments of developmental panic are increased and intensified. Quite suddenly it seems as if anxiety, hysteria, and the borderline status come together and induce fundamental doubts about existence: Who am I? What am I doing? Where am I going? How am I to get there? Will I be adequate? Will tomorrow be different? Will I be less anxious, less confused, less emotional? And what will it be like when I grow up and become just like other people?

Children, whether they are anxious, borderline, or hysterical, all express doubts and worries of this kind. There is one way in which they differ from adults: even in the worst of their predicaments, they have a hopefulness about the next day that adults have often lost and therapists who deal with children must surely regain if they are to be successful with them.

Something of these complex emotions that affect children at critical moments along the way to becoming grown up is reflected in this poem by a young boy at the far end of childhood:

Oh, where are my feelings, where have they gone,
Maybe they will come in the next three dawns,
Why can't I feel like all the other people,
It makes me feel like an ant so small and so feeble.
I seem to be lost in a big giant maze,
When will I be able to clear all the haze,
I am stuck up against a big giant wall,
One day soon I'll make that wall fall.
One day soon that day will come,
I'll find my feeling on the rising sun.

It is such feelings that sustain the child through the ordeals of childhood and adolescence, and it is such feelings that sustain the therapist in his work with them.

REFERENCES

Anthony, E.J. (1967) Taxonomy is not one man's business. *Intl. J. Psychiatry*, 3:173–178.
Boswell, A.J. (1934, 1965). *Life of Johnson*, Vols. 1–6. London: Oxford University Press.
Weil, A.M. (1978). Maturational variations and genetic-dynamic issues. *J. Am. Psychoanal. Assn.*, 26:461.

Index

THE LIBRARY
UNIVERSITY OF CALIFORNIA
San Francisco
666-2334

THIS BOOK IS DUE ON THE LAST DATE STAMPER BELOW
Books not returned on time are subject to fines according to the Library
Lending Code. A renewal may be made on certain materials. For details
consult Lending Code.

14 DAY OCT 5 1982	14 DAY JUN 17 1986	14 DAY SEP - 7 1990
RETURNED OCT 6 1982	RETURNED JUN 17 1986	RETURNED SEP 4 1990
14 DAY SEP - 6 1983	14 DAY JAN 21 1990	14 DAY OCT 1 8 1991
RETURNED SEP - 4 1983	14 DAY FEB - 4 1990	RETURNED OCT 1 1991
14 DAY MAR - 9 1984	RETURNED FEB 11 1990	
RETURNED MAR - 9 1984		Series 4128